Myth and Mythmaking

Myth and Mythmaking

Edited and with an Introduction by

HENRY A. MURRAY

BEACON PRESS   BOSTON

The following essays were originally published in *Daedalus,*
the Journal of the American Academy of Arts and Sciences,
under the general editorship of Gerald Holton:

THE HISTORICAL DEVELOPMENT OF MYTHOLOGY by Joseph
Campbell

RECURRENT THEMES IN MYTHS AND MYTHMAKING by Clyde
Kluckhohn

THE YEARNING FOR PARADISE IN PRIMITIVE TRADITION by
Mircea Eliade

THEORIES OF MYTH AND THE FOLKLORIST by Richard M. Dorson

SOME MEANINGS OF MYTH by Harry Levin

THE WORKING NOVELIST AND THE MYTHMAKING PROCESS by
Andrew Lytle

WORLD INTERPRETATION AND SELF-INTERPRETATION: SOME BASIC
PATTERNS by Ernst Topitsch

THE THREE ROMES: THE MIGRATION OF AN IDEOLOGY AND THE
MAKING OF AN AUTOCRAT by Robert Lee Wolff

MYTH AND IDENTITY by Jerome S. Bruner

MYTH AND MASS MEDIA by Marshall McLuhan

International Standard Book Number: 0–8070–4679–5

9   8   7   6   5   4

Printed in the United States of America

Contents

Myth and Mythmaking

Myth and Mythmaking

Introduction

HENRY A. MURRAY

To EXPLAIN how it came about that a rank amateur in the domain of myth should be introducing this select assemblage of papers by eminent professionals is to describe, by way of apology for his presence here, the conditions of the bringing forth of these illuminations of one of the darkest of all fields of inquiry.

Assignment to my present role came as the last move in an inescapable, fateful chain of interactions set off two years ago by my reluctant-rash consent to act as chairman of a small committee to organize a preliminary symposium on myth under the auspices of the American Academy of Arts and Sciences. Already I had reached the point of no retreat, for somebody, of course, had to play the part of chargé d'affaires at the symposium itself which, with the support of the Carnegie Corporation, took place at the House of the Academy in May, 1958. The lively and abundant exchanges of facts, speculations, and opinions generated by the addresses delivered at that meeting settled the question of publication in the Journal of the Academy, and this, according to custom, meant that somebody had to serve as guest editor under Mr. Holton, editor-in-chief. The result was the 1959 Spring issue of *Daedalus*, entitled "Myth and Mythmaking," which was composed of four provocative papers prepared for the 1958 symposium (those by Messrs. Bruner, Kluckhohn, Levin, and McLuhan), six most welcome additional contributions (those of Messrs. Campbell, Dorson, Eliade, Lytle, Topitsch, and Wolff) —of which some were specially requested and some vouchsafed the editors by a timely providence—and then, for dessert, four virtually indispensable passages from the writings of Mann, Schorer, and Sorel.

The number of favorable responses to this issue of *Daedalus* was deemed sufficient warrant for its presentation in book form to a larger public, particularly since there was some reason to believe that certain other scholars had compositions cooking in their ovens which, if finished and offered in the near future, would fit nicely into a few of the conspicuously vacant places and give the book a greater amplitude. This meant, in turn, that somebody had to be appointed editor. Hence my presence here, an embarrassed tyro in this company of experts yet proud of having had a hand in drawing forth such valuable supplements and complements to the already garnered riches as the papers by Miss Ackerman and Messrs. Frye, Hatfield, Marcus, Rieff, and Weisinger.

The volume that lies ahead of you is notable in the main for its scope, diversity, import, scholarship, and style. This is apparent from the start, since Mr. Campbell's brilliant chapter, written as his introduction to a work in progress—no less than a world-embracing history of mythology in four volumes—possesses all these qualities and something more, the vision of an emergent, energy-releasing frame of mind for those who are disposed and capable. Beginning with the earliest known patternings of myth in the Orient and Near East, Mr. Campbell carries us swiftly down the ages with eloquence and apt citations through daemonic and metaphysical mythology to the humanistic, poetic mythology of Greece, and finally to our current situation, leaving us with the seminal idea of extending Huizinga's conceptions of the "play-sphere" to the whole realm of myth.

Although Mr. Campbell mentions the global distribution of certain mythic themes, in this volume it is Mr. Kluckhohn who with the skill of gift and discipline brings his encyclopedic and exact knowledge of primitive cultures to bear upon the question of cross-cultural universals in the field of myth as well as upon the problem of the psycho-sociological function of mythic imaginations. His substantial chapter, full of sage comments, now constitutes our most dependable basis for the reconstruction, among other things, of certain features of contemporary psychoanalytic theory.

In contrast to these two authors, the equally knowledgeable and comprehensive Mr. Eliade has chosen to concentrate on a single integrate of myths, those descriptive of Paradise, the immortality of primordial man, his communion with God, his fall, the origin of death, and the discovery of the "spirit." With signal clarity and distinction, both of feeling and of thought, Mr. Eliade portrays the intimate relationship of this mythic compound with the ecstatic trances of shamanism, as well as the ideological continuity between this most elementary form of mystical experience and Christian mysticism.

In the next chapter, Mr. Dorson, our foremost champion of the folklorist's point of view and methods, draws his sharp sword of reason and of satire and attacks the Hydra of monomaniac theories relative to the proper interpretation of myths. Here, for many of us, his special service consists in highlighting the absurdity and faddishness of some of our latest ideas, by juxtaposing, for example, the extravagances of the currently fashionable psychoanalytic school of interpreters with the more patent, discredited extravagances of the old solar school. Most pertinent in this connection is Miss Ackerman's elegant, compact, and discriminating essay in which—by substituting a more restricted and more valid theory for the hypertrophied theories of the past and sustaining it with telling particles drawn from her vast store of applicable learning—she succeeds in restoring to their proper place the once prodigiously inflated and then punctured and ostracized astronomical interpretations of certain mythic compositions.

Next in order is Mr. Levin's learned, graceful, and witty addition to our knowledge of the diverse referents, from Homer to modern times, of "myth," the chameleonic term that most of us are employing as if it pointed to one and the same class of entities. Mr. Levin's nicely-woven history of the word appears at this point, instead of where it stood originally at the beginning of the

symposium, in order to provide a clarifying prelude to the succeeding chapters of this book. Mr. Levin is clearly less concerned
with primitive myths—either of the ancient Orient and Near
East or of contemporary non-literate societies—than he is with
"myth" when used in connection with literary works or political
ideologies of the Western world. The notion of "myth" as contrary
to fact and reason, and as capable, in certain of its forms (e. g.
Fascism), of producing infectious and malignant psychic inflam-
mations has proved sufficient ground for Mr. Levin's resolution to
remain a member of the society of mythoclasts along with the
majority of scholars. At this juncture, then, the reader might be
well advised to turn to the Appendix and read, as an impressive
contrast, the definition of myth elaborated by Mr. Schorer. Mr.
Schorer—perceptive interpreter of the visions of William Blake—
is more hopeful of the beneficent potentialities of the imagination
than he is fearful of its dangers—chief requirement for membership in the smaller but more exuberant society of mythophiles,
which includes Mr. Campbell, Mr. Lytle, Mr. Bruner, D. H.
Lawrence, Thomas Mann, and possibly a few others represented
in this volume.

The conscious or unconscious role of myth in the creation of
literature is the topic of the valuable chapters by Mr. Frye, Mr.
Weisinger, and Mr. Lytle. Taking off from Aristotle's unelabo-
rated comment that dramatic and epic poetry, because of its
concern with universals, is more philosophical than history, Mr.
Frye, in felicitous and explicit language, elucidates with copious
examples the nature of poetic thought, in what respects it is
similar and in what respects dissimilar to other kinds of thought
—metaphysical, metahistorical, historical, and scientific. As illustrations of mythic configurations and patterns which have provided poets with the necessary structure for the arrangement of
their images and image-phrasings, Mr. Frye orders in an astonishing manner some of the favored cosmologies of literature—
various hierarchical stratifications of regions from the highest
(heaven) to the lowest (hell), including the ascensions and
descensions of different orders of beings from one region to

another. In the course of this adroit exposition of his subject-matter, Mr. Frye manages to behead with three sharp sentences those who have held that the poet's cosmology is extraneous to his craft, that the *Divine Comedy* is the metaphysical system of St. Thomas translated into imagery, and that poetry is simply a form of permissible lying.

Mr. Weisinger, who has profound understanding of the historic transformation of sacred ritual into secular tragic drama, offers us a revealing and even-handed, tightly knit review of recent endeavors of literary critics to interpret the works of Shakespeare in terms of the death-and-renewal *ur*-myth of the Near East. The disparity of these generally far-fetched interpretations might well have been predicted, each being the resultant of a different man's attempt to reach the interior of an author's mind by empathy or inference, capacities which are dependable in none of us. These capacities, however, need not be strained or even exercised when we come to an author who is brave enough to expose for our benefit the more salient features of the order of mental processes that occurred during the composition of a book. This is precisely what Mr. Lytle generously agreed to do in response to petitions from several members of this company, and so our collection of papers is now happily enriched by his absorbing account of the operation of myth in the mind of a novelist at work.

Of a wholly different sort is the enlightenment to be gained from the superb chapter by Mr. Topitsch, packed as it is with illustrations of highly consequential imaginal projections into the universe—that is, into "what is remote, unknown, or difficult to understand"—of conceptual images derived from the domain of social and productive action—that is, from "what is near, well known, and self-evident." Even more remarkable are the numerous instances cited by Mr. Topitsch of the subsequent retro-jection (or introjection) of these same projections—actual cities are built according to the model of the imagined "heavenly city," and so forth—and also, among other trenchant observations, examples of the projection of incompatible dispositions and powers into the personality of God and of the creation in this way, by man himself, of momentous, insoluble problems calling for solution, the creation, in other words, of a state of affairs conducive to obsessional neurosis.

This brings us to Mr. Wolff's fascinating, substantial, and convincing story of the emergence and propagation of the flattering image of the Russian Tsar as "the sole Emperor of all the Christians in the whole universe." Here is myth in the form of a vainglorious, wish-fulfilling vision, if not of a full-fledged delusion of grandeur, operating in the service of a national ideology. Of similar psychic fabric and tenor, though more preposterous and pathological, were the myths of the Nazi epidemic, the roots and cancerous growth of which constitute the subject matter of Mr. Hatfield's comprehensive, interesting, and vitally important essay.

Here would be the timely place to experience two moving and instructive passages to be found in the Appendix: first, the excerpt from Sorel's *Reflections on Violence,* and second, that from Mann's *Doctor Faustus.* The latter will implant in sensitive minds an indelible impression of the intoxicating effects of a grandiose mythology once a desperate and reckless minority has become possessed by it. Today, after the debacle of Nazi-ism, we have a salutary *deterrent* social myth, conforming to the classic pattern of arrogant pride (hubris) and retribution (nemesis).

With this in view should we not be mindful of the nearly universal human tendency, mentioned by Mr. Levin, to denounce "myth as falsehood from the vantage point of a rival myth"? What is our myth?

Mr. Marcus does not precisely specify, his purpose being to point to what is characteristic of all powerful Western myths—including Fascism and Communism—as compared to Oriental myths, namely, a linear time-perspective combined with a conviction of election and of the necessity of participating in an historical process moving inexorably towards an ultimate consummation. To do justice to the intensity with which future-oriented myths of this messianic type—whether Christian or anti-Christian—have been experienced and believed, and do justice to the power of such visions of destiny to mobilize and orient social action, Mr. Marcus has chosen the term "mystique." The essence of the mystique is the conviction that the ideal is not only immanent in history but has actually been embodied in one or more particular myth-events (e. g. Fall of the Bastille, October Revolution in Petrograd, etc.). Mr. Marcus' vivid and zealous description of the role of an activist mystique of movement in giving the individual the sense of a meaningful relationship to his world and of obligation to history-in-the-making constitutes a striking contrast to the state of affairs in America today, especially as represented by the half-hearted, directionless, lonely peer-groups of our schools and colleges. The reader leaves this thought-evoking essay with the picture of a new Orient and new Africa, both infected with the inflammatory germs of a host of competing mystiques derived from the aggressive West, their traditional circular time-perspectives having been replaced by a consciousness of history and of destiny—all this at the very moment when the West, distrustful of fanatical leaders of fanatical herds, is vainly searching for a realizable vision of world harmony and peace.

Having given due consideration to the mysteriously propelling power of a variety of social myths—the enormities committed in their names—readers who still retain a sturdy faith in the possibility of beneficent imaginations will be in the best temper to appreciate the virtues of the two succeeding chapters, the first by Mr. Rieff, the second by Mr. Bruner. Both are in the main concerned with the genesis, form, or function of one or more individual *exemplar* myths, myths, that is to say, which serve as an invitation to a way of life or as a model for the orientation of self-development. Mr. Rieff—against the background of his recently completed, masterful analysis of Freud, the moralist—examines with his wonted penetration the products of the fervent need for myths in D. H. Lawrence, that other charismatic moralist who was preoccupied from first to last with sex and always aiming—more outspokenly than his medical predecessor—at a transvaluation of values relative to this then-harmfully-restricted form of psychic energy.

In the next essay, Mr. Bruner, sparkling wtih propitious thoughts communicated in arresting diction, discusses the complementarity of the grammar of experience and the grammar of myth. The thesis he upholds, with numerous telling illustrations from classical and modern literature, is that a corpus of myth is functional in so far as it offers to each individual person a variety of possible identities or, seen from another angle, a "library of scripts" with which "the internal drama of his multiple identities" can be critically compared. This stimulating chapter ends with brief references to two emerging myths: that of the "hipsters" and the "squares," and that of the "full, creative man." The excerpt (in the Appendix) from Thomas Mann's thoughtful "Freud and the Future"—in the background of which Jung's ideas are more prominent than Freud's—can be read most relevantly at this point, partly as a further elaboration of Mr. Bruner's abbreviated exposition of exemplar myths and partly as contrast to the modernity of Mr. Bruner.

To readers who have yet to be advantaged by familiarity with the striking and engaging style and content of Mr. McLuhan's recent writings, the next chapter is likely to stand out as most novel, intriguing, and, in some respects, bewildering. Dealing as it does with a so-far-unmentioned, yet important, determinant of both the nature and effect of every "myth" (as the term is used by most members of this company), this essay is unique, though what it has to say is applicable to the substance of all preceding essays. As I understand it, Mr. McLuhan's thesis is first, that language, in the usual sense (say the English language), shapes the character of what is thought, felt, and said by the people who use it; second, that the introduction of a new mode of communication (say the invention of the phonetic alphabet or the invention of TV) changes the current language drastically and hence the character of what is thought, felt, and said: third, that language, in the usual sense, is a form of mass medium, and that a mass medium, in the usual sense (say the movies), is a form of language; fourth, that the language, or medium, *is* the message and its effect is determined by its form; and fifth, that a language, or medium, may be called a "macromyth," a single "myth" being an image, photograph, "still" shot, or static abstraction of a macromyth in action. From this I would infer that what counts in Mr. McLuhan's mythological scales is not at all the *content* (referent, meaning) of any given mental product but the *mode* (language, style, technique) by which it is transmitted. Whether or not this inference corresponds to Mr. McLuhan's settled semantic stance is a question whose answer does not affect the validity of his main thesis, namely, that our moving in recent years from the predominantly "segmental, lineal space of literacy" (e. g. book reading at different times in private) into "the auditory, unified field of electronic information" (e. g. listening simultaneously to a TV program) has conferred on modern culture a "formal auditory character" and is thereby serving to restore, to some extent, preliterate modes of apprehension. Mr. McLuhan is a hive of suggestiveness whose abundance resists reduction to a few segments of the "lineal space of literacy."

Here I shall rest, trusting that I have given you just enough of the salt and savor of each portion of the feast that lies ahead of you to whet your appetite and no more.

In the last chapter I shall raise the moot question of the possibility of a vital "mythology" to come, though not till I have wrestled with the prior question of whether or not "modern myth" is a contradiction in terms, myths being, by one authoritative definition, *prehistoric* stories about the gods recited in conjunction with a sacred ritual.

1. The Historical Development of Mythology*

JOSEPH CAMPBELL

I

THE COMPARATIVE STUDY of the mythologies of the world compels us to view the cultural history of mankind as a unit; for we find that such themes as the Fire-theft, Deluge, Land of the Dead, Virgin Birth, and Resurrected Hero have a world-wide distribution, appearing everywhere in new combinations, while remaining, like the elements of a kaleidoscope, only a few and always the same. Furthermore, whereas in tales told for entertainment such mythical themes are taken lightly—obviously in a spirit of play—they appear also in religious contexts, where they are accepted not only as factually true but even as revelations of the verities to which the whole culture is a living witness and from which it derives both its spiritual authority and its temporal power. No human society has yet been found in which such mythological motifs have not been rehearsed in liturgies; interpreted by seers, poets, theologians, or philosophers; presented in art; magnified in song; and ecstatically experienced in life-empowering visions.

Indeed the chronicle of our species, from its earliest page, has been not simply an account of the progress of man the toolmaker

* This essay is based on the Introduction of a projected four-volume work entitled *The Masks of God* (New York: The Viking Press), the first volume of which was published in 1959. Copyright © 1959 by Joseph Campbell. Reprinted by permission of The Viking Press.

but—more tragically—a history of the pouring of blazing visions into the minds of seers and the efforts of earthly communities to incarnate unearthly covenants. Every people has received its own seal and sign of supernatural designation, communicated to its heroes and daily proved in the lives and experiences of its folk. And though many who bow with closed eyes in the sanctuaries of their own tradition rationally scrutinize and disqualify the sacraments of others, an honest comparison immediately reveals that all have been built from the one fund of mythological motifs —variously selected, organized, interpreted, and ritualized according to local need, but revered by every people on earth.

A fascinating psychological as well as historical problem is thus presented to us by our science. Man, apparently, cannot maintain himself in the universe without belief in some arrangement of the general inheritance of myth. In fact, the fullness of his life would even seem to stand in a direct ratio to the depth and range, not of his rational thought, but of his local mythology. Whence the force of these unsubstantial themes, by which they are empowered to galvanize populations, creating of them civilizations, each with a beauty and self-compelling destiny of its own? And why should it be that whenever men have looked for something solid on which to found their lives, they have chosen, not the facts in which the world abounds, but the myths of an immemorial imagination— preferring even to make life a hell for themselves and their neighbors, in the name of some violent god, rather than to accept gracefully the bounty the world affords?

Are the modern civilizations to remain spiritually locked from each other in their local notions of the sense of the general tradition? Or can we not now break through to some more profoundly based point and counterpoint of human understanding? For it is a fact that the myths of our several cultures work upon us, whether consciously or unconsciously, as energy-releasing, life-motivating, and directing agents; so that even though our rational minds may be in agreement, the myths by which we are living—or by which our fathers lived—can be driving us, at that very moment, diametrically apart.

No one, as far as I know, has yet tried to compose into a single picture the new perspectives that have been opened in the fields of comparative symbolism, religion, mythology, and philosophy by the scholarship of recent years. The richly rewarded archaeological researches of the past few decades; astonishing clarifications, simplifications, and coordinations achieved by intensive studies in the spheres of philology, ethnology, philosophy, art history, folklore, and religion; fresh insights in psychological research; and the many priceless contributions to our science by the scholars, monks, and literary men of Asia—all have combined to suggest a new image of the fundamental unity of the spiritual history of mankind. Without straining beyond the treasuries of evidence already on hand in these widely scattered departments of our subject, therefore, but simply gathering from them the *membra disjuncta* of a unitary mythological science, I shall attempt in the following pages the first sketch of a natural history of the gods and heroes, such as in its final form should include in its purview all divine beings—just as zoology does all animals, and botany all plants—not regarding any as sacrosanct or beyond its scientific domain. For, just as in the visible world of the vegetable and animal kingdoms, so also in the visionary world of the gods: there has been a history, an evolution, a series of mutations, governed by laws. To show forth such laws is the proper aim of science.

Moreover, just as our science of biology came to maturity only when it dared to reckon man among the beasts, so will that of mythology only when God is reckoned among the gods. It is true that the ultimate nature and being of what has been called God are beyond all human knowledge and consequently beyond science; but so also are the ultimate nature and being of the gods —and of the bees and flowers. Books have been written, however, not only about God, but also about his commandments, program for mankind, and arrangements for eternity; thrones and altars have been fixed upon the tablets of his law; services instituted in his name. It is to such historical curiosities that our science will be addressed, leaving the ineffable unnamed.

II

Like the aim of Bacon's *Advancement of Learning*, that of our work will be "to point out what part of knowledge has been already labored and perfected, and what portions left unfinished or entirely neglected." To that end the subject can be conveniently divided into four parts: The Psychology and Archaeology of Myth; Oriental Mythology; Occidental Mythology; and Poetic Mythology.

THE PSYCHOLOGY AND ARCHAEOLOGY OF MYTH

"Very deep," wrote Thomas Mann at the opening of his mythological tetralogy, *Joseph and his Brothers,* "very deep is the well of the past. Should we not call it bottomless?"

The question points to the problem of the relationship of history to psychology. Is the psyche a function of history, or vice versa? Shall we find, in tracing our mythological themes to their points of origin, that these can be identified in discoverable strata of the well of history? Or shall we find, rather, when the bottom of the deep well has been reached and even broached, that the origin or ground of myth will not have been attained? If the latter, then we shall be justified in asserting that at least some of the archetypes on which the wonder tales and religions of mankind have been founded derive not from any fund of human experience in time but from some structuring principle antecedent to history—or even the cause of history: namely, the form of the psyche itself, as a function of the biology of the human body.

"The deeper we sound," wrote Thomas Mann, "the further down into the lower world of the past we probe and press, the more do we find that the earliest foundations of humanity, its history and culture, reveal themselves unfathomable."

Our initial task must be to ask if this is true. And to this end we shall explore, first, the psychological aspect of our question, to learn whether in the human psychosomatic system there have been found any structures or dynamic tendencies to which the origins of myth and ritual might be referred; turning only then to the archaeological and ethnological evidences, to learn what the earliest discoverable patterns of mythological ideation may have been.

However, as Thomas Mann has already warned, concerning the foundations for which we shall be seeking: "No matter to what hazardous lengths we let out our line they still withdraw, again and further into the depths." The first depth will be the archaeological: that of the beginnings of the high cultures of Mesopotamia, the Nile, Guatemala, and Peru. The second depth will be the paleontological and ethnological: of primitive man, the hunter and early planter. But there will be a third depth even below that—below the ultimate horizon of humanity: for we shall find the ritual dance among the birds, the fishes, the apes, and the bees. And we shall therefore have to ask the evidence whether man, like those other members of the animal kingdom, does not possess any innate tendencies to respond compulsively, in strictly patterned ways, to certain signals flashed by his environment and his own kind.

ORIENTAL MYTHOLOGY

Having viewed the open question of the origins and earliest patternings of myth through the balanced lenses of archaeology and psychology, we shall find the next natural division of our subject in the highly developed systems of the Orient: the rich yet essentially unified major province represented by the philosophical myths and mythological philosophies of India, Southeast Asia, China, and Japan—to which should be joined the much earlier yet spiritually closely related mythological cosmologies of archaic Mesopotamia and Egypt. In all of these hieratically organized civilizations will be recognized the basic mythology of a universe not progressing toward any end, but rendering manifest to the contemplative mind, here and now, the radiance of a divine power, which, though transcendent, is yet immanent in all things. Certain aspects of the Greek and even of the pagan Celto-Germanic mythological systems belong to this fundamentally contemplative order of mythopoetic thought. However, the

Greeks themselves felt that there was a notable difference
between their approach to life and that of the more ancient
peoples toward the south and east; and we too generally find it
normal to think of the Occident and the Orient under separate
heads. The next convenient division of our subject, then, will be:

OCCIDENTAL MYTHOLOGY

But the watershed, or dividing line, between the lands of the
early Oriental and the more recent Occidental traditions must
be drawn—for the field of mythology, at any rate—not at the
longitude of the Aegean (with Greece immediately to the west
and modern Turkey, or ancient Anatolia, eastward) but through
Iran. For the first formulation of the new mythology upon which
the Occidental world view was to be founded appeared in the
reforms of the Persian prophet Zoroaster (c. 660 B.C.), whose
fundamentally progressive concept of history and ethical challenge to the individual to become voluntarily engaged in the
furtherance of the Kingdom of God (Ahura Mazda) on Earth
overcame for the West the earlier mythology of the endless,
spontaneously self-generating, cosmic cycle of Eternal Return.

According to the earlier cyclic view, which is the basic view of
the great Orient to this day, there was never a time when time
was not, nor will there be a time when time will have ceased to
be; for the daily round of the sun, the waxing and waning of the
moon, the cycle of the year, and the rhythm of birth, death, and
new birth in the organic world, represent a principle of continuous creation that is fundamental to the nature of the universe.
We all know the myth of the four ages—of gold, silver, bronze,
and iron—where the world is represented as declining from its
golden age, growing ever worse. It will disintegrate, presently,
in chaos—only to burst forth again, however, fresh as a flower,
and to recommence spontaneously the inevitable course. There is
therefore nothing to be gained, either for the universe or for man,
through individual originality and effort. Those who have identified themselves with the body and its affections will necessarily
find that all is painful, since everything—for them—must end.

But for those who have found the still point of eternity, around which all—including themselves—revolves, everything is glorious and wonderful just as it is. The first duty of man, consequently, is to play his given role—as do the sun, the moon, the various animal and plant species, the waters, the rocks, and the stars— without fault; and then, if possible, so to order his mind as to identify it with the inhabiting essence of the whole.

The reform of Zoroaster broke the dreamlike spell of this contemplative, metaphysically oriented tradition, where light and darkness alternated and danced together in a world-creating cosmic shadow play. The first principle of the reform was expressed in Zoroaster's radical separation of light and darkness, together with his assignment to each of an ethical value, the light being pure and good, the darkness foul and evil. Before the creation of the world, he taught, these two were apart. But the violent powers of the dark overwhelmed the light, and a cosmic battle ensued—which was, precisely, the universe. Hence the universe was to be known as a compound of wisdom and violence, light and dark, wherein good and evil were contending fiercely for the victory. And the privilege of man—who, being himself a part of creation, was a compound of good and evil—was to elect, voluntarily, to join the battle in the interest of the light. With the gospel of Zoroaster (announced, it was believed, twelve thousand years following the creation of the world) an epochal turn was given to the conflict in favor of the good: and when he returned (after another twelve millennia) in the person of the messiah Saoshyant, there would take place a mighty battle and cosmic conflagration, through which he would annihilate all darkness, utterly. Whereupon all would be light, there would be no further history, and the Kingdom of God would have been realized forever.

It is obvious, surely, that we have here a potent mythical formula for the reorientation of the human spirit—pitching it forward along the way of time, summoning man to an assumption of responsibility for the reform of the universe in God's name, and thus fostering a new, potentially political philosophy of holy war. The first sociological expression of this new force was in the prodigious Persian empire of Cyrus the Great (*d.* 529 B.C.) and Darius the Great (*c.* 521-486? B.C.), which in a few decades reached from the bounds of India to those of Greece, and under the protection of which the postexilic Hebrews not only rebuilt their temple (Ezra 1:1-11) but also both reconstructed and reinterpreted their ancient Mosaic inheritance. The second formidable socio-political expression of the new progressive myth is therefore to be found in the Hebrew application of its message to themselves. The next application appeared in the world mission of Christendom, and the fourth in that of Islam.

"For the children of the desolate one will be more than the children of her that is married, says the Lord. Enlarge the place of your tent, and let the curtains of your habitations be stretched out; hold not back, lengthen your cords and strengthen your stakes. For you will spread abroad to the right and to the left, and your descendants will possess the nations and will people the desolate cities." (Isaiah 54:1-3)

"And this gospel of the kingdom will be preached throughout the whole world as a testimony to all nations; and then the end will come." (Matthew 24:14)

"And slay them wherever you catch them, and turn them out from where they have turned you out; for tumult and oppression are worse than slaughter. . . . And fight them on until there is no more tumult or oppression, and there prevail justice and faith in God; but if they cease, let there be no hostility except to those who practice oppression." (Koran 2: 191; 193)

The Greeks, in a measure, participated in this mythos of the war of the Sons of Light with the Sons of Darkness. We find it reflected in some of the later developments of the mythology of Dionysos. Many conflicting earlier and later legends were told of the birth and deeds, death and resurrection of this great deity of the plant world, whose cult of divine ecstasy became the rage in Greece in the seventh century B.C. The ultimate origins of the wild rites are lost in the depths of an unrecorded past: indeed, as we shall see, they are certainly very much older than the history, or even the prehistory, of Greece itself. But we know a good deal concerning the later mutations through which the worship passed before the figure of the great lord of the grain and the vine—of bread and wine, of divine rapture, and of resurrection—became merged with that of Jesus in the sacramental system of the early Church.

According to one important version of his miraculous birth, death, and resurrection[1], when the great goddess of the operations of agriculture and of the fruitful soil, Demeter, came to Sicily from Crete with her daughter Persephone, whom she had conceived of Zeus, she discovered a cave near the spring of Kyane. There she hid the maiden, setting to guard her the two serpents that were normally harnessed to the maiden's chariot. And Persephone there commenced weaving a web of wool, a great robe on which there was to be a beautiful picture of the universe; while her mother, Demeter, contrived that the girl's father, Zeus, should learn of her presence. The god approached his daughter in the form of a serpent, and she conceived of him a son, Dionysos, who was born and nurtured in the cave. The infant's toys were a ball, a top, dice, some golden apples, a bit of wool, and a bull-roarer.[2]

That is the first part of the story of the god Dionysos. The second tells of his death and resurrection. The infant in the cave was given a mirror, and while he was gazing into it, delighted, there approached him stealthily from behind two Titans, who had been sent by the goddess Hera, the jealous wife and queen of Zeus, to slay him. Now the Titans were divine beings of an earlier generation than the gods. They were the children of the Sky and the Earth, and from two of their number, Kronos and Rhea, the gods themselves, the Olympians, were born. The Titans and their mythology derived from an earlier stratum of thought and religion than the classical pantheon of the Olympians, and the episodes in which they appeared frequently had traits of an extremely primitive tone.

For example, in the present case, the two Titans stealing into the cave were painted with white clay or chalk—like the cannibals, whom we shall presently be meeting, at their feasts of ritual sacrifice. The Titans pounced upon the playing child, tearing him into seven parts, which they boiled in a cauldron supported by a tripod and then roasted on seven spits.[3] But when they had consumed their sacrifice—all except the heart, which had been rescued by the goddess Athene—Zeus, attracted by the odor of the roasting meat, entered the cave, and when he beheld the scene, slew the white-painted cannibal Titans with a bolt of lightning. The goddess Athene thereupon presented the rescued heart in a covered basket to the father, who accomplished the resurrection, according to one version of the miracle, by swallowing the precious relic and himself then giving birth to his son.

The primitive aspects of this myth can be rediscovered, ritually enacted in a gruesome series of rites still practiced among the cannibals of the primitive equatorial regions. But for the present, let us turn our attention to the manner in which the crude inheritance was spiritually transformed and reinterpreted in the image of the concept of man's nature as a battleground of good and evil.

The chief channels through which this mythology was preserved and developed from the sixth century B.C. until about the fourth A.D. were the numerous, widely scattered Orphic conventicles, which, as we know, exercised a considerable influence on both the philosophical and the religious speculations of that crucial time. A direct and powerful line leads from the Orphic schools through Pythagoras (c. 582-c. 507 B.C.) and the Eleatic philosophers to Plato (427?-347 B.C.), the Alexandrian mystery cults, and the great Neoplatonic thinkers, not only of the first millennium A.D. but also of the high Middle Ages and the Renaissance.

According to an important Orphic version of the myth of the killed and eaten infant Dionysos, it was from the ashes of the annihilated Titans that mankind arose. Man, therefore, is of mixed origin, containing a divine principle (Dionysos) and a wicked (that of the Titans). The image is analogous to that of the origin of the universe described by Zoroaster, and is actually an expression of the same idea of man's obligation to engage in a struggle of ethical significance, to release the godly substance from the grip of the dark and evil. However, in the Greek version of the problem we do not find any progressive, potentially political mythos of the ultimate salvation of the world. As in the Orient, we hear, rather, of the "cycle of birth or becoming" (*kyklos tēs geneseōs*); and the call to the individual is to save, not the world, but himself: to purge away the wicked portion of his nature and to cultivate the godly, by vegetarianism, asceticism, and assidious practice of the Orphic rituals through many lives.

We cannot pause at this point to probe the relationships to one another of the Orphic, Zoroastrian, and remoter Eastern traditions. Suffice it to say that, for any basic study of the foundations of Occidental mythology, this is a fundamental question to be faced. And the second question will be that of the interplay of the two contrary themes of the personal (Orphic) and the universal (Zoroastrian) salvation throughout the history of Occidental religion—the first retaining the archaic concept of the never ending cosmic cycle, but with a view of the world rather as evil than as divine: the second foreseeing, on the other hand, an end to it all and the ultimate realization of the Kingdom of God on Earth.

But the Orphic transformation of the Dionysian tradition—which, though it hardly touched the Synagogue, exerted a considerable influence on the Church and for a time even touched the Mosque—was not the only, or even the most important, Greek contribution to the development of mythological thought and practice in the West. For the more typical and more challenging influence was in the sphere, not of religion, but of art; and this we must study according to a completely different set of rules, thoughts, and deep concerns, and under a totally different rubric, namely:

POETIC MYTHOLOGY

The great Greeks from Thales (*c.* 640-546 B.C.) to Zeno (336?-264? B.C.) well knew that the mythological inheritance was composed in the language of the past. As F. M. Cornford has observed:[4]

> The Zeus of Aeschylus still bears the name of the polygamous father of the gods and men, whose temper made his consort an expert in the arts of wifely deceit; but it is clear that Aeschylus did not believe that such a person guided the destinies of the world. A great part of the supreme god's biography had to be frankly rejected as false, or reinterpreted as allegory, or contemplated with reserve as mysterious myth too dark for human understanding. But the very clearness of unmistakable detail in the Homeric picture made it a hard task to distort the contents of myth in the sense of a revised morality.

We can understand the problem; for we are now facing it ourselves, twenty-six hundred years later, in our own mythological inheritance of the Bible and ecclesiastical dogma. The completely unforeseen and still unpredictable findings of modern science have blasted forever the geocentric universe, where a Joshua could have caused the sun to stand at Gibeon and the moon in the valley of Ajalon, while the Creator assisted him in the slaughter of his enemies by tossing down great stones upon them from a heaven just above the clouds (Joshua 10:12-13)—to which, twelve hundred years later, Jesus and his virgin mother would magically ascend.

By many of the Greeks—as by many of ourselves—the archaic mythopoetic inheritance continued to be revered: its festivals were celebrated and its gods were addressed in prayer, as though they enjoyed some sort of independent life apart from the human imagination. However, among the poets, artists, and philosophers, such direct belief in the literal truth of a poetically conceived mythology was impossible. They knew that, just as they were themselves coining and developing myths, so in the remote past the inherited mythology had also been composed—under the influence of divine inspiration, no doubt, yet by the hands and labors of functioning poets.

An important distinction must be drawn in our studies of mythology between the attitudes toward divinities represented on the one hand by the priest and his flock, and on the other by the creative poet, artist, or philosopher. The former tend to what I should like to call a positivistic reading of the imagery of their cult. Such readings are fostered by the attitude of prayer, since in prayer it is extremely difficult to retain the balance between belief and disbelief that is proper to the contemplation of an image or idea. The poet, artist, and philosopher, on the other hand, being themselves fashioners of images and coiners of ideas, realize that all representation—whether in the visible matter of stone or in the mental matter of the word—is necessarily conditioned by the fallibility of the human organs. Overwhelmed by his own muse, a bad poet may fall into the posture of a prophet —whose utterances we shall define (for the present) as "poetry overdone," overinterpreted—whereupon he becomes the founder of a cult and the generator of priests. But so also a gifted priest may find his images deepening, changing form, or even dissolving: whereupon he will possibly become either a prophet or, if more greatly favored, a creative poet.

Three major metamorphoses of the motifs and themes of our subject, therefore, have to be recognized as fundamentally differing even though fundamentally related, namely: the true poetry of the poet, the poetry overdone of the prophet, and the poetry done to death of the priest. Whereas the history of religion is largely a record of the latter two, the history of mythology includes all three, and in doing so it brings not only poetry but also religion into a fresh and healthily vivified relationship to the wellsprings of creative thought. For there is a tendency in poetry ("poetry underdone") to rest in the whimsies of personal surprise, joy, or anguish before the realities of life in a universe man never made; whereas in religion the opposite tendency may prevail—that of rendering no personal experience whatsoever, but only clichés.

It was the miracle of the Greeks to have stood for creative thought—that is to say, poetic thought—in a world in which for some four thousand years the same old themes had been worked and reworked, served this way and that; but always in the ways either of prophecy and religion, or, on the other hand, of mere moral instruction or entertainment, as, for example, in the fable or in the wonder tale. The category of art—not as a form of anonymous craftsmanship in the service of either luxury or religion, but as a vehicle of individual insight and experience—the world owes, apparently (or, at least, so far as the evidence at present available suggests), to a certain peculiar circumstance in the character and society of the Greeks, of which they themselves were both aware and proud. And this is the *second* great distinction to be noted at the heart of our Occidental mythological tradition; the first having been the ethically toned progressive principle, announced in the Zoroastrian mythos of the battle of the powers of darkness and the powers of light. Once again we may take our lead from F. M. Cornford:[5]

Greek theology was not formulated by priests nor even by prophets, but by artists, poets, and philosophers. The great civilizations of the East were dominated by a sacerdotal caste, and the temple became for them the center of intellectual, no less than of religious life. In Greece nothing of this sort ever happened. There was no priestly class guarding from innovating influence a sacred tradition enshrined in a sacred book. There were no divines who could successfully claim to dictate the terms of belief from an inexpugnable fortress of authority. One consequence was that the conception of deity could be dissociated from cult, and enlarged to include beings and things which no one ever dreamed of connecting with the obligation of worship.

And so it is that, although in the Far and Middle East a rich tradition of storytelling flourished and, in the later periods, an elegantly turned and polished art of the literary myth, any systematic study of the aesthetic approach to mythology as a fundamental factor in the development of a cultural ideal for man must begin with the Greeks. With Alexander's invasion of India (327 B.C.) and the founding of the brief-lived but highly influential Hellenistic states of Bactria (*c.* 250-*c.* 135 B.C.) and the Punjab (*c.* 200-*c* 58 B.C.),[6] a reflection of the Greek humanistic ideal played for a time over the arts of the Oriental courts. But even there, the forces of the priest and the yogi come finally to preponderate—except in China and Japan, where the Confucian poet-scholar and Taoist poet-sage developed a mythologically inspired aesthetic orientation, which in the modern world is the most forceful counterplayer to the poetic tradition of the West.

In the Celto-Germanic mythologies of the high Middle Ages, an extremely sophisticated handling of symbols and aesthetic forms, based rather on bardic than on priestly thought and experience, lets us know that the lesson of the Greeks was never lost in the West. The contemporary poetry and philosophy of Islam also carried a great charge of humanistic inheritance. And then, finally, in the Renaissance, it was the poets, artists, and philosophers of Europe who carried not the West alone, but mankind, into the new chapter of civilization, where every mythological theme of the past that is not transmuted into poetry (poetic truth) is doomed to become simply a provincial relic.

In our natural history of the gods and heroes it will be our task to search for the laws of the alchemy of that transmutation.

III

In the primitive world, where the clues to the origin of mythology must be sought, gods and demons are not conceived in the way of hard and fast, positive realities. The phenomenon of the primitive mask, for example, is a case in point. The mask is revered as an apparition of the mythical being that it represents, yet everyone knows that a man made the mask and that a man is wearing it. The one wearing it, furthermore, is identified with the god during the time of the ritual of which the mask is a part. He does not merely represent the god: he *is* the god. The literal fact that the apparition is composed of (a) a mask, (b) its reference to a mythical being, and (c) a man, is dismissed from the mind, and the presentation is allowed to work without correction upon the sentiments of both the beholder and the actor. In other words, there has been a shift of view from the logic of the normal secular sphere, where things are understood to be distinct from each other, to a theatrical or play sphere, where they are accepted for what they are *experienced* as being, and the logic is that of "make-believe"—"as if."

We all know the convention, surely! It is a primary, spontaneous device of childhood: a magical device, by which the world can be transformed from banality to magic in a trice. And its inevitability in childhood is one of those universal characteristics of man that unite us in one family. It is a primary datum, consequently, of the science of myth, which is concerned precisely with the phenomenon of self-induced belief.

Leo Frobenius wrote in a celebrated paper on the force of the daemonic world of childhood:[7]

A professor is writing at his desk and his four-year-old little daughter is running about the room. She has nothing to do and is disturbing him. So he gives her three burnt matches, saying, "Here! Play!" and, sitting on the rug, she begins to play with the matches: Hansel, Gretel, and the witch. A considerable time elapses, during which the professor concentrates upon his task, undisturbed. But then, suddenly, the child shrieks in terror. The father jumps. "What is it? What has happened?" The little girl comes running to him, showing every sign of great fright. "Daddy, Daddy," she cries, "take the witch away! I can't touch the witch any more!"

Frobenius further observes:

An eruption of emotion is characteristic of the spontaneous shift of an idea from the level of the sentiments (*Gemüt*) to that of sensual consciousness (*sinnliches Bewusstsein*). Furthermore, the appearance of such an eruption obviously means that a certain spiritual process has reached a conclusion. The match is not a witch; nor was it a witch for the child at the beginning of the game. The process, therefore, rests on the fact that the match *has become* a witch on the level of the sentiments and the conclusion of the process coincides with the transfer of this idea to the plane of consciousness. The observation of the process escapes the test of conscious thought, since it enters consciousness only after or at the moment of completion. However, in as much as the idea *is*, it must have *become*. The process is creative, in the highest sense of the word; for, as we have seen, in a little girl a match can become a witch. Briefly stated, then: the phase of *becoming* takes place on the level of the sentiments, while that of *being* is on the conscious plane.

We may take this observation as a clue, not only to the origins of myth and of the fabulous rituals by which men and women have allowed themselves to be tortured as by demons, but also to the radical distinction between mythology as read by the Greek poets, artists, and philosophers and mythology as functioning in the primitive sphere.

Three categories are to be distinguished for mythology proper: daemonic, metaphysical, and humanistic. The first is characteristic of the earliest high civilizations, as well as of all primitive societies and folk cultures; the second achieved its apogee in medieval India, China, and Japan; while the last distinguishes the classical inheritance of the West.

According to the first, the gods and daemons represent something with a life and consciousness of its own, a "something not ourselves" (to quote Cornford's felicitous paraphrase of the Greek term *theos,* "god"),[8] which, though it is rather a force than a shape and works invisibly, yet appears in shapes. It appears in visions, where it works upon the spirit of the individual; and it appears in the paraphernalia of the ritual, to work upon the spirit of the group. Furthermore, many, if not all, rites have taken their rise from individual vision.

The Judeo-Christian-Islamic prophetic inheritance must be regarded (if we are to retain an objective distance) as a powerful variant of this first category of myth, wherein the daemons of Abraham, Jesus, Paul, Mohamet, and the rest, have been over-interpreted, not as personal patrons (like the daemon of Socrates) nor even as tribal patrons (like the deities of the Navaho), but as the father-creator of the universe, with a single program for the entire human race, to be administered by the representatives of this special visionary tradition. In fact, we may say that, just as the second of our categories of myth, the metaphysical, reached its apogee in the Far East and South Asia, so did the first, the daemonic, in the variously developed monotheistic theologies of the Synagogue, the Church, and the Mosque.

The second view, the metaphysical, seems to have taken its rise in the hermit groves and philosophically cultivated courts of India, in the eighth and seventh centuries B.C. It developed then, with increasing subtlety and sophistication as well as range of schools and peoples involved, until by the ninth century A.D. the whole of the Orient was a great symphony of metaphysical references.

We read already in the *Brihadāranyaka Upanishad* (eighth to seventh centuries B.C.):[9]

This that people say, "Worship this god! Worship that god!"— one god after another! This is his creation, indeed, and he himself is all the gods. . . . He has entered into everything, even to the fingernail tips, as a razor would be hidden in a razor case, or fire in a fire holder. Him they see not; for, as seen, he is incomplete. When breathing, he is named the breath; when speaking, the voice; when seeing, the eye; when hearing, the ear; when thinking, the mind: these are merely the names of his acts. Whoever worships one or another of these—he knows not; for he is incomplete in one or another of these. One should worship with the thought that he is one's very Self; for therein all these others become one. But that thing, namely, this Self, is itself but the footprint of this All: by it one knows this All, just as, verily, one finds [one's quarry] by a footprint. . . . So, whoever worships another divinity than his Self, thinking "He is one and I another," he knows not. He is like a sacrificial animal for the gods. Verily, indeed, just as many animals can be of service to a man, even so each single person is of service to the gods. And if even one animal is taken away, it is not pleasant. What, then, if many? Therefore, it is not pleasing to the gods that men should know this.

Much the same insight can be sensed in the sayings of the Greek Xenophanes of Colophon (fl. 536 B.C.), the reputed founder of the Eleatic school from which Plato derived certain mythologically colored strains of his philosophy. He said:[10]

There is one God, greatest among gods and men, neither in shape nor in thought like unto mortals. . . . He is all sight, all mind, all ear.... He abides ever in the same place motionless, and it befits him not to wander hither and thither. . . . Yet men imagine gods to be born, and to have raiment, voice, and body, like themselves. . . . Even so the gods of the Ethiopians are swarthy and flat-nosed, the gods of the Thracians, fair-haired and blue-eyed. . . . Even so Homer and Hesiod attributed to the gods all that is a shame and a reproach among men—

theft, adultery, deceit, and other lawless acts. . . . Even so oxen, lions, and horses, if they had hands wherewith to carve images, would fashion gods after their own shapes and make them bodies like to their own.

Or again, we have the words of Antisthenes (born *c.* 444 B.C.): "God is not like anything; hence one cannot understand him by means of an image."[11]

In the Orient the tendency of the philosophical development was to retain the atmosphere of myth, employing its symbols and rites as adequate means by which to ready the mind for intuitive insights into the ineffable mystery of the universe:

> There the eye goes not;
> Speech goes not, nor the mind.
> We know not, we understand not
> How one should teach It.
>
> For It is other, indeed, than the known,
> And, moreover, above the unknown.[12]

In the Occident, however, the tendency has been progressively toward such a definitively humanistic point of view as that epitomized in Nietzsche's volume of disillusionment, *Human, All Too Human*, where he writes that all—morality and religion, art and prophecy—in spite of their pretensions to supernatural authority, transcendental insight, and ineffable inspiration, are finally "human, all too human," and are to be read, consequently, in terms rather of psychology than of theology or metaphysics. One may, if one likes, regard these two views—the metaphysical and the humanistic, these two poles of philosophy in the modern world—as representing a play in the human mind of Niels Bohr's principle of complementarity; as a pair of opposites, or a pair of aspects, beyond which (as beyond the clashing rocks of the Symplegades) an ultimate truth of some sort must abide (awaiting perhaps our heroic arrival). But for the present systematization of the materials available to a natural history of the gods and heroes, the view of Nietzsche will suffice. And we shall have to com-

mence, furthermore, far back of the great period of the differentiation of our cultures into Orient and Occident, with the
primitive dancing ground of the gods and the mystery of the
primitive mask.

What was the attitude toward their deities of the participants
in those festivals, and what the background from which their
gods must have first appeared?

IV

Frobenius' example of a child's seizure by a witch while in the
act of play may be taken to represent an intense degree of the
daemonic mythological experience. However, the attitude of
mind represented by the game itself, before the seizure super-
vened, also belongs within the sphere of our subject. For, as J.
Huizinga has pointed out in his brilliant study of the play element in culture, the whole point, at the beginning, was the *fun*
of play, not the rapture of seizure. "In all the wild imaginings of
mythology a fanciful spirit is playing," he writes, "on the
border-line between jest and earnest."[13] "As far as I know, eth-
nologists and anthropologists concur in the opinion that the
mental attitude in which the great religious feasts of savages are
celebrated and witnessed is not one of complete illusion. There is
an underlying consciousness of things 'not being real.' "[14] And he
quotes, among others, R. R. Marett, who, in his chapter on
"Primitive Credulity" in *The Threshold of Religion,* develops the
idea that a certain element of "make-believe" is operative in all
primitive religions. "The savage," wrote Marett, "is a good actor
who can be quite absorbed in his role, like a child at play; and
also, like a child, a good spectator who can be frightened to death
by the roaring of something he knows perfectly well to be no
'real' lion."[15]

"By considering the whole sphere of so-called primitive culture
as a play-sphere," Huizinga then suggests, in conclusion, "we pave
the way to a more direct and more general understanding of its
peculiarities than any meticulous psychological or sociological

analysis would allow."[16] I concur wholeheartedly with this judgment, only adding that we should extend the consideration to the entire field of our present subject.

In the Roman Catholic mass, when the priest, quoting the words of Christ at the Last Supper, pronounces the formula of consecration, with utmost solemnity, first over the wafer of the host (*Hoc est enim Corpus meum:* "For this is My Body"), then over the chalice of the wine (*Hic est enim Calix Sanguinis mei, novi et aeterni Testamenti: Mysterium fidei: qui pro vobis et pro multis effundetur in remissionem peccatorum:* "For this is the Chalice of My Blood, of the new and eternal Testament: the mystery of faith: which shall be shed for you and for many unto the remission of sins"), it is to be supposed that the bread and wine become the body and blood of Christ: that every fragment of the host and every drop of the wine is the actual living Savior of the World. The sacrament, that is to say, is not conceived to be a *reference,* a mere sign or symbol to arouse in us a train of thought, but is God himself, the Creator, Judge, and Savior of the Universe, here come to work upon us directly, to free our soul (created in his image) from the effects of the Fall (the Titan substance).

Comparably, in India it is believed that in response to consecrating formulas, deities will descend graciously to infuse their divine substance into the temple images, which are then called their throne or seat (*pitha*). It is also possible—and in some Indian sects even expected—that the individual himself should become a seat of deity. In the *Gandharva Tantra* we read, for example: "No one who is not himself divine can successfully worship a divinity." And again: "Having become the divinity, one should offer it sacrifice."[17] Or finally, one may even discover that everything—absolutely everything—has become the body of a god: or rather, reveals the omnipresence of God as the ground of all being.

There is a passage recorded among the conversations of the nineteenth-century Bengalese spiritual master Ramakrishna, in which he described such a vision. "One day," he is reported to have said, "it was suddenly revealed to me that everything is Pure Spirit. The utensils of worship, the altar, the door frame—all Pure Spirit. Men, animals, and other living beings—all Pure Spirit. Then like a madman I began to shower flowers in all directions. Whatever I saw I worshiped."[18]

Belief, or at least a game of belief, is the first step toward such a divine seizure. The chronicles of the saints abound in accounts of their long ordeals of difficult practice, which preceded their moments of being carried away; and we have also the more spontaneous religious games and exercises of the folk (the amateurs) to illustrate for us the principle involved. The spirit of the festival, the holiday, the holy day of the religious ceremonial, requires that the normal attitude toward the cares of the world should have been temporarily set aside in favor of a particular mood of dressing up. The world is hung with banners. Or in the permanent religious sanctuaries—the temples and cathedrals—where an atmosphere of holiness hangs in the air, the logic of cold, hard fact must not be allowed to intrude and spoil the spell. The gentile, the "spoilsport," the positivist who cannot or will not play, must be kept aloof. Hence the guardian figures that stand at either side of the entrances to holy places: lions, bulls, or fearsome warriors with uplifted weapons. They are there to keep out the "spoilsports," the advocates of Aristotelian logic, for whom A can never be B; for whom the actor is never to be lost in the part; for whom the mask, the image, the consecrated host or tree or animal, cannot become God, but only a reference. Such heavy thinkers are to remain without. For the whole purpose of entering a sanctuary or participating in a festival is that one should be overtaken by the state known in India as "the other mind" (Sanskrit, anya-manas: absent mindedness, possession by a spirit), where one is "beside oneself," spellbound: set apart from one's logic of self-possession and overpowered by the force of a logic of indissociation, wherein A is B, and C also is B.

"One day," said Ramakrishna, "while worshiping Shiva, I was about to offer a bel-leaf on the head of the image, when it was revealed to me that this universe itself is Shiva. Another day, I had been plucking flowers when it was revealed to me that each plant was a bouquet adorning the universal form of God. That was the end of my plucking flowers. I look on man in just the same way. When I see a man, I see that it is God Himself, who walks on earth, rocking to and fro, as it were, like a pillow floating on the waves."[19]

From such a point of view the universe is the seat (*pitha*) of a divinity from whose vision our usual state of consciousness excludes us. But in the playing of the game of the gods we take a step toward that reality, which is ultimately the reality of ourselves. Hence the rapture, the feelings of delight, and the sense of refreshment, harmony, and re-creation! In the case of a saint, the game leads to seizure, as in the case of the little girl to whom the match revealed itself to be a witch. Contact with the orientation of the world may then be lost, the mind remaining rapt in that other state. For such it is impossible to return to this other game, the game of life in the world. They are possessed of God: that is all they know on earth and all they need to know. And they can even infect whole societies so that these, inspired by their seizures, may themselves break contact with the world and spurn it as delusory or as evil. Secular life then may be read as a Fall, a Fall from Grace—Grace being the rapture of the festival of God.

But there is another attitude, more comprehensive, which has given beauty and love to the *two* worlds: that, namely, of the *līlā*, "the play," as it has been termed in the Orient. The world is not condemned and shunned as a fall, but voluntarily entered as a game or dance, wherein the spirit plays.

Ramakrishna closed his eyes. "Is it only this?" he said. "Does God exist only when the eyes are closed, and disappear when the eyes are opened?" He opened his eyes. "The Play belongs to Him to whom Eternity belongs, and Eternity to Him to whom the Play belongs. . . . Some people climb the seven floors of a building and cannot get down; but some climb up and then, at will, visit the lower floors."[20]

The question then becomes only: how far down or up the ladder can one go without losing the sense of a game? Huizinga, in his work already referred to, points out that in Japanese the verb *asobu*, which refers to play in general—recreation, relaxation, amusement, trip or jaunt, dissipation, gambling, lying idle, or being unemployed—also means to study at a university or under a teacher; likewise, to engage in a sham fight; and finally, to participate in the very strict formalities of the tea ceremony. He writes:[21]

The extraordinary earnestness and profound gravity of the Japanese ideal of life is masked by the fashionable fiction that everything is only play. Like the *chevalerie* of the Christian Middle Ages, Japanese *bushido* took shape almost entirely in the play-sphere and was enacted in play-forms. The language still preserves this conception in the *asobase-kotoba* (literally, play-language) or polite speech, the mode of address used in conversation with persons of higher rank. The convention is that the higher classes are merely playing at all they do. The polite form for "you arrive in Tokyo" is, literally, "you play arrival in Tokyo"; and for "I hear that your father is dead," "I hear that your father has played dying." In other words, the revered person is imagined as living in an elevated sphere where only pleasure or condescension moves to action.

From this supremely aristocratic point of view, any state of seizure, whether by life or by the gods, must represent a fall or drop of spiritual *niveau:* a vulgarization of the play. Nobility of spirit is the grace—or ability—to play, whether in heaven or on earth. And this, I take it—this *noblesse oblige*, which has always been the quality of aristocracy—was precisely the virtue (*aretē*) of the Greek poets, artists, and philosophers, for whom the gods (whether of the Homeric, the Orphic, or the Zoroastrian strains) were true as poetry is true. We may take it also to be the primitive (and proper) mythological point of view, as contrasted with the heavier positivistic; this latter is represented on the one hand by religious experiences of the literal sort, where the impact of a daemon, rising to the plane of consciousness from its place of birth on the level of the sentiments, is taken to be objectively real, and on the other, by science and political economy, for which only measurable facts are objectively real. For if it is true that "God is not like anything: hence no one can understand him by means of an image," or that

> It is other, indeed, than the known
> And, moreover, above the unknown!

then it must be conceded, as a basic principle of our natural history of the gods and heroes, that whenever a myth has been taken literally its sense has been perverted; but also, reciprocally, that whenever it has been dismissed as a mere priestly fraud or a sign of inferior intelligence, truth has slipped out the other door.

But what, then, is the sense that we are to seek, if it is neither here nor there?

The reader will perhaps recall that Immanuel Kant, in his *Prolegomena to Every Future System of Metaphysics*, states very carefully that all of our thinking about final things can be only by way of *analogy*. "The proper expression for our fallible mode of conception," he says, "would be: that we imagine the world *as if* its being and inner character were derived from a supreme mind."[22]

Such a highly played game of "as if" frees our mind and spirit on the one hand from the presumption of theology, which pretends to know the laws of God, and on the other from the bondage of reason, whose laws do not apply beyond the horizon of human experience.

I am willing to accept the word of Kant as the view of the metaphysician. And applying it to the range of festival games and attitudes just reviewed—from the mask to the consecrated host and temple image, transubstantiated worshiper and transubstantiated world—I can see, or believe I can see, that a principle of release operates throughout the series by way of the alchemy of an "as if"; and that, through this, the impact of all so-called "reality" upon the psyche is transubstantiated. The play state and the rapturous seizures sometimes deriving from it represent, therefore, a step *toward* rather than away from the ineluctable truth; and belief—acquiescence in a belief that is not quite belief —is the first step toward the deepened participation that the festival affords in that general Will to Life which, in its metaphysical aspect, is antecedent to, and the creator of, all of life's laws.

The opaque weight of the world—both of life on earth and of death, heaven and hell—is dissolved, and the spirit freed . . . not *from* anything, for there was nothing from which to be freed except a myth too solidly believed, but *for* something, something fresh and new, a spontaneous act.

From the position of secular man (*Homo sapiens*), then, we are to enter the play sphere of the festival, acquiescing in a game of belief, where fun, joy, and rapture rule in ascending series. The laws of life in time and space—economics, politics, and even morality—will dissolve. Whereafter, re-created by that return to Paradise before the Fall, before the knowledge of good and evil, right and wrong, true and false, belief and disbelief, we are to carry the point of view and spirit of man the player (*Homo ludens*) back into life: as in the play of children, where, undaunted by the banal actualities of life's meager possibilities, the spontaneous impulse of the spirit to identify itself with something other than itself, for the sheer delight of play, transubstantiates the world—in which, after all, things are not quite as real or permanent, terrible, important, or logical as they seem.

REFERENCES

1. *Nonni Dionysiaca* 6.121; *Orphei Hymni* 39.7; *ibid.* 253.
2. O. Kern, *Orphicorum fragmenta* (Berlin, 1922), 34.
3. *Ibid.* 34, 35.
4. F. M. Cornford, *Greek Religious Thought from Homer to the Age of Alexander* (London: J. M. Dent and Sons, Ltd.; New York: E. P. Dutton & Co., Inc., 1923), pp. xv-xvi.
5. *Ibid.*, p. xiii.
6. E. J. Rapson, ed., *The Cambridge History of India* (New York: The Macmillan Company, 1922), Vol. I, pp. 434-461; 541-561.
7. Leo Frobenius, *Paideuma, Umrisse einer Kultur- und Seelenlehre* (3 Aufl., Frankfurt, 1928), pp. 143-145.
8. Cornford, *op. cit.*, pp. x-xii.
9. *Brihadāranyaka Upanishad* 1.4.6-10.
10. H. Diels, *Die Fragmente der Vorsokratiker* (Berlin, 4th ed. 1922), Vol. I.
11. Cited by Clement of Alexandria, *Exhortation to the Greeks,* p. 61 P.
12. *Kena Upanishad* 1.3.
13. J. Huizinga, *Homo Ludens*, trans. R. F. C. Hull (London: Routledge and Kegan Paul, Ltd., 1949), p. 5.
14. *Ibid.*, p. 22.
15. *Ibid.*, p. 23, citing R. R. Marett, *The Threshold of Religion* (New York, 1914), p. 45.
16. *Ibid.*, p. 25.
17. Zimmer, *Philosophies of India* (New York: Pantheon Press, 1951), pp. 581 ff.
18. Swami Nikhilananda, trans., *The Gospel of Sri Ramakrishna* (New York: Ramakrishna-Vivekananda Center, 1942), p. 396.
19. *Ibid.*, p. 396.
20. *Ibid.*, pp. 778-779.
21. Huizinga, *op. cit.*, pp. 34-35.
22. Kant, *Prolegomena zu einer jeden künftigen Metaphysik, die als Wissenschaft wird auftreten können* (*Werke*, Leipzig, 1838-1842, Theil 3), Paragraph 58. (Italics added.)

2. Recurrent Themes in Myths and Mythmaking

CLYDE KLUCKHOHN

It is the purpose of this paper to draw together some information on and interpretation of certain features of mythology that are apparently universal or that have such wide distribution in space and time that their generality may be presumed to result from recurrent reactions of the human psyche to situations and stimuli of the same general order. Addressing a group from a wide range of disciplinary affiliations, I shall utilize recent writings that are, as yet, generally familiar only to anthropologists and folklorists. I shall also add a modest effort on my own part to sample independently the distribution of a small number of mythic elements. The result makes no pretensions to completeness or indeed to more than approximate accuracy on the materials surveyed. But even a crude and tentative synthesis may have some interest and provide some stimulation to more comprehensive and precise research.

Literary scholars, psychiatrists, and behavioral scientists have, of course, long recognized that diverse geographical areas and historical epochs have exhibited striking parallels in the themes of myth and folklore. Father-seekers and father-slayers appear again and again. Mother-murder appears in explicit and in disguised form (see Bunker, 1944). Eliade (1949) has dealt with the myth of "the eternal return." Marie Bonaparte (1947) has presented evidence that wars give rise to fantasies of patently similar content. Animal stories—at least in the Old World—show likenesses in many details of plot and embellishment: African tales and Reynard the Fox, the Aesop fables, the Panchatantra of India and the Jataka tales of China (see Herskovits and Herskovits, 1958, p. 118). The Orpheus story has a sizable distribution in the New World (Gayton, 1935).

In considering various parallels, some elementary cautions must perforce be observed. First, levels of abstraction must be kept distinct. It is true, and it is relevant, to say that creation myths are universals or near-universals. But this is a far more abstract statement then are generalizations about the frequency of the creation of human beings by mother earth and father sky, or by an androgynous deity, or from vegetables. Second, mere comparisons on the basis of the presence or absence of a trait are tricky and may well be misleading. Although there are cases where I have as yet no positive evidence for the presence of the incest theme, there is no corpus of mythology that I have searched carefully where this motif does not turn up. Even if, however, incest could be demonstrated as a theme present in all mythologies, there would still be an important difference between mythologies preoccupied with incest and those where it occurs only incidentally and infrequently. Nevertheless, the methodological complications of reliable ratings upon the centrality or strength of a given theme are such that in this paper I must deal almost exclusively with sheer presence or absence.

Most anthropologists today would agree with Lévi-Strauss (1955) that throughout the world myths resemble one another to an extraordinary degree; there is, indeed, an "astounding similarity between myths collected in widely different regions." The differences are there too, of course, between cultures and culture areas, even between versions of "the same" myth collected on the same day from two or more individuals of a particular culture. Some myths appear to have a very limited geographical distribution; other themes that have a very wide or perhaps universal distribution are varyingly styled, weighted, and combined. These differences are very real and very massive, and there must be no tacit attempt to explain them away. For some purposes of inquiry the focus must be upon questions of emphasis, of inversion of plot, of selective omission and addition, of reinterpretation, of every form of variation. The similarities, however, are also genuine, and it is upon these that I shall concentrate. After all, presumably no two events in the universe are literally identical. But there are formal resemblances at varying levels of abstraction that are interesting and significant.

Let us begin with some broad universals. I have already mentioned the creation myth.* This may seem so broad a category as to be empty. Yet Rooth (1957) on analyzing three hundred creation myths of the North American Indians finds that most of them fit comfortably into eight types and that seven of these types appear likewise in Eurasia. She interprets the similarities in types and in congruence of detail motifs between North America and Eurasia (and also some between Peru, Meso-America, and the Pacific Islands) as due to historic diffusion. Were this inference to be demonstrated as valid in all respects, there would still remain the fact that these plots and their details had sufficient psychological meaning to be preserved through the centuries.

There are two ways of reasoning that bulk prominently in all mythological systems. These are what Sir James Frazer called the "laws" of sympathetic magic (like causes like) and holophrastic magic (the part stands for the whole). These principles are particularly employed in one content area where the record is so full and so exceptionless that we are justified in speaking of genuine cultural universals. I know of no culture without myths and tales relating to witchcraft, and the following themes seem to appear always and everywhere.

* Myths of the creation of the world are infrequent in some areas (e. g., Melanesia and Indonesia). But stories of the creation of mankind appear to be universal. Many themes recur in widely separated areas but do not approach universality: the first parents are sun and moon or earth and sky; the first impregnation comes from the rays of the sun; the first humans are fashioned from earth by a creator or emerge as vegetables from the earth and cannot at first walk straight. Destruction of an old world and creation of a new is likewise a frequently recurring story.

1. Were-animals who move about at night with miraculous speed, gathering in witches' sabbaths to work evil magic.
2. The notion that illness, emaciation, and eventual death can result from introducing by magical means some sort of noxious substance into the body of the victim.
3. A connection between incest and witchcraft.

So far as I have been able to discover, the only cultural variability here concerns minutiae: details of the magical techniques; which animals are portrayed; what kinds of particles are shot into the victim or what kinds of witchcraft poisons are employed. It is, to be sure, conceivable that once again we are dealing with diffusion: that all known cultures derive eventually from a generalized Paleolithic culture in which these items of witchcraft lore were already evolved. But, again, their persistence cannot be understood except on the hypothesis that these images have a special congeniality for the human mind as a consequence of the relations of children to their parents and other childhood experiences which are universal rather than culture-bound.

While a comprehensive interpretation of any myth or of mythologies must rest upon the way in which themes are combined—upon, as Lévi-Strauss (1955, 1957) says, "a bundle of features"—nevertheless the mere recurrence of certain motifs in varied areas separated geographically and historically tells us something about the human psyche. It suggests that the interaction of a certain kind of biological apparatus in a certain kind of physical world with some inevitables of the human condition (the helplessness of infants, two parents of different sex, etc.) bring about some regularities in the formation of imaginative productions, of powerful images. I want to consider examples of these, only mentioning some but discussing others at a little greater length. I have selected themes that have been stated by various students of comparative mythology to be nearly universal in distribution.

In most cases we cannot say strictly that these images are universal, either because of incomplete evidence or because of known exceptions, but we can say that some are known from all or almost all of the major culture areas of the world. To avoid egregious sampling errors and generally to make the inquiry more systematic, I have used Murdock's (1957) "world ethnographic sample." He presents a carefully selected sample of all the cultures known to history and ethnography, classified into sixty culture areas. Richard Moench and I tried to cover one culture from each of these areas but were able to work through only fifty—and this not exhaustively. The fifty are, however, distributed about evenly among Murdock's six major regions (Circum-Mediterranean, Negro Africa, East Eurasia, Insular Pacific, North America, South America). To the extent that time permitted, we used standard monographic sources on the cultures in question (or excerpts from these sources in the Human Relations Area Files at Harvard). We also had recourse to certain compendia: the Hastings *Encyclopaedia of Religion and Ethics, Myths of All Races,* Stith Thompson's *Motif Index,* and others.

Our results are far from satisfactory, but they do represent a start. On the positive side, they ought to be almost completely trustworthy. That is, where we report, for example, that brother-sister incest is a mythological theme in Micronesia, this can be regarded as established. It is on the negative side that doubt must be raised. For instance, we did not discover an androgynous deity in the mythology of the Warrau. This, unfortunately, does not necessarily mean that no such deity exists in Warrau mythology—only that we discovered no reference in the one original source and in the compilations we checked. Without question, a more intensive search than we were able to conduct would enlarge—we cannot guess by how great a factor—the number of features to be tabulated as "present."

Flood. We found this theme—usually, but not always, treated as a punishment—in thirty-four of our fifty mythologies. The distribution is not far from equal in five of the six regions, but we encountered only one reference from Negro Africa. There is the possibility that some of these tales take their ultimate source from the mythology of the Near East and, specifically, Jewish-

Christian mythology, although many ethnographers are careful to discriminate explicitly between those that may have this derivation and others that seem definitely "aboriginal." Li Hwei (see Bascom, 1957, p. 114) has traced fifty-one flood myths in Formosa, South China, Southeast Asia, and Malaysia that it hardly seems plausible to attribute to Jewish-Christian sources.[*] At any rate, if one adds earthquakes, famines, plagues, etc., it is likely, on present evidence, that "catastrophe" can be considered as a universal or near-universal theme in mythology.

Slaying of Monsters. This theme appears in thirty-seven of our fifty cultures, and here the distribution approaches equality save for a slightly greater frequency in North America and the Insular Pacific. Not infrequently, the elaboration of the theme has a faintly Oedipal flavor. Thus in Bantu Africa (and beyond) a hero is born to a woman who survives after a monster has eaten her spouse (and everyone else). The son immediately turns into a man, slays a monster or monsters, restores his people —but not his father—and becomes chief.

Incest. This is overtly depicted in thirty-nine mythologies. In three cases (Celtic, Greek, and Hindu) mother-son, father-daughter, and brother-sister incest are alluded to; eleven cases mention two forms of incest; the remaining twenty-five mythologies apparently deal with only a single type. In our sample we encountered only seven references to mother-son incest (none in Negro Africa and only one in East Eurasia). In other reading we did find an additional seven reports—one more from East Eurasia but still none from Negro Africa. Brother-sister incest was easily the most popular theme in the sample (twenty-eight cases). There are twelve cases of father-daughter incest. In creation stories, the first parents are not infrequently depicted as incestuous, and there are numerous references to the seduction of a mother-in-law by her son-in-law (or vice versa).

[*] Lord Raglan (1956) relates the flood myth to the flooding of rivers and the whole problem of subsistence in newly agricultural civilizations. But it occurs in many nonliterate societies, including some that do not have even incipient agriculture.

Sibling Rivalry. We discovered thirty-two instances of this theme, which appears from all six "continental" regions but—so far as our sample goes—is appreciably more frequent in the Insular Pacific and in Negro Africa. The rivalry between brothers is portrayed far oftener than any other, and usually in the form of fratricide. There were only four cases of brother-sister quarrels (one resulting in murder) and only two of sister-sister. There are some indications in the data that a larger sample and a finer analysis would reveal some culturally distinctive regularities as regards the age order of siblings depicted as rivalrous. For example, in parts of Negro Africa it appears that it is always two siblings born in immediate sequence who are chosen as protagonists.

Castration. We found only four cases where actual castration is mentioned in the myths, and one of these (Trobriand) is self-inflicted castration, ostensibly as a reaction to guilt over adultery. There were in addition five cases in which the threat of castration to boys is mentioned in myths as a socialization technique. There are also instances (e.g., Baiga) where there are reports of severed penes and injured testicles. However, if one counts themes of "symbolic castration," then there is an approach toward universality. The subincision rites of the Australian aborigines have been so interpreted. And in our browsing (beyond our sample) we encountered the *vagina dentata* motif among the following peoples: Arapaho, Bellabella, Bellacoola, Blackfoot, Comox, Coos, Crow, Dakota, Iroquois, Jicarilla, Kwakiutl, Maidu, Nez Percé, Pawnee, San Carlos Apache, Shoshone, Shuswap, Thompson, Tsimshian, Walapai, Wichita; Ainu; Samoa; Naga; Kiwai Papuan.

Androgynous Deities. From our sample we can document only seven cases (all from Circum-Mediterranean, East Eurasia, and North America). Eliade (1958[a], p. 25) says that divine bisexuality is not found "in really primitive religions." The numerous examples he gives (1958[b], pp. 420-425) are all from "advanced" religions, though we could add a few from "primitive" cultures.

OEDIPUS-TYPE MYTHS

Let us now turn to a brief examination of two patterns in which themes are combined. The Oedipus story has long haunted European literature and thought, even if in very recent times the myth of Sisyphus may have replaced that of Oedipus in popularity (see Kafka, Camus, and many others). Jones (1954) has tried to show that *Hamlet* is basically an Oedipal plot. Others insist that Great Mother or Mater Dolorosa tales are simply special variants.

At all events, some scholars have regarded the Oedipal tale as prototypical of all human myths. Critical scrutiny of this generalization, and particularly one's conclusions as to the prevalence of Oedipus-type myths outside the areas the story may have reached through historical diffusion, will rest on how much credence one is prepared to give to psychoanalytic interpretations of latent content, on the one hand; and on how many elements of the Greek myth one demands be replicated, on the other. Thus Róheim's (1950, pp. 319-347) contention that certain Navaho myths are Oedipal strikes many as strained. The main emphasis is upon the father killing his own children—even here Róheim must argue that it is the father's *weapon* that is used (by another). And he must contend that the giant who makes amorous advances to the mother and is killed by the sons is a *father substitute*.

Actually, the forty-eight Oedipal myths in the Euro-Asiatic area analyzed by Rank (1952) and Raglan (1956) do not show a very striking fit in detail (see Bascom, 1957) to the Greek myth. In only four of these does the hero marry his mother. Indeed, in only eight others is an incestuous theme of any kind explicitly present. Again, in only four of the forty-eight myths does the hero cause the death of his father. In nine other cases the hero kills (or in one case is killed by) a close relative (grandfather, uncle, brother, etc.). One can make a good case for "antagonism against close relatives—*usually* of the same sex" as a prominent motif, and a fair case for physical violence against such relatives. But neither parricide nor Raglan's regicide motifs will stand up literally without a great deal of farfetched interpretation.

In a very interesting paper Lessa (1956) has suggested that the Oedipus-type story spread by diffusion from the patriarchal Euro-Asiatic societies to Oceanic peoples with whom the situation is very different. He writes:

> ... we find such stories limited to a continuous belt extending from Europe to the Near and Middle East and southeastern Asia, and from there into the islands of the Pacific. It seems to be absent from such vast areas as Africa, China, central Asia, northeastern Asia, North America, South America, and Australia [page 68].

In an examination of several thousand Oceanic narratives Lessa found twenty-three that bore some resemblance to the Oedipus tale. He points out, however, that none meet all three of his major criteria* (prophecy, parricide, and incest) or his minor criteria (succorance from exposure, rearing by another king, fulfillment of prophecy); only a third meet the combination of parricide and incest. Lessa also calls attention to various "substitutions": mother's brother for father, father's sister for mother, son kills father rather than the other way round, incest merely threatened rather than consummated, baby abandoned but without hostility.

Nevertheless, even if one grants Lessa's inference of diffusion (with culturally appropriate substitutions), I do not think one can at present assent to his main argument without exception. Róheim's (1950) case for Oedipal pattern in the myths of Australian aborigines, Yurok, Navaho, and others does indeed involve too much reliance upon "unconscious ideas" and "real motifs." And yet, in my opinion, something remains that cannot altogether be explained away. Lessa asserts flatly that Oedipal tales are absent from Africa, but they are found among the Shilluk (Bascom, 1957, p. 111); and the Lamba (central Bantu) have

* Lessa's criteria are those of the Aarne-Thompson classification of folk tales.

a story of a son killing his father, in which there is a fairly overt motif of sexual rivalry for the mother.

Herskovits and Herskovits (1958, p. 94) make two significant points as regards testing generalizing conclusions about the Oedipus myth in cross-cultural perspective. The first (abundantly confirmed by the present small study) is neglect of rivalry between brothers. Then they say:

In analyzing the motivating forces underlying the myth clusters that fall into the Oedipus category, we must take into account not only the son's jealousy of the father, but also the father's fear of being displaced by his son. Parent-child hostilities, that is, are not unidirectional. As manifest in myth, and in the situations of everyday experience, they are an expression of the broader phenomenon of intergenerational competition. These tensions, moreover, begin in infancy in the situation of rivalry between children of the same parents for a single goal, the attention of the mother. This rivalry sets up patterns of interaction that throughout life give rise to attitudes held toward the siblings or sibling substitutes with whom the individual was in competition during infancy, and it is our hypothesis that these attitudes are later projected by the father upon his offspring. In myth, if the psychological interpretation is to be granted validity, we must posit that the threat to the father or father-surrogate is to be seen as a projection of the infantile experience of sibling hostility upon the son. It may be said to be the response to the reactivation of early attitudes toward the mother under the stimulus of anticipated competition for the affection of the wife.

The hypothesis that the main direction of hostility is from father to son received much confirmation from our reading from the following: fourteen North American peoples; four Circum-Mediterranean peoples; five from East Eurasia; three from the Insular Pacific; four from Africa. These were noted incidentally in searching for material on our selected themes. In many cases the myth states as an explicit motif the father's fear of being killed or displaced by his son. In some instances a prophecy is mentioned. Sometimes the son is expelled by the father rather than killed. An Azande father is depicted as destroying an

incestuous son by magic. An Alor father orders his wife to kill the
next child *if* male. There are many variants, but the basic theme
is certainly a prevalent one.

THE MYTH OF THE HERO

It strikes me that the Oepidal pattern may best be considered
as one form of a far more widespread myth, which has been
treated by Rank (1952), Raglan (1956), and Campbell (1956).
Rank abstracts the following pattern in thirty-four myths from
the Mediterranean basin and western Asia:

> The hero is the child of most distinguished parents; usually the son
> of a king. His origin is preceded by difficulties, such as continence, or
> prolonged barrenness or secret intercourse of the parents, due to
> external prohibition or obstacles. During the pregnancy, or antedating
> the same, there is a prophecy in the form of a dream or oracle, cau-
> tioning against his birth, and usually threatening danger to the father,
> or his representative. As a rule, he is surrendered to the water, in a
> box. He is then saved by animals, or lowly people (shepherds) and is
> suckled by a female animal, or by a humble woman. After he is grown
> up, he finds his distinguished parents in a highly versatile fashion;
> takes his revenge on his father, on the one hand, and is acknowledged
> on the other, and finally achieves rank and honors [page 61].

Raglan's first thirteen (of twenty-two) points correspond strikingly to this formula. In a world-wide context Campbell develops
essentially the same pattern in a more sophisticated form, tied
neither to the doctrinaire psychoanalysis of Rank nor to the
limited and culture-bound theories of Raglan.

From the reading done by Moench and myself, many details
not cited in any of the above three publications could be added:
numerous instances of parricide in myth; virgin and other kinds
of miraculous birth; newborn child in basket or pot; care of the
infant by animals or humble women; and the like. This would,
however, be more of the same fragmentary information. Rather,
I shall add to the record two recent pertinent studies that are
more systematic.

Ishida (1955) shows the prevalence in the Far East of all of this "bundle" of themes except prophecy. There are, of course, certain cultural embellishments that are characteristically different, but the plot is patently similar except for the omission of prophecy and the addition of a theme not present in the Rank formula: greater emphasis upon the mother of the hero, and often the worship of her along with her divine son.

But Ishida's research deals with the same continental land mass from which Rank and Raglan draw their data. Let us therefore take an example from the New World, Spencer's (1957, see esp. pp. 19, 73) analysis of Navaho mythology. The following similarities may be noted:

1. These are also hero stories: adventures and achievements of extraordinary kind (e.g., slaying monsters, overcoming death, controlling the weather).
2. There is often something special about the birth of the hero (occasionally heroine).
3. Help from animals is a frequent motif.
4. A separation from one or both parents at an early age is involved.
5. There is antagonism and violence toward near kin, though mainly toward siblings or father-in-law. This hostility may be channeled in one or both directions. It may be masked but is more often expressed in violent acts.
6. There is eventual return and recognition with honor. The hero's achievements are realized by his immediate family, and redound in some way to their benefit and that of the larger group to which the family belongs.

Contrasts between the Old World and New World forms are clearly reflected in content and emphasis. The themes of social hierarchy and of triumph over (specifically) the father are absent in the American Indian version, and the Navaho theme of anxiety over subsistence is absent from the Euro-Asian plot. Yet at a broad psychological level the similarities are also impressive. In both cases we have a form of "family romance": the hero is separated but in the end returns in a high status; prohibitions and portents and animals play a role; there are two features of

the Oedipus myth as Lévi-Strauss (1955) has "translated" it—
"under-estimation and over-estimation of near kin."

Of constant tendencies in mythmaking, I shall merely remind
you of four that are so well documented as to be unarguable,
then mention two others:

1. Duplication, triplication, and quadruplication of elements. (Lévi-
   Strauss, 1955, suggests that the function of this repetition is to
   make the structure of the myth apparent.)
2. Reinterpretation of borrowed myths to fit pre-existing cultural
   emphases.
3. Endless variations upon central themes.
4. Involution-elaboration.

The psychoanalysts have maintained that mythmaking exemplifies a large number of the mechanisms of ego defense. I agree,
and have provided examples from Navaho culture (Kluckhohn,
1942). Lévi-Strauss (1955, 1957) suggests that mythical thought
always works from awareness of binary oppositions toward their
progressive mediation. That is, the contribution of mythology is
that of providing a logical model capable of overcoming contradictions in a people's view of the world and what they have
deduced from their experience. This is an engaging idea, but
much further empirical work is required to test it.

In conclusion, it may be said that this incomplete and explora-
tory study adds a small bit of confirmation to the finding of
others that there are detectable trends toward regularities both
in myths and in mythmaking. At least some themes and the
linking of certain features of them, while differently stylized and
incorporating varying detailed content according to culture and
culture area, represent recurrent fantasies that have held the
imaginations of many, if not most, social groups.

REFERENCES

Bascom, William, "The Myth-Ritual Theory," *Journal of American Folklore*, 1957, 70: 103-115.

Bonaparte, Marie, *Myths of War*. London: Imago Publishing Company, Ltd., 1947.

Bunker, H. A., "Mother-Murder in Myth and Legend," *Psychoanalytic Quarterly*, 1944, 13: 198-207.

Campbell, Joseph, *The Hero with a Thousand Faces*. New York: Meridian Books, 1956. (1st edn., New York: Pantheon Books, 1949; Bollingen Series, 17.)

Eliade, Mircea, *Le myth de l'éternel retour*. Paris: Gallimard, 1949. (Engl. trans. W. R. Trask, New York: Pantheon Books, 1954; Bollingen Series, 46.)

————, *Birth and Rebirth*. New York: Harper & Brothers, 1958a.

————, *Patterns in Comparative Religion*. New York: Sheed & Ward, 1958b.

Gayton, A. H., "The Orphic Myth in North America," *Journal of American Folklore*, 1935, 48: 263-293.

Herskovits, M. J., and F. S. Herskovits, *Dahomean Narrative*. Evanston, Ill.: Northwestern University Press, 1958.

Ishida, Eiichiro, "The Mother-Son Complex in East Asiatic Religion and Folklore," in *Die Wiener Schule der Voelkerkunde, Festschrift zum 25 jährigen Bestand* (Vienna, 1955), pp. 411-419.

Jones, Ernest, *Hamlet and Oedipus*. New York: Doubleday Anchor Books, 1954. (Published first as an article in the *American Journal of Psychology* in 1910; again in 1923 as Ch. 1 in *Essays in Applied Psycho-Analysis;* revised edn., London: V. Gollancz; New York: W. W. Norton, 1949.)

Kluckhohn, Clyde, "Myths and Rituals: A General Theory," *Harvard Theological Review*, 1942, 35: 45-79.

Lessa, William, "Oedipus-Type Tales in Oceania," *Journal of American Folklore*, 1956, 69: 63-73.

Lévi-Strauss, Claude, "The Structural Study of Myth," *Journal of American Folklore*, 1955, 68: 428-445.

————, "Structure et dialectique," in Morris Halle (compiler), *For Roman Jakobson* (The Hague: Mouton, 1957), pp. 289-294.

Murdock, G. P., "World Ethnographic Sample," *American Anthropologist*, 1957, 59: 664-688.

Raglan, Lord, *The Hero: A Study in Tradition, Myth and Drama*. New York: Vintage Books (Alfred A. Knopf), 1956. (1st edn., London: Methuen and Company, 1936.)

Rank, Otto, *The Myth of the Birth of the Hero,* trans. F. Robbins and S. E. Jellife. New York: Robert Brunner, 1952. (1st edn., *Der Mythus von der Geburt des Helden,* Leipzig-Wien: F. Deuticke, 1909.)

Róheim, Géza, *Psychoanalysis and Anthropology.* New York: International Universities Press, 1950.

Rooth, A. G., "The Creation Myths of the North American Indians," *Anthropos,* 1957, *52:* 497-508.

Spencer, Katherine, *Mythology and Values.* Memoir 48, American Folklore Society, Philadelphia, 1957.

3. The Yearning for Paradise in Primitive Tradition*

MIRCEA ELIADE

In his book on the myths of the African peoples Hermann Baumann sums up the myths of a primeval paradisial era. In those times, he says, men did not know of death: they understood the language of the animals and were at peace with them; they did not work, and found abundant nourishment at hands' reach. Following upon a certain mythical event—which we will not undertake to discuss—this paradisial stage ended and humanity became what we know it to be today.[1]

We encounter the "paradise myth" all over the world in more or less complex forms. Besides the paramount paradisial note, it always has a certain number of characteristic elements, chiefly the idea of immortality. These myths may be classified into two great categories: first, those concerning the primordial close proximity between Heaven and Earth; and second, those referring to an actual means of communication between Heaven and Earth. This is not the place to analyse the many variations of each of these two types, nor to give precise indications of the areas of their distribution or their chronology. For our purposes, a single feature concerns us: in describing the primordial situation the myths reveal its paradisial quality by the fact that *in illo tempore* Heaven is said to have been very near Earth, or that it was easy to reach it by means of a tree, a vine, or a ladder, or by

* Reprinted from the Summer 1953, issue of *Diogenes*, which is published in the United States by the University of Chicago Press.

climbing a mountain. When Heaven was rudely "separated" from Earth, when it became "distant" as it is today, when the tree or the vine leading from Earth to Heaven was cut, or the mountain which touched Heaven was levelled—the paradisial state was over and humanity arrived at its present state.

Actually, all these myths show primitive man enjoying blessedness, spontaneity, and liberty, which he has most annoyingly lost as the consequence of the "fall," that is, as the result of a mythical occurrence which has brought about the rupture between Heaven and Earth. *In illo tempore,* in that paradisial time, the gods descended to Earth and mingled with men, and men could ascend to Heaven by climbing a mountain, a tree, a vine, or a ladder, or have themselves carried there by the birds.

A careful ethnological analysis will throw light on the cultural context of each of these two types of myths. For example, it may be possible to show that the myths about the extreme nearness of Heaven and Earth are found primarily in Oceania and in southeast Asia and are in some way connected with a matriarchal ideology.[2] And again, it might show that the mythical symbol of an *Axis mundi*—mountain, tree, vine, which occupies the "centre of the Earth" and connects Earth with Heaven, a symbol already found among the most primitive tribes (Australia, pigmies, Arctic regions, etc.)—has been developed principally in pastoral and sedentary cultures, and has been handed on to the great urban cultures of Eastern antiquity.[3] But we need not go into these ethnological analyses. For the purposes of this article the classification of the myths will suffice.

Let us enumerate the specific characteristics of the man of the "paradisial" period without considering their respective contexts: immortality, spontaneity, liberty, the ability to ascend to Heaven and "easy access" to the gods, friendship with the animals and knowledge of their language. This combination of privileges and powers was lost in consequence of a primordial event: the "fall" of man may be interpreted equally well by an ontological mutation in his own state as by a cosmic rupture.

It is, however, not uninteresting to find that through the exercise of special techniques the shaman tries to overcome the actual conditions of human life—those affecting "fallen man"—and to reconstitute the state of primordial man as we know it by the "paradisial myths." We know that among the other manipulators of religion in archaic cultures the shaman is the specialist in ecstasy *par excellence*. It is because of his ecstatic power—thanks to the fact that he can at will leave his material body and undertake mystical journeys anywhere in the cosmos—that the shaman can be healer and guide as well as mystic and visionary. None but the shaman can follow the wandering and lost soul of the diseased, capture and restore it to its body. It is he who accompanies the souls of the dead to their new dwellings. No other than he may undertake the long ecstatic journeys to Heaven to lay before the gods the soul of the sacrificed animal and pray for the divine blessing. In a word, the shaman is the expert in "matters of the spirit"; he, above all others, knows the various dramas, risks, and perils that concern "the soul." For "primitive" societies, the whole complex "shaman" represents what, in more elaborated religions, we have agreed to call mysticism and mystical experience.

The shamanic séance usually contains the following elements: (1) call of the auxiliary spirits (for the most part these are animals) and conversation with them in a secret language; (2) drum playing and dancing in preparation for the mystic journey; (3) the trance (feigned or real) during which the soul of the shaman is considered to have left his body. The goal of the whole shamanic séance is to arrive at ecstasy, for only in ecstasy can the shaman "fly" through the air, or "descend into Hell," in other words, fulfill his mission of healer and psychic guide.

It is significant that in order to prepare for the trance the shaman makes use of a "secret language," or, as it is called in some regions, "the language of animals." On the one hand, the shaman imitates the behaviour of the animals; on the other, he tries to imitate their cries, above all those of birds. Shieroszewski has observed it among the Yakutsk shamans:[4]

Mysterious noises are audible sometimes from above, sometimes from below, sometimes in front of, sometimes behind the shaman. . . . You seem to hear the plaintive call of the lapwing mingled with the croaking of a falcon interrupted by the whistle of the woodcock, all that is the voice of the shaman, varying the intonations of his voice— you hear the screaming of eagles mingled with the plaints of the lapwing, the sharp tones of the woodcock and the refrain of the cuckoo.

Castagné describes the *baqça* of the Kirghiz-Tatars, "Imitating with remarkable fidelity the songs of the birds and the sound of their wings."[5] As Lehtisalo has observed, a good share of the words used by the shaman during the séance have their origin in the cries of birds and other animals. This is particularly true with regard to the refrains and the yodelling, most frequently founded on onomatopeia, on phonemes and trills which plainly show that they come from the calls as well as the songs of birds.[6] In general, the shaman speaks during the séance with a high voice, a head tone, a falsetto, as if to emphasise that it is not he who speaks but a "spirit" or a "god." But we must note at this point that the same high voice is used as a rule for intoning magic formulas. "Magic" and "song"—especially song like birdsong—are often designated by the same word. The Germanic term for the magic formula is *galdr* used with the verb *galan,* "to sing," which is applied more particularly to the cries of birds.

If one takes into account the fact that during his initiation the shaman is supposed to meet an animal who will reveal to him certain secrets of his profession, teach him "the language of animals," or become his "helper-spirit" (familiar) it is easier to understand the relations of friendship and familiarity which are established between the shaman and the animals: he speaks their language and becomes their friend and their master. We must say at once that to obtain the friendship of the animals so that they freely accept his control over them does not, to the mind of the primitive, imply any regression on the part of the shaman to a lower biological rank or stage. In one respect the animals are the bearers of a symbolism and mythology very significant for the religious life; to have contact with them, to speak their language, to become their friend and master means the possession of a spiritual life much more abundant than the simple human life of an ordinary mortal. In another sense, and as viewed by primitive man, animals possess considerable prestige, inasmuch as they know the secrets of life and of nature and even possess the secrets of longevity and immortality. Thus, in returning to the condition of the animals, the shaman comes to share their secret knowledge and enjoys the fuller life which is theirs.

We should emphasise this fact: friendship with the animals and knowledge of their language represents a "paradisial" syndrome. *In illo tempore,* before the "fall," such friendship was an integral part of the primordial situation. The shaman restores part of the "paradisial" situation of primordial man and he does this by recovering animal spontaneity (imitating animal behaviour) and speaking animal language (imitation of animal sounds). It is important to state that the dialogue with the animals or their "incorporation" by the shaman (a mystic phenomenon not to be confused with "possession") constitutes the pre-ecstatic stage of the séance. The shaman cannot abandon his body and set out on his mystic journey before he has recovered, by his intimacy with the animals, a blessedness and a spontaneity inaccessible to his profane, every-day state. The vital experience of this friendship with the animals advances him far beyond the general situation of "fallen" humanity, while it permits him to return to *illud tempus* of the "paradisial" myths.

As for the state of ecstasy itself, it comprises, as we have seen, the abandonment of the body and the mystical journey to Heaven or to Hell. Here one fact is of supreme interest: namely, that the shaman's ascent to heaven is accomplished by the instrumentality of a tree or upright pole, symbols of the Cosmic Tree or Pole. Thus the Altaic shaman uses for the seance a young birch tree with its lower branches lopped and seven, nine, or twelve steps cut into the trunk. The tree symbolises the Tree of the World, the seven, nine, or twelve steps represent the seven, nine or twelve Heavens, in other words, the different celestial levels. After having sacrificed a horse, the shaman climbs the steps, one after the other, till he reaches the ninth Heaven where Bai Ulgan, the supreme God, resides. As he ascends he describes to his audience,

in great detail, everything he sees in each one of the Heavens.
Finally, in the ninth Heaven he falls down before Bai Ulgan and
offers him the soul of the sacrificial horse. This episode is the
climax of the ecstatic ascent of the shaman: he collapses ex-
hausted. After some time, he rubs his eyes, as though waking
from deep sleep and greets the audience as though returning
after long absence.[7]

The symbolism of the heavenly ascension by means of a tree is
also clearly exemplified by the initiation ceremony of the Buriat
shamans. The candidate clambers up a birch tree inside the hut,
reaches the top and exits through the vent made for the smoke.
But this vent for the smoke is known to represent the "hole" made
by the polar star in the firmament. (Among other races the tent
pole is called "Pole of the World" and likened to the polar star
which also holds the tent of heaven like a pole and is called "Nail
of Heaven.") Thus the ceremonial birch inside the hut is a representation of the "Cosmic Tree" which is located in the "Centre of
the World" and at the top of which shines the polar star. By
climbing it, the candidate enters Heaven, and that is why, when
he has left the tent by the vent, he shouts to invoke the help of
the gods; up there he is in their presence.[8]

A similar symbolism explains the role of the shamanic drum.
Emsheimer has shown that the dreams or initiation ecstasies of
the future shamans signify a mystic journey on the Cosmic Tree
at whose summit resides the Lord of the World. From one of the
branches of that tree, dropped by the Lord for that purpose, the
shaman fashions the cylinder of his drum.[9] We know that the
Cosmic Tree is supposed to be at the "Centre of the World" and
that it connects Heaven and Earth. Because the cylinder of the
drum comes from the very wood of the Cosmic Tree, the shaman,
while drumming, is magically brought close to that tree, that is,
to the Centre of the World, where there is a possibility of going
from one cosmic level to another.

Accordingly, whether he climbs the seven or nine steps cut into
the ceremonial birch tree, or whether he beats his drum, the
shaman is on his way to Heaven. In the first case, he laboriously

mimics the ascent of the Cosmic Tree; in the second, he "flies" to the tree by the magic action of his drum. "Shamanic flight" is in any case very frequent and often identified with the ecstasy itself. Among the numerous variations of "shamanic flight" we are chiefly interested in the "flight" to the "Centre of the World"; there we find the Tree, the Mountain, the Cosmic Pole, which connect Earth with Heaven. And it is there that we find the "hole" made by the polar star. As he climbs the Mountain, as he ascends the Tree, as he flies or comes up through the "hole" to the summit of the heavenly vault, the shaman effects his ascent to Heaven.

We know that *in illo tempore*, in the mythical time of "Paradise," there was a Mountain, a Tree, a Pole, or a Vine which connected Earth with Heaven and that primordial man could readily pass from one to the other by climbing them. Communication with Heaven was easy *in illo tempore*, and the meeting with the gods took place in actuality. The memory of these "paradisial" days is still very lively among "primitive" people. The Koryaks remember the mythical era of the hero Great-Crow when men could ascend to Heaven without trouble; they add that in our days only the shamans can do this. The Bakairi of Brazil believe that for the shaman Heaven is no higher than a house, and therefore he can reach it in the twinkling of an eye.[10]

This means that during this ecstasy the shaman recovers the "paradisial" state. He re-establishes the easy communications as *in illo tempore* between Heaven and Earth. For him the Mountain or the Cosmic Tree again becomes the actual method of attaining Heaven, such as it was before the "fall." For the shaman, Heaven again comes close to Earth; no higher than a house, just as it was before the primordial rupture. Furthermore, the shaman re-establishes friendly relations with the animals. In other words, the ecstasy restores, though only provisionally and for a restricted number of persons—the "mystics"—the initial state of all humanity. Thus the mystic experience of "primitive" peoples is equivalent to a *return to the beginning*, a reversion to the mythical days of a "Lost Paradise." For the shaman in the state of ecstasy, this world, this fallen world—which according to modern terminology is governed by the laws of Time and History—no longer exists. True, there is a great difference between the situation of primordial man and that restored by the shaman during ecstasy; the shaman can only temporarily abolish the rupture between Heaven and Earth. He ascends to Heaven "in spirit," no longer *in concreto* as did primordial man. He does not abrogate death (all the ideas of immortality found among primitive peoples imply—as they do among civilised ones—a preliminary death; that is to say, that the immortality is always a post-mortem, "spiritual" one).

To sum up: the paramount mystic experience of primitive societies, that is to say, shamanism, reveals this "yearning for Paradise," the wish to return to a state of blessedness and liberty such as existed before the "fall," to restore contact between Heaven and Earth; in a word, it reveals the wish to abolish everything which has changed in the structure of the Cosmos itself and in the manner of man's existence since the primordial break. The ecstasy of the shaman recovers largely the paradisial situation: he has regained the friendship of the animals; by his "flight" or by his ascension he has again linked Heaven and Earth; up there in Heaven he meets again face to face the celestial Being and speaks to him in person as he was wont to do *in illo tempore.*

One finds an analogous situation in the most recent and most elaborate mysticism in existence, namely in Christian mysticism. Christianity is dominated by the yearning for Paradise. Turning to the East during prayer is connected with paradisial themes— it appears as an expression of the yearning for Paradise.[11] The same symbolism of paradise is attested in the ritual of baptism: "Contrasted with Adam, who falls under the domination of Satan and is driven from Paradise, the catechumen is as though freed from such domination by the New Adam and led back to Paradise."[12]

Christianity thus appears as the realisation of Paradise. "Christ is the Tree of Life" (Ambrosius, *De Isaac,* 5, 43) or the "fount of

Paradise" (Ambrosius, *De Paradiso*, 3, 272, 10). But this realisation of Paradise is on three successive levels. Baptism is the entrance into Paradise (Cyril of Jerusalem, *Procatech.* P. G. xxxiii, 357A); the life of mysticism is a deeper penetration into Paradise (Ambrosius, *De Paradiso*, I, I); finally death conducts the martyrs into Paradise (*Passio Perpet.*, P.L. III, 28a). It is indeed remarkable that we find this paradisial vocabulary applied to these three aspects of the Christian life.[13]

It is mysticism, then, that best reveals the restoration of the paradisial life. The first syndrome of this restoration is the renewed control over animals. As is well known, Adam at the beginning was told to provide names for the animals (Genesis, II, 19); for to name them is the same as to dominate them. Saint Thomas thus explained the power of Adam over creatures not endowed with reason: "The mind commands by its rule the sensitive appetites, such as the passions of anger and of desire which, in a certain way, do obey reason. *Hence* in the state of innocence, man by his command ruled over the other animals."[14] But, "both giving names and changing names played an equally important role in eschatological pronouncements. . . . The Messianic kingdom brings about a moral conversion in men and even in animals . . . conversions characteristic of the world made by the hand of God."[15] In the mystic state the animals are often subject to the saint as they were to Adam. "The history of the early Fathers of the monastic era shows—such cases are not infrequent—that they were obeyed by the wild beasts which they fed as they would domestic animals" (Dom Stolz, *op. cit.*, p. 31). Saint Francis carries on the tradition of the desert Fathers. Friendship with wild beasts and control over animals by their own consent are manifest signs of the return to a paradisial state.

In the same way we can observe the paradisial symbolism of the churches and the monastic garden. The landscape which surrounds the monk represents the earthly paradise: in a certain way it anticipates it. But it is above all the mystical experience as such which interests us. As Dom Stolz has very well shown, the typical Christian mystical experience is the ascension to

Heaven of Saint Paul: "I knew a man in Christ above fourteen years ago (whether in the body, I cannot tell; or whether out of the body, I cannot tell: God knoweth;) such an one caught up to the third heaven. And I knew such a man (whether in the body or out of the body, I cannot tell: God knoweth;) How that he was caught up into paradise and heard unutterable words, which it is not lawful for a man to utter." (Second Epistle to the Corinthians, xii. 2, 3, 4.) We need not dwell here on the ascensional symbolism of Christian mysticism: in it the Ladder to Paradise plays an important role. The various degrees of contemplation are the steps in the ascent of the soul toward God. However, Saint Paul has stated precisely that this mystical ascension brings man to Paradise: the "unutterable words" which he has heard, are they not the words of God Himself? For Adam in Paradise, as Saint Gregory tells us, "delighted in frequent communion with God" (Dom Stolz, *op. cit.*, p. 111).

Accordingly, although Christianity was permeated with the yearning for Paradise, only the mystics were able to achieve its partial restoration: friendship with the animals, ascension to Heaven and meeting with God. We find the same situation in ancient religions: a certain "yearning for Paradise" appears at all levels of the religious life[16] but it shines out with greatest brilliance in the mystic experience, that is to say, in the ecstasy of the shaman. The specific characteristics of the restoration of *illud tempus* are the same: friendship with the animals, ascension to Heaven, conversation with God in Heaven. Just as does the Christian saint, the shaman in ecstasy recovers Paradise only provisionally; for neither of them can abolish death, in other terms, neither of them can re-establish the condition of primordial man.

Finally, one might remember that for Christian tradition Paradise has become all the more inaccessible because of the fire which surrounds it, or, which amounts to the same thing, because its approach is guarded by angels with flaming swords. "God," says Laetantius (*Divin. Instit.*, II, 12), "has expelled man from Paradise and surrounded it with fire so that men may no longer enter." This is what Saint Thomas means when he explains that

Paradise is no longer accessible to us, principally "because of the heat which keeps it away from our lands" (Dom Stolz, *op. cit.*, p. 24). For this reason he who wants to enter Paradise must first cross the flames surrounding it. "In other words, only he who has been purified by fire may thereupon enter paradise. Thus the cleansing process precedes the mystic union, and the mystics do not hesitate to put this purification of the spirit on the same level as the purifying fire which leads to paradise. . . ." (Dom Stolz, *ibid.* p. 32).

These few citations will suffice to sum up and demonstrate the doctrine of the purifying fire which guards the entrance to Paradise. We will not go into a discussion of the symbolism of fire in Christian mysticism and theology. It is significant, however, that a similar symbolism may be observed in quite a number of shamanic techniques: witness the well-known "mastery of fire." In fact, the shamans are always and everywhere considered "the masters of fire": during the séances they swallow live coals, they touch the burning flame, they tread on fire. The shamans of the earliest cultures already bear witness to this mastery of fire; it is as much a part of shamanism as the ecstasy, the ascent to Heaven, and the understanding of animal language. The ideology implied by this mastery of fire is not easy to unravel: the primitive world (indeed all popular cultures in general) makes a distinction between the "spirits" and human beings on the ground of the formers' "insensitivity to fire," that is to say, their ability to resist the heat of the live coals. The shamans are said to have got beyond the condition of man and to share in the condition of the spirits: just like spirits, they become invisible, they fly in the air, they ascend to Heaven, they descend to Hell. And finally they, too, enjoy "insensitivity to fire." This mastery of fire transposes their "transcendence of human conditions" into terms perceptible to the senses; here as elsewhere the shaman proves that he has adopted a "spiritual state," that he has become—or may become during the séance—a "spirit."

If one compares the purifying fire of Christian tradition as it surrounds Paradise with the "mastery of fire" as practised by the shamans, one notes at least one common feature: in both cases the act of braving the fire without harm is the sign that the human state has been overcome. But for Christianity, just as for the archaic cultures, the present state of humanity is the result of the "fall." Consequently to do away with this state, even if only provisionally, is equivalent to re-establishing the primordial condition of man, in other words, to banish time, to go backward, to recover the "paradisial" *illud tempus*. How precarious this recovery of primordial condition is, is shown, above all, by the circumstance that the shaman obtains it by imitating the state of the "spirits." We have already noted this in connexion with other shamanic techniques; during the trance, it is not the shaman who flies to the Heavens but only his "spirit." A similar situation prevails in Christian mysticism: only the "soul," purified by fire, may enter Paradise.

The analogies which we have just stated seem important: it follows as a corollary that there is no break of continuity between the ideology of the "primitive" mystic experience and Judeo-Christian mysticism. Among the "primitive" peoples, just as among the saints and the Christian theologians, mystic ecstasy is a return to Paradise, expressed by the overcoming of Time and History (the "fall") and the recovery of the primordial state of Man.

Let us make it clear: in uncovering these similarities we do not pretend to make value judgments on the content of the various mystical experiences, whether "primitive" or otherwise. All we mean is that their ideologies contain as a kernel, a focal point, "the yearning for Paradise." Of course such a conclusion does not exclude the many differences between primitive and Judeo-Christian mysticism as well as those among the various schools of Christian mysticism. On the other hand, we have purposely chosen to compare Christianity and the most ancient type of mystic experience, omitting the great tradition of the East: although the "setting aside of Time" and the abolition of History are the essential elements of every mystical experience and therefore also of Eastern mysticism, it seems to us that the "paradisial" elements are better preserved in the archaic mysticisms. In certain ways, the comparisons between the forms of "primitive" mysticism and Christian mysticism have a stronger basis than those between the latter and the Indian, Chinese, and Japanese mysticisms.

Although we cannot attempt to give in these few pages a comparative study of mysticism, the chief result of our inquiry should be stressed: the complete ideological continuity between the most elementary forms of mystical experience and Christianity. At the "beginning" as well as at the "end" of the religious history of Man, we find the same "yearning for Paradise." If we take into account the fact that the "yearning for Paradise" is equally discernible in the general religious attitude of early man we have the right to assume that the mystical memory of a blessedness without history haunts man from the moment he becomes aware of his situation in the cosmos. Thus there opens a new perspective for the study of archaic anthropology. This is not the place to enter upon such a study. Suffice it to say that, in the light of all that has been noted above, certain features of "primitive" spirituality which were considered "aberrant" are not indeed to be considered as such. The imitation of animal cries by the shamans, so impressive to the observer, has at times been considered by anthropologists as manifesting a pathological "possession" whereas, on the contrary, they reveal the wish to recover friendship with animals and thus to re-establish the primordial "paradise." The ecstatic trance, no matter what its phenomenology, is "aberrant" only if its spiritual significance is disregarded. In reality, the shaman, as we have seen, is seeking to re-establish the contact between Heaven and Earth which the "fall" disrupted. The "mastery of fire" likewise is not a "savage superstition" but, on the contrary, shows how the shaman partakes of the state of the "spirits."

Viewed from its own angle, all the strange behaviour of the shaman reveals the highest form of spirituality; it is actually part of a coherent ideology, possessing great nobility. The myths which make up this ideology are among the richest and most beautiful we possess, they are the myths of Paradise and the "fall," the immortality of primordial man and his communion with God;

of the origin of death and of the discovery of the "spirit" (in every sense of that word). All this is not without significance for the understanding and evaluation of the "primitive" and, in general, of the nature of non-European man. Too often Western man allows himself to be moved by the *manifestation* of an ideology, while ignoring the one thing which he should know, the ideology itself, that is to say, the myths that constitute it. The *manifestations* depend on local customs and cultural styles, and the latter may or may not be directly accessible. Impression, accordingly, determines judgment: a ceremony with masks is judged "beautiful," a certain form of dance is "sinister," an initiation rite is "savage" or "aberrant." But if we take the trouble to understand the ideology which underlies all these "manifestations," if we study the myths and the symbols which condition them, we may abandon the subjectivity of "impressions" and arrive at a more objective viewpoint. At times the comprehension of the ideology is sufficient to re-establish the "normality" of a certain behaviour. Recall one single example: the imitation of animal cries. For over a century, the strange cries of the shaman were felt to prove his mental aberration. But their basis was quite different: it was the yearning for Paradise, which haunted the minds of Isaiah and of Virgil, sustained the sainthood of the Fathers of the Church and came to glorious flower in the life of Saint Francis of Assisi.

REFERENCES

1. Hermann Baumann, *Schoepfung und Urzeit des Menschen im Mythos Afrikanischer Voelker* (Berlin, 1936), pp. 236 *et seq.* In Africa a certain number of paradisial myths have become myths of creation; actually they explain the origin of death. Cf. Hans Abrahamson, *The Origin of Death, Studies in African Mythology,* Upsala, 1951.

2. H. Th. Fischer, "Indonesische Paradiesmythen," *Zeitschrift fuer Ethnologie,* xiv, 1932, pp. 204-245; Franz Kiichi Numazava, *Die Weltanfaenge in der japanischen Mythologie,* Paris-Luzern, 1946.

3. Mircea Eliade, *Le Mythe de l'Eternel Retour* (Paris, 1949), p. 21.

4. W. Shieroszewski, "Du chamanisme d'après les croyances des Yakoutes," *Revue de l'Histoire des Religions,* xlvi, 1902.

5. J. Castagné, "Magie et exorcisme chez les Kazak-Kirghizes et autres peuples turcs orientaux," *Revue des Etudes Islamiques,* 1930, pp. 53-151, p. 93. See also Mircea Eliade, *Le chamanisme et les techniques archaiques de l'extase* (Paris, 1951), pp. 180 *et seq.* and *passim.*

6. T. Lehtisalo, "Beobachtungen ueber die Toder," *Journal de la Societé Finno-Ougrienne,* xlviii, 1936-1937. Eliade, "Techniques de l'extase et langages secrets," *Conferenze del Istituto italiano per il medio ed estremo Oriente,* Vol. ii, 1951-1952.

7. M. Eliade, *Le chamanisme et les techniques archaiques de l'extase,* pp. 175 *et seq.*

8. Eliade, *ibid.,* pp. 116 *et seq.*

9. E. Emsheimer, "Schamanentrommel und Trommelbaum," *Ethnos,* 1946, pp. 166-181; Eliade, *Le chamanisme,* pp. 159 *et seq.*

10. Eliade, *Le chamanisme,* pp. 235 *et seq.,* 419 *et seq.;* cf. also *ibid.,* pp. 227, 295.

11. Jean Daniélou, S. J., *Bible et Liturgie* (Paris, 1951), p. 46.

12. *Ibid.,* p. 47.

13. ———, *Sacramentum futuri* (Paris, 1950), p. 16.

14. Dom Anselme Stolz, *Théologie de la mystique* (Chevetogne, 1947), p. 104.

15. Daniélou, *op. cit.,* p. 6.

16. Cf. Eliade, *Traité d'Histoire des religions* (Paris, 1949), pp. 321 *et seq.*

4. Theories of Myth and the Folklorist

RICHARD M. DORSON

STUDENTS OF MYTH and folklore once occupied some common ground. In his often reprinted collection of essays called *Custom and Myth*, first published in 1884, Andrew Lang spelled out the relationship as seen by the anthropological school of English folklorists who so spiritedly advanced the cause of folklore science in the late nineteenth century. Two bodies of material intrigued Lang and his fellows. Around them they beheld archaic survivals among the British—and European—lower classes, in the form of village festival, agricultural rite, and household charm, so anomalous in the midst of the progressive, industrial, scientific England of the Victorian age. From missionaries, travelers, colonial officers, and the new anthropological fieldworkers they learned about "savage" myths, usages, and beliefs in remote corners of the world. The equation between peasants and savages provided "The Method of Folklore," the title of Lang's opening chapter. Savage myth embodied in fresh and vivid form the withered superstitions and desiccated rites now faintly visible in peasant customs. The folklorist could reconstruct their original full-fleshed shapes, and the prehistoric world in which they functioned, by close comparisons with the myths of primitive peoples.

These bodies of living myths further explained to the folklorist the irrational elements in myths of civilized peoples. Lang puzzled over the question why classical Greece preserved in her mythology such barbarous ideas, and found his answer in the new anthropology of E. B. Tylor. Greek myths were survivals and distorted mirrors of an earlier culture when cannibalism and human sacrifice did indeed prevail. To see such customs intact in his own day, the folklorists need simply turn to the Andaman Islanders, the African Hottentots, the Australian Noongahburrahs, and similar newly exposed areas of primitive life. Now the ugly Greek myth of Cronus becomes meaningful. Cronus cruelly castrated his father Uranus, who was about to embrace his mother Gaea. A Maori myth from New Zealand gives the key, depicting Heaven and Earth as a wedded couple, Heaven lying on Earth and imprisoning their children between them. Finally one child, the forest god, forces them asunder, freeing the off-spring for their godly duties over the various elements. So did Cronus secure the separation of Heaven (Uranus) and Earth (Gaea), although the Hellenic Greeks had forgotten the original sense of the nature myth.[1]

Behind this method of folklore inquiry lay an enticing theory, transferred from Darwin's biology to the young science of an-thropology and thence to folklore. Lang and his co-workers, G. L. Gomme, E. S. Hartland, and Edward Clodd, all accepted the unilinear view of cultural evolution. Mankind had climbed from his simian ancestry upward to the state of polished civilization by successive stages. All peoples ascended the evolutionary ladder in exactly the same manner. The savages of today were the Victorians of tomorrow, simply arrested by local circumstance, and conversely the Victorians of the contemporary moment were the savages of yesteryear.

In his far-reaching study of *The Legend of Perseus* (three volumes, 1894-1896), Edwin Sidney Hartland engaged upon the most sweeping application of the folklore method to a single classical myth. By slicing the Perseus myth into component epi-sodes, such as the notions of the Supernatural Birth, the Life Token, the Witch and her Evil Eye, and pursuing their appear-ances throughout the world-wide collections of fairy tales, sagas, and savage mythologies, Hartland was able to demonstrate the substratum of primitive ideas underlying the literary myth. In the refined versions by Ovid and Strabo, Pausanias and Lucian, coarse traits essential to the primitive saga had dropped out: the external soul of the ogre, the lousing of the sleeping hero by his maiden-lover.

Another leading member of the anthropological school, Edward Clodd, examined the relationship between myth and the new study of folklore in his *Myths and Dreams* (1885).[2] The title of a preliminary lecture expresses more completely his point of view: "The Birth and Growth of Myth, and its Survival in Folk-Lore, Legend, and Dogma." Clodd saw in the concept of "myth" not merely the label for a narrative of the gods or the creation of the universe, but also the designation of an entire period in the stage of man's intellectual development, "a necessary travailing through which the mind of man passed in its slow progress towards certitude."[3] In this stage, prehistoric man corresponded to the child, taking dreams for reality, endowing inanimate objects with life, crediting animals with the power of speech.

While the anthropological school of folklorists depended on myths, in this broad sense, to document their major hypotheses, they were at the same time vigorously battling a rival group of myth interpreters. The philological school of comparative mythology, championed in England by Max Müller, unlocked the secrets of myths with the new key of Vedic Sanscrit. In his famous essay on *Comparative Mythology* in 1856, Müller outlined the principles governing the proper explication of myths. All Aryan tongues stemmed from the Sanscrit, which transferred to its offspring the names of gods, all referring to celestial phenomena. The basic equation lay in Dyaus = Zeus, uniting the two chief gods of the Vedic and Hellenic pantheons. Through a "disease of language," the original meanings and myths of the inherited names were forgotten and barbarous new myths arose to take their place. These myths had revolved around the sky (Dyaus) and the sun, the dawn and the clouds, and now comparative mythology could reconstruct these primary meanings buried within revolting Aryan mythologies.

So did solar mythology make its persuasive plea. Among the

solarists who followed Müller's lead, George Cox outstripped all others in the sweep of his claims. Every mythical hero—from Herakles, Perseus, Theseus, Oedipus, Samson, down to Beowulf and King Arthur and the humbler heroes and heroines of the fairy tales, the Frog Prince, Cinderella, Hansel and Gretel— embodied the same solar deity or children of the dawn. One plot underlay all the primary myths and fairy tales, from the siege of Troy to the Song of Roland, the struggle of the sun against the powers of darkness. The sun hero battled monsters and ogres and armies, and suffered frightful trials in the nether regions, just as the sun toiled his way across the sky in the face of clouds and tempests. The gold he found at the end of his quest was the golden sunlight, and his magic swords, spears, and arrows were the sun's darting rays. All mythology revolved around the conflict between day and night.

The science of comparative mythology thus strove to incorporate into its system the narrative traditions prized by the folklorists. In leading the counterattack, Lang called repeated attention to the inner disagreements among the celestial mythologists. Müller read the dawn into his Sanscrit etymologies; others deciphered the storm, fire, the sky, raindrops, the moon. Who was right? The anthropologists also employed the weapon of ridicule, showing how readily "A Song of Sixpence" could be interpreted as solar myth: the pie is the earth, the crust the sky, the four and twenty blackbirds the hours; the king is the sun, and his money the golden sunshine.[4]

By the turn of the century the solar mythologists were fairly routed. Four years after George Cox's *An Introduction to the Science of Comparative Mythology and Folklore,* there appeared in 1885 a rival volume faithfully presenting the anthropological point of view, *An Introduction to Folk-Lore,* by Marian Roalfe Cox, whose study of Cinderella constituted the first extensive comparative investigation of a folk tale. The anthropological school controlled the Folk-Lore Society and dominated its publications during the remaining years of "the great team of English folklorists."[5]

Half a century following the elaboration of Müller's theory another symbolism descended on myth and sought to annex folklore. The sun and the dawn yield to the son and the mother. A new dispensation, Freud's *Interpretation of Dreams*, replaces Müller's *Comparative Mythology*, and psychoanalysis succeeds philology as the handmaiden of myth, laying bare the secret lore of the unconscious, as Vedic Sanscrit had opened the ancient wisdom of the East. Oedipus now leads the pantheon, embracing Jocasta as heaven had formerly clutched earth. In the myths, the toiling sun and the darksome night abandon their ceaseless contention, giving way to the energetic phallus and the enveloping womb. Where light had vanquished darkness, now, in the words of Jung, consciousness triumphed over unconsciousness.[6] In the specific terms of Freud, the hero is a wish fulfillment, and the Devil personifies the "repressed unconscious instinctual life."[7] No longer are the meanings of the myths writ large in external, visible nature, but rather they are sunk deep in man's unfathomed inner nature.

The Viennese psychoanalytical school could scarcely have avoided familiarity with the German nature mythologists, and the extent of their reading is seen in Otto Rank's study of *The Myth of the Birth of the Hero*. Rank cites a shelfful of writings by the older school, disparaging them but adopting their method of interpretation. Only the symbols change. How transparent the myth of Cronus now is![8] And how appropriate that the word "incest" comes from the Sanscrit![9]

In Rank's gallery of heroes, the Freudian symbols fall neatly into place. The myth hero corresponds to the child ego, rebelling against the parents. The hostile father, projecting back his son's hatred, exposes the child in a box or basket in the water; the box is the womb, and exposure in water is known in dreams to signalize birth. (The Flood myths are thus the hero myth amplified; the Ark is the box-womb.) The fact that birth has already occurred in the myth-story is easily explained away by Freud, who finds natural acts and fantasies from the unconscious peacefully succeeding each other in dream-myths. So the mythmakers are reconstructing their own childhood fantasies. The myth proves to be the delusion of a paranoiac resenting his father, who has pre-empted the mother's love.

Dreams, myths, and fairy tales tell one common story, a genital-anal saga. Thread is semen, wheat is the penis, salt is urine, gold is feces.[10] Defecation is itself symbolic of sublimated or rejected sexuality. "Jack and the Beanstalk" was once a pleasant lunar myth-tale, with the moon as the bean of abundance which Jack climbs to the wealth of the morning light. Now it is a masturbation fantasy, in which the beans and the stalk symbolize testicles and penis.[11] Little Red Riding Hood, erstwhile a dawn maiden, has become a virgin ready for seduction; her red cap is a menstrual symbol, and her wandering in the woods a straying from the path of virtue; the wolf eating the girl is the sex act. But beyond this simple and obvious symbolism, Fromm finds subtler meanings, a "pregnancy envy" shown by the wolf (man), who fills his belly (womb) with the living grandmother and the girl, and is properly punished when Little Red Riding Hood stows stones, the symbol of sterility, in his insides. This copulation drama turns out to be a tale of women who hate men and sex.[12]

Just as the celestial mythologists wrangled over the primacy of sun, storms, and stars, so now do the psychoanalytical mythologists dispute over the symbols from the unconscious. Formerly it was Müller, Kuhn, Preller, Goldziher, Frobenius, who recriminated; now it is Freud, Jung, Ferenczi, Fromm, Kerényi, Róheim, Reik. The shifts and twistings of symbolism can be seen clearly enough in the crucial figure of Oedipus. In the solar orthodoxy of Cox, Oedipus the sun hero defeated the schemings of the thundercloud Sphinx that hung threateningly over the city of Thebes; he reunited with his mother Jocasta, the Dawn, from whom he had been parted since infancy; unwilling to see the misery he had wrought, he tore out his eyes, meaning that the sun had blinded himself in clouds and darkness; his death in the sanctuary of the Eumenides was the demise of the sun in the Groves of the Dawn, "the fairy network of clouds which are the first to receive and the last to lose the light of the sun in the morning and the evening."[13] Oedipus was hurried irresistibly on his predestined course, just as the sun journeyed compulsively onward.

In his revelation of the Oedipus complex Freud disclosed the wish fulfillment of our childhood goals, to sleep with our mothers and kill our fathers. Yet already in 1912, twelve years later, Ferenczi has added adornments. True both to Freud and to the older philological mythologists, he accepts Oedipus as the phallus, derived from the Greek "swell-foot"; the foot in dreams and jokes symbolizes the penis, and swelling signifies erection. But Ferenczi also worked in the castration complex, represented in Oedipus' blinding himself. The eyes, as paired organs, symbolize the testicles. Oedipus mutilated himself to express horror at his mother-incest, and also to avoid looking his father in the eye. Ferenczi reads this additional motive in the reply of Oedipus to the appalled Chorus, that Apollo fills his measure of woe. Apollo, the sun, is the father symbol. Hence Oedipus, formerly the sun hero, is now son of the sun god, and thus, if both readings are accepted, has become his own father.[14]

Erich Fromm shifted the burden to a conflict between matriarchy and patriarchy, revealed in the whole Oedipus trilogy, with Oedipus, Haemon, and Antigone upholding the matriarchal order against the tyranny of Creon. Fittingly Oedipus dies in the grove of the matriarchal goddesses, to whose world he belongs. Jung, moving farther afield, is bitterly castigated by Freud for exciding the libido from the Oedipus complex, and substituting for the erotic impulses an ethical conflict between the "life task" that lies ahead and the "psychic laziness" that holds one back, clinging to the skirts of an idealized mother and a self-centered father.[15]

Fairy tales, regarded by the mythologists as truncated myths, occasion the same discords. When Müller solarized "The Frog King," first of the Grimms' *Kinder- und Hausmärchen*, he saw the frog as one more name for the sun, and worked out a derivation from the Sanscrit. People in the mythopoeic age called the frog the sun when they saw it squatting on the water. Ernest

Jones, the voice of Freud, recognizes the frog as the penis. So the unconscious regards the male organ in moments of disgust, and the fairy-tale moral is the gradual overcoming of the maiden's aversion to the sex act. In the chaster, archetypal reading of Jung, according to Joseph Campbell, the frog is a miniature dragon-serpent, loathsome in appearance but representing the "unconscious deep" filled with hidden treasures. He is the herald summoning forth the child from her infantile world to the land of adventure, independence, maturity, self-discovery, and at the same time filling her with anxiety at the thought of separation from her mother. Her golden ball lost in the well is the sun, the deep dark spring waters suggest the night; so the older symbolism overlays the newer.[16]

Even in their joint commentaries on the Winnebago trickster, the contemporary mythologists differ. Kerényi sees the ubiquitous Indian scapegrace and culture hero as the phallus; Jung and Radin find in him god, man, woman, animal, buffoon, hero, the amalgam of opposites, the reflection of both consciousness and unconsciousness.[17]

Toward the new symbolism of the psychoanalytical schools, the folklorist of today takes a position similar to that held by Lang and his fellows of yesterday. The language of the unconscious is as conjectural and inconclusive as Sanscrit, when applied to myths and tales. The tortured interpretations differ widely from each other; which is right? The psychoanalysts, like the philologists, come to the materials of folklore from the outside, anxious to exploit them for their own a priori assumptions. The folklorist begins with the raw data of his field and sees where they lead him. He can admire the symmetrical structure reared by Joseph Campbell from many disparate materials, but the folk literatures that occupy him cannot all be prettily channeled into the universal monomyth.[18] The issue between contemporary mythologists and folklorists has, however, never been joined, because the one subject they could have debated, myth, has dropped from the vocabulary of folklore.

The English anthropological school of folklore did not long enjoy their conquest of the solar mythologists. Their own theory of survivals soon collapsed before the detailed field inquiries of modern anthropology.[19] Leadership in folklore studies passed to the Continent, centering in the historical-geographical technique of the Finnish scholars. Collecting, archiving, and the comparative study of branching variants became, and still are, the order of the day. In the United States a division of labor has resulted between humanistic folklorists, who would abandon the term "myth," and cultural anthropologists, who would discard the term "folklore."[20] It is no accident that the keenest review of current theories of myth has been provided by the anthropologists Melville and Frances Herskovits, who test them empirically against their field materials.[21] The collectors of folk traditions in contemporary America encounter almost all forms of traditional narrative—legend, anecdote, ghost story, *Märchen,* animal tale, jest, dialect story, tall tale, dirty joke, cante-fable—save only myth. The word "myth" is still flourished, say, at the mention of Davy Crockett or Paul Bunyan, but in the same fuzzy sense indistinguishable in common usage from "legend" or "folklore."[22] Cultural historians like Henry Nash Smith or Richard Hofstadter employ "myth" with the quite separate meaning of a popularly accepted cluster of images.[23]

The progress of field collecting shows that mythologists and folklorists are dealing with different classes of material. In writing on Greek gods and heroes, Kerényi prefers sacred myths of the priests and poets to the heroic saga of the folk. The folklorist exhibits just the opposite preference. Heroic saga is the very stuff of folk tradition, and the Chadwicks in their exhaustive studies have explained the formation of folk epics in terms eminently sensible to the folklorists.[24] The hero is not the sun, or the penis, or superconsciousness, but a great warrior around whom legends gather. The gold he wins is neither sunlight nor dung, but the same legendary gold that inspires countless treasure quests in real life, among down-East lobstermen, Southern Negroes, and Western cowhands.

The Crockett tradition follows in detail after detail the Chadwicks' analysis, even given the special conditions of American history. From the frontier setting issues a Heroic Age society; Crockett is the historical figure to whom oral and written legends fasten; he undergoes adventures similar to those of all folk-epic heroes—single combats, wanderings, love affairs. He possesses famed weapons, utters fierce boasts, displays precocious strength, and meets death against great odds, like the other Heroic Age champions. His printed tales, close to their oral substratum, reveal him as a clownish hero, again in keeping with the Chadwicks' findings, but the first step in the literary process leading to epic dignity can be seen in the almanac embroidery of the tradition.[25]

The recent Disney-inspired revival of Crockett had nothing to do with the folk figure, but like the Paul Bunyan story was packaged by the mass media for popular consumption. These assembly-line demigods, numbering now nearly a dozen, belong to the "folklore of industrial man," as Marshall McLuhan has called it in *The Mechanical Bride,* discussing themes that are not folklore at all but "pop kutch." At the bottom of the Paul Bunyan fanfare lies the slenderest trickle of oral taletelling, and this has vanished in the sands of journalistic, advertising, radio, and juvenile-book regurgitation of Bunyan antics. Paul Bunyan has entered the vocabulary of journalism as a convenient humorous symbol for mammoth size and gargantuan undertakings, but the readings of the symbol vary widely. The lumber industry sees in him the exemplar of giant production, the *Daily Worker* finds in him the spirit of the workingman, artists extract from him the sheer brute strength of the American genius, resort promoters exhibit a big dummy to attract tourists.[26]

A recent essay claims that the rebellious youth-idol hero, a composite of Marlon Brando, James Dean, and Elvis Presley, is the lineal descendant of Crockett and Bunyan. There can be no direct connection between a hero of oral folk tradition and the idol of teen-age mass adoration, but as mass-culture heroes, Crockett and Brando shocking the dudes, Superman and James

Dean hurtling through space, Tarzan and Elvis Presley grunting and grimacing, do have an affinity.[27]

Also in the domain of "pop kutch" belong the Paul Bunyan-sized treasuries of "folklore," assembled most vigorously by Benjamin A. Botkin. These bargain packages use folklore as a bright label for their miscellany of local gags, schmalz, nostalgic reminiscences, and journalistic jokes, clipped from second-hand sources, with all coarse and obscene elements excluded, and a wide geographical area covered, to insure large distribution. There is a bit of sentiment and fun for everybody in these BIG American albums.

The problems in American folklore studies today are to separate the folklore of the folk from the fake lore of industrial man, and to establish among many specialists a common ground based on the unique circumstances of American history. There is a need to secure general acceptance of scholarly procedures in collecting and reporting the raw materials of folklore. In these respects American folklorists have a good deal of catching up to do to reach the solid platform of their English predecessors. The question of myth is far afield. But when it is posed, the lesson taught by Andrew Lang still holds, and the folklorist looks with a jaundiced eye at the excessive strainings of mythologists to extort symbols from folk tales.

REFERENCES

1. Andrew Lang, "The Myth of Cronus," in *Custom and Myth* (London, 1901), pp. 45-63.
2. London, published by the Sunday Lecture Society, 1875.
3. *Myths and Dreams* (London, 1891), pp. 5-6.
4. E. B. Tylor, *Primitive Culture* (3rd edn., London, 1891), Vol. I, p. 319.
5. As I have described them in an article of that title in the *Journal of American Folklore*, LXIV (1951), pp. 1-10. My discussion of the Lang-Müller controversy, "The Eclipse of Solar Mythology," appeared in the same journal, LXVIII (1955), pp. 393-416, in a special symposium on myth, edited by Thomas A. Sebeok. Titled *Myth: A Symposium*, this group of papers also appears as Volume 5 in the Bibliographical and Special Series of the American Folklore Society (Philadelphia, 1955), and has been reprinted by the Indiana University Press (Bloomington, Indiana, 1958).
6. C. G. Jung and C. Kerényi, *Essays on a Science of Mythology*, trans. R. F. C. Hull (New York: Pantheon Books, 1949), p. 119.
7. *The Interpretation of Dreams*, in *The Basic Writings of Sigmund Freud*, trans. and ed. A. A. Brill (New York: The Modern Library, 1938), p. 308; S. Freud and D. E. Oppenheim, *Dreams in Folklore*, trans. A. M. O. Richards (New York: International Universities Press, 1958), p. 39.
8. Otto Rank, *The Myth of the Birth of the Hero, A Psychological Interpretation of Mythology*, trans. F. Robbins and S. E. Jelliffe (New York: Robert Brunner, 1952, 2nd ed. 1957), p. 93, note 97.
9. Ernest Jones, *Essays in Applied Psycho-Analysis*, Vol. II, "Essays in Folklore, Anthropology and Religion" (London: Hogarth Press, 1951), p. 19.
10. See, e. g., Jones, "The Symbolic Significance of Salt," *ibid.*, pp. 22-109; Freud and Oppenheim, "Feces Symbolism and Related Dream Actions," *op. cit.*, pp. 36-65.
11. Angelo de Gubernatis, *Zoological Mythology* (2 vols., New York and London, 1872), Vol. I, p. 244; William H. Desmonde, "Jack and the Beanstalk," *American Imago*, VIII (1951), pp. 287-288.
12. Erich Fromm, *The Forgotten Language, An Introduction to the Understanding of Dreams, Fairy Tales and Myths* (New York: Rinehart & Co., 1951), pp. 235-241.
13. George W. Cox, *An Introduction to the Science of Comparative Mythology and Folklore* (London, 1881), p. 126.

14. Freud, *The Interpretation of Dreams,* in *The Basic Writings of Sigmund Freud* (New York: The Modern Library, 1938), pp. 307-309; Sándor Ferenczi, "The Symbolic Representation of the Pleasure and the Reality Principles in the Oedipus Myth," *Imago,* I, 1912, reprinted in *Sex in Psychoanalysis,* trans. Ernest Jones (New York: Robert Brunner, 1950), pp. 253-269.

15. Fromm, "The Oedipus Myth," in *The Forgotten Language,* pp. 196-231; Freud, *The History of the Psychoanalytic Movement,* in *The Basic Writings of Sigmund Freud,* p. 974. Rival psychoanalytic systems are considered in Patrick Mullahy, *Oedipus, Myth and Complex* (New York, 1948; reprinted in Evergreen Edition, 1955).

16. Max Müller, *Chips from a German Workshop* (New York, 1872), Vol. II, pp. 244-246; Ernest Jones, "Psycho-Analysis and Folklore," *op. cit.,* Vol. II, p. 16; Joseph Campbell, *The Hero with a Thousand Faces* (New York: Pantheon Books, 1949), pp. 49-53.

17. Paul Radin, *The Trickster, A Study in American Indian Mythology,* with commentaries by Karl Kerényi and C. G. Jung (New York: Philosophical Library, 1956). Cf Kerényi, pp. 183-185, with Radin, p. 169, and Jung, p. 203.

18. Joseph Campbell's achievement in *The Hero with a Thousand Faces* rests on equal familiarity with folklore, psychoanalysis, literature, and theology. His brilliantly written "Folkloristic Commentary" to the Pantheon Books edition of *Grimm's Fairy Tales* (New York, 1944), pp. 833-864, shows his mastery of folk-tale scholarship.

19. The psychoanalytical mythologists evinced considerable interest in the survival theory. Freud saw the savage as well as the child in adult dreams and neuroses (Ernest Jones, *The Life and Work of Sigmund Freud,* Vol. II, New York: Basic Books, Inc., 1955, p. 272), and made elaborate analogies between savages and neurotics in *Totem and Taboo.* Speaking at a congress of the English Folklore Society, Ernest Jones referred to "survivals" in the individual unconscious of totemistic beliefs, corresponding to survivals in racial memory ("Psycho-Analysis and Folklore," p. 7).

20. Stith Thompson, "Myths and Folktales," in *Myth: A Symposium,* pp. 482-488; William R. Bascom, "Verbal Art," *Journal of American Folklore,* LXVIII (1955), pp. 245-252.

21. Melville J. and Frances S. Herskovits, "A Cross-Cultural Approach to Myth," in *Dahomean Narrative* (Evanston, Ill.: Northwestern University Press, 1958), pp. 81-122. See also the review by M. J. Herskovits of Fromm, *The Forgotten Language,* in *Journal of American Folklore,* LXVI (1953), pp. 87-89.

22. E.g., Stuart A. Stiffler, "Davy Crockett: The Genesis of Heroic Myth," *Tennessee Historical Quarterly*, XVI (1957), pp. 134-140.

23. Thus H. N. Smith, *Virgin Land, The American West as Symbol and Myth* (Cambridge, Mass.: Harvard University Press, 1950); R. Hofstadter, "The Agrarian Myth and Commercial Realities," in *The Age of Reform* (New York: Alfred A. Knopf, Inc., 1956), pp. 23-59.

24. C. Kerényi, *The Gods of the Greeks* (London and New York: Thames & Hudson, 1951); H. M. and N. K. Chadwick, *The Growth of Literature* (3 vols., Cambridge: Cambridge University Press, 1932-1940).

25. I developed this idea in "Davy Crockett and the Heroic Age," *Southern Folklore Quarterly*, VI (1942), pp. 95-102.

26. My evidence for the journalistic treatment of Bunyan is given in "Paul Bunyan in the News, 1939-1941," *Western Folklore*, XV (1956), pp. 26-39, 179-193, 247-261. The only full scholarly treatment is by Daniel G. Hoffman, *Paul Bunyan, Last of the Frontier Demigods* (Philadelphia: University of Pennsylvania Press, 1952).

27. Robert S. Brustein, "America's New Culture Hero," *Commentary*, XXV (February 1958), pp. 123-129. Leo Gurko considers the muscle-bound quality of American mass heroes in "Folklore of the American Hero," in *Heroes, Highbrows and the Popular Mind* (Indianapolis and New York: Bobbs-Merrill Co., 1953), pp. 168-198.

5. Stars and Stories

PHYLLIS ACKERMAN

A FEW YEARS ago a young Orientalist was employed by a small museum to catalogue Ancient Near Eastern material. It was a fortunate opportunity and the work began with happy zest. But it soon ran into a dilemma. Falsifications? No; the collection had been assembled in the good old days, no eyebrows could be raised against it. *This* was a really serious problem, warranting 175 miles of railroad travel for consultation.

The trip was taken, the facts placed before a more experienced Orientalist of similar cultural background. The verdict was instant and final: "For God's sake! Don't mention *stars!*"

Now to you, or me, or—let us say—a Professor of English Literature stars might seem quite a normal, decent item, whether painted on a prehistoric pot or mentioned in a verse; but a suspicion of stellar references, almost an intellectual astrophobia, has haunted most scholars under Germanic intellectual influence in the last four or five decades if they were concerned with mythology, religions or iconography in the Near East, from prehistoric times to the Muslim period. Yet meanwhile, Cumont in France, to cite only one of various exceptions, was contributing rich insights into astromythological traditions in this area.

This emotional deflection, which was transferred all too easily into American scholarship, derived from the errors of one German Orientalist, the late Alfred Jeremias. Jeremias, due to causes unknown, became, it would seem, enamored of the solar zodiac. To this concept and the associated planets, he devoted his scholarly attention, convinced that in solar zodiacal astronomy lay the Master Key to early Near Eastern religions and their expressions and diffused perpetuations.

Thus in the beginning of this century he wrote, concerning early Babylonian religion: "The science of the stars formed the basis of all intellectual culture . . . the zodiac is considered the most important part of the whole universe. . . . The moving stars [planets] were regarded as interpreters of the Divine will. The heaven of fixed stars was related to them like a commentary written on the margin of a book of revelation." And ranging far afield, Jeremias affirmed: "The Babylonian doctrine . . . has spread over the whole world. We find it again in Egypt, in the religion of the Avesta, and in India; traces of it are discovered in China as well as in Mexico and among the savage nations of South America."[1]

This is, of course, far from fact. The solar zodiac was a late invention. The Egyptian decan-system was non-zodiacal, non-planetary. The Avestic star-gods have no zodiacal character, and in both Assyrian and Mazdean belief planets were evil.

A vigorous Assyrian text attacks, characteristically, the malign planetary forces:

"The Seven are born in the mountains of the West,
 The Seven go down in the mountains of the East,
 Their throne is in the depths of the earth. . . .
 They are the instruments of the wrath of the gods,
 Disturbing the highroad they encamp by the way,
 The foes, the foes:
 Seven are they! Seven are they! Seven are they! . . .
 They are the day of mourning and of noxious winds!
 They are the day of fate, and the devastating wind which precedes it!
 They are the children of vengeance, the sons of revenge,
 They are the forerunners of the plague. . . .
 They are the instruments of the wrath of Nin-kigal [Death goddess],
 They are the flaming pillar of fire which works evil on earth.[2]

The rationale of their evil reputation comes out clearly in the opening lines: these are night-sky bodies that do not conform to the regular predictable pattern of the dark heavens. It was the invariability of the movements of other stellar bodies which constituted their value and their importance. Thereby, once the pattern had become familiar, the sky served at night as both clock and compass. And this was (and still is) important because, through the summer months, relentlessly hot virtually all over the Near and Middle East, most of life is, and for countless centuries has been, lived in the comparative cool of night hours, principally on the flat roofs with the stars just above, glowing near and golden bright. And travel is confined to night. Planets roaming about, defying the rest of the sky system, would be confusing, and could lead an unwary traveller, mistaking one for a regular star, even unto death. Such was the basis of the Ancient Near Eastern fear and rejection of the planets, which Jeremias extolled as "interpreters of the divine will."

In India the zodiac was not, as Jeremias implied, the solar zodiac with which he was concerned, but the much older and very different lunar zodiac. Ancient Chinese astromythology emphasized the Pole Star and Four-Quarters foci, and also gave great attention to an Orion/Antares opposition. New World astronomical traditions had varied emphases: Ursa Minor and the Pleiades are often conspicuous—the former having, of course, no zodiacal connections, the latter connected with the zodiac only as a detail of Taurus.

Yet Jeremias' arbitrary and erroneous theory, because he had official prestige and productive energy, enjoyed for some time a considerable vogue, though almost entirely in Germany. When the extent and seriousness of his errors were finally all too manifest, the negative reaction was proportionately energetic and far more persistent, epitomized by the earnest advice protectingly imposed on the uncertain young cataloguer: "For God's sake, don't mention stars!"

But stars are ancient, in cultural records as in fact. The name of the primordial Sumer-Akkadian Great God, founder of the pantheon, is "An," which means "Above." He lived in Heaven and Heaven was then, as now (even to the intellectually sophisticated, save by virtue of conscious critical effort) the sky.

In the semi-pictographic signs which were the first approach to writing, the "Above" for which An was named might have been indicated by a radiant sun. The sun, when it is "above," has the distinctive advantage of being up there in the sky sole and alone. Or "An," "Above," could have been written with a moon, the largest object in the night-sky—perhaps less satisfactory as pictograph than the sun because of its changing form, but, on the other hand, offering a more distinctive figure, for many objects might be indicated as a disk, but only the moon is naturally and typically a crescent.

Yet "An" as "Above" and the designation of the first, and long-supreme Great God of the Sumer-Akkadian pantheon was not expressed pictographically with either a sun or a moon. The word and the god were indicated by a star. Moreover, this conventional star (and its successive derivatives, gradually developed into a hieroglyph) became the qualification of all names of divinities, the sign of status as a god or goddess.

For when we first met An he was already one of many divinities. He, however, was the ultimate ancestor of them all. Hence they must all have been in the sky and of the same nature as An. This hints at an early stellar pantheon; yet, conversely, the star-pictograph for "An" implies a possible embarrassment: if the members of his derivative pantheon all had astral "embodiments," if all the gods were up in the night-sky, why was An alone called "Above"?

The answer is, to be sure, obvious: there is one star that is above—in relation not only to the terrestrial gazer, but likewise to all other stars: the Polar Star, of course, often called in the hemisphere of which we are speaking the North Star. This second name, moreover, emphasizes the practical importance of this star: it is a permanent immobile point of spatial reference. Likewise, being the one fixed point in the night sky, it is the focus for all other stellar references.

In the rush, however, to disclaim Jeremias and his confusions no such significant considerations prevailed. Lurking fears promoted an anxious fashion to be safely and conspicuously anti-stellar; and this old constriction still controls the thinking of many whose interests touch this field—amateurs and professionals alike—though frequently they do not know how, a half-century ago, it became "correct" to scoff at astro-mythology.

In the interval this Germanic intellectual embarrassment has not deflected real scholars, serene in objectivity. Louis de Saussure, for example, established a valuable framework by tracing stellar myths in Chinese sources and on beyond, especially the Orion-Antares opposition mythic pattern; but he died too soon to rectify and develop his work. Both Flinders Petrie and W. Max Müller had already assembled extensive, soberly documented material on stellar relations of Egyptian divinities, with data on their great antiquity. Pyramid texts, for instance, give conclusive proof of the identification of both Osiris and Horus with the constellation that we, accepting a Greek myth, call "Orion," while the relation of Isis to the star Sirius is matter-of-fact. Nor are stellar foci limited to this one divine family in Ancient Egyptian thought. Safekht, for instance—goddess of writing, named as early as Pyramid times—is represented wearing as her head-dress a seven-pointed star, which, moreover, is one of the earliest Egyptian symbols of divinity-as-such. Again, Pyramid texts report that the gods dwell in the malachite lakes (or lake), but malachite powder falls from the stars; and another Pyramid text tells of "a great island in the Field of Sacrifices on which the great gods rest, the never-vanishing stars"—i.e. the circumpolar stars.

Epet Ta-Ueret (The Great One) was one of the important personages in the Field of Sacrifices, for we find her specifically identified as representing the constellation that we call "Boötes." Similarly, the astral foci of a number of other Egyptian divinities are available; when they are not thus verbally recorded they can be discovered by various kinds of internal evidence, including especially iconographic indications.

The Babylonian epic, the so-called *Enuma elish* . . . , identifies the divine hero Marduk with the constellation "Orion," his great bow being our "Canis Maior," which they called the "Bow-star"; and it does closely resemble a drawn bow with the arrow set, even on an astronomically scientifically conceived star-map, such as the large-scale one issued by New York's Hayden Planetarium.

Iranian texts identify stars of the Four Quarters and the Center: the rain-god Tishtriya represented the East at Sirius, the Great Bear represented the North; the identifications of the western and southern stars—called, respectively, Vanand and Satavaesa—have been disputed. Vanand was the "home" of the drought-god, Apaosha, with whom Tishtriya had violent contests, a standard Rain-versus-Drought myth, in which the evil personality usually represented the red star, Antares. But this old Iranian astro-divine pattern differs from the usual formula in having as "Guardian" of the north a polar constellation, Ursa Maior (at long intervals the polar star is Alpha Ursae Maioris— "Dubhe"). Given this deviation in the northern point, Apaosha would more probably be, not in Antares, but in another of the old opponent-foci, the constellation Sagittarius, or one of the stars therein, perhaps Nunki. No successful guess has been offered for the old Iranian southern Guardian, "Vanand," but the rectangular Four-Quarters-cross would be correctly completed if Vanand were either Aries or Cetus.

The Great One Called Gah in the middle of the sky has scarcely been discussed, but its identification would have varied, according to the date in question. If the concept is very old, this Middle Great One must have been in the first instance Thuban (Alpha Draconis) or, more accurately, in the blank space between Alpha and Iota Draconis; but the existing document is late and hence that must refer to our own Polaris in Ursa Minor. The Iranian mythic material in relation to three of these stars—the north, center and southern points—has faded away, leaving only the tale of enmity and battle between Sirius/Tishtriya and Sagittarius (?)/Apaosha.

Greek mythology is rich in (non-zodiacal) astral associations, some specifically documented, others implied; yet it is impossible in modern surveys of Hellenic mythology or cults to find any coherent presentation of these star-relations and their significance. Indeed, most of the familiar accounts of Greek mythology, including serious scholarly publications, entirely disregard astronomical elements.

This is true even of extended analyses of the god Dionysus; yet various classic texts, both early and late, present, more or less emphatically, his stellar character. Thus Macrobius (*Sat.* I, 18)—to reverse the time sequence of these texts—claims that the dappled fawn-skin worn by the god (as well as, sometimes, by his followers) was dotted with countless circles to portray the stars. This is indeed a dubious interpretation on Macrobius' part, but it shows that in his time astronomical values in the Dionysiac cult were taken for granted. Plutarch (*On the Ei at Delphi*) calls Dionysus "the Night Sun." Pindar hails the God as "the Joy-god Dionysus, the pure star/ That shines amidst the gathering of the fruit." Sophocles in his *Antigone* calls him "The leader of the fire-breathing stars."

When pan-solarism was rampant amongst historians of religion, "The Night Sun" was interpreted as the "Chthonic sun"! By this was meant the sun while it was passing under the earth—according to the cosmological conceptions of the time—though why a god should be given a special designation and honors at the moment when his supposed functions were inoperative was not discussed. What the phrase meant, of course, was the brightest star in the night sky—the celestial body that, by night, was outstanding, as was the sun by day; this is confirmed and specified by the quotations from Pindar and Sophocles. Pindar's phrase shows that Dionysus' star was conspicuous in the sky at the vintage season; Sophocles gives the direct clue.

For "the Leader" was a Babylonian name (*"Kaksidi"*) for a star, which Sayce long ago identified as the star Sirius. And Sirius would be the "night sun" as the brightest star in our heavens; moreover, it also was conspicuous at the vintage season (when it was about to set). The relation of Dionysus/Sirius to "Fire-breathing stars" (or "Stars aflame with fire," in another possible translation) is essentially the same as the relation of Tishtriya/Sirius to rain-storms: Sirius and the stars round it are brilliant during the stormy season when the skies are lit with the fires of lightning.

But there is also another specific fire-association possible here: the Celts celebrated Beltane, "The Fire of the God Bel," with rites which centered round the kindling of a fire on the day (originally May Day) when the Pleiades rose at dawn. The Hindus saw the Pleiades-cluster as a flame, and called it the Seven Mothers of their ancient Fire-god, Agni. Specifically, then, in this association, the "stars aflame with fire" of which Dionysus as Sirius was Leader were the Pleiades.

These two night-sky features—Sirius and the Pleiades—might seem rather far apart to be Leader and Followers, but the possibility of the relation is confirmed by the intimate connection between Dionysus and the second cluster near the Pleiades, the Hyades. After Dionysus, as Zagreus, was torn apart by the Titans, then reassembled and revivified by Rhea, Hermes, on instructions from Zeus, took the infant and put him in charge of the Hyades—the cluster sometimes being called, in consequence, the Nurses of Dionysus.

Dionysus could be so signally associated with both the Pleiades and the Hyades, despite the fact that his principal astral seat was some distance away in the star Sirius, because he had also a bull form which was in the constellation Taurus; and the Hyades are in Taurus, the Pleiades immediately contiguous, or sometimes construed as the tassle on the Bull's tail.

Moreover, Dionysus was also syncretized with Osiris, who, we have seen, was identified by Pyramid texts with the constellation Orion. But Osiris was the focus of a special cult at the city of Canopus, where they worshiped his detached head (relic of the dismemberment episode in his mythic cycle) set in a rich vase, and this severed head was identified with the star Canopus. Thus Osiris (at least at a relatively late period) was conceived as extending astrally from the star Canopus, as his head, through Orion.

Intervening, however, is the constellation Lepus—The Hare. This, too, however, fits into the Osirian complex; for as Leader of the Dead, Osiris was called *"Oun Nefer"* (Gr. *"Onophris"*), "The Good Being," and the hieroglyph for *"Oun"* is based on the figure of a hare. Many tapestry-woven inset ornaments from Egyptian-woven linen burial garments (dating mostly from the 5th and 6th centuries A.D.) show hare, which seem never to have been explained: they refer to Osiris as "The Good Being," and they help to commend the soul of the deceased to Osiris as the ancient Judge of the Dead.

In a late period, then, the astral Osiris extended from Canopus, his head—sometimes called "The Star of Osiris"—through Lepus, symbol of his "goodness," through Orion. But, he, too, had a bull (or ox) avatar; hence his astral presence swept across the sky from Canopus through Taurus. And in this wise Dionysus and Osiris were astrally commingled. And they were, correspondingly, literarily and cultically syncretized—recognized in the Alexandrian period, and thereafter, as essentially one god.

The function of Sirius and the holy divinity associated with it as Leader has another interesting reflection. It is quaintly employed in a Sumerian myth, creating a stylistic device which seems gauche and distracting until one understands its deliberate purpose as a definitive clue. The hero of this poem is Enlil: Lord (*En*) Air (*lil*). In the Sumerian pantheon he comes just after An, the god "Above," whose name is written with a single star, the single star "Above" all others being, as we have already noted, the Polar Star. Enlil's stellar character is emphasized by repeated conspicuous references to his bright eyes—stars being often expressed as "eyes."

Enlil is a storm god: as the celestial fire which Dionysus "leads" is, in one major aspect, lightning, so Enlil's powerful "Word" or "Voice" is thunder. Moreover, this thunder-voice of Enlil's is connected not only with the crop-stimulating values of the accompanying rains; it has general creative power—it is a primitive forebear of the Logos concept. Hence Enlil was probably the hero of the original Sumerian Creation myth, and fragmentary texts show parts of his creative prowess, notably his work in organizing the skies by moving the upper (northern) heaven—*an,* "above"—from the lower (southern) heaven—*ki,* "below," a process that has been misunderstood by modern Sumerologists as the act of separating heaven from earth; the creation of Earth actually was to come only later.

Enlil is reported, in the Sumerian poem now under consideration, as being in the city of Nippur—a cosmic, celestial Nippur, antedating the creation of the earth, but destined to serve ultimately as the model of the terrestrial Nippur, for the Sumerian cosmic pattern was, in general, designed on the principle of Heaven (Sky)/Earth parallelism.

The celestial city of Nippur is on a pure, Wide River—Sirius is on the edge of the Milky Way, which appears in astromythologies as sometimes a sea (e. g., *tamtu*) or a river (e. g., the Nile-in-the-Sky). The city has a Vine Quay, and a boat-quay called the Quay of Dreams—each of which probably had astral identifications familiar at the time; now—star map in hand—they can provide a good guessing game. For instance, the next civic feature, a canal described as "a glittering stream," might be the familiar river-constellation, Eridanus, which runs close to Orion, not far, as astral distances go, beyond Sirius.

The Dramatis Personae are Enlil, the maiden Ninlil (Lady of the Air) and her mother (Nunbarshegunu, a Grain-goddess)—a scheming old woman of flexible morality who advises her daughter to go bathing in the river and then walk along the Glittering Stream so that she will be seen by Enlil, the "bright-eyed." The ruse works and Ninlil, as a result, is pregnant, and Enlil leaves town. Ninlil, however, has—understandably—no intention of letting him get away, and this creates the circumstances in which Enlil becomes "*Kaksidi,*" the Leader. Ninlil, "so bright, so shining" (she was probably Procyon), follows him relentlessly and he leads her a merry chase—and leads, and leads, but punctuating the process with recurrent pauses for renewed intercourse.

Remote from this in all respects, but again with strong emphasis on the *Kaksidi* motif, is a story so familiar in theme that the original form is often forgotten; but this is especially interesting because here the *Kaksidi* is not a god impersonating a star but is the star itself, and the "leading" motif is almost equally clear—allowing for the brevity of the narrative.

"When Jesus was born in the days of Herod, the King, there came wise men from the east to Jerusalem, saying, where is he that is born King of the Jews? for we have seen his star in the east and are come to do him honor. Herod sent them to Bethlehem and said, Go and search diligently for the young child; and the star which they saw in the east *went before them till it came and stood over where the young child was.* When they saw the star, they rejoiced with exceeding great joy"—which is, as one need hardly say, the story (condensed) as Matthew (I.2) records it. But the *Infancy of Jesus Christ,* a second-century Gnostic version, adds that "the wise men came from the East to Jerusalem according to the prophecy of Zaradascht (Zoroaster) . . . and . . . the Lady Mary took one of his swaddling clothes . . . and gave it to them. . . . And at the same time there appeared to them an angel in the form of that star, which had before been their guide in their journey, the light of which they followed till they returned into their own country."

Here is *Kaksidi* leading the Magi, both according to the account of Matthew, and again, at greater length, in the second-century Gnostic account, where, indeed, the Angel of the Star manifests himself and continues to lead them all the way back to Persia. Certainly the second-century Gnostic writer took for granted that the star which we commonly call, vaguely, the "Star of Bethlehem," was Sirius, the Leader (*Kaksidi*); and the Mazdean angel of that star, Tishtriya, was himself in direct charge of leading the Magi to see and shower with gifts the infant Jesus—a fitting mission for Tishtriya, a beneficent divinity who played a major role in the faith and mythology of the Magi.

The last several pages of this summary discussion offer some specific astral interpretations, chosen almost at random out of several possible volumes of immediately available material, in order to answer in advance any query as to what a study of possible astral relations might contribute to interpreting and evaluating mythic material. Actually, the potential utility of understanding astral implications radiates irregularly into unexpected extensions. Thus astromythology is decisive for identifying central factors, as well as various incidental details, in Grail legendry. It contributes essential insights to unraveling Tarot history. There is an undetermined amount of work to be done assessing the influences of astromythological assumptions—different selections and combinations therefrom, their geographic and chronological range, their variety of incidence and divergence in effects.

No one with pretensions to responsible interest in the history of ideas and cultures can continue to avoid astromythology, even though Jeremias did, a half century ago, disseminate errors concerning cultic influences of the solar zodiac and the planets. The precautionary fiat, "For God's sake, don't mention stars!" must, and will be supplanted by some such admonition as "Look sharp! Any stellar factors?"

REFERENCES

1. A. Jeremias, *Ages of the World (Babylonian)*, Hasting's Encyclopaedia of Religion and Ethics, I (1908), p. 184.
2. Eliza M. Butler, *Ritual Magic* (New York: Cambridge University Press, 1949), p. 6, quoting: K. Kiesewetter, *Der Occultismus des Altertums* (Leipzig, n.d., I), p. 10.

6. Some Meanings of Myth

HARRY LEVIN

A FAMOUS WORK of American mythology, which affords an object-lesson to those rash enough to go fishing for mythical monsters, is introduced by a Sub-Sub-Librarian, who presents a sequence of more or less relevant extracts and cross-references. Such is the role allotted to me in the ensuing discussion. If my handful of citations suggests the range and richness of our subject, or if it indicates hazards which we might do well to avoid, it will have served its purpose. As a reminder of earlier speculations and a welcome to further contributions, much of what I have to say will be obvious and all of it will be provisory.

We could hardly begin without recognizing that we are beset on all sides by the temptations of verbalism. We cannot even talk about our subject without indulging in "the myth of myths," as we have been admonished by Paul Valéry, for whom the very essence of myth was talk. "Myth," according to Valéry, "is the name for everything that exists, or subsists, only to the extent that speech is its cause." That is a fairly objective definition of the non-mythical as whatever exists independent of speech; it invites us to pursue the mythical into subjective realms, and to pin it down with a more detailed semantic inquiry.

The original meaning of our word is "word": *mythos*. Add *logos,* and you get "mythology." Thus, in a certain sense, the science of myth also means "the word of words," which should be a caveat against tautologies and other excesses of verbiage. An exploded example is the hypothesis of Max Müller that all myths were originally derived from words through a species of allegorical etymology. We may agree that language conditions thought; but may we agree that language antedates thought? Rather, we must assume that both language and thought are shaped by habits of prelogical or metaphorical thinking—primitive metaphysics as systematized by Ernst Cassirer in the second volume of his *Philosophy of Symbolic Forms.* It is an incidental irony that, although Max Müller did not succeed in accounting for myths by words, he circulated a word which went on to create a myth, the dangerous word "Aryan."

Mythos is used for "word" or "speech" in Homer and the Greek poets, as differentiated from *logos,* "tale" or "story." As such, it became a technical term of literary criticism, signifying "plot," which Aristotle held to be the most important feature of tragedy. The Latin equivalent, *fabula,* may signify the whole dramatic work, and has its own derivative in "fable," which comes down to us with moralistic overtones. Dr. Murray's point is well taken when he takes exception to the phrase, "purely fictitious," in the primary definition of the Oxford English Dictionary. Here, I suspect, the lexicographers have superimposed a conception more germane to a later rationalism. Vico was at pains to point out that *mythos* is often glossed by the ancients as *vera narratio.* Invention, exaggeration, and falsification were subsequent meanings.

Tragedy, which began in ritual, drew its fabulous plots from an inherited body of narrative lore, which was regarded as roughly true on the plane of universalized experience. The notion that writers should create their own plots, *ad hoc* and *ex nihilo,* is relatively modern and possibly wrong. Shakespeare, although his sources were much more eclectic than those of the Greeks, would not have thought of inventing the stories he dramatized any more than Sophocles. The late Gilbert Murray, through a searching comparison between Hamlet and Orestes, has supplied us with a striking instance of that recurrence of themes which Mr. Kluckhohn has termed "cross-cultural universals."

Whereas the derivatives from *logos* have attached themselves to the sciences, or "-ologies," *mythos* and its verbal congeners have been associated with religion. Retrospectively and scientifically, we stress the etiological aspect of things, and look upon myths as symbolic answers to questions raised by man's curiosity about causes: e. g., the thunder must be the voice of Zeus. Theogony and cosmogony, not to mention metaphysics, abound in discredited hypotheses for explaining natural phenomena—which, of course, are supernatural until they have been satisfactorily explained. Even the metamorphoses fabled by poets can be regarded as prescientific gropings toward biological evolution. Perhaps we read back our own concern with etiology, in asking ourselves the why, whence, and how of myth.

The process is obscure enough to deserve the designation of *mythopoesis,* a technical term for imagination at work. *Poesis* is neither more nor less than making; a poet, etymologically, is a maker; and poetry is, quite literally, make-believe. The term "fabulation," which some of us have used to designate the storytelling faculty, should make clearer how the function of myth-making relates to other forms of mental activity; for *la fonction fabulatrice,* as Bergson locates it, stands midway between the strictly cognitive and the vaguely intuitive; and it is out of that limbo between rational intelligence and the unconscious that fictions are generated.

Now there are two ways of looking at a fiction: we can either consider it as a deviation from fact or as an approximation to fact. Fact must always be the criterion; and when the facts are under control, we emphasize the degree of deviation; but when we are out of touch with the facts, we utilize fiction to explain the unexplainable by some sort of approximation to it. "For as hieroglyphics came before letters," Bacon has said, "so parables came before arguments." We might well add that Plato's myths are notable examples of argument reverting to parable. Continually, in some such fashion, we must rely on imaginative constructs to fill in the gaps of our knowledge.

By and large, the writers of Greece and Rome were rather Pickwickian in their acceptance of mythology. So far as they could, they moralized or rationalized or allegorized the embarrassing misbehavior of their Olympians. Ovid's mythography—or, for that matter, the Norse pantheon of Snorri Sturlason—is highly sophisticated, if not downright skeptical. At its most serious, it asks for no more than that willing suspension of disbelief which Coleridge would call poetic faith. It was precisely because the classics were based upon fictive themes that they survived the mythoclastic rigors of early Christianity. Myths were pagan, and therefore false in the light of true belief—albeit that true belief might today be considered merely another variety of mythopoeic faith. Here is where the game of debunking starts, in the denunciation of myth as falsehood from the vantage-point of a rival myth.

Classical myths could be rescued by allegory, prefiguration, or other methods of reinterpretation; but they could not be accepted literally. For Yeats, as for so many other poets, they would frankly be "embroideries." They had long been the *ornements reçus*, the conventional embellishments recommended by neo-classical critics. On the other hand, Boileau had declared that the Christian mysteries were improper subjects for works of fiction, which should properly deal with the fictitious, and not with the truths of revealed religion. Milton disregarded that injunction, at his peril, in *Paradise Lost*; yet, though he made a personal allusion to Galileo, Milton fell back upon the quasi-mythical system of Ptolemy when he came to describe the machinery of the cosmos.

This accords with the assumption of many evolutionary theories of culture that poetry is essentially the product of a primitive age, and that it will in due course be superseded by the application of reason to the various fields of human endeavor. Such theorists as Comte and Hegel come to mind in this connection; yet the attitude was already formulated during the Battle of the Ancients and Moderns in the latter years of the seventeenth century. The pioneering modernist Fontenelle, in his essay *On the Origin of Fables*, suggested then that mythology was a kind of ignorant philosophy. He himself would become a kind of culture-hero to the anthropologists, for having likewise suggested that classical myths and those of the American Indians be studied comparatively.

Fontenelle's rationalistic tendency had been anticipated by an ancient author whose name has been handed on as a virtual synonym for mythoclast, or dispeller of myths, Euhemerus. The lost work of Euhemerus seems to have been devoted to an exposure of the gods as deified men: Zeus turns out to have been an actual king of Crete, long dead and buried and apotheosized. Curiously enough, that euhemeristic tract seems to have been cast in the form of a romance, some sort of imaginary journey. The attitude it projected, euhemerism, reduces myth to legend; and legend, after all, can easily be reduced to exaggerated history.

The historical approach was expressly set forth in 1725 by the monumental treatise of Giambattista Vico, *Principi di una scienza nuova intorno alla natura delle nazioni.* Vico proposed that mythology be read as protohistory. He discerned in myth not only the outlines of his spiral theory of progress, but a key to the so-called Homeric problem and a working model for the development of law. The personification of forces of nature through the Olympian deities represented a naïve stage of knowledge, which Vico called "poetic wisdom." Just as the early peoples had founded the arts during the childhood of the race, so later generations gave birth to philosophers who were maturely developing the sciences.

Vico's ardent disciple, Benedetto Croce, has claimed that his master resolved the age-old quarrel between poetry and philosophy. If he accomplished that object, he did so by apologizing for mythopoesis. He remained a man of the Enlightenment, and shared its interest in disentangling fact from fiction; but he showed how mythoclasm could be employed, not simply as a means of exposing imposture, but as a technique for interpreting phantasmagoria. It would be wielded as a scholarly instrument for the examination of superstitious yet significant misconceptions, when Ottfried Müller brought out his *Prolegomena zu einer wissenschaftlichen Mythologie* in 1825.

Mankind, having outgrown its mythical adolescence, felt itself able to get along without myths. If the other religions were mythical, so was Christianity, David Strauss maintained in his *Life of Jesus*. As for poetry, it was interesting enough, from an esthetic or archeological standpoint; but it was technologically obsolescent. Poets lamented, with increasing pathos, that great Pan was dead, that the gods of Greece had gone into exile or underground, or that the woods and streams had lost their nymphs and naiads. Myth itself was believed to be defunct, a thing of the past; and the realization engendered another myth, the nostalgic myth of pastoralism.

Karl Marx, heavily committed to material progress, announced that any mythology was bound to be incompatible with the results of the Industrial Revolution. Indeed, the distance was vast between Mount Olympus and the city of Manchester. Yet when Ralph Waldo Emerson visited Manchester in 1848, he clair-voyantly noted in his journal that a modern mythology would have to be industrial, mechanical, parliamentary, commercial, and socialistic; moreover, that its "mythagogic names" would be Astor, Fulton, Arkwright, Peel, Russell, Rothschild, Stephenson, and Fourier. Emerson's generalization stands up better than most of his illustrations; for the men he names were primarily con-trivers, and not exemplars.

Emerson was really seeking tutelary spirits, lay saints for a secular epoch, in accordance with principles laid down in "Uses of Great Men," the introduction to his *Representative Men*. His friend Carlyle came closer to the mark—that is to say, the signifi-cance of public roles, the relationship between myth and cult— in his comparable set of case-histories, *Heroes and Hero-Worship*. One of their common illustrations, common to all minds formed in the nineteenth century, was that of Napoleon, who was both contriver and exemplar, and who managed to become the mythog-rapher of his own myth.

The romantic movement—to sum it up in our terms—may be conceived as a mythopoeic revival. Ideologues like Herder argued the need; critics like Friedrich Schlegel pointed the way;

metaphysicians like Schelling reconstructed a transcendental world-view; philologists like the brothers Grimm resurrected the old Nordic war-gods. It is no mere historic accident that this impetus originated in Germany, or that it found itself pitted against the more classicized culture of France. Nativism led to nationalism, as we can unhappily bear witness, with Wagner's tetralogy for its artistic climax and Hitler's Nazism for its political *Götterdämmerung.* "Poetic politics" had been Vico's polite expression for what we have come to recognize as the Big Lie.

Georges Sorel was the theoretician of myth who placed it in its ideological context. To his *Reflections on Violence,* which expounded the syndicalist doctrine of the general strike, he appended a postscript which analyzed Lenin's myth of world-revolution; and he lived to confer his benediction on Mussolini's legend of Rome restored. Sorel perceived that social movements enlisted their adherents by envisioning themselves as struggles on behalf of an ultimately triumphant cause. This did not mean that the test would be the future; whether utopian or millennial, that would be pie in the sky. "Myths must be judged as means of acting upon the present," asserted Sorel—in other words, for their effectiveness as propaganda.

I leave it to our colleagues among the social scientists to face the ambivalent consequences of this view. I shall only venture to remark, in passing, that it is characteristically Gallic in the stress it puts upon the factors of contrivance and calculation. It is instrumental rather than apocalyptic, in treating the myth as a means rather than as an end. With the Germans, the very opposite seems to be the case; and, consequently, they have tended to be a nation of mythopoets or—at least—mythophiles; whereas one has only to read the newspapers in order to realize that the French are a nation of mythoclasts. The current regime of General de Gaulle is a desperate effort to reverse their habitual direction.

In the standard French dictionary of Littré, the third meaning given for *le mythe* is "that which has no real existence." Whereupon the lexicographer has set down an afterthought: "It is said

that, in politics, justice and good faith are myths." This edifying
sentiment may help us to understand why French schoolboys are
so frequently cynical. A recent critic, Roland Barthes, in a book
entitled *Mythologies*, discusses sports, films, gadgets, slogans,
elections, advertisements, and the sensations of metropolitan
journalism. "Mythology," M. Barthes theorizes, "is an accord with
the world, not as it is, but as it wants to be."

It was the absence of the deflated myths of the Old World,
and the comparative mythlessness of the New World, that inspired our American Dream; and it was—as it happened—a
French immigrant to this hemisphere, Crèvecoeur, who voiced
the most poignant hope for a new breed of men, *homo
americanus*. In the third of his *Letters from an American Farmer*,
Crèvecoeur asked, "What is an American?," and answered by
sketching out his ideal portrait, a cross between savagery and
civilization which would have Cooper's Leatherstocking as its
fictional protagonist, Walt Whitman as its messianic bard, and
F. J. Turner as its historiographer.

The emergent figure has been much exploited, notoriously in
the case of Davy Crockett, the politician presenting himself as
folk-hero. Henry Nash Smith has chronicled numerous other
heroes of the backwoods and the frontier in his comprehensive
study of the West as symbol, *Virgin Land*. A suggestive sequel
is the monograph by R. W. B. Lewis on the concept of native
innocence, *The American Adam*. Both of those closely interrelated myths, it would appear, have been extinct for some time.
Even the Horatio Alger myth, *The Dream of Success*, which
Kenneth Lynn has retraced through the writings of the muck-
raking naturalists, has been losing conviction. We Americans
have experienced the Fall, for better or for worse, and have lost
our intellectual virginity. At the moment, our favorite myth
seems to be that of Original Sin.

Mr. Lewis' theme, the American Adam, converges with an apt
statement from Victor Hugo, who compares the formation of
types in art with the creation of Adam in life itself. Inevitably,
we shall be discussing Jung's archetypes and—it has been inti-

mated—probing beyond them into the ultimate Ur of unconsciousness; so we may be well advised to stick, as long as we can, to the level of literary consciousness. Hugo, the mythopoet of the Napoleonic myth who became its mythoclast, offers this insight into Shakespeare: "A lesson which is a man, a man with a human face so expressive that it looks at you and its look is a mirror, a parable which nudges you, a symbol which warns you, an idea which is nerve, muscle, and flesh . . . a psychic conception which has the concreteness of fact . . . that is a type."

That is how Shakespeare's exemplary figures—Romeo, Shylock, Falstaff—have succeeded in embodying their respective ways of life. And that is why Russian writers of the nineteenth century, while creating Adams of their own, recreated "A Lear of the Steppes," "A Hamlet of the Shchigri District," and "A Lady Macbeth from Mtsensk." Richard Chase, in his dissertation, *Quest for Myth*, has given us a lively and informative survey of accumulated opinion; but when Mr. Chase equates myth with literature, he has been carried away by the zeal of the mythological critic for linking everything with everything else. Myth may be unwritten literature, if you like; and if that is a contradiction in terms, it has been made meaningful by the researches of Milman Parry and Albert Lord into the bardic composition of the oral epic.

Myth, at all events, is raw material, which can be the stuff of literature. Insofar as this implies a collective fantasy, it must be shared. The ontogeny of dream recapitulates the phylogeny of myth—to restate a well-known Jungian axiom, an alternative to diffusionism, and a possible explanation why the individual psyche can be so deeply receptive to certain trains of imagery. Yet if we have lived through all of the world's mythologies in embryo, then the synthetic and syncretic "monomyth" of *Finnegans Wake* proves—if it proves nothing else—how difficult it is to recapture our foetal memories. Conversely, we may wonder whether any single person—even so intense a poet as William Blake—can fabricate and promulgate his own mythology? Must not a private myth, rather, be labelled a pseudomyth? And is

pseudomyth the desideratum that some of our critics would
propose?

We can test these paradoxes when we discuss mythical parallels in contemporary literature. Such parallels have been forth-
coming whenever the moderns have conjured with the classics:
the hybrid Euphorion, created by Goethe in the image of Byron,
identifies himself with his classical prototype in his dying breath:
"Icarus! Icarus!" Similarly, Joyce's artist-hero, Stephen Dedalus,
sees his fate prefigured in his mythagogic name. Through these
devices of identification, T. S. Eliot has told us, the modern
world is made possible for art. But, when they have been so
explicitly sustained by artists so consciously versed in psychology or anthropology, they impress us as commentaries rather
than texts.

Thomas Mann's lecture, "Freud and the Future," which deals
more directly with Mann and the past, speaks for "the mythically
oriented artist." The prelude to the first volume of his Joseph
cycle, correctly titled *Tales of Jacob* in the British edition, is a
remarkable excursion into the racial memory. Yet *Joseph and his
Brothers*, as a whole, is a sophisticated version of Genesis, not a
primitivistic reversion to it. It is not dissimilar, in that respect,
to many other adaptations from the Bible, such as Racine's
Esther and *Athalie*. Indeed it follows the curve that Flaubert
projected for later novelists when, bored with the nondescript
subject-matter of his own day, he immersed himself in
hagiography.

Conscious revivals may prove to be less revelatory than unconscious survivals. Literary achievements are never quite so
personal or original as they may seem, and generally more
traditional or conventional. The most powerful writers gain
much of their power by being mythmakers, gifted—although
they sometimes do not know it—at catching and crystallizing
popular fantasies. Thus Dickens' novels enthrall us again and
again by taking us back, recurrently and obsessively, to the old
folktale about the Babes in the Woods. Little Nell, David
Copperfield, Esther Summerson, Pip, and his other waifs have to

cope with the wicked witches of sullen bureaucracy and greedy industrialism. And *Hard Times* might almost be Dickens' response to Emerson's plea for a myth of Manchester.

In a stimulating footnote to his book of essays on magico-religious symbolism, *Images et symboles*, Mircea Eliade exclaims: "What an exalting enterprise it would be to disclose the true cultural role of the nineteenth-century novel, which—in spite of all the scientific, realistic, and social formulas—has been the great reservoir of debased myths!" Professor Eliade's idea is luridly illuminated by Mario Praz's *Romantic Agony*, which shows the extent to which devils and vampires and other survivors from demonology still pervade the decadent fiction of the eighteen-nineties. We are still inclined to think of the novel as the most immediate, circumstantial, and individualized of artistic forms, the faithful mirror of actualities. We need to be reminded that it contains the elements, and continues the functions, of myth.

This may encourage us to believe that the underlying patterns are timeless, however their ephemeral contexts may change; or it may imply that modernity, which has become so much less modern than we used to believe, has not yet dispensed with the sociocultural processes behind folklore. Such a *motif* as the Otherworldly Bride may be forgotten, except by professional folklorists or medieval antiquarians. Yet some antiquarians of the future, looking back at Emma Bovary, Anna Karenina, Hedda Gabler, and Carol Kennicott, may discover that all of those heroines exemplify one of the most persistant *motifs* of the past century: *la femme incomprise, die misverstandene Frau*, the Misunderstood Wife or—since English does not convey the ambiguous implication—the Unappreciated Woman.

Myth is profoundly receptive to the permutations of history. The contrast between Homer's Odysseus and Tennyson's Ulysses is nearly as complete as if the two had no genetic affinity. Moreover, when the latter sums up his credo—"To strive, to seek, to find, and not to yield"—he seems to be affirming a temporal kinship with an altogether different protagonist, Goethe's Faust.

Faust is probably the most elaborate literary crystallization of any myth we have had—or, more exactly, any legend—stemming as it does from a vaguely historic personage and surrounded as it is with numerous and revealing analogues. By comparing it with varying versions, we can distinguish the hard core of the mythic entity from traits acquired through the impact of successive reworkings.

All the accretions ultimately belong: the Protestant warning of the Lutheran *Faustbook,* the catalogue of Renaissance learning in Marlowe's *Dr. Faustus,* the self-fulfillment of the nineteenth-century individualist with Goethe, the relapse into guilty genius with Mann. Faust is throughout a *magus,* an intellectual and a heretic, who obtains through magic what he cannot through Christianity; in breaking the taboo against such knowledge, he comes to resemble the primordial Adam or the Titan Prometheus. The predicated consequence, damnation, withers away with the fading of orthodox eschatology. The eternally feminine component seems to enter the story at a late date. Much of this may seem accidental or idiosyncratic; yet the resulting complex of themes is so typical that Spengler employs the epithet "Faustian" to cover the trend of western civilization.

In this part of the latter twentieth century, face to face with a decline in the literate arts and a rise in the extraliterary and audiovisual media, myth should be more influential than ever, as students of communication and public opinion can demonstrate. Meanwhile, one final quotation should subsume and underline the basic distinction I have been trying to draw between mythoclasm and mythopoesis. "Science is the critique of myths," wrote W. B. Yeats in a letter to his fellow poet, Sturge Moore. "There would be no Darwin, had there been no Book of Genesis." When a society comprising as many scientists as the American Academy of Arts and Sciences entertains such a topic sympathetically as well as critically, it is a perspicuous sign of the times. The pallid Sub-Sub-Librarian now concludes and withdraws, leaving his colleagues to embark upon their oceanic adventure.

7. New Directions from Old

NORTHROP FRYE

IN HIS ESSAY on Edgar Allan Poe's *Eureka*, Paul Valéry speaks of cosmology as one of the oldest of literary arts. Not many people have clearly understood that cosmology is a literary form, not a religious or scientific one. It is true of course that religion and science have regularly been confused with, or more accurately confused by, cosmological structures. In the Middle Ages the Ptolemaic universe had close associations with contemporary theology and science as well as with poetry. But as science depends on experiment and religion on experience, neither is committed to a specific cosmology, or to any cosmology at all. Science blew up the Ptolemaic universe, and Christianity, after feeling itself cautiously all over, discovered that it had survived the explosion. The situation is very different in poetry. It is a gross error to study the cosmology of the *Commedia* or *Paradise Lost* as extraneous obsolete science, for the cosmology of these poems is not simply a part of their subject-matter, but inseparably a part of their total form. Dante's love of symmetry, of which so many critics speak, is not a personal predilection, but an essential part of his poetic craftsmanship.

Even in times when science gives little encouragement for it, poetry shows a tendency to return to the older cosmological structures, as Poe's *Eureka* itself shows. In chemistry the periodical table of elements may have replaced the old tetrad of fire, air, water and earth, but it is the traditional four that reappear in the Eliot Quartets. The universe of Dylan Thomas's "Altarwise by owl-light" sonnets is still geocentric and astrological; the

structure of *Finnegans Wake* is held together by occult correspondence; no reputable scientist has had the influence on the
poetry of the last century that Swedenborg or Blavatsky has had.
Critics have often remarked on the archaic, even the atavistic,
tendencies of poets, and nowhere are these tendencies better
illustrated than in the reckless cosmological doodling that may
be traced in poetry from Dante's *Convivio* to Yeats's *Vision*. A
principle of some importance is involved here, nothing less in
fact than the whole question of poetic thought, as distinct from
other kinds of thought. Either Peacock's thesis is correct, that
poets are a barbaric survival in a scientific age that has outgrown
them, or there are requirements in poetic thinking that have
never been carefully studied by critics. The graduate-school
cliché that Dante's *Commedia* is the metaphysical system of
St. Thomas translated into imagery is a melancholy example of
how helpless criticism is to deal with one of its own subjects.

We are all familiar with the Aristotelian argument about the
relation of poetry to action. Action, or *praxis*, is the world of
events; and history, in the broadest sense, may be called a verbal
imitation of action, or events put into the form of words. The
historian imitates action directly: he makes specific statements
about what happened, and is judged by the truth of what he
says. What really happened is the external model of his pattern
of words, and he is judged by the adequacy with which his
words reproduce that model.

The poet, in dramas and epics at least, also imitates actions
in words, like the historian. But the poet makes no specific statements of fact, and hence is not judged by the truth or falsehood
of what he says. The poet has no external model for his imitation, and is judged by the integrity or consistency of his verbal
structure. The reason is that he imitates the universal, not the
particular; he is concerned not with what happened but with
what happens. His subject-matter is the kind of thing that does
happen, in other words the typical or recurring element in action.
There is thus a close analogy between the poet's subject-matter
and those significant actions that men engage in simply because

they are typical and recurring, the actions that we call rituals. The verbal imitation of ritual is myth, and the typical action of poetry is the plot, or what Aristotle calls *mythos*, so that for the literary critic the Aristotelian term *mythos* and the English word myth are much the same thing. Such plots, because they describe typical actions, naturally fall into typical forms. One of these is the tragic plot, with its desis and lysis, its peripety and catastrophe, as charted in the *Poetics*. Another is the comic plot with its happy ending; another is the romance plot with its adventures and its final quest; another is the ironic plot, usually a parody of romance. The poet finds increasingly that he can deal with history only to the extent that history supplies him with, or affords a pretext for, the comic, tragic, romantic or ironic myths that he actually uses.

We notice that when a historian's scheme gets to a certain point of comprehensiveness it becomes mythical in shape, and so approaches the poetic in its structure. There are romantic historical myths based on a quest or pilgrimage to a City of God or a classless society; there are comic historical myths of progress through evolution or revolution; there are tragic myths of decline and fall, like the works of Gibbon and Spengler; there are ironic myths of recurrence or casual catastrophe. It is not necessary, of course, for such a myth to be a universal theory of history, but merely for it to be exemplified in whatever history is using it. A Canadian historian, F. H. Underhill, writing on Toynbee, has coined the term "metahistory" for such works. We notice that metahistory, though it usually tends to very long and erudite books, is far more popular than regular history: in fact metahistory is really the form in which most history reaches the general public. It is only the metahistorian, whether Spengler or Toynbee or H. G. Wells or a religious writer using history as his source of *exempla*, who has much chance of becoming a best-seller.

We notice also that the historian proper tends to confine his verbal imitations of action to human events. His instinct is to look always for the human cause; he avoids the miraculous or the providential; he may assess various non-human factors such as climate, but he keeps them in his "background." The poet, of course, is under no such limitation. Gods and ghosts may be quite as important characters for him as human beings; actions may be cause by *hybris* or nemesis, and the "pathetic fallacy" may be an essential part of his design. Here again metahistory resembles poetry. Metahistorical themes often assume an analogy, or even an identity, with natural processes. Spengler's *Decline of the West* is based on the analogy of historical cultures and vegetable life; Toynbee's "withdrawal and return" theme turns on the analogy of the natural cycle; most theories of progress during the last century have claimed some kind of kinship with evolution. All deterministic histories, whether the determining force is economics or geography or the providence of God, are based on an analogy between history and something else, and so are metahistorical.

The historian works inductively, collecting his facts and trying to avoid any informing patterns except those that he sees, or is honestly convinced he sees, in the facts themselves. The poet, like the metahistorian, works deductively. If he is going to write a tragedy, his decision to impose a tragic pattern on his subject is prior, in importance at least, to his decision to choose a specific historical or legendary or contemporary theme. The remark of Menander that so impressed Matthew Arnold, that his new play was finished and he had only to write it, is typical of the way the poet's mind works. No fact, however interesting, no image, how-. ever vivid, no phrase, however striking, no combination of sounds, however resonant, is of any use to a poet unless it fits: unless it appears to spring inevitably out of its context.

A historian in the position of Menander, ready to write his book, would say that he had finished his research and had only to put it into shape. He works toward his unifying form, as the poet works from it. The informing pattern of the historian's book, which is his *mythos* or plot, is secondary, just as detail to a poet is secondary. Hence the first thing that strikes us about the relation of the poet to the historian is their opposition. In a sense the historical is the opposite of the mythical, and to tell a historian that what gives shape to his book is a myth would sound to him vaguely insulting. Most historians would prefer to believe, with Bacon, that poetry is "feigned history," or, at least, that history is one thing and poetry another, and that all metahistory is a bastard combination of two things that will not really combine. But metahistory is too large and flourishing a growth to be so easily weeded out, and such oversimplifying would eliminate Tacitus and Thucydides equally with Buckle and Spengler. It would be better to recognize that metahistory has two poles, one in history proper and the other in poetry. Historians, up to a point, know what the province of history is and what its dependable methods are; but literary critics know so little of the province or methods of either poetry or criticism that it is natural for the historian to feel that one pole of metahistory is real and the other imaginary, and that whatever is poetic in a historical work destroys its value as history. This is to assume that poetry is simply a form of permissible lying, but that is an assumption that critics have never done much to refute.

Because of its concern with the universal rather than the particular, poetry, Aristotle says, is more philosophical than history. Aristotle never followed up this remark, to the extent at least of working out the relation of poetry to conceptual thought. Perhaps, however, we can reconstruct it along lines similar to his discussion of the relation of poetry to action. We may think, then, of literature as an area of verbal imitation midway between events and ideas, or, as Sir Philip Sidney calls them, examples and precepts. Poetry faces, in one direction, the world of *praxis* or action, a world of events occurring in time. In the opposite direction, it faces the world of *theoria*, of images and ideas, the conceptual or visualizable world spread out in space, or mental space. This world may be imitated in a variety of ways, most commonly in words, though composers, painters, mathematicians and others do not think primarily in words. Still, there is a large area of discursive writing, or works of science and philosophy, which makes up the primary verbal imitation of thought. The discursive writer puts ideas and images into words directly. Like the historian, he makes specific statements, or predications; and, like the historian, he is judged by the truth of what he says, or by the adequacy of his verbal reproduction of his external model.

The poet, similarly, is concerned, not with specific or particular predications, but with typical or recurring ones: "What oft was thought," in other words. The truism, the sententious axiom, the proverb, the *topos* or rhetorical commonplace, the irresistibly quotable phrase—such things are the very life-blood of poetry. The poet seeks the new expression, not the new content, and when we find profound or great thoughts in poetry we are usually finding a statement of a common human situation wittily or inevitably expressed. "The course of true love never did run smooth" is from a Shakespearean comedy, and such sententious comments have been a conventional feature of comedy at least since Menander, whose stock of them was raided by St. Paul. The pleasure we get from quoting such axioms is derived from the versatility with which they fit a great variety of situations with an unexpected appositeness. There are serious works on theology and economics that use a quotation from *Alice in Wonderland* as a motto for each chapter.

Again, the poet has more in common with the constructive elements in thought, and less in common with its descriptive elements. Versified science, whether obsolete or up to date, as we have it in various encyclopedic poems from medieval times onward, never seems able to get beyond a certain point of poetic merit. It is not that the poets are unskillful, but that there is something wrong with the organizing form of the poem. The unifying theme of the *Ormulum* or *The Pastime of Pleasure* is not itself poetic in outline. We may compare the versified historical chronicles of Robert of Gloucester or William Warner, in which we also retain only a languid literary interest, and for the same reason. Poetry seems to have a good deal more affinity with speculative systems, which from Lucretius to *The Testament of Beauty* have consistently shown a more poetic shape. It looks as though there were something of the same kind of affinity between poetry and metaphysics that there is between poetry and metahistory. Of late years we have become much more impressed with the element of *construct* in metaphysical systems, with the feature in them that seems most closely to resemble the poetic. There are logicians who regard metaphysics as bastard logic, just as there are historians who regard metahistory as bastard history. Everything is most properly symmetrical.

The only defect in the symmetry is that metaphysics seems to work mainly with abstractions, and poetry has a limited tolerance for abstractions. Poetry is, in Milton's words, more simple, sensuous and passionate than philosophy. Poetry seeks the image rather than the idea, and even when it deals with ideas it tends to seek the latent basis of concrete imagery in the idea. A discursive nineteenth-century writer will talk of progress and advance in history without noticing, or deliberately ignoring, the fact that his idea has been suggested by the invention of the railway. Tennyson will say "Let the great world spin for ever down the ringing grooves of change," getting his mechanical facts wrong, as poets will, but hitting his conceptual target straight in its sensational bullseye. Literary criticism finds a good deal of difficulty in dealing with such works as *Sartor Resartus*, which appear to employ philosophical concepts and seem to be stating propositions, and yet are clearly something else than actual philosophy. *Sartor Resartus* takes the structure of German Romantic philosophy and extracts from it a central metaphor in which the phenomenal is to the noumenal world as clothing is to the naked body: something which conceals it, and yet, by enabling it to appear in public, paradoxically reveals it as well.

The "ideas" the poets use, therefore, are not actual propositions, but thought-forms or conceptual myths, usually dealing with images rather than abstractions, and hence normally unified by metaphor, or image-phrasing, rather than by logic. The mechanical or diagrammatic image referred to above is a clear example of the poetic element in thought. We sometimes get explicit diagrams in philosophical thought, such as Plato's divided

line and Aristotle's middle way, but the great chain of being is
more typically a poetic conceptual myth, because it is a device
for classifying images. The chain is only one of a great variety of
mechanical models in poetic thought, some of them preceding by
centuries the machines that embody them. There are the wheels
of fate and fortune, mirrors (the word "reflection" indicates how
deeply rooted the conceptual world is in the mechanism of the
eye), internal combustion or vital spark metaphors, the geared
machinery of so much nineteenth-century scientism, the thermo-
stat and feedback metaphors which, since at least Burke's time
and certainly long before "cybernetics," have organized most
democratic political thought.

Just as we are initially aware of an opposition between the
historical and the mythical, so we are initially aware of an opposition between the scientific and the systematic. The scientist starts
out empirically, and tries to avoid hampering himself with such
gigantic constructs as "universe" or "substance." Similarly, the
idea "God," taken as a scientific hypothesis, has never been anything but a nuisance to science. God himself, in the Book of Job,
is represented as warning man of this when he points out to Job
that the conception "creation," as an objective fact, is not and
never can be contained by human experience. Such constructive
concepts are at least metaphysical, and metaphysics, as its etymology indicates, comes after physical science. In theology the
deductive tendency has completely taken over, as there can
hardly be such a thing as empirical theology. The next step
brings us to poetic mythology, the concrete, sensational, figurative, anthropomorphic basis out of which the informing concepts
of discursive thought come.

II

In its use of images and symbols, as in its use of ideas, poetry
seeks the typical and recurring. That is one reason why throughout the history of poetry the basis for organizing the imagery of
the physical world has been the natural cycle. The sequence of

seasons, times of day, periods of life and death, have helped to provide for literature the combination of movement and order, of change and regularity, that is needed in all the arts. Hence the importance, in poetic symbolism, of the mythical figure known as the dying god, whether Adonis or Proserpine or their innumerable allotropic forms, who represents the cycle of nature.

Again, for poets, the physical world has usually been not only a cyclical world but a "middle earth," situated between an upper and a lower world. These two worlds reflect in their form the heavens and hells of the religions contemporary with the poet, and are normally thought of as abodes of unchanging being, not as cyclical. The upper world is reached by some form of ascent, and is a world of gods or happy souls. The most frequent images of ascent are the mountain, the tower, the winding staircase or ladder, or a tree of cosmological dimensions. The upper world is often symbolized by the heavenly bodies, of which the one nearest us is the moon. The lower world, reached by descent through a cave or under water, is more oracular and sinister, and as a rule is or includes a place of torment and punishment. It follows that there would be two points of particular significance in poetic symbolism. One is the point, usually the top of a mountain just below the moon, where the upper world and this one come into alignment, where we look up to the heavenly world and down on the turning cycle of nature. The other is the point, usually in a mysterious labyrinthine cave, where the lower world and this one come into alignment, where we look down to a world of pain and up to the turning cycle of nature. This upward perspective sees the same world, though from the opposite pole, as the downward perspective in the vision of ascent, and hence the same cyclical symbols may be employed for it.

The definitive literary example of the journey of ascent is in the last half-dozen cantos of Dante's *Purgatorio*. Here Dante, climbing a mountain in the form of a winding stair, purges himself of his last sin at the end of Canto 26, and then finds that he has recovered his lost youth, not his individual but his generic youth as a child of Adam, and hence is in the garden of Eden, the

Golden Age of Classical mythology, a lower Paradise directly
below the moon, where Paradise proper begins. This point is as
far up as Virgil can go, and after Virgil leaves Dante the great
apocalyptic vision of the Word and the Church begins. We are
told in Canto 28 that Eden is a *locus amoenus,* a place of perpetually temperate climate, from which the seeds of vegetable
life in the world below proceed, and to which they return—in
other words Eden is at the apex of the natural cycle. In Eden
Dante sees the maiden Matilda, who, he says in the same canto,
makes him remember where and what Proserpine was, when her
mother lost her and she lost the spring flowers. Earlier, in
Canto 27, the dying god's conventional emblem, the red or purple
flower, is dropped into the imagery with a reference to Pyramus
and Thisbe. As a garden is a place of trees, the tree itself is, like
the mountain-top, a natural symbol of the vision of ascent, and
enters Dante's vision, first in Canto 29 in the form of the seven
candlesticks, which look like golden trees at a distance, and later
in Canto 32 as the tree of knowledge, which turns purple in color.

The Gardens of Adonis episode in Book Three of *The Faerie
Queene* is a familiar English example of *locus amoenus* symbolism. The Gardens of Adonis are spoken of as a "Paradise," and
are, again, a place of seed from which the forms of life in the
cycle of nature proceed, and to which they return. In Spenser
we have the dying god Adonis, the purple flower amaranthus
(associated with Sidney, whose fatal thigh-wound made him a
favorite historical embodiment of Adonis) and a grove of myrtle
trees on top of a mountain. One of Spenser's earliest and acutest
critics, Henry Reynolds, suggests, in the easy-going fashion of
his time, an etymological connection between Adonis and Eden,
but Spenser does not make any explicit link between this garden
and Eden, which is the kingdom of Una's parents in Book One.
Nor does he explicitly locate the Gardens at the apex of the
cyclical world just below the moon, though he does speak of
Adonis as "eterne in mutabilitie," which reminds us of the
Mutabilitie Cantoes and of the dispute between Mutability and
Jove, held in the sphere of the moon at the boundary of Jove's

world. In this poem the evidence brought forward by Mutability in her favor, which consists of various aspects of the natural cycle, proves Jove's case instead, because it is evidence of a principle of stability in flux. In any case the upper location of the Gardens of Adonis seems to be in Milton's mind when in *Comus* he introduces the Attendant Spirit as coming from the Gardens of Adonis, which according to the opening line are "Before the starry threshold of Jove's Court." Milton also places Eden on a mountain-top, protected by a "verdurous wall," and the world into which Adam is exiled is spoken of as a "subjected plain."

In Biblical typology the relation between Eden and the wilderness of Adam's exile is closely parallel to the relation between the Promised Land and the wilderness of the law. Here again the Promised Land is thought of as being "above" the wilderness, its capital being Jerusalem, the center of the world and the city on the mountain, "whither the tribes go up." The same kind of language enters the prophetic visions: Ezekiel's wilderness vision of dry bones is in a valley, while the panorama of the restored Jerusalem with which the prophecy concludes begins with the prophet seated "upon a very high mountain." In *Paradise Regained* Christ's temptation in the wilderness is really a descent into hell, or the domain of Satan, terminated by his successful stand on the pinnacle of Jerusalem, which prefigures his later conquest of the lower world of death and hell, much as Satan prefigures his own success in Eden when he sits "like a cormorant," in the tree of life, the highest point in the garden. Christ's victory over Satan also, Milton says, "raised" Eden in the wilderness. The forty days of the temptation are commemorated in Lent, which is immediately followed in the calendar by Easter; they also correspond to the forty years of wilderness wandering under the law, which was terminated by the conquest of the Promised Land by Joshua, who has the same name as Jesus (cf. *Paradise Lost* xii, 307-314).

T. S. Eliot's *Ash Wednesday* is a poem founded on Dante's *Purgatorio* which at the same time glances at these Biblical and liturgical typologies. The central image of the poem is the winding stair of Dante's mountain, which leads to a Paradisal garden. Overtones of Israel in the wilderness ("This is the land. We have our inheritance."), of Ezekiel's valley of dry bones, and of course of Lent, are also present. As the poet is preoccupied with ascent, we get only fitful glimpses of the natural cycle on the way up: "a slotted window bellied like the fig's fruit," "hawthorn blossom," and a "broadbacked figure drest in blue and green," the last reappearing in a subdued form as a silent "garden god" in the *locus amoenus* above. In the final section the poet returns from the universal past to the individual past, from "the violet and the violet" of the garden to a nostalgia symbolized among other things by "lost lilacs."

In view of the explicit and avowed debt of this poem to the *Purgatorio,* the parallels in imagery may not seem very significant. It is all the more interesting to compare the treatment of the "winding stair" image in Yeats, as there, whatever influence from Dante there may be, the attitude taken towards the ascent is radically different. Two of Yeats's poems, A *Dialogue of Self and Soul* and *Vacillation,* turn on a debate between a "soul" who wants only to ascend the stair to some ineffable communion beyond, and a "self" or "heart" who is fascinated by the downward vision into nature, even to the point of accepting rebirth in its cycle. In the former poem the "self" focuses its gaze on the dying-god symbol of the Japanese ceremonial sword wrapped in silk embroidered with flowers of "heart's purple." In *Vacillation* the symbol of ascent and separation from the cycle, the uncorrupted body of the saint, is contrasted with the cycle itself of death and corruption and rebirth, represented by the lion and honeycomb of Samson's riddle. Here, however, it is the symbol of the tree, associated with "Attis' image" and, somewhat like Dante's candlestick vision, "half all glittering flame and half all green," that dominates the poem, and that seems to combine in itself the images of ascent and cycle. Similarly in *Among School Children* the contrast between the nun and the mother, the "bronze repose" of direct ascent and the cyclical "honey of generation," is resolved in the image of the chestnut tree.

There are other examples of the green world at the top of the natural cycle in modern poetry. Wallace Stevens, for instance, gives us a very clear description of it in *Credences of Summer*:

> It is the natural tower of all the world,
> The point of survey, green's green apogee,
> But a tower more precious than the view beyond,
> A point of survey squatting like a throne,
> Axis of everything.

But in the twentieth century, on the whole, images of descent are, so to speak, in the ascendant. These derive mainly from the sixth book of the Aeneid, and its progenitor in the eleventh book of the Odyssey. Here also one is confronted with two levels, a lower world of unending pain, the world of Tantalus and Sisyphus and Ixion, and an upper world more closely connected with the natural cycle. In Virgil there is a most elaborate development of cyclical and rebirth symbolism, introducing speculations of a type that are rarely encountered again in Western poetry before at least Romantic times. In the vision of descent, where we enter a world of darkness and mystery, there is more emphasis on initiation, on learning the proper rites, on acquiring effective talismans like the golden bough. The main figures have a strongly parental aura about them: in Virgil the prophet of the future of Rome is Aeneas' father, and the maternal figure is represented by the Sibyl. In Homer, Odysseus' mother appears, and the figure corresponding to Virgil's Sibyl is Circe, whom Homer calls *potnia*, which means something like reverend. At the top of the winding stair one normally attains direct knowledge or vision, but the reward of descent is usually oracular or esoteric knowledge, concealed or forbidden to most people, often the knowledge of the future.

In romance, where descent themes are very common, the hero often has to kill or pacify a dragon who guards a secret hoard of wealth or wisdom. The descent is also often portrayed as a mimic, temporary or actual death of the hero; or he may be swallowed by the dragon, so that his descent is into the monster's belly. In medieval treatments of the Christian story some of these

themes reappear. Between his death on the cross and his resurrection Jesus descends into hell, often portrayed, especially in
fresco, as the body of a huge dragon or shark, which he enters
by the mouth, like his prototype Jonah. Again there are two
levels in the lower world: hell proper, a world of endless torment,
and the upper limbo which is "harrowed," and from which the
redeemed, among whom the parental figures Adam and Eve
have an honored place, return to the upper world. The monster's
open mouth recurs in *Ash Wednesday* as "the toothed gullet of
an agèd shark," and as the symbol of the "blue rocks" or
Symplegades, whose clashing together has similar overtones.

For obvious reasons, visions of descent in medieval and Renaissance poetry are usually infernal visions, based on Virgil but
ignoring his interest in rebirth. Only with Romantic poetry do
we begin to get once more the oracular or quest descent, where
the hero gets something more from his descent than a tragic tale
or an inspection of torments. In Keats's *Endymion* there are
adventures in both upward and downward directions, the upward ones being mainly quests for beauty and the downward
ones quests for truth. The Gardens of Adonis in this poem seem
to be down rather than up, as they do at the conclusion of
Blake's *Book of Thel*, though in that conclusion there is a sudden
reversal of perspective. Shelley's *Prometheus Unbound* is a more
striking example of a cosmology in which everything beneficial
comes from below, and everything sinister from above. The contrast here with the cosmology of Dante and Milton is so striking
that it deserves more examination.

In Dante, in Spenser, in Milton, the foreground of symbols
and images seems to be portrayed against a background of
roughly four levels of existence. I need a word for this background, and am strongly tempted to steal "topocosm" from
Theodor H. Gaster's *Thespis*, though he uses it in a quite different sense. The top level is the place of the presence of God,
the empyreal heaven, which operates in this world as the order
of grace and providence. The next level is that of human nature
properly speaking, represented by the garden of Eden or the
Golden Age before the Fall, and now a world to be regained

internally by moral and intellectual effort. Third is the level of physical nature, morally neutral but theologically fallen, which man is born into but can never adjust to, and fourth is the level of sin, death and corruption, which since the Fall has permeated the third level too. Throughout this period it was traditional to symbolize the top level by the starry spheres, the spiritual by the physical heaven. Dante's upper Paradise is located in the planetary spheres, and in Milton's *Nativity Ode* the music of the spheres, symbol of the understanding of unfallen man, is in counterpoint to the chorus of descending angels.

After the rise of Copernican astronomy and Newtonian physics, the starry sky becomes a less natural and a more perfunctory and literary metaphor for the spiritual world. The stars look increasingly less like vehicles of angelic intelligences, and come to suggest rather a mechanical and mindless revolution. This shift of perspective is of course already present in a famous passage in Pascal, but it does not make its full impact on poetry until much later. A deity at home in such a world would seem stupid or malignant, at best a kind of self-hypnotized Pangloss. Hence the variety of stupid sky-gods in Romantic poetry: Blake's Urizen, Shelley's Jupiter, Byron's Arimanes, Hardy's Immanent Will, perhaps the God of the Prologue to *Faust*. Blake, the closest of this group to the orthodox Christian tradition, points out that there is more Scriptural evidence for Satan as a sky god than for Jesus. Even more significant for poetic symbolism is the sense of the mechanical complications of starry movement as the projection or reflection of something mechanical and malignant in human nature. In other words, the Frankenstein theme of actualizing human death-impulses in some form of fateful mechanism has a strong natural connection with the sky or "outer space," and in modern science fiction is regularly attached to it. At the same time poets in the Romantic period tend to think of nature less as a structure or system, set over against the conscious mind as an object, and more as a body of organisms from which the human organism proceeds, nature being the underlying source of humanity, as the seed is of the plant.

Hence with Romanticism another "topocosm," almost the

reverse of the traditional one, begins to take shape. On top is the bleak and frightening world of outer space. Next comes the level of ordinary human experience, with all its anomalies and injustices. Below, in the only place left for any *locus amoenus*, is the buried original form of society, now concealed under the historical layers of civilization. With a modern Christian poet this would be the old unfallen world, or its equivalent: thus in Auden's *For the Time Being* the "garden" world is hidden within or concealed by the "wilderness" of ordinary life. With a poet closer to Rousseau this buried society would be the primitive society of nature and reason, the sleeping beauty that a revolutionary act of sufficient courage would awaken. On the fourth level, corresponding to the traditional hell or world of death, is the mysterious reservoir of power and life out of which both nature and humanity proceed. This world is morally ambivalent, being too archaic for distinctions of good and evil, and so retains some of the sinister qualities of its predecessor. Hence the insistence in Romantic culture of the ambivalent nature of "genius," or an unusual degree of natural creative power, which may destroy the poet's personality or drive him to various forms of evil or suffering, as in the Byronic hero, the *poète maudit*, the compulsive sinner of contemporary Christian and existential fiction, and other varieties of Romantic agony.

Against this "topocosm" the action of *Prometheus Unbound* seems logical enough. In the sky is Jupiter, the projection of human superstition with its tendency to deify a mechanical and sub-human order. Below is the martyred Prometheus; below him Mother Earth (in whose domain is included the world of death, which has a mysterious but recurring connection with the *locus amoenus* in Shelley), and at the bottom of the whole action is the oracular cave of Demogorgon, who calls himself Eternity, and from whom the power proceeds that rejuvenates Earth, liberates Prometheus, and annihilates Jupiter. (On the mythical structure of *Prometheus Unbound* see, now, Harold Bloom, *Shelley's Mythmaking*, a study not available to me when writing this essay.)

The Romantic "topocosm," like its predecessor, is, for the poet, simply a way of arranging metaphors, and does not in itself imply any particular attitudes or beliefs or conceptions. The traditional infernal journey naturally persists: Eliot's *Waste Land* and the first of Pound's *Cantos* are closely related examples, the former having many Aeneid echoes and the latter being based on the Odyssey. In Pound the characteristic parental figure is Aphrodite, called "venerendam," an echo of Homer's *potnia*, who bears the "golden bough of Argicida," in other words of Hermes the psychopomp. In Eliot the parallel figure to this combination of Hermes and Aphrodite is the hermaphroditic Teiresias, the seer who was the object of Odysseus' descent.

The "topocosm" of Dante was closely related to contemporary religious and scientific constructs, and to a much lesser degree the same is true of the post-Romantic one. We get our "up" metaphors from the traditional forms: everything that is uplifting or aspiring about the spiritual quest, such as the wings of angels or the ascension of Christ or the phrase "lift up your hearts," is derived from the metaphorical association of God and the sky. Even as late as the nineteenth century, progress and evolution were still going up as well as on. In the last century or so there has been a considerable increase in the use of approving "down" metaphors: to get "down" to bedrock or brass tacks or the basic facts is now the sign of a proper empirical procedure. Descent myths are also deeply involved in the social sciences, especially psychology, where we have a subconscious or unconscious mind assumed, by a spatial metaphor, to be underneath the consciousness, and into this mind we descend in quest of parental figures. The Virgilian inspiration of modern scientific mythology is not hard to see: the golden bough of the sixth book of the Aeneid supplies the title and theme for Frazer, and the famous line spoken by Juno in the seventh, that if she cannot prevail on the high gods she will stir up hell (fletere si nequeo superos, Acheronta movebo), is the apt motto of Freud's *Interpretation of Dreams*. But now that politics and science at least are beginning to focus once more on the moon, it is possible that a new construct will be formed, and a new table of metaphors organize the imagery of our poets.

8. An Examination of the Myth and Ritual Approach to Shakespeare

HERBERT WEISINGER

QUIETLY, BUT STEADILY and stubbornly, in the face of outright opposition and even deadlier smiling scepticism, the myth and ritual approach to literature, and to Shakespeare specifically, has been attracting increasing numbers of recruits who, though they may think of themselves as cut off from each other and besieged on all sides, add up in fact to a goodly corps of criticism. Indeed, one can almost name the date when the trumpet call to arms was first sounded: if we omit the suggestive but unsystematic insights concerning the use of myth in literature thrown off by the German romantic critics and their English fellow-traveller Coleridge, we can locate the rallying place and time by the work of the English anthropological school of the nineteenth century, first with Tylor and Robertson Smith, but, far above all others, with Frazer, followed hard on by Crawley, Hartland, and Lang. Among the very first to recognize the value of the discoveries of the new anthropology to other fields was Freud—repaid, incidentally, for his interest in Frazer by a cutting indifference—so that the bond of anthropology and psychoanalysis was cemented at the very foundation of both disciplines, and therefore simultaneously of modern myth study. The first students of literature to take advantage of this fascinating and fruitful union were the classicists, particularly those belonging to the so-called Cambridge school—Harrison, Murray, Cook, Cornford, and Thomson. In turn, the method was applied to ever-widening circles of literature by such critics as Auden, Burke, Cauldwell, Chase, Eliot, who said as early as 1923: "it is a method for which the horoscope is auspicious," Fergusson, Frye, Graves, Hyman, Mann, Raglan, Read, Schorer, Tindall, Wheelwright, Weston, and Yeats. The pioneer, full-scale treatment of Shakespeare in the light of the myth and ritual approach was achieved by the still-neglected Colin Still, but he has been followed by other, better-known names: Barber, Bland, Bodkin, Chambers—the references to Frazer in *The Medieval Stage* are critical but the influence is unmistakable and pervasive—Danby, Frye, Heilman, Knight, Speight, Spencer, Traversi and the *Scrutiny*-Penguin group, Stirling, and Wincor.

Those who hold to the myth and ritual approach to Shakespeare are almost unanimously agreed that the pattern of rebirth and reconciliation is fundamental to virtually the whole of Shakespeare's plays. "Birth, struggle, death, and revival," the late Theodore Spencer wrote, "these are not only the themes of the individual final plays, they are the themes which describe the course of Shakespeare's work as a whole, from his earliest plays through *King Lear* to *The Tempest*." Tillyard has said of the last plays: "Regeneration emerges dominant from the total tragic pattern," and he sums up this pattern as a ". . . general scheme of prosperity, destruction, and re-creation. The main character is a King. At the beginning he is in prosperity. He then does an evil or misguided deed. Great suffering follows, but during this suffering or at its height the seeds of something new to issue from it are germinating, usually in secret. In the end this new element assimilates and transforms the old evil. The King overcomes his evil instincts, joins himself to the new order by an act of forgiveness or repentance, and the play issues into a fairer prosperity than had first existed." Barber has characterized the comedy before Hamlet as giving ". . . form to feeling and knowledge by a movement which can be summarized in the formula: *through release to clarification*"; the middle plays, and particularly *Measure for Measure,* have been interpreted as analogies of the doctrine of atonement, as has been *Othello;* while Wincor suggests that ". . . Shakespeare's last plays may be best understood by comparing them with the old festival plays that celebrate the return of spring after a barren winter." And, summing up some two decades of devotion to Shakespeare, Knight describes what he has found to be ". . . the habitual design of Shakespearean tragedy: from normalcy and order, through violent conflict to a spiritualized music and then to the concluding ritual." In sum, then, we see that the bulk of Shakespeare's plays has been found to conform to the myth and ritual pattern.

Recently I attempted an epitome of the myth and ritual approach to tragedy as follows: ". . . the structure of tragic form, as derived from the myth and ritual pattern, may be diagrammed in this way: the tragic protagonist, in whom is subsumed the well-being of the people and the welfare of the state, engages in conflict with a representative of darkness and evil; a temporary defeat is inflicted on the tragic protagonist, but after shame and suffering he emerges triumphant as the symbol of the victory of light and good over darkness and evil, a victory sanctified by the covenant of the settling of destinies which reaffirms the well-being of the people and the welfare of the state. In the course of the conflict there comes a point where the protagonist and the antagonist appear to merge into a single challenge against the order of God: the evil which the protagonist would not do, he does, and the good which he would, he does not; and in this moment we are made aware that the real protagonist of tragedy is the order of God against which the tragic hero has rebelled. In this manner is the pride, the presumption which is in all of us by virtue of our mixed state as man, symbolized and revealed, and it is this *hybris* which is vicariously purged from us by the suffering of the tragic protagonist." I then went on to examine Shakespeare's plays in the light of their adherence to or departure from this pattern and I came to the conclusion that ". . . while the last plays of Shakespeare do indeed carry forward the tragic pattern established in *Hamlet, Othello, King Lear,* and *Macbeth,* they neither heighten nor deepen it but on the contrary reject and even destroy it. In fact, I would go so far as to argue that the tragic pattern in the tragedies themselves is scarcely maintained equally strongly over each of the plays." For, if we take the myth and ritual pattern as fundamental and anterior to tragedy, as either the normal or ideal paradigm of tragedy, then it must follow, I insist, ". . . that Shakespeare's tragic vision, which he was able to sustain but tentatively in *Hamlet,* most fully in *Othello,* barely in *King Lear,* and hardly at all in *Macbeth,* failed him altogether in the last plays."

In my own formulation can be found the major weaknesses of the myth and ritual approach to literature, and to Shakespeare in particular, the major methodological problems which it has yet to solve. I must confess that conversion to the method tends to bring with it the euphoria of conversion which enthusiastically overlooks defects and difficulties and sees only the light of conviction, but the problems exist and persist, and they must be confronted honestly and then eliminated before the method can take its place as a fully articulated instrument of criticism. The first problem, then: there is no agreement as to what the myth and ritual pattern actually is. Not only is this true of students of literature who must, after all, take their materials from the anthropologists, archaeologists, pre-historians, psycho-analysts, historians of religion, folklorists, and classicists, but it is equally true of the very experts in those fields. I know from personal observation that Frankfort turned livid at the sound of Frazer's name, Rose savages Graves, Graves gores Jung, Guthrie deplores Cornford, and bound volumes of *The Journal of American Folklore* are thrown at Raglan and Hyman for criticizing Thompson. As a matter of fact, no myth and ritual pattern as such exists or ever existed in any real sense; it is a modern, scholarly reconstruction of diverse materials drawn from divergent sources. Moreover, and this is even more exasperating, there is no agreement as to the meaning of myth itself. To Whalley, a myth ". . . is a direct metaphysical statement beyond science. . . . Myth has as its purpose, its source and end, revelation"; to Watts, it is the *philosophia perennis;* to Wheelright, "it is . . . a set of depth-meanings of perduring significance within a widely shared per-

spective"; to Graves, it is ". . . the reduction to narrative short-
hand of ritual mime performed on public festivals" or, contrariwise, the antique story of the White Goddess, or, even more
contrariwise, politico-religious history; and as a final example,
myths are ". . . mistaken explanations of phenomena . . . founded
on ignorance and misapprehension they are always false, for
were they true, they would cease to be myths," and this, ironically
enough, was Frazer's opinion.

The second problem: assuming for the moment that such a
pattern as the myth and ritual pattern does in fact exist, there is
no satisfactory way of explaining how Shakespeare got at it. The
best case which can be made out for the transmission of the
pattern to Shakespeare is along the lines of the materials collected
in Chambers' *The Medieval Stage* and *The English Folkplay*
which suggest that the ideological atmosphere in which Shakespeare worked was drenched with Christian versions of the pattern, though Chambers himself says nothing about this in his
life of Shakespeare. This is the tack taken by Barber, Philpotts,
Murray, and Wincor; I myself struck a more cautious note: "But
the most that can be claimed for the influence of the pattern is
that, in an atmosphere where the drama of redemption as symbolized in the death and resurrection of Christ was made the
very heart of universal faith, it is not surprising that the pattern
was given expression in an almost endless variety of ways and
forms . . . it means only that the medieval climate of opinion was
in a large degree sympathetic to the pattern because of the per-
vading effect of its Christian shape." But this is too close to
begging the question for more daring spirits; so, for example,
Frye writes: "Or again, we have, in myth, the story of Proserpine,
who disappears into the underworld for six months of every year.
The pure myth is clearly one of death and revival; the story as
we have it is slightly displaced, but the mythical pattern is easy
to see. The same structural element often recurs in Shakespearean
comedy, where it has to be adapted to a roughly high level of
credibility." It seems to me that the leap between the second
and third sentences of this statement is precisely the point at

issue: how does an ancient Near Eastern myth—for the Proserpine version is a late redaction—become the basis of a Renaissance play? Are we to take Frye's assertion as merely analogously illustrative; but, if it is only an analogy, how can it be made to bear the weight of the function assigned to it? Serious methodological questions are involved here: how does myth get into works of art—are there demonstrable historical steps involved, or demonstrable psychological steps? Is the form of myth inherent in the form of works of art? If it is, how does one distinguish between them? According to my own reconstruction of the myth and ritual pattern, a reconstruction which tries to take in the variations in the pattern which recent scholarship has uncovered and which must be taken into account, though they blunt the vivid sharpness and convincing exactitude of a monolithic and universal formulation, it contains nine elements, but, at the same time, of these tragedy has eliminated four, reduced two more to subordinate roles, and retained only three of the original nine; in addition, certain other significant changes have been made as well. Are we not getting to the point where the differences are more important than the similarities? Moreover, is the use of the myth and ritual pattern a conscious, deliberate, aesthetic decision of the artist himself? The myth and ritual approach seems to suggest that the artist is no more than the torpid holder of the pen which the myth and ritual pattern in some arcane fashion guides. "For the craft of the poet is light and winged and holy, and he is not capable of poetry until he is inspired and out of his mind and there is no reason in him. Until he gets into this state, any man is powerless to produce poetry and to prophesy." This is not G. Wilson Knight speaking, but the Plato of the *Ion*.

The third problem: at the moment there appears to be no agreement among those who advocate this view as to the aesthetic and ethical effects of the pattern on the plays themselves. There are, in fact, two opposing points of view: one which holds that the pattern enabled Shakespeare to convert the chaos of evil into an orderly world of understanding and reconciliation, the other which sees Shakespeare's plays as moving altogether in the reverse direction, in which the brute fact of evil implacably and finally overcomes whatever is good and great in men. One makes Shakespeare out a Christian Olympian, a kind of Sophocles of the *Oedipus at Colonus* or a Goethe of the second part of *Faust* or a Beethoven of the last quartets; the other turns him into a tired, disillusioned old man, playing technical tricks in the last plays for his cynical amusement. For the first group, *The Tempest* ". . . distills the poetic essence of the whole Shakespearean universe"; for the other it is merely silly. Substitute Dowden for Knight and Strachey for James and it would seem that fifty years of scholarship and criticism have been unable to reconcile themselves over the plays of reconciliation. All that has changed is the vocabulary, for one side cannot forget that Prospero promises to break his staff, the other that in fact he does not do so. His final assurance to deliver all ends the play on just the right note of ambiguity calculated to perpetuate another fifty years of disagreement. But is it necessary that the myth and ritual approach to Shakespeare force him into the narrow mold of a doctrinaire Christian? Indeed, is it necessary that the method be manipulated to recast all the works of literature it considers into exhibiting the same progression from despair to affirmation, an affirmation couched in specifically Christian terms? But if the method can detect affirmation, it can also discover denial, and in fact it is this very nicety of discrimination which gives the myth and ritual approach its subtlety and universality of application. To limit it to Christian affirmation alone is to confine and reduce not only the method but, what is worse, the variety and vitality of literature itself.

The fourth and final problem: what is the critical validity of a method which in effect sets up a pattern derived from sources outside the texts and then judges their success and failure in terms of their approach to or distance from conformity to that pattern? Can we in fact judge a work of art by standards quite unsuspected by its maker? To what an extremity this point of view may be pushed is illustrated by my own article, in which I was forced to the conclusion that Shakespeare failed to write a single successful tragedy—by my standards, that is. Such dogmatism, and it is no excuse that other advocates of the myth and ritual approach are as dogmatic, though about other convictions, as I was, is, however, not inherent in the method, and reflects the extra-critical preconceptions of the critic, and reveals them, too. But it is not a question of striking off Knight's Anglicanism against my scepticism, but of doing justice to the work of art itself, though I must confess that we often seem to be using Shakespeare or Milton as sticks to shake against ourselves, to the detriment both of literature and of criticism. As a corrective to the dogged and dull empiricism of much of Shakespearean scholarship, the myth and ritual approach offers the relief of a provocative and integrated point of view, but its more ardent devotees are often like the dictators of *haute couture:* they force a dogmatic shape upon the individual reluctant body for the sake of a general theoretical ideal.

And yet all that I have been saying against the myth and ritual approach to Shakespeare can, with equal justice, be directed against any unified and consistent critical system. For all our seeming forward motion, we have fallen right back into the midst of that ancient quarrel between the idealists and empiricists, and we must choose sides; either Plato or Aristotle, no matter what new name may be printed on the label. Of course, we like to think of ourselves as being very scientific in our methods and we are all presumably dedicated to the postulate that a generalization can be no more than the exact sum total of all the individual inferences by which it is constituted. So we may believe, but we don't act that way. There is never any moment at which it may be confidently stated that all the facts are finally in, nor can a principle ever encompass within the confines of a single proposition all the single details which it is intended to cover. To start from the ultimate, irrefutable fact and painstakingly build upward may be the Baconian dream, but, after all, the function of a dream is to allow us to do symbolically what we cannot do in reality. In criticism, as in politics, it is legitimate to delude others; it is fatal to delude one's self. For all his hard-headedness, the empiricist pursues a phantom with which he can never catch up.

The myth and ritual approach to Shakespeare cannot possibly encompass in all their rich variety the totality of Shakespeare's plays. But it can, and does, place the plays in an exciting and vital context which does have the effect of renewing them for us; it is the context which Gilbert Murray once spoke of as ". . . the strange, unanalyzed vibration below the surface" of such plays as the *Agamemnon* or *Electra* or *Hamlet*, ". . . an undercurrent of desires and fears and passions, long slumbering yet eternally familiar, which have for thousands of years lain near the root of our most intimate emotions and been wrought into the fabric of our most magical dramas." To have done this for Shakespeare, to have linked him to the most fundamental, and oldest, of man's attempts to create an understandable place for himself in an indifferent universe, is no small accomplishment, and this I think the myth and ritual approach to Shakespeare has successfully done. To be sure, it is a method which seems to demand the wholehearted allegiance of its adherents, and it is therefore subject to the extremes which all true believers perpetrate. It is a committed point of view and so cantankerous, obstreperous, irritating, wrong on details, and dictatorial, but it is passionate and alive and has something to say. And these, after all, are the virtues of literature as well.

9. The Working Novelist and the Mythmaking Process

ANDREW LYTLE

WHEN I first began thinking about the book which was to become *The Velvet Horn*,* I was thinking consciously: that is, rationally. I could almost say falsely, except that the creative act uses all the mind's faculties. I thought I wanted to do a long piece of fiction on a society that was dead. At the time I saw the scene as the kind of life which was the Southern version of a life that, discounting the sectional differences, had been common everywhere east of the Mississippi and east of the mountains. That life seemed to me to be what was left of the older and more civilized America, which as well retained the pattern of its European inheritance. The Civil War had destroyed that life; but memory and habit, manners and mores are slow to die.

As a boy I had witnessed its ghostly presence, and yet the people which this presence inhabited were substantial enough. They were alive in their entire being. They seemed all the more alive because their culture was stricken. The last active expression of this society seemed to fall somewhere between 1880 and 1910. Those decades seemed the effective turning point of the great revolution which was to diminish a Christian inheritance. The mechanics of the change are obvious to all; the most effective

---

* *The Velvet Horn* (New York: McDowell, Obolensky Inc., 1957), is set in the Cumberland hill country in the nineteenth century, and revolves round the passionate-natured Cropleigh family. Besides its poetic descriptions and its sensitivity to speech rhythms, the novel, marked for its use of symbolism, is rich in metaphor and allusiveness.—EDITOR.

was the automobile, since it uprooted the family by destroying its attachment to place. In the South, certainly, family was the one institution common to all its parts. There was great variety to the South's homogeneity, which the false myths about it never understood. There has been no part of this country so afflicted with "galvanized" myths which presumed to interpret it, but it was family as institution which best expressed its culture. By family, I mean all the complex interrelationships of blood and kin, the large "connections" which extended to the county lines and by sympathy overlapped the states.

I take the automobile as the supreme agency in the destruction of attachment to place, since the railroads did not destroy the communities; they merely connected them more readily. Family and place, as I said, go together. It was the sense of both which set the South apart in this country, but too much was asked of the family as institution. It should have been one among many institutional expressions of culture; it was called upon to do more than its form allowed. But the artist works by means of such limitations. So it seemed to me as I began. I had no intention, no sense of dealing with a myth which forever recurs within the human scene.

This conscious approach is merely one way in, or down. The writer may begin with anything, a mood, a scene, an idea, a character, a situation. Whatever sets him going generally appears suddenly in that suspension of attention which is like the aftereffect of shock. It is a condition of the psyche when it finds itself outside time. This condition may be the occasion for vision or dream. In the Middle Ages any man might know it. Dreams remain, but vision commonly fails us today. We are helpless before the condition in which dreams appear; but vision strikes the state of consciousness. This stroke and that mysterious sense of being possessed largely remain for the artist, the point being that presumably he suffers this intrusion when he is conscious. Presumably, because the aftereffect of shock allows for a certain awareness of what is going on around outside, but the consciousness does not respond in action. It is suspended before the intuitive and instinctive action taking place within the mind. Somehow, through a fissure, the unconscious pierces the consciousness, and from below streams the image, or whatever it is, that sets the artist to work. The shock is a true shock. It paralyzes the rational mind momentarily. It is mysterious. The cause, the source, can in no way be discovered by natural or positive means. But the experience is true, and forever denies to mere formula a rendition of the knowledge which is experience.

The creative act is, then, both a rational and an intuitive performance. What comes up from below through this fissure generally relates to the subject, but for me at least it always seems at first to be the essence of the subject. It can be this, but it rarely is. It must contain the essence, however; and it is just here that the conscious use of the craft of fiction comes in. The craft is the lesser part, but nevertheless crucial. Without its procedure of arranging, finding relationships between structural parts, and all such matters, as well as the tedious search for the right word or phrase, there would be no art of language as fiction.

It is curious, but for as long as I have written, I am always surprised afresh, after much sorrow and trouble to get a story going, that the idea may merely be related to, not be, the subject. Each time I have to learn afresh that it is either a segment of a larger idea or an idea too big for the action, as it shows itself. The resistance to its dissolution in the action is enormous, partly because it retains the excitement of the moment of inspiration. This inspiration is a momentary vision of the whole. It quickly sinks into the abyss from which it arose, leaving the idea as a kind of clue, the end of the thread which leads into the labyrinth. No matter how firmly the critical sense has explored the idea's limitations, the moment the artist engages himself, he cannot but take it to mean more than it does. An idea is so inflexible; it tends so easily toward the conceptual. It *must* turn flesh before it is fiction. Fiction above all should give the illusion of life, of men and women acting out some one of the eternal involvements we all know, resolving, not solving. Only God may solve. A character or a situation would be the simpler way to begin. It would lead more directly into the conflict. It is rarely my way.

I feel there is an advantage to beginning with an idea rather than a situation or a mood. This advantage is suggested by its very irrefrangibility. If the idea is universal, in action it becomes archetypal. Therefore, to render it describes more nearly a whole action; and the artist must not tell any story but the *one* story which the people and situation demand. I would like to distinguish at this point between an opinion about behavior and archetypal representation. Opinion is the vulgarity of taste. It is never a true idea, because it is either topical or partial. It distorts any action, since it is blind to the fullest complexity of that action. No matter how disguised, opinion always has a "message," it always wants to prove something instead of making experience show itself. Its selection of incidents, therefore, is often obviously arbitrary. This is the failure of the realistic school of fiction, if school it is.

To begin by wanting to resuscitate a dead society, it seems to follow, involves the writer in a great risk. It gets in the way of bringing his people alive. For the first hundred pages or so he is in danger of being misled by opinion. He is saved by the creative act; that is, he is saved by his people showing life. The moment comes when the actors in the stress of the situation will come "alive," will make a response that reveals them. In the light of this response the writer can go back and rectify, revise, remove the scaffolding. Then he is able to examine, to criticize the impulse which set him going. He can do this without impairing the life evoked. He can do it because life is there. It is at this point that the conscious and the intuitive practice of the craft work most easily together. The mechanics for this is cleaning up as you go along. Ford Maddox Ford taught me this method. Many practice it, but not all. You do the day's stint, let it set, and next morning look at it again. Tighten it up, change things about, and then proceed. As the action grows, each day's work moves closely out of what has gone before. In the beginning it is not always clear which of the threads of complication holds the center. Cleaning up at last shows it. This is a decisive moment. Such a process stimulates natural growth most unnaturally: that is, it has about it the mystery of all growth, and yet is artificial. The common miracle of life is the seasonal change. It is so common, and of necessity must be so, else we would be too aware of living in a state of constant miracle. This would strain the amenities. So it is in the practice of a craft. But there are moments when the craft is overborne by the stroke of life. This is the flash of miracle. This is the artist's reward, almost the only lasting reward, for it is an assurance that the work is moving as it should. Perhaps it was of this that Blake was thinking when he said the artist continues the act of God.

How gradually does this bemusement with the strict idea lift. I do not now remember at what stage it became clear again that you do not write about a society living or dead. You write about people who live within the constraint of some inherited social agreement. They are already involved when you take them up, for there is no natural man. He has never anywhere been seen, certainly not within historic time. But what is natural or common to all men has been changed from birth by manners and mores, institutions, all the conventions and laws of a given society. It is the restraint of decorum, propriety, taste, the limits of estates and classes—all such which distort, repress, guide the instincts, impulses, passions, the unruly demands of the blood toward the multifold kinds of behavior. All forms of intercourse rely upon faith and belief. This is a platitude of statement, but as working knowledge for the author it shows itself with the fresh light of truth.

And this working knowledge was already informing, changing from a concept to the movements of life, the idea of a dead society. I was not only rationally seeing fuller implications; that is, I was not only seeing of what this society was composed as action, which had already taken it out of a conceptual stage; I was comparing it to the cycles which other societies go through. The decline of civilizations, for example, of necessity follows the failure of belief, the cultural forces gradually withdrawing made manifest in the hardening of traditional laws and forms, foreshadowing rigidity: that is, death. But out of death comes life, as appositely death is the conclusion to life. Within the circling

spiral of such change lies the belief in immortality and continuance. At some point it came to me that it is the archetypes which
forever recur, are immortal, timeless; it is only the shapes in
which these appear that seem to harden and die, that is, the
manners and mores that are unique to a given society; and these
shapes are the appearances of reality, the world's illusion moving
within the illusion of time. What a shock this was to my partial
and emotional view of the South!

Now the South was a mixed society, and it was a defeated
society; and the defeated are self-conscious. They hold to the
traditional ways, since these ways not only tell them what they
are but tell them with a fresh sense of themselves. Only defeat
can do this. It is this very self-consciousness which makes for the
sharpened contemplation of self. It is comparable to euphoria.
The sudden illumination made life fuller and keener, as it made
life tragic. But it stopped action. The very heightening of self-
awareness made for a sudden withdrawal of the life force. What
was left of it remained in the surface forms. The forms were
shattered, but because of this force they held their shape briefly.
The shed skin for a while shines with life, but the force of life is
already on its night sea journey. I did not know how to define
this force at the time; I only felt it vaguely, as I felt the vacuum
beneath, which is the atmosphere of chaos. I was slow to connect
this basic energy with the repetitive thrust out of chaos into the
surrounding void, but I felt I knew that chaos is the underlying
condition of any artifice, whether it was the state or the family
or a work of art. Mythically, for so far only did I read the myth,
it seemed the state Adam and Eve found themselves in after Eve
had been taken from Adam's side. Their expulsion from the
earthly paradise seemed to put them into the disorder of chaos.
Actually, they were confronted by a natural order which was a
multiplicity of the conflicts of opposites. This is not chaos but life
as we suffer it, and we fall into it as the child falls into the world.
Continuance depended upon the exercise of the will and especially the crafts, not only to survive but to try to restore, to bring
together the two halves which make a whole. Together, man and

woman serve as the basic symbol for the life drama. How old is the sentence we hear every day, "This is my better half."

It was some years after I had been working on the as yet unnamed *The Velvet Horn* that I realized I was treating an aspect of this ancient drama. The brothers and sister, under the guidance of the eldest, withdrew from the stresses of formal society in an effort to return to the prenatural equilibrium of innocence and wholeness. This is an habitual impulse, the refusal to engage in the cooperating opposites that make life. It is also as illusory as any Golden Age, and forbidden by divine and human law. Therefore, it is the grounds for one of the oldest forms of search and conflict. The symbol for this is incest. It need not be fact; but it is symbol, also one having a literal counterpart; in one instance in the story it happened as fact as well.

For many years it has seemed to me that incest was a constant upon the Southern scene. There was plenty of circumstantial evidence. The boys' and girls' rooms seemed too obviously separated. I remember in old houses the back stairs with solid paneling to hide ankles and lower legs as the girls came down. Call it prudery, but what is prudery? The fear of incest, if incest it was, was perhaps not overt, but I knew of whore houses where too many of the girls had been ravished by fathers and brothers. Even if these were extreme instances—I had no way to know how general they may have been—still they were indicative. But the actual union between close kin was not my interest. It was the incest of the spirit which seemed my subject, a spiritual condition which inhered within the family itself. I did not have to look very far, no farther than both sides of my own house, to know this. It was clearest in the county family, where the partial isolation meant an intimacy and constancy of association in work and play which induced excessive jealousy against intrusion from the outside. Often enough a partiality for one child went beyond the needs of parental care, bringing about all kinds of internal stresses within the family circle. This jealousy, this love, extended to the land and to natural objects with a possessiveness lasting even generations. I know of a family that today will engage in ritualized quarrels for hours on end over whether a field has been let grow up in sprouts, while the guests sit as at a play. These are all love quarrels, and the land is as much subject as object.

But to return: once I had got well into the first section of the novel, I had completely forgotten that I had wanted to bring a dead society to life. What part incest would play had, as well, moved to the edge of my attention. I was involved in the first pressures of making a world, peopling this world into which the young nephew, Lucius, would be guided by his uncle. The surface action seemed to be the initiation of the boy, culminating in his first sexual experience, although this was by no means his only adventure. The world he was entering, I felt, must seem out of the world, withdrawn, mysterious, of a strange look to him and refreshing, since in climbing the Peaks of Laurel, he left behind a dry and sterile place, burning under excessive drought. Of course he was climbing into his entanglement with life, which his father's suicide would rebegin. The seeming accidental reason for the climb was to witch a well: find water. It bore a literal as well as symbolical meaning.

Gradually I became aware of the need for this double usage as far as fiction is concerned. The symbol should always have its literal or natural counterpart. It should never rely upon the Platonic ideal image; this is a concept. Since fiction is an action in which nothing must be left inert, a concept of perfection, say, cannot be known actively. Perfection can only be sought out of imperfection, out of the fallen state of man represented by the cooperating forces of good and evil. The reinterpretation of myth by such people as Jung and Zimmer has done much to make this clear, but I think it has always been known by a certain kind of artist, if only intuitively. It was the yeast which worked the dough. An image seemed, then, not an imperfect reflection of perfection, but an action derived from the shattering of a whole into parts, which in all myths of origin begins the world drama. The end of this would be a reunion of the parts into a whole, but a whole no longer innocent. But this reunion never takes place in the world, else the drama would end. Here was the clue to the end of my novel, however, although I in no way saw it. The action had not moved sufficiently to inform me.

Anyway, the action itself must be symbolic of the archetypal experience. This, I consider, was the most important thing *The Velvet Horn* taught me. The symbol must be more than an inert sign or emblem. Where symbols appear—and there will be one to contain them all in their relationships—they represent the entire action by compressing into a sharp image or succession of images the essence of meaning. For example, in animal nature, the horn stands for both the masculine and feminine parts of being, the two aspects of the apposites which make a whole: the two in one contained by a single form. Add the velvet to this and you posit the state of innocence, that suspension before the act which continues the cycle of creation. At a certain moment the buck, out of the mystery of instinct, rubs the velvet off against the tree, and then he is ready for the rutting season. The velvet grows about the feminine end of the horn, and it bleeds as it is rubbed away. The blood is real, but the act symbolizes what the other end of the horn will do. In human nature the horn's counterpart would be the hermaphrodite, Hermes and Aphrodite contained within the one form. Their separation, Eve taken from Adam's side, at another level continues the cycle of creation. Both forms exist within the constancy of the seasonal turn of nature. The entire range of imagery relates to these.

So used, the image as symbol becomes the clue to reading, the means by which all the parts are related to the structure. It is not inert but active, being both root and crown of a particular living experience. This is technically called the controlling image; and once discovered, it allows the reader to read, not read *into* a book his own preconceptions and preoccupations. It also guides the judgment as it analyzes the rendition. When an action eschews the partial or topical, it is always symbolic, that is archetypal, whether the author knows it or not. To see a fiction either as so-called realism or symbolism is to commit the literal error, either as writing or reading. Realism distorts or diminishes the full action by plotting beforehand a beginning, middle, and end.

How can this be done without inhibiting the creative act? How can a writer know beforehand what his people will do, until he has put them into action and so let the kind of thing they do show them for what they are; and upon this ground proceed partly creatively and partly deliberately? I rather imagine that when such fiction is successful, the author allows his creative sense to abandon the rigid plotting or the parts of it which get in the way. On the other hand you find the symbol misused as sign. Sign as symbol will be inserted in place of the concretion, the motion of action. It will be made to stand for the action instead of the actors in conflict showing it. To let the bare boards of the Cross stand for the Crucifixion is one thing; the Cross as image releasing the action of the Passion in the mind and heart is the other, the fictive way.

The writer working out of some form of myth will accept the supernatural as operating within nature. He does not take the world as the end in itself. His form will be some form of myth. Myth: symbol: archetype—the structure: the image: the conflict of the ever recurring human experience. In the Garden of Eden section of *The Velvet Horn* ("The Water Witch") there are three parts that represent the three stages of Eden as symbol of the world drama. Adam alone, the hermaphrodite, is the entire creature isolated within himself, the stasis of innocence, the loss of which is the beginning of action. When the woman is taken out of his side (symbolic: not according to nature as we know it), the separation begins the perpetual conflict. Incest is the symbol for this next stage. The third is the continuing action of the drama, the effort to fuse the parts into a wholeness which is complete knowledge. The symbol for this is the serpent, the old intruder. But there is another symbol for wholeness, the *uroboros,* the serpent eating its tail, lying about the waters of chaos. This is one of the oldest symbols, and out of it comes the only perfect figure, the circle. You will find it all over the world. In our hemisphere it encircles the Mexican calendar stone. To shift the image, Adam within his form contains the *uroboros,* both the masculine and feminine parts. Once separated, the feminine in

Adam becomes Eve, the masculine the Serpent. All the goods and evils grow out of this separation, and one of the images of it is the caduceus, the two serpents entwining sickness and health. There are numerous forms of the separation, the dragon fight, where destructive nature takes its fire-breathing, scaly shape without the human creature; or the Medusa; or Moses' staff. This, I should think, is repeated endlessly in myth.

Of course reading has helped me tremendously, but I read not as a scholar but as an artist. The wonder of it is its accidental nature. I did not look to books for help. I happened to be reading certain authors at the time of writing—some even before I began, Frazer years ago, more recently Zimmer, Jung, particularly *Psychology and Alchemy,* and Neumann's *Origin and History of Consciousness.* This accidental reading comes close to mystery, but anyway the first real surge of conscious direction and awareness came out of it. The curious part is that, as I looked back over what already had been done, I found little to change. The action was doing its own work. Whether it would have continued or not I cannot say. Of course there was rearrangement but the intrusion from the depths, where the subject lay, had already painfully and haltingly been moving in its own direction, its own autonomous way. The conscious help from me was ambiguous. I thought I was helping another kind of story; then at a certain moment I took hold consciously. The invisible form showed only streaks of substance, but I was able to *feel* the subject shaping its form. And I had my controlling image well fixed in the top part of my head: incest, the act symbolic of wholeness, not the wholeness of innocence but the strain toward a return to this state of being. Was not the brotherhood of man most supremely defined by the love of brother and sister, at least in symbolic terms? If they represented the two parts of the whole of experience, the effort to become one again must contain every kind of love which the separation had scattered throughout the world as man struggled to escape his fallen condition. Through love and the act of will he could escape it, but only temporarily as far as the flesh was concerned. The irony of the central conflict lay just

here. It is most surely known in the act of love, when flesh and
spirit surcharge each other, in that brief annihilation of every
separate faculty, the annihilation being the act of fusion, the
disembodiment within the body, which was the suspension in
chaos before the fall. The moment in which this could be felt
had nothing to do with time, but with its opposite, the knowing
of eternity which under-stands, that is stands under or outside
time, the brief insight into the unmoving Mover.

I now saw my two working parts of the structure: the moving
present tense which is the world's illusion, and the eternal present
tense which knows nothing of past or future but always is. We
know it best in the images of dreams. But the myth and fairy
tale all operate through and represent this sense of the eternal.
Once upon a time; Long, long ago in a far kingdom—these beginnings by their tone and meaning speak of no time, no country.
They are outside time; they are always and forever about what
is constant in human experience. The seeming tone of the far
past is the announcement of the timeless held within the point
of a moment. To emphasize this, there is little or no natural
landscape, no recognizable cities, in myth or fairy tale. This is a
crucial distinguishing feature between myth and fiction which
deals with myth. They have the archetypes in common, but in
fiction the action must be put in a recognizable place and society.
The moment I say this, Kafka appears. Except for the intrusion
of his moral rage, he more nearly approaches the ideal form of
myth. But morality as we know it has little to do with myth.

As soon as I began to feel the right limits of the structure, I
could deal with its formalities. Within the various levels and
distinctions of the mind, especially where it oscillates between
conscious and unconscious, I could put the sense of eternity, the
images of the past which are not past but forever quivering with
immediacy. Opposed to this, by closing the mind and letting the
action take place as upon a stage, I could use the moving present
tense, the action in time. But this last was not to proceed in a
continuous movement of surface beginning, middle, and end.
Each of the five sections was to be nearly complete within itself,

the tensions of the action evoked by eternal knowledge acting against time's knowledge. The movement in time would allow the sections to be dramatically connected, each showing a whole but differently, involving, I hoped, the fullest possibilities of the central image: incest. Not until the end of the book would the shock of meaning connect all the parts and the action be complete. There would be no way to turn to the end of the book and find out what had happened. This puts a handicap upon reading, this juxtaposition and accumulation rather than the steady advance of a conflict, which is the way of naturalism and the oldest form of all, the simple art of narrative.

By now I also had a firm grasp upon the point of view, and I knew who the protagonist was. Everybody was the hero and heroine, but only Jack Cropleigh, the brother and uncle, could represent them, for Jack, the spiritual hermaphrodite, contained them all in his mind. He alone could suffer the entire myth. The point of view would therefore be that of the Roving Narrator, where the variety of the action might lie within the levels of his consciousness as it met the unconscious: time and eternity. Having set him apart with no life of his own, other than his entanglement with all life viewed by family and community, he was best suited to control as central intelligence, and his office as victim-savior could bring it all to a focus by his death. The irony I intended, or recognized when it happened, lay in how little his victimage could offer. He could save nobody, not even his beloved nephew, by proxy. He could only save his nephew from running away from life. All he could tell him was that no matter how far you run you are always there. As archetype of victim-savior, Jack, I'm afraid, denies the efficacy of the Mass. His death implies that for heroes, at any rate, the sacrifice must be forever repeated, actually as well as symbolically. This perhaps is theological heresy but mythical truth, and certainly fictional truth. The feeling and knowledge he suffers throughout pass progressively through the three phases of the Garden's drama, renewing through the nephew, the inheritor, the same perpetual cycle.

The nephew Lucius, the bastard child of incest, is in a sense then the youthful counterpart of Jack, or if you like of all his uncles and mother. I think this was the reason I was so long in finding the protagonist. I had begun with Lucius so the tale opens out of his eyes and mind. Jack takes over in the next section, and the view remains with him throughout for the reasons given, in spite of the fact that it roves again to Lucius and even to Pete Legrand, the old intruder. In the roving point of view it is only necessary, I feel, for one mind to dominate throughout the story, so that no matter where the view shifts, it might seem to belong to one central intelligence, that intelligence and sensibility alone equal to the fullest knowledge. The success of this depends upon how you write it, and especially upon the transitions from section to section. (The roving is no good written in chapters.) For example, although the view is with Lucius at the beginning, Jack so fills the pages, especially toward the end, that when he takes over in the next section the reader should feel no jar and without question follow, as he was now entering a fuller complexity of the complication. If he did not feel that what had gone before was actually in Jack's mind, he could feel that it might have been. This was tricky, I know, but if it could be made to go smoothly, then what follows could also seem an extension of the central intelligence, as every mind is equal to the total experience, the difference being that only one can know the fullest meaning in suffering for all. Anyway, this is how it worked out—how successfully, it is not the author's place to say.

I can only feel that it comes off. My pace of writing is generally very slow, with constant cleaning up and structural revisions. Too often I will spend a day on a paragraph; a page is a good day's work. But as I drew toward the end, the last thirty pages or so, the artifice completely usurped my mind. It possessed me. There is no other word for it, and I've never quite felt it before. I became merely an instrument. I wrote three or four pages a day, scarcely changing a word. It was as if I had divided myself into two persons, one watching and one doing. The physical presence seemed a shadow. I felt disgust for its demands, and appetite had lost its savor. My impulse was to remain at the typewriter and not get up until the book was done, but this would be too long for my strength. Food and sleep were necessary, and the tactical considerations of how much changed from day to day. I could not bear to be touched or noticed. My nerves had drawn into the tissue of the skin. I forced myself to eat as in a dream. I would go to bed at seven or eight o'clock and rise each morning earlier, until I was getting up at two. In a kind of half-awareness I knew that I had to watch this expense of energy, or I would give out before the end. I sensed that if I did, I would lose it, that once this possession of me by the actors was broken, it would never return. It was as if there were only so many words left, and each had its place, if I could hold out to receive them. The last day my breath was all in the front part of my mouth, and each word had weight. Then in the final hour or so they began to fade, the substance of meaning growing lighter. When it was all done, the final period made a final expulsion of breath. I leaned back in the chair. I felt that all that had gone before was right, or the illusion of the last acts being not fiction but life would not have seized me.

This is the way it was done, to the best of my recollection. There is such cunning in the way the creative part uses the conscious craft that it is hard to follow the twisted windings of the journey. It seems just that. You must act as if it is real, and yet know you are acting; but the acting is lost in the act. How it is sustained over so long a time, in this instance over nine years, is a mystery and a cause for shame, as is the setting down of what seems to be the procedure.

This fresh interest in myth derives, perhaps, from a weakening of the formal authority of the Church. Everywhere the Satanic acceptance of matter as the only value, the only fulfillment, has been shaken. We sense again that people cannot live, except in some belief outside themselves. The cycles of cultures seem to show that when belief hardens into formalism, leaving the center dry and hollow, it is a time, as Yeats says, of the trembling of the veil of the temple. But before some new faith breaks through, there is a withdrawal into the source. This I believe to be the archetypal conflicts of myth which precede the formalized rituals and dogmas of institutional religion. This is a statement only an artist can make. And he can make it only vaguely, as it affects his work, for the artist is a cannibal of Gargantuan appetite who does not exclude himself, if he is lucky.

10. *World Interpretation and Self-Interpretation: Some Basic Patterns*

ERNST TOPITSCH

THE ENORMOUSLY VARIED conceptions and postulates by which human beings have tried to understand their enviroment and themselves have not lent themselves either to classification in accordance with a single principle, or to a derivation from a single principle. Nevertheless, a group of thought models has emerged. And, although it can in no way claim exclusiveness, it has played an important part in the development of mythology as well as of philosophy. The examination of these models in this essay may be useful toward a better understanding of the methods by which we look for an interpretation of the world and of ourselves, as well as toward the elimination of numerous pseudo problems that still exist in traditional philosopy as remnants of prescientific thought patterns.

I

Man for the most part conceives of what is remote, unknown, or difficult to understand in terms of what is near, well known, and self-evident. As a rule, this is the significant factor in practical life as well as in anything that is emotionally effective.[1] That is to say, it is the most striking and impressive vital, social, and artistic processes and productions that most often serve as explanations by analogy for the universe as a system. Thus the world may appear as a social structure, a family, a clan, or a state ruled by a king and ordered in accordance with a law. Or it may be manifested as a work of art, a building, or a city; or as a divine musical instrument resounding in the harmony of the spheres. These and similar conceptions play an important part in mythology, and especially in the astral myths of the great cultures of antiquity, from Egypt to China. Furthermore, they may be found to be still prevalent today among primitive races. Here the phylogenetic and ontogenetic findings agree. For example, in his psychology of development, Jean Piaget has shown that the child also conceives of the world as existing in analogical relation to his wishes and actions, his social connections, and his handling of things in general.

Not only are certain conceptual images from the domain of social and productive action projected outward into the universe, but also the cosmos itself in this anthropomorphic interpretation may be retrojected into its original image, that of human action. The terrestrial state and terrestrial law must be assimilated to, or modeled upon, the cosmic state and law; the human ruler is the image, the son or deputy of the divine ruler of the world. Places of worship and cities are built according to the model of the supposed "world edifice" or "heavenly city," and music should be an echo of "the harmony of the spheres."

Such conceptions were developed in the major cultures of the ancient East to become a mythology of great power and influence; in the Hellenistic age they fused with Greek thought; and they had their repercussions in Europe far on into the New Era. The conception of the ecclesiastical edifice as an image of the "Heavenly Jerusalem" or even of the cosmos was still familiar to the architects of the Gothic period and the Renaissance, so that an unbroken tradition leads from the Solar Kingdom of Egypt to that of Louis XIV. Moreover, astrology (which for thousands of years, far from being mere superstition, was a conception of the world equal in rank to philosophy) was founded on the same process of projecting conditions of immediate earthly reality into the cosmos (as in the naming of the stars), and then of retro-jecting the "macrocosmos" so interpreted into the "microcosmos" of human existence.

Whether the original doctrines of Greek philosophy were influenced by Oriental myths of this kind is not certain; but it is definitely established that the pre-Socratics employed these same models in forming their conception of the world. Thus the world is taken to be a state, similar to the Greek *polis*, or a well-organized farm, or an edifice designed in conformity with definite aesthetic principles. The atomistic system of Demokritos may have originated in technological conceptions—above all, those concerning the behavior and divisibility of matter—as well as the simple truth exemplified in architecture, namely, that out of the same stones various buildings can be constructed, one after another.

The analogies borrowed from artistic creation were significant to both Plato and Aristotle, as many scientific investigators have realized. The Idea must not be regarded as a universal concept of neutral value, but as a paradigm, as a representative work project, which should imply a correspondence, just as a work of art corresponds to the artist's plan. The Aristotelian dual concepts of form and matter, of potency and act, are likewise borrowed from artistic production. Above all, the interpretation of causality (the doctrine of four causes) was based on the process followed in creative handcraft, by which the master produced (*efficit*) a work according to a form (*forma*) planned by him for a definite purpose (*finis*) out of a given material (*materia*). Aristotle used these models and concepts not only in the realm of organic nature but also in the theory of knowledge and, to a certain extent, in logic.

Thus the Aristotelian distinction between a passive, receptive intellect and an active, form-giving one (later called respectively *nous pathetikos* and *nous poietikos*) presupposes the technomorphic model of the formation of a material. Thomas Aquinas makes this distinction: by the ability to work on the part of the active intellect (*intellectus agens*) and by the imparting of a

form—represented by thought (*species intelligibilis*)—the work-
man (the human being, or the soul) creates the work (the idea)
out of a material (the passive intellect, or *intellectus possibilis*).
These conceptual models were still effective even in Kant's
writings. In recent times T. W. Adorno has indicated the importance of the work process to the foundations of Hegel's metaphysics of knowledge.[2]

Still more striking than in these rather special considerations
is the effectiveness of the analogies borrowed from production
and the social order in the outlining of extensive world conceptions. The Stoics in particular created a world picture of this kind
by fusing certain Platonic and Aristotelian traditions with corresponding forms in the Oriental mythology of antiquity. At least
in its fundamental characteristics, it remained a conclusive one
for Christianity: the universe is a single, powerful state, organized in accordance with a rational law, governed by a divine
ruler whose authority determines all events down to the minutest
detail and whose principle is that of true justice. In another
interpretation, it is a work of art, designed and constructed by a
superhuman master or foreman.

The tendency to interpret the cosmos and the individual alike
as a picture, so to speak, of the social or technological modes of
human behavior sometimes overlaps another tendency: the *antitype* of human limitations and transitoriness, it gives rise to the
idea of a perfect entity. This entity (the "Supreme Being" or
however it may be termed), superior to all limitations such as
the imperfections and frustrations typical of human existence, is
above every form of will and activity, and ultimately even above
man's thought. It cannot be defined by means of concepts or
comprehended through the medium of language; that would be
incompatible with its perfection. Furthermore, it is beyond any
kind of contaminating relation to the empirical world. The adherents of this doctrine, however, do not acknowledge that it
owes its conception to the antitype of this empirical world.

These hypotheses have engendered a number of problems. If
the structure of the universe, of universal nature, or of human

nature is subject to a "law of order" superior to all positive statutes, of what does this law consist? Furthermore, if a just Power dominates the cosmos without restriction, how can we account for injustice, and still more for the apparent irrationality of values in the world process? And if this Power represents the cause of all events and consequently of all human will and activity, how can the human being be responsible for his actions when in fact they are not his? Finally, if the divine entity transcends all human conception and is unrelated to the empirical world, how can one speak of it? What is its role in the exegesis of the world?

Traditional metaphysics has for many centuries been occupied with such problems of natural law, with theodicy, with freedom of will and the *analogia entis*, yet it has never solved them. The reason is obvious as soon as the presuppositions are revealed. The first three problems are based on the projection of models, drawn from the domain of human activity, into the cosmos, and on their reflection from there onto this domain. If we abandon this typically prescientific way of explaining the world, these problems also disappear—the problem of freedom of will disappears in at least one of its numerous versions. The impossibility of solving the problem of the *analogia entis* may, in principle, be ascribed to the fact that the concept of the "most perfect entity" is founded on conceptions of perfection that contradict one another; and to the further fact that the postulate of perfection, of a being beyond human knowledge, comes into conflict with the desire for knowledge.

The fact that these so-called eternal problems are pseudo problems when seen from this point of view can be gathered from their history and from the methods used in dealing with them. For more than two millennia, a variety of socio-ethical and political ideals and requirements, often in complete contradiction to one another, have been established under the title of "natural law," without any success in settling this "plurality of natural laws" or even any likelihood of settling them. This must be ascribed quite simply to the fact that any arbitrary ethico-political postulate may be set forth as an expression of "universal law" or of "human nature" and then may be deduced from the latter subsequently—a fact of which the pioneer advocates of the various doctrines of natural law were by no means conscious.

If, finally, the doctrine of natural law involves tautologies and vicious circles, then the problem of theodicy (or cosmodicy) arises as a result of the presupposed contradiction existing between the assumption of the omnipotence of a just world principle (or one directed toward values of any sort) on the one hand, and on the other, the multiplicity of actual evils in the ordinary course of life. This unresolvable contradiction could be concealed only by modifying or rejecting, as inconspicuously as possible, at least one of the incompatible hypotheses. Thus either the omnipotence of the divine principle became restricted, or, alternatively, the attempt was made to deny the existence of evil. Precarious methods were sometimes adopted by arguing thus: reality and values must in any case coincide, and if it is impossible to adapt reality to values, then values must be adapted to reality.

The fact that the ensuing conflict between theodicy and ethics never broke out in full force must be ascribed to the circumstance that the former was for the most part restricted to a contemplative reconciliation with, or adjustment to, the inevitability of evil, while in daily life the customary rules of moral conduct were complied with. Nevertheless, the divergence between practical ethics and a contemplative admiration of the cosmos (or of its ruler) has led to the most significant expression from the philosophical standpoint of the problem of the freedom of the will. On the one hand, the perfection and sublimity of the cosmocrator implied omnipotence and universal causality; on the other, the thesis that sin was also caused by the cosmocrator threatened the foundations of morality. Here also the contradiction was included in the premises, so that solution was impossible. It was necessary to be satisfied with the alternative of making considerable concessions in respect to one or another of the postulates by way of illogical compromises. The case of the *analogia entis* (likewise unresolvable as a result of the contradiction in the premises) was similarly dealt with.

II

Not only are thought patterns from the sphere of social production and reproduction in life projected into the cosmos, but they are also used in explaining the individual and are sometimes even introjected into the "soul"—if this expression of Freud's may be used in a somewhat different sense. Since a smaller number of facts that can be objectively tested exist in this domain as compared with the physical world, fantastic speculations are rendered possible. But it must be emphasized that belief in the soul has never represented a single consistent doctrine, but rather a reservoir containing extremely varied ideas, which could be systematized only with great difficulty by priest-thinkers and philosophers. Although originally conceptions of the soul were probably modeled only in part, if at all, on social events, even in prehistoric times such conceptions were strongly influenced by social conditions.

This is shown by the belief in the survival of the personality after death. In many cases, the kinship of the clan continues beyond the grave.[3] In so far as they are remembered, the deceased members, together with the living, constitute a unit with reciprocal rights and obligations. A deceased member of a family or clan is entitled to provisions and to deference on the part of the survivors. On the other hand, he can intervene in the fate of the living members, and above all, he can protect his clan in case of distress. The Greek cities had their protectors. In the German Middle Ages, when a settlement was exposed to peril from pagan invasion, the dead were said to have risen and averted the calamity. The conception of the life to come as a continuation of earthly social order has been kept alive in feudal and monarchical forms of society. The tombs of nobles and their rulers were provided with arms and servants, in order that even after death they might maintain a way of life consistent with their

rank. If the Athenian democracy restricted pomp at the burial
of nobles, the question was not merely one of "combating luxury," but rather of depriving the dead of the means of continuing
a privileged existence in the world to come.

With many peoples, moreover, survival after death represented
a privilege of the nobility: only they were endowed with an immortal soul, whereas ordinary people had nothing to which to
look forward. Even commoner was the differentiation of fate in
the life to come from the point of view of rank and dignity: the
souls of the nobles and the rulers ascended to heaven, but those
of ordinary human beings were permitted only to stagnate in
shadowy Hades. Among the Egyptians, survival after death was
exclusively a privilege of lords and rulers, that is, those who
could secure residence and maintenance throughout eternity by
means of costly tombs and their appurtenances; the poor were
merely buried in the sand without any offerings. In Egypt, the
intimate association between the political system and a belief
in the survival of the soul was additionally attested to by the
fact that as soon as dignitaries received their appointments, they
were honored by the king with the *Ka*, a special type of soul. In
course of time this group of the privileged was expanded to
include a wider range of social strata.

As the "realm of the dead" took shape in conformity with the
terrestrial state, the souls of common people were also allowed to
enter the other world, in order that servants and administrative
machinery should be at the disposition of rulers and officials even
after death. China, the other great bureaucracy of the ancient
world, also developed the idea of a "realm of the dead." The ruler
of Hades had his staff of subordinates and servants, like a great
terrestrial potentate, and officiated at a tribunal of justice by
apportioning rewards or punishments to the deceased souls. Thus
a government of "dead souls" developed as a pendant to that of
the living.

The idea of the "tribunal of the dead," one of the most important social elements of belief in the soul, had originally no meaning on the ethical plane. In Egypt, it was primarily the tribunal

with which the dead menaced the violators of graves, and which ruled on whether the dead had been buried according to ritual, and also whether the deceased had performed his duties as dignitary. Only in course of time did the tribunal of the dead acquire a more and more pronounced moral character. The moralization of the conceptions of the hereafter did not always imply humanization. On the contrary: the penalties imposed by the tribunal of the next world were often based on the cruel *jus talionis*, on the desire for revenge on the part of persecuted religious communities that derived satisfaction from the assurance that in the next world their present persecutors would suffer throughout eternity the agonies they had imposed on others.

The belief in the transmigration of souls was also given a new moral interpretation. This belief arose from ethically neutral conceptions, such as the hereditary nature of vital energy or the reincarnation of the dead in the newborn of their clan and—last but not least—the transmigration of the souls of the dead into animals and plants. Later on, this belief was invoked primarily to reconcile the apparent contradiction between the manifold injustices in earthly life on the one hand, and the idea of an equitable world order on the other. The disparity between merit and good fortune was explained as punishment for some offense committed in a previous existence, or else as the promise of compensation in a future reincarnation of the sufferer. Here, as elsewhere, the soul was an instrument of a function of society: the guilty subject, and the object of retaliation.

In other respects, also, social thought patterns have been of importance to the development of ideas concerning the soul. Like the cosmos, the individual and his soul were interpreted in terms of the social hierarchy. The Pythagorean physician, Alkmaion of Kroton, conceived of human nature as analogous to the state; health was guaranteed by the equality of rights (*isonomia*) of the forces manifest in the body, whereas illness was caused by the autocracy (*monarchia*) of any one of these forces. In the writings of Demokritos (Fragm. B 34), both the individual and the cosmos represent corresponding social hierarchies. Finally,

Plato outlined in detail the picture of the "soul state." For him (at least in the *Republic* and *Timaios*) the soul represented a hierarchial system consisting of the components of the soul, a system in which reason (*logistikon*) was supposed to rule over desire (*epithymia*), and the common people in the soul state, with the aid of a strong will (*thymoeides*), were similar to a police force (*doryphoroi*). If this order prevailed, then justice ruled. On the other hand, the revolt of the "lower spiritual forces" implied civil war (*stasis*) in the soul—or, more simply, evil.

This "social model of the soul" continued to be effective in the history of philosophy, from Aristotle to the Stoics and neo-Platonists, and it is still to be discerned in such an enlightened thinker as Freud. With him the superego appears, to control and tyrannize over the ego. The function of the latter is in many ways similar to that of an executive manager of a large firm: it compromises, harmonizes, organizes, adapts, and encourages adaptation in other physical domains. Furthermore, on the basis of examples derived from sociology, Freud shows that the extreme suppression of a minority of rebels effects the elimination not of the group itself but rather of its activities; this is more dangerous, since the activities are driven underground. As F. Hacker stated in a recent lecture, many fundamental concepts of psychoanalysis seem influenced by specifically Austrian social conditions:

Where else does a censorship exist or has ever existed in which— although it is incorruptible and strict—everything can be arranged in accordance with a definite purpose, or a police force which controls the frontiers between the conscious and the unconscious, but which relaxes during the night so far as to facilitate the smuggling of contraband goods—whereby dreams arise?

It is tempting, and indeed necessary, to analyze the explanatory power and function of such conceptions more exhaustively than has been done hitherto. As G. H. Mead has pointed out, the human self and our interpretation of self are socially influenced to a high degree. Ideological motives, however, also play a considerable part in these questions.

Many of these conceptions are not only introjected into the "soul" from the domain of social relations, but the idea of the "soul state" thus realized reacts upon society just as in the case of the "cosmic state." Even the above-mentioned view of Alkmaion suggests that only the republic of nobles with its *isonomia* constitutes the "sane" and therefore the appropriate form of state, whereas monarchy represents a pathological and consequently an erroneous form. Plato makes this quite clear. He first places his ideal of the state in the "soul," then claims that the human state must correspond to the "soul state." Moreover, that ideology according to which the social order prevailing on this side of the grave is continued in the hereafter may react upon the social structure. But here the existing conditions are not always clear. This idea that a "compensatory justice" (or one that atones) prevails in the other world—as compared with the belief that the privileges of the ruling classes persist beyond death—may be a revolutionary one; but on the other hand, it may serve in this world to prevent subjugated peoples from resorting to revolutionary measures. Max Weber has shown convincingly that the Indian doctrine of the transmigration of souls was closely connected with the caste system and tended to preserve it.

The impossibility of testing statements concerning destiny in the next world led to the same result as did the empty formulae of "natural law." Up to a certain point, everyone could adapt these conceptions to his own desires and ends. The rich and powerful awaited a continuation of their seignorial existence, the poor and oppressed hoped for compensation for their misery, while the priests were certain they would dominate the great of this world and, in the meantime, forced the latter to make abundant gifts by threatening them with the torments of hell. The manifold forms of desire for aggression, revenge, and retaliation that could not be satisfied in this life found an outlet in the various conceptions of the next world. It is thus understandable that descriptions of hell in literature are much more convincing than those of heavenly bliss.

But the concept of the soul may be interpreted by technomorphic analogies: for instance, Aristotle represents it as *forma corporis*. Living beings, then, represent the products that result from a process of artistic handcraft, by which they are produced from a given material by virtue of a principle of form effective from within (the soul), and are dedicated to their own specific type of perfection. Thus we have here, above all, the question of a technomorphic explanation of certain definite uniformities in organic nature, such as morphogenesis and the continuity of species. Moral attitudes are, in the first place, as foreign to this "biological" theory as to the doctrine of the atomists, according to which the soul, based on the mechanical model, consists of material particles, possibly of extraordinarily fine and mobile atoms of fire. Even when no "soul substance" is assumed, the psychical functions are often conceived of as analogous to the mechanics of medium-sized bodies. Conceptions of this kind were applied particularly in the so-called psychology of association, but they are still traceable in psychoanalysis, as, for instance, in Freud's theory of the drives, according to which the spiritual processes occasionally seem to take place in a manner similar to the mechanics of waterworks. Like the social, the technomorphic thought patterns have a certain value as heuristic principles, and also as a means of description and elucidation. On the other hand, they may be completely misleading.

No less important than these analogistic conceptions of the soul, determined in part by the fundamental forms in which human beings come to practical terms with their environment, is another form that seeks its own ways of overcoming the pressure imposed by the surrounding world: shamanism. It is not just by chance that this conception predominates in the Arctic, the region where human beings are most intensely affected and thwarted by environment.[4] But in more southerly cultures the type of the ecstatic magician is likewise to be found, and it is undecided whether and to what extent there is any general connection with shamanism. In any case, it is true that in all these cases certain definite experiences of a superiority to the surrounding world occur, usually in the ecstatic state engendered by appropriate drugs—hashish, mescaline, and the like—and also by means of rhythmic dances, a curtailment of respiration, and other such practices.[5] In states of this kind, the human being experiences the feeling of being independent of the limitations of space, time, and his own bodily existence. The resistance of the things he tries or fails to surmount is easily overcome. The harm caused by social conflicts, especially by feelings of guilt, suddenly disappears. Hopes and desires the realization of which would otherwise seem improbable attain fulfillment. In the last resort, the human being imbued with this euphoria feels himself superhuman, possessing divine power—even a god. Inasmuch as he believes these ecstatic experiences to be real, the possessed man becomes convinced that he is capable of extraordinary achievements (and his fellow men are likewise so convinced). The shaman possesses magic powers over his enviroment: he is able to heal the sick, to reveal secrets, and to avert misfortune and suffering; his soul, separating itself from his body, has access to the realm of the dead and to the kingdom of heaven, and can journey far and wide in any direction on this earth.

Here again a process of fading, dwindling, and spiritualizing has more recently been at work. The outward and visible effects of ecstasy were renounced wherever belief in magical forces diminished, or where the magic that aimed at external effects was unnecessary, or where an aversion to humiliating and disillusioning consequences existed, or, finally, where the pressure of environment was so overwhelming that to overcome it in the practical sense could no longer be expected. No longer was any attempt made to diminish the discord between individual desires and evaluations on the one hand, and the facts opposing the latter on the other, through the attempt to change facts by magic. Instead, the same end was sought by altering the individual spiritual state and emotional attitude to things. To quote Freud, the aims of these desires were transferred in such a way that they were no longer frustrated by reality.[6]

III

Thus the idea developed that the soul, or at least its essence, is independent of and superior to its environment (including the body). It can be redeemed from its "imprisonment in matter" by various rites, and in the case of the more philosophical types of these myths, it suffices for redemption that the human being become aware of the divinity of his "true ego." A doctrine of the "higher soul" or "mind" emerges, by which the latter is fundamentally different from our empirical self, so closely entangled with our environment. The characteristics of this "mind" are precisely defined by its superiority to the injuries that may threaten us from our own psychophysical organism, from nature, and from our fellow creatures. The "mind" is immortal, free from suffering, and devoid of guilt—in so far as it is detached from the contaminating contact with matter.

This conception of the soul or ego has played an important part in the doctrines of the mystic and gnostic philosophers of India and the Occident. In addition to these social and technomorphic models of the soul, however, we also find the interpretation of the soul as an animating force, and finally the beginnings of a scientifically descriptive psychology. In many cases these various conceptions of the soul coexist in the doctrines of one and the same philosopher, who then makes use of whichever he needs in a particular context. Even some of the greatest philosophers were not always aware of the ensuing contradictions. Here, only a few difficulties may be pointed out. Even social and technomorphic conceptions are often incompatible with one another. The soul as *forma corporis* is not the agent of conscious action, and for this reason it cannot be held accountable for conscious actions. Neither is it conceivable in the social role of the avenger or in that of the penitent. Indeed, this conception of the soul cannot render conceivable any form of continuity of the individual after death. The mechanical model of the soul, in the narrower sense, is always indifferent to morality and repudiates survival after death. After the death of the body, the atoms of the soul are redispersed throughout the universe.

Still more intense is the discord between social and mystical conceptions. In mysticism the "true soul" is good; it is timeless, immaterial, and exempt from suffering. For this reason it cannot be imagined in the role of a representative of guilt and expiation. Its "freedom" consists in its state of redemption from the pressure of reality; its freedom is not that of the individual who decides between good and evil and is held accountable for such decisions. Inasmuch as this soul is timeless, it cannot be subjected to the sequence of guilt and expiation. Because it is above all suffering, no punishment in the form of pain can be inflicted upon it. Indeed, the objection to an immaterial soul, in the strictest meaning of the term, is sometimes based on the fact that because it has no corporeal form, it cannot be punished.

Quite other inferences were drawn from the belief that the "true ego" was above all guilt and misery, in so far as this doctrine, which originated in the domain of contemplative uplift, was applied to that of practical activity. As a result of the belief that this "higher soul" could not in any way be sullied or defiled, the human being might commit any outrage whatsoever without either injuring his "true self" or running the risk of being punished in the next world. Moreover, because that self was unaffected even by torture and death, the human being might torment and kill his fellow men without pangs of conscience— inasmuch as he did not cause them any real harm. Thus in certain cases these mystic doctrines were used to abrogate morality, and Indian despots saw in them a welcome opportunity of justifying their acts of cruelty.[7]

These and kindred problems have exercised traditional philosophy—or theology, which is in essence the same thing—for millennia. Under the protection of powerful institutions and by virtue of the manifold possibilities of formulation accessible to those institutions, metaphysical theories concerning the soul have exercised considerable influence almost to the present day. Even Kant's theory of the ego represents, in the final resort, an attempt to achieve a compromise between mystic contemplative conception on the one hand, and the moral idea of the "true self" on the other. The "intelligible ego," which as the "thing in itself" is superior to the physical world, is defined in terms of the proposition that it is always striving for what is morally good. Thus a link between mysticism and morality is forged—a link that, however, does not prove to be a firm one, since the intelligible ego is incapable of deciding between good and evil, and consequently cannot be the object of merit or culpability.

It is only in our century that, as a result of the dwindling of belief in the soul and in immortality, interest in philosophical speculation in regard to the soul has diminished. This is perhaps the reason why it is possible only today to analyze the metaphysics of the cosmos and the soul in a scientific and truly objective manner.

REFERENCES

1. The ideas in this first section are more explicitly elaborated in my book, *Vom Ursprung und Ende der Metaphysik. Eine Studie zur Weltanschauungskritik* (Vienna, 1958).
2. T. W. Adorno, *Aspekte der Hegelschen Philosophie* (Frankfurt am Main, 1957), pp. 24 ff.
3. Many examples of these facts are to be found in the *Lehrbuch der Religiongeschichte* by Chantepie de la Saussaye (4th edn., Tübingen, 1925). H. Schreuer gives a well-documented account of the belief in legal relations beyond the grave in his "Das Recht der Toten. Eine germanistische Untersuchung," *Zeitschrift für vergleichende Rechtswissenschaft*, Vols. 33 and 34, 1916.
4. The influence of shamanism on the view of the world in higher cultures is shown by K. Meuli in "Scythica," *Hermes*, Vol. 70, 1935; by E. R. Dodds in *The Greeks and the Irrational* (Berkeley: University of California Press, 1951; Boston: Beacon Press, 1957), pp. 135 ff.; and by F. M. Cornford in *Principium Sapientiae* (Cambridge, England: Cambridge University Press, 1952), pp. 88 ff.
5. J. H. Leuba, *Die Psychologie der religiösen Mystik* (Munich, 1927).
6. Sigmund Freud, *Das Unbehagen in der Kultur* (Vienna, 1930), p. 29; E. Spranger, *Die Magie der Seele* (2nd edn., Tübingen, 1949), p. 120.
7. W. Ruben, *Die Philosophen der Upanishaden* (Bern, 1947), pp. 227 ff.

11. The Three Romes: The Migration of an Ideology and the Making of an Autocrat

ROBERT LEE WOLFF

I

IN RECENT YEARS the Western world has given increasing attention[1] to the ideas expressed in a passage taken from a letter written by an early sixteenth-century Russian churchman, Philotheus (or Filofey) of Pskov, to Tsar Vassily III (reigned 1505-1534). An approximate translation reads thus:

> The church of the Old Rome fell because of the Apollinarian heresy; the gates of the church of the Second Rome, Constantinople, have been hewn down by the axes of the infidel Turks; but the present church of the Third, New Rome, of thy sovereign Empire ... shines in the universe more resplendent than the sun. ... All the empires of the Orthodox Christian Faith have come together in thy single Empire. Thou are the sole Emperor of all the Christians in the whole universe. ... For two Romes have fallen, but the Third stands, and a Fourth shall never be.[2]

Arnold Toynbee uses this passage in his essay, "Russia's Byzantine Heritage," to illustrate and demonstrate the persistence in Russia of two features that he singles out as characteristic of the Byzantine empire: a conviction of complete rightness in controversy, and a messianic sense of manifest destiny.[3] Some have embraced and embroidered the thesis, and others have challenged and ridiculed it. Those who would like a single simple explanation of the difficulties between the West and the U.S.S.R. have perhaps seized on it too eagerly. Those who are skeptical as to the importance of ideology, who doubt the continuity of ideology over the watershed of the Russian Revolution, or who are concerned with defending *Russia* as such and with attributing to communism alone the problems that face us, have perhaps dismissed it too swiftly. Whether attacked or defended, however, the idea has caught on and penetrated, usually without much preliminary reflection, into the consciousness of many Americans. Thus, Wallace Stevens wrote in 1947:*

> Say this to Pravda, tell the damned rag
> That the peaches are slowly ripening,
> Say that the American moon comes up
> Cleansed clean of lousy Byzantium.

The following remarks are intended as a gloss on the passage from Philotheus of Pskov. What is its ideology? Whence derived? And what has been the relationship of that ideology to Russian political behavior? In trying to answer the last question, I have assumed that men often adopt an ideology in order to justify some course of action already undertaken or planned, and that thereafter the political practitioner may become the victim of his own ideology. If it has been generally accepted, or expanded, or popularized, it may seize hold of him and force him to act in a way no longer advisable for other reasons. For example, Mussolini's ideology of *Mare Nostrum*, of a revived Roman empire in the Mediterranean, served in the beginning as a nationalist spur to rebuild seaports, to create a merchant fleet and a navy; and it caused him to embark on the African and Albanian adventures—all projects he had long contemplated. But after the Fascists had spread through all available channels the idea that they were "Romans," they had to act as they themselves had

* Reprinted from "Memorandum" (*Opus Posthumous,* p. 89) by Wallace Stevens by permission of Alfred A. Knopf, Inc. Copyright, 1957, by Elsie Stevens and Holly Stevens.

insisted Romans must act: they had to move toward Mediterranean revisionism (Corsica, Nice, Tunisia, Savoy) and toward
Hitler, and away from the Western democracies and the preservation of the status quo, where their interests actually lay.
Political theory and political action are difficult to disentangle;
but surely, if practice initially gives birth to theory, then theory
in turn may eventually dictate practice.

We may immediately identify the passage from Philotheus as
another example of the mystic and somehow satisfying pronouncements about the third member of a series: the churches
of Rome, Constantinople, and Moscow. The churches of two of
these have fallen, but that of the third stands fast: there can be
no fourth. It was perhaps Joachim of Fiore (1145-1202), a
Calabrian monk, who was most responsible for popularizing this
way of thinking in triads. His third age of the universe, the age
of the third member of the Trinity, would find its revelation in
a third Testament, as the first two ages had been respectively
that of the Father and the Old Testament, and that of the Son
and the New. Recent students of the astonishing impact of
Joachite influence on the European mind have instanced, as late
reappearances of the same fantasy, the Comteian idea of history
as moving successively through theological, metaphysical, and
scientific phases; the Hegelian process of thesis, antithesis, and
synthesis; the Marxian dialectic of primitive communism, class
society, and final communism, in which the state will wither
away; and even Hitler's Third Reich, whose title was invented
by the nationalist Moeller van den Bruck as early as 1923, but
was taken over by the Nazis because they sensed that it retained
the age-old emotional impact of the third and final member of
a triad.[4] One need not for a moment argue that Philotheus of
Pskov had read Joachim of Fiore, but only that he did not have
to do so: the Joachite concept was in the air, and the church
of the Third Rome repeats the fantasy.

For the ideology of the first Rome, ruler of the world, center
of the universal power, destined to last until the end of time, we
need only turn to Virgil (*His ego nec metas rerum nec tempora*

pono / Imperium sine fine dedi. . . .—Aeneid I, 278-279); and to appreciate the extraordinary vigor of the tradition, we turn to one of the last of the pagan poets, Rutilius Namatianus, who echoes Virgil even in the fifth century A.D., when the entire structure of Roman society was in fact crumbling before the barbarians. In Virgil's day the transformation that turned the elected Roman chief magistrate into a deified monarch on the Hellenistic pattern had taken place. By the fifth century, the disappearance of the emperor from Rome left a vacuum the Popes would eventually fill by expressing the old ideas of primacy and eternity on their own behalf.

Meanwhile, Constantine's transfer of the seat of empire to Byzantium and his own conversion to Christianity naturally led to a transfer and a modification of the ideology. Constantine intended Constantinople to be a second Rome. There he founded a new senate, transplanting many ancient aristocratic Roman families, placing *Urbs Roma, Populus Romanus*, and the she-wolf on his coinage along with Constantinople's goddess of fortune, even seeking to find in the new capital the ancient topographic features of the old—the seven hills, the fourteen regions. As early as 381 A.D., the Second Ecumenical Council, held at Constantinople, declared that the Bishop of Constantinople ranked second only to the Bishop of Rome, "because Constantinople is new Rome." This was reaffirmed in 451 at the Fourth Ecumenical Council at Chalcedon, which simultaneously extended the ecclesiastical jurisdiction of Constantinople, though this was specifically challenged by Pope Leo I, who strongly objected. Even St. Augustine agreed, however, that "God permitted Constantine to found another city like a daughter of Rome herself." Byzantine writers regularly called their city "New Rome." Though they were Greeks writing in Greek, they always referred to themselves as "Romans" (*Rhomaioi*), never as "Hellenes," which had come to mean "pagans." Constantinople had become the capital of a state that regarded itself as ecumenical, or universal, embracing the whole inhabited world. Again and again throughout the centuries the writers of Constantinople claimed that the city was stronger and more vigorous than the old Rome. The court poet writing the epithalamium for the wedding of Manuel I (1143-1180) to the princess of the Holy Roman Empire, Bertha of Sulzbach, says:

If Old Rome supplied the bride, you [i.e., Byzantium or New Rome] supplied the bridegroom, and since "the head of the woman is the man" [1 Cor. 11, 3] so are you too the head, and the Old Rome only a limb of yours.

And from the West the *versus Romae* lament: "Flourishing Constantinople is called New Rome; Old Rome, thou art falling, both walls and ways of life [*moribus et muris*]."[5]

After Constantine, the emperor is of course no longer God, but he is the earthly reflection of the single God in heaven, divinely ordained, and as time passes he is bound by a code of etiquette so complicated and rigid that every waking moment is governed by its particular protocol. Fountainhead of law and justice, master of his subjects, who are called by a term that literally means slaves, he needs to consult with no one, but resides in a sacred place, set apart. Equal to the Apostles, he presides over the councils of the Church and gives the force of law to the decisions of the ecclesiastics. Sometimes he even pronounces on matters of dogma *without consulting* the opinion of the bishops. When he does so, he may fairly be called Caesaro-papist, since he is literally acting both as Caesar and as Pope. But even when he takes council with the bishops, his Church remains a department of state. Seldom in the long course of Byzantine history is an emperor successfully challenged by a patriarch, and very seldom do we find the proposition that in the West becomes a commonplace of papal theory: that the wielder of the spiritual power, the patriarch, should be regarded as equal to the emperor, a claim that logically leads directly to an assertion of superiority. (The idea did appear in the ninth-century law book called the *Epanagoge*, in a passage probably written by the Patriarch Photius, but it had little impact on Byzantine thinking or action.[6])

It is true that in practice the emperor often fails to force through policies that might offend the religious susceptibilities of the people of Constantinople; it is true that when he disobeys the divine laws the people have the sanction of revolution; it is true that the throne eventually becomes the prize in a struggle between the landed aristocrats and the imperial bureaucracy; and true that in the period just before the successful overturn of the empire by the Crusaders in 1204, the power of the central government has weakened, local anarchy prevails, and hated Western influences are penetrating everywhere. But these developments take place in the harsh world of actuality; the Byzantine theory of the state does not alter, and its ecumenical claims are put forward with the same calm assurance during the two centuries after the Greeks have recaptured their capital in 1261 and while their empire is in fact little more than another Balkan state.

It is little wonder, perhaps, that in the period of Byzantine greatness the image of the Byzantine state should have exerted a compelling attraction on all the barbarian peoples; it is startling that the image lost little of its power even after the reality had faded, and that Bulgarians, Serbs, and Russians were held as spellbound by it in the fourteenth and fifteenth centuries as they and others had been five hundred years earlier.

Between the Second Rome and the First the sources of disagreement were many. In their desperate efforts to solve the theological controversies of the first Christian centuries—controversies in which expressions of views contrary to those put forward in Constantinople thinly veiled the national hatred of the restless Egyptians or Syrians for their Greek rulers—the Byzantine emperors often encountered grave opposition from the Popes, who did not understand (or, in some cases, want to understand) the imperial political problems in the East. So the schism over Zeno's efforts to appease the Monophysites in the last quarter of the fifth century was followed by the troubles over Justinian's attempt to legislate on dogma in the middle of the sixth century, and by renewed hostility over Heraclius' last efforts before the Arab conquests in the seventh century. And when the image-breakers put their candidates on the throne in the eighth century, and the Popes opposed their views, the emperors subtracted southern Italy and Illyricum, with their rich revenues, from papal jurisdiction, and gave the quarrel between the First Rome and the Second real political and economic content.

To these issues was added, in time, the growing discovery, easily exploited for purposes of propaganda, that different practices had grown up in the Eastern and Western churches. So in the ninth century for the first time it became a burning issue that the Latin church of the West had "added" to the creed the word *filioque*, "and from the Son," with reference to the procession of the Holy Ghost, who in the Greek church proceeds from the Father only. These issues, some major, some minor, multiplied until in 1054 one of the periodic controversies over them culminated in a break that proved permanent. Among the issues was that of the azymes: the West used unleavened bread for the communion wafer, the East leavened bread. The Greeks argued that the yeast in the leaven of their communion bread symbolized the human nature that the Word of God had assumed when taking flesh. To use unleavened bread was to deny the human nature of Christ. This was the heresy of Apollinaris of Laodicea, and the Roman church was guilty of it. And this is what Philotheus meant when he said that the church of the Old Rome "fell because of the Apollinarian heresy." Actually, of course, the church of Old Rome had not fallen, nor has it fallen yet; but it was convenient for Philotheus' argument to assert that it had.

II

At the end of the tenth century, the Prince of Kiev, Vladimir, accepted Christianity from Byzantium. The Kievan princes were members of a group of Scandinavian origin, ruling over a Slavic population. They shared with the Germans the tradition of the war-band, Tacitus' old *comitatus*, the *Gefolge*—in Russian, *druzhina.* The members of the war-band had the traditional right to be consulted on major questions, and they also enjoyed the celebrated right of departure to serve some other prince whenever they were sufficiently discontented. Nothing could be more unlike the pattern of Byzantine autocracy. Despite the important cultural influences that entered Russia with Christianity and imbued the new church with Byzantine traditions, Kiev did not borrow extensively from the Byzantine imperial ideology; indeed, its dynastic ties were largely Western. Only toward the very end of the Kievan state, in the last quarter of the twelfth century, do we find in literature the first traces of this borrowing: one of the Russian chronicle texts takes over a passage about the good prince from a rather pedestrian and conventional sixth-century Byzantine work by Agapetus on the proper character of a ruler.[7]

So it is not until a much later period, after the collapse of the Kievan state, under pressure from outside forces and as the result of internal fragmentation, and after the long years of Tatar domination, during which much of Russia was largely cut off from Western influences, that we find emerging in the princes of Moscow the dynasty to which both the political theory of the heritage of Rome and the political practice of the Byzantine autocrat would make their appeal. First as agents of the Tatar khan, the princes of Moscow profited by the connection to assess Tatar weaknesses; then they emerged as national champions against the Tatars: a grasping, able line of princes who established the principle of primogeniture, expanded their territorial holdings, and consolidated their power.

Watching this process, the Russian church singled out the princes of Moscow as its most promising allies. In 1326 the Metropolitan chose Moscow as his official residence, and advised the Prince that if he would build a church of the Virgin and bury him in that church, the city would become celebrated above all other Russian cities, and that its resident bishops would help him defeat his enemies. A few years later, in 1339, the scribe of a manuscript of the Gospels was already comparing the prince of Moscow to the Byzantine emperors Constantine, Justinian, and

Manuel Comnenus: the Russian church was beginning to seek in the only tradition it knew, that of Byzantium, for precedents to make great the prince whom it had decided to support and on whom its own future depended. More and more the complexion of the church itself was becoming Russian; after the Tatar invasions the Metropolitan was more and more frequently a native Russian; direct communication with Byzantium had ceased to be easy, for during the fourteenth century the Byzantines themselves were beset by the Turks.

In 1393 we find the Patriarch of Constantinople himself complaining to the Prince of Moscow that the Russians pay insufficient honor to the Byzantine Emperor:

Once more with grief I have heard that your highness has said certain things about the Emperor in derogation. . . . That is bad. The Emperor is not like local and provincial rulers and sovereigns. The Emperors convoked the ecumenical councils; by their own laws they sanctioned what the divine canons said about the correct dogmas and the ordering of the Christian life; they determined by their decrees the order of the episcopal sees and set up their boundaries. The church ordained the Emperor, anointed him, and consecrated him Emperor and Autocrat of all the Romans, that is, of all Christians. My most exalted and holy autocrat is by the grace of God the eternal and orthodox defender and avenger of the church. It is not possible for Christians to have a church and not to have an Emperor.[8]

This lesson in Byzantine political theory did not inspire the Russians to render fuller obedience to distant Constantinople, itself now nearly powerless. But the lesson was not lost: the ambitious Muscovite church and state were learning what it was to be absolute.

So long as the Byzantine Empire lasted, the Second Rome was in being, and Moscow could hardly claim to have superseded it. Two crucial events of the fifteenth century, however, made possible the development of the complete ideology. At the Council of Ferrara-Florence, in 1439, the representatives of the Byzantine Empire, now under intolerable pressure from the Turks, agreed to a new union with Rome, officially ending the schism. They did this, of course, with the utmost reluctance, in the hope of obtaining from the West sufficient help against the enemy. As in the case of the other official attempts at reunion with the Roman church, Byzantine public opinion repudiated it. Although the Russian representative at the council, the Greek Isidore of Kiev, accepted the union, he was repudiated too. In 1441 Tsar Vassily II ousted him, declaring that the old faith had been altered by the agreement with Rome, and that the dreadful teachings of the *filioque* and the unleavened bread must not be allowed to corrupt the faith.[9] The ouster of Isidore virtually put the Russian church and empire out of communion with Constantinople, which now stood charged with dealing with schismatics. Only a dozen years later, in 1453, came the vengeance of the Lord some Russians had been predicting: the Turks took Constantinople and put an end to the Byzantine Empire. The Second Rome had disappeared: the gates had been hewn down by the infidel Turks, the Byzantines had been punished for their agreement with Rome. It was also clear who must be their successors.

In Russia, as everywhere else in the Christian world, the fall of Constantinople made a deep impression. A certain Nestor, a Russian who had been converted to Islam and was actually present in the Turkish armies outside the city, reported that during the siege he had seen a great flame burst from the dome of Saint Sophia and rise up into the air: this was proof that the grace of God had abandoned Byzantium. Fables figuring the eventual victory of Christianity over Islam circulated widely, despite the temporary triumph of the Muslims; prophecies were rife, and one effort to interpret obscure passages in Ezekiel even led to a prediction that it was the Russians who were destined to rescue Constantinople in the end, after 365 years of bondage.[10] Though these ideas may not have had much practical effect at the time (there was no thought, for example, of a Russian attack on the formidable Ottoman Turks), the Russian church at least as early as 1461 echoed the old Byzantine political theory of the emperor in its description of Vassily II as

the man chosen by God, beloved by God, respected by God, enlightened by God, and sent by God, who governs you in the righteous
ways of laws appointed by God, that divinely wise student of the holy
law, only supporter of the true Orthodoxy, invested by God and
ruling in his greatness, Vassily, crowned by God in his orthodoxy,
Tsar of all Rus.[11]

Ivan III, son of this Vassily, in 1472 married Sophia (or Zoë)
Palaeologina, niece of the last Byzantine emperor—a marriage
curiously enough sponsored in the first instance by the Pope, who
hoped that Sophia, as the representative of the recently concluded union between the Greek and Latin churches, would
bring Russia over to Rome. When Sophia set out for Russia, the
Pope gave her a splendid retinue headed by a papal legate, who
wore a scarlet robe, had a crucifix carried before him in the
Roman manner, and did not venerate the icons. As the procession
approached Moscow, the news spread that a schismatic churchman was about to arrive. An assembly of Russian nobles was
held to debate whether to receive him; the deciding argument
was provided by the Metropolitan of Moscow:

Such honors [he said to Ivan III] may not be rendered to a legate of
the Pope. If he comes in one gate of your city of Moscow preceded
by his cross, I, your spiritual father, will leave by another.[12]

Messengers set out at once, and forced the legate to abandon his
cross, Sophia herself intervening against him. Here the homeless
daughter of the conquered Second Rome, sponsored by the
splendid Renaissance prince who was Pope of the First Rome,
symbolically repudiated him and accepted the Orthodox and
Byzantine principles of the nascent and still unavowed Third
Rome—then little more than a collection of log huts huddled
together in the boundless plain, lacking the characteristic towers
and domes with which she and her husband and the Italian
architects they imported would soon begin to embellish it.
    Among the Byzantine sources, one most suggestive phrasing of
the feeling of superiority of the Second Rome over the First is

to be found in a twelfth-century verse chronicler, Constantine Manasses, writing, like all ancient chroniclers, a complete history of the world since creation. When he comes to the sack of Rome by the Vandals in 455, some 700 years before his own day, he describes its horrors and then remarks:

This is what happened to Old Rome. Ours, however [i.e., Constantinople], flourishes, thrives, is strong and young. May it continue to grow eternally, O Lord of all, since it has so great an Emperor, whose light shines far abroad, victor in a thousand battles, Manuel, the golden glowing scarlet rose, with whose brilliance a thousand suns cannot compare.

Two centuries after it was written, the chronicle of Manasses was one of those Byzantine books translated into Slavonic in neighboring Bulgaria, at a time when Byzantium was weakening and Bulgaria was enjoying a revival. When the translator reached the passage about the sack of Rome, he yielded to the obvious temptation. The Vandal sack, he said, happened to Old Rome, but then he attributed to the Bulgarian capital, Tirnovo, and the Bulgarian Tsar, Asen Alexander, all the glory that Manasses had reserved for Constantinople and the Emperor Manuel:

This happened to Old Rome, but our new imperial city flourishes, thrives, is strong and young. It will remain so to the end of time because it is under the dominion of the high Tsar of the Bulgarians, the generous, the noble, the friend of the monk, the great Tsar, Asen Alexander, whose lordship cannot be outshone by numberless suns.

In one of the manuscripts there is even a portrait of Asen Alexander dressed in full Byzantine imperial regalia, receiving a crown from an angel. Before Bulgaria fell to the Turks in the late fourteenth century, the Manasses chronicle, as well as other literary monuments, had been transmitted direct to Russia in a new wave of that South Slavic cultural influence to which Muscovite culture and ideology owed so much. By 1512, we have it in a version in which the native Russian scribe has yielded to the temptation that beset his Bulgarian predecessor, and has ascribed

to Moscow and to Ivan III the role claimed for the Byzantines by
Manasses. The elements needed for the ideology expressed by
Philotheus of Pskov are now all present: the political theory of
the Third Rome is complete.[13] In fact, he may himself have
written the words of the Russian version.

In the years after Philotheus, of course, the doctrine received a
variety of elaborations and adornments, refinements and addi-
tions. Philotheus himself once represented the church as the
woman of *Revelations* 12: 1, "clothed with the sun and the moon
under her feet and upon her head a crown of twelve stars." She
had fled from Old Rome because of the heresy of the unleavened
bread, but had found no peace in New Rome because its church
had united with the Latins. "But then she fled to the Third Rome,
that is Moscow in new great Russia. Now she shines, the holy
apostolic church, more brightly than the sun in the whole world
and the great and pious Russian Tsar alone protects her."[14] In
one of the cycles of popular stories, there appear the insignia of
empire, originally belonging to Nebuchadnezzar of Babylon himself, and transferred in a carnelian (or sardonyx) box to Byzantium, and thence by Vladimir, ancestor of the tsars of Moscow,
to Kiev. Here the storyteller pushes the roots of Muscovite imperial legitimacy back into the Old Testament period, in accordance with the deep and widespread interest of the Russians in
the Old Testament. In the "Legend of the Princes of Vladimir,"
written down in the late fifteenth century, we find the Emperor
Augustus sending his entirely legendary brother Prus to the banks
of the Vistula to organize that part of the world; fourteen generations later the Russians invite Prus's direct descendant Rurik
to come and rule over them; and of course the Muscovite tsars
are directly descended from Rurik. Here, too, material regalia—
a piece of the True Cross and the Byzantine imperial crown—
enter the story, as presents sent to the tsar by the Byzantine
emperor, who begs to be left in peace.

The "Legend" identifies the tsar receiving the insignia as
Vladimir (972-1015), adding that after he received them he took
the name Monomakh, after the Byzantine Emperor Constantine

Monomachus. Of course, like the rest of the account, this is pure fable: Constantine IX Monomachus (1042-1055) reigned several decades later than Vladimir, who never took the name Monomakh; while the true Vladimir Monomakh (1113-1125) reigned a half-century later still, and got his name from his Byzantine mother. Uneasy because of their own defiance of chronology, the Russian storytellers invented the additional feature that the regalia were not to be used until such time as God should send a worthy ruler to the Russians. Later still, they shifted the name of the Byzantine imperial donor to Alexius I (1081-1118), a true contemporary of Monomakh. In the sixteenth century, the Muscovite tsars began to be invested on their coronation with a short cap and jacket of Byzantine manufacture, which were declared to be the actual objects sent so many centuries earlier by Constantine Monomachus, and held in reserve until now. They were in fact used down to the coronation of Nicholas II in 1894, and were regarded as the living "proof" of the truth of the legends. Here then, in false genealogies of a kind first popularized by the South Slavs, who also claimed Augustus or Constantine the Great as ancestors of their rulers, and in regalia and myths about regalia, the church disseminated the fictions that helped establish the Tsar. On the one hand, the Prus legend is solemnly cited as historic fact in a treaty with the Poles; on the other, popular ballads proclaim about the tsar (in this case, Ivan the Terrible, 1534-1584): "I brought the regalia from Tsargrad [Constantinople],/Put on the imperial purple,/ Took the mace of Empire in hand./I shall drive the traitors out of Moscow."[15] So the ideology penetrated into the popular consciousness at all levels of sophistication.

Nor did the church neglect itself. Simultaneously it went back to an old and spurious claim, originally invented by the Byzantines for the church of Constantinople, that the Apostle Andrew, the first-called, the elder brother of Peter, who had introduced Peter to Our Lord, had undertaken a mission to the Scythians. He had blessed the site where Kiev would rise, and had declared that this Russian land would in the far-distant future maintain the true faith. So the churchmen provided for their own institution a direct claim to apostolic foundation, and that by Peter's *elder* brother.[16] What more could one ask for the center of orthodoxy, the only possessor of the truth in all the world?

III

It remains to suggest some of the ways in which the new ideology affected Russian political behavior. After Ivan III and Sophia had been married in 1472, he used the title "tsar" (almost surely derived from "Caesar"), and adopted the Byzantine double-headed eagle as the symbol of the Russian monarchy. Though actually a fairly distant relative, Sophia called herself heiress to Byzantium, and signed an embroidery "Empress of Byzantium." Like the Byzantine emperors, Ivan was crowned with imperial splendor; he made his sons co-rulers during his lifetime; he began to use the title *samoderzhets*, the precise equivalent of the Byzantine *autokrator*, the man who rules by himself, the autocrat. The imperial couple built the Kremlin, the Muscovite version of the Byzantine sacred palace, the residence set apart, where the emperor lived. Ivan began to isolate himself and to make decisions without consulting his nobles. He began to deny them the right to depart and serve another master. He punished them for protesting against his autocratic behavior.

So under Ivan the older Kievan Scandinavian relationship between ruler and fellow warriors was replaced by the imperial pattern suitable to the supreme master of the Christian world. The nobles of course objected, and went on objecting. Indeed, one of the most frequently repeated themes in Russian political life, for three centuries after Ivan III, was the noble's claim that he had a right to be consulted. When one of the leading Russian boyars, Prince Kurbsky, fled in the 1560's, from Ivan IV (the Terrible), he claimed that he was exercising the ancient right of departure, and wrote polemical pamphlets demanding that the tsar consult his nobles as a matter of right. In his response, Ivan referred to all his subjects by the word that means slaves. He strengthened his ringing affirmation of absolutism on the Byzantine pattern by opening a reign of terror against the great nobles.

In 1606, when a certain Prince Shuysky, representative of the class of the great boyars, managed to become tsar briefly during the so-called "Time of Troubles," the oligarchy whom he represented extracted from him the promise to consult with them, and not to punish them arbitrarily. Even after Peter the Great (1689-1725) had to all appearances riveted the shackles of universal state service upon all the nobility, regardless of their origin, the boyars of ancient birth emerged again after his death. In 1730 they imposed on the new Empress Anne, as a condition for her mounting the throne, a set of "articles" that revealed how little their program had changed: she promised to consult them—that is to say, a small council of great nobles—before taking any fundamental decisions. For a few brief weeks, until Anne realized that the newer military-service gentry would support her against the boyars of ancient birth, she governed according to the "articles." Then she tore them up. When Catherine the Great called her legislative commission in 1766 and the representatives of the different classes had their opportunity to put forward their views on Russian life in general, Prince Shcherbatov—far from a reactionary, indeed later a great admirer of George Washington —advanced opinions and claims in no way different from those of Prince Kurbsky two centuries earlier. Despite the repeated blows dealt to the old boyars—by Ivan IV; by the Time of Troubles, in which they were discredited as the friends of Poland; by Peter the Great, who forced them to amalgamate as a class with the upstart service gentry; and by the foreign advisers of Peter's successors—the old Kievan tradition died extremely hard.

Despite boyar objections (and, of course, there was no parallel to this in Byzantium), the autocracy, new in the fifteenth century, was even then firmly established in Russia. We find Ivan III in 1489 writing to the Austrian emperor, whose subject, Poppel, had just discovered Russia, and who had injudiciously offered to give Ivan a royal crown:

By God's grace we have been lords in our land since the days of our earliest ancestors. God has elevated us to the same position which they held, and we beg him to grant us and our children our rulership in eternity as now. We have never wished for and do not wish for confirmation of this from any other source.[17]

When a German traveler, Herberstein, visited Moscow under Vassily III (1505-1534), Philotheus' Tsar, son of Ivan III, he commented:

In the power which he exercises over his subjects he easily outstrips the rulers of the whole world. He makes use of his authority in spiritual as well as temporal affairs; he freely and of his own will decides concerning the lives and property of everybody; of the councilors whom he has, none is of such authority that he dares to disagree or in any way to resist. They say publicly that the will of the prince is the will of God.[18]

Ivan the Terrible's arbitrary autocratic rule hardly needs comment. And despite the anguish of the autocracy and the nation during the Time of Troubles (1605-1613) and the appearance of a kind of national assembly, the *zemsky sobor,* which tided Russia over the dynastic break and elected a new dynasty in 1613, the autocracy as such remained unchallenged. By the end of the seventeenth century, the *zemsky sobor* had disappeared.

In their relations with the church, the tsars outdid the Byzantine emperors. In 1589, when the Metropolitan of Moscow was made patriarch, the Patriarch of Constantinople himself performed the consecration, and spoke in the very words of Philotheus of Pskov:

Since the old Rome fell because of the Apollinarian heresy, and the Second Rome, which is Constantinople, is possessed by the godless Turks [the masters of the speaker himself], thy great Russian Tsardom, pious Tsar . . . is the Third Rome . . . and thou alone under heaven art called the Christian Tsar in the whole world for all Christians; and therefore this very act of establishing the Patriarchate will be accomplished according to God's will. . . .

Even the exceptions prove the rule. Twice in the seventeenth century the tsar granted the patriarch the title of "Great Sovereign," together with major political responsibilities. But the episodes came about almost by accident. In the first case, the patriarch actually was the tsar's own father, and had almost been elected to the throne some fifteen years before his son. In the second case, Tsar Alexis Romanov (1645-1676) admired and trusted his Patriarch Nikon. But Nikon had read the wrong Byzantine book, the *Epanagoge*, with its introduction by Photius, which led him to claim temporal as well as spiritual supremacy over the tsar, actually quoting Photius' own words written eight centuries earlier.

This sounded the unmistakable danger signal. Not only was Nikon deposed—thus proving dramatically that the power remained in the hands of the tsar—but Tsar Alexis Romanov's own son, Peter the Great, eventually (1721) went so far as to abolish the patriarchate as an institution, declaring that he did so in order that no second Nikon might ever arise to make such claims again:

For the common people [says Peter's decree] do not understand the difference between the spiritual power and that of the autocrat; but, dazzled by the splendor and glory of the highest pastor, they think he is a second sovereign of like power with the autocrat or even more, and that the spiritual post is another and better sovereignty. If then there should be any difference of opinion between the Patriarch and the Tsar, it might easily happen that the people, perhaps misled by designing persons, should take the part of the Patriarch in the mistaken belief that they were fighting for God's cause.[19]

For the patriarch, he substituted the "clerical college" or the Holy Synod, a committee of bishops that soon came under the direction of a lay procurator. Here the principle of Caesaro-papism triumphed as it had never done at Byzantium.

I am well aware that some scholars minimize the importance of Byzantine influence in helping to shape Muscovite absolutism, and point instead to the Tatar khanate, for so long the overlord

of all northeast Russia, including Moscow, as supplying the
model for autocracy. Nor would I exclude the importance of the
Tatar precedents. Yet the weight of the evidence seems to me
overwhelming that the church's doctrine of the Third Rome and
its popularization of Byzantine political theory, stimulated by
the Byzantine marriage of Ivan III, gave the princes of Moscow
precisely the ideological assistance they needed in transforming
themselves into autocrats. Indeed, much of Moscow's success in
overcoming the Tatars depended precisely upon the fact that the
Muscovite princes could put themselves forward as the champions
of Christianity and of Russia. If it was indeed the Tatar khan on
whom they were modeling themselves, can one contest the fact
that Byzantine ideology enabled them to succeed? And if, as
seems to me more likely, it was rather the vanished supreme
master of the Christian *oikoumene*, the emperor of Rome or of
Byzantium, whom they were aping, was not his political theory
all the more essential to their success?

Finally, one may note the way in which the ideology of autocracy establishes its own tyranny: if a state rests on generally
accepted assumptions, it is almost impossible to challenge those
assumptions without damaging the structure of the state. As
Russian history passes before us, even those tsars of the greatest
good will and most liberal tendencies find themselves in a way
the prisoners of Muscovite ideology. Catherine II and her grand-
son Alexander I play at being liberals, but neither can be sure of
anything in the end except the tsars' divinely appointed mission.
Catherine's admiration for Montesquieu and Beccaria and Black-
stone vanishes like a puff of smoke in the first drafty current of
air from the French Revolution; she toughens and becomes reactionary, murmuring something reminiscent of Herberstein
about the huge size of her dominions and the unsuitability of any
except an autocratic government.

Alexander's tricolor cockade, sported on the day the Bastille
fell, was a young man's whim. As tsar, he and his Secret Committee of intimates, including the young Stroganov, an ex-member
in good standing of the Jacobin Club of Paris, found themselves
hesitant to do much except smoke cigars and drink brandy after

dinner; Speransky's careful plan for subordinating the tsar to the law died aborning; it was Madame de Krüdener and Metternich who eventually prevailed over Alexander, filling him full of satisfying mysticism, manifest destiny, and legitimacy; and it was the brutal Arakcheev who in the end administered the domains of this autocrat *malgré lui.* In the last two centuries after Peter the Great, only Alexander II, under the lash of circumstances, ever made a serious attempt to modify the social and political institutions associated with autocracy, and he was assassinated before he could consolidate his work.

Meanwhile the positive supporters of autocracy were never silent. In the Slavophiles it found a kind of advocacy that even won many liberals. Repudiating as alien the "materialistic" West and all its ways, as well as Peter the Great, who had wanted to "corrupt" the purity of Russian institutions, they proclaimed the unique virtues of Byzantine Christianity, longed for a paternal and responsible autocracy that had in fact never existed, and urged a revival of the *zemsky sobor* with which the ruler might consult, instead of the creation of a parliament that might serve as a check upon him. It is arresting to turn to the works of Pobedonostsev, tutor and intellectual preceptor of the last two tsars, setting down at the turn of the twentieth century an impassioned defense of the purest theory of divinely ordained absolutism. It is fantastic to discover the Empress Alexandra, wife of Nicholas II, writing (in the English that all Victoria's grandchildren preferred) to her beloved husband at the front during the First World War:

> ... thank God our Emperor is an *Autocrat* ... only you must show more power and decision.
> How they all need to feel an *iron will & hand*—it has been a reign of gentleness & now must be the one of power & firmness—you are the Lord & Master in Russia & God Almighty placed you there & they shall bow down before your wisdom & firmness, enough of kindness, wh. they were not worthy of & thought they could hoist you around their finger.... Lovy you must be firm....
> You are the head & protector of the Church.... Show your fist,

chastisen [sic], be the master and the lord, you are the *Autocrat* &
they dare not forget it.

   ... they are nothing and you are all, anointed by God. Be Peter the
Great, John the Terrible, Emperor Paul—crush them all under you....[20]

Silly though the Empress was ("now don't you laugh, noughty
[sic] one," she appends to the last injunction), these letters
(written in 1915 and 1916, while the Russian forces were dying
in their millions on the front, while the hapless and dedicated
Duma politicians and civil servants strove to combat the corruption and intrigue that centered round her friend Rasputin), none
the less reflect her deeply felt convictions—and she had enormous
personal influence. On the the very eve of the Revolution of 1917,
the Muscovite ideology still flourished.

   Even the masses of the Russian population, tried though they
so often were beyond bearing and to the point of revolt, in a
curious way subscribe to the ideology. So the earlier uprisings
(Bolotnikov's in 1605, Razin's in 1676, Pugachev's in 1773, to
mention only three) take on the same pattern: discontented serfs
combine with unruly Cossack frontiersmen; they burn the manor
houses and kill the landlords and officials. But the rebels never
proclaim that the tsar must go, or direct their forces against him.
Either they maintain that the tsar is on their side and would be
horrified if he only knew what crimes his officials and the landlords have been perpetrating, or their leaders announce that they
are in fact the tsar: false Dmitris, false Alexises, false Peter III's
on their way to join their loving Catherine, and the like. In 1825,
fifty years after Pugachev, who had gone the way of the others
despite his intellectual superiority and strategic ability, when the
Decembrists, in accordance with the liberal principles they had
learned in France, start a revolution from above, they find that
they must lie to the troops and revolt in the name of the "legitimate" Tsar Constantine in Warsaw, for whom they have no more
liking than for Nicholas I himself. When Muraviev-Apostol, of
the southern branch of the revolutionary society, reads aloud to
the peasants in a Ukrainian village a ringing denunciation of the

Tsar, and declares that Christ and Christ alone can be the proper ruler, the peasants inquire in bewilderment *what* tsar it is to whom they should take their oath. And fifty years later still, in the 1870's, when the idealistic Western-oriented reformers and revolutionaries "go to the people" and dedicate themselves to the welfare of the peasantry and try to educate them as to their grievances against the tsar, the peasants turn the Populists over to the tsar's police by the hundred.

Is it too much to say that the adoption, at the end of the Tatar period and the beginning of the tsardom, of a Byzantine imperial ideology in some measure helped determine the character of the rulers' own behavior, and shaped their own and their people's attitudes toward the nature of their society and the role of the autocrat within it?

REFERENCES

1. The best study of the subject remains Hildegard Schaeder, *Moskau das dritte Rom* (Hamburg, 1929), Osteuropäische Studien herausgegeben vom Osteuropäischen Seminar der Hambürgischen Universität, Heft 1. The following more recent works deal more or less directly with the central problem: N. S. Chaev, " 'Moskva—Tretii Rim' v politicheskie praktike Moskovskogo Pravitel'stva XVI veka," *Istoricheskie Zapiski* 17 (1945), 3-23; G. Olšr, S.J., "Gli ultimi Rurikidi e le basi ideologiche della sovranità dello stato russo," *Orientalia Christiana Periodica* 12 (1946), 322-373; E. Denisoff, "Aux origines de l'église russe autocéphale," *Revue des Etudes Slaves* 23 (1947), 66-68; H. Rahner, *Vom ersten bis zum dritten Rom* (Innsbruck, n.d. [1950]), his inaugural address as Rector of the University of Innsbruck; O. Ogloblin, *Moskovs'ka Teoriya III Rimu v XVI-XVII stol* (Munich, 1951); W. K. Medlin, *Moscow and East Rome, A Political Study of the Relations of Church and State in Muscovite Russia* (Geneva, 1952), Etudes d'Histoire Economique, Politique et Sociale, I; D. Strémooukhoff, "Moscow the Third Rome: Sources of the Doctrine," *Speculum* 28 (1953), 84-101; C. Toumanoff, "Moscow the Third Rome: Genesis and Significance of a Politico-Religious Idea," *The Catholic Historical Review* 40 (1955), 411-447. Chaev writes from the Soviet point of view; Olšr, Denisoff, Rahner, Strémooukhoff and Toumanoff from the Roman Catholic; and Ogloblin from the Ukrainian. I have not seen M. de Taube, "A propos de 'Moscou, troisième Rome,' " *Russie et Chrétienté* 3-4 (1948), 17-24.

2. V. Malinin, *Starets Eleazarova Monastyrya Filofei i ego Poslaniya* (Kiev, 1901), pp. 50 and 55 of the third, separately paginated, portion of the work, which gives the original Old Slavonic texts of two versions of the letter. I have substituted "infidel Turks" for the original "Agarenes" (descendants of Hagar), the usual term for Muslims at Byzantium. The quotation as given here, and as usually cited by scholars, requires a conflation of passages from the two variants of the text—a point they do not mention. I have not been able to consult the version published in *Pravoslavnyi Sobesednik* of Kazan for January, 1863. Philotheus' letters to Munekhin, official under Vassily III (see Malinin, pp. 266 ff.), still further elaborate the theme. See below.

3. First published in *Horizon,* August 1947; reprinted in *Civilization on Trial* (London, 1948), pp. 164-183. For a thoughtful challenge to Toynbee (not, however, convincing to me) see D.

Obolensky, "Russia's Byzantine Heritage," *Oxford Slavonic Papers* I (1950), 37-63.

4. See, most recently, Norman Cohn, *The Pursuit of the Millennium* (Fair Lawn, N. J.: Essential Books, Inc., 1957), pp. 99 ff. and 391-392.

5. Among the very numerous recent works on Constantine, see H. Dörries, *Das Selbstzeugnis Kaiser Konstantins* (Göttingen, 1954), Abhandlungen der Akademie der Wissenchaften in Göttingen, Philosophisch-historische Klasse, Folge 3, Nr. 34; and L. Voelkl, *Der Kaiser Konstantin* (Munich, 1957); also, J. M. C. Toynbee, "Roma and Constantinopolis in Late Antique Art," *Journal of Roman Studies* 37 (1947), 135-144. Regarding the rank of the city after Rome, see A. Grillmeier and H. Bacht, eds., *Das Konzil von Chalkedon* II (Würzburg, 1953), pp. 433-562, articles by T. O. Martin, E. Herman, and A. Michel, with many references to other literature. For St. Augustine, *De civitate dei*, V, 25; the Epithalamium for Manuel I in C. Neumann, *Griechische Geschichtsschreiber und Geschichtsquellen im zwölften Jahrhundert* (Leipzig, 1888), p. 55; the *Versus Romae* most conveniently in Monumenta Germaniae Historica, *Poetae Latinae* III (Berlin, 1896), pp. 555 ff.; for discussion, W. Hammer, "The New or Second Rome in the Middle Ages," *Speculum* 19 (1944), 50-62, especially p. 53, n. 6.

6. J. Scharf, "Photius und die Epanagoge," *Byzantinische Zeitschrift* 49 (1956), pp. 385-400, with bibliographical references.

7. Sevčenko, "A Neglected Byzantine Source of Muscovite Ideology," *Harvard Slavic Studies* II (1954), pp. 142-179.

8. Metropolitan Peter's advice to Ivan I in 1326 is cited from E. Golubinsky, *Istoriya Russkoi Tserkvi* (2nd edn., Moscow, 1901-1911), II, 1, p. 144; the eulogy of Ivan and the comparison with the Byzantine emperors is taken from a manuscript of Siisk by I. I. Sreznevsky, "Svedeniya i zametki o maloizvestnykh i neizvestnykh pamyatnikakh," *Zapiski Imperatorskoi Akademii Nauk* 34 (1879), *Prilozhenie*, pp. 145 ff., no. 86. For relations with Byzantium, see D. Obolensky, "Byzantium, Kiev and Moscow," *Dumbarton Oaks Papers* XI (1957), 21-78. The Patriarch's letter in the Greek text is in F. Miklošich and I. Müller, *Acta et Diplomata Graeca Medii Aevi* II (Vienna, 1862), p. 191.

9. See especially M. Cherniavsky, "The Reception of the Council of Florence in Moscow," *Church History* 24 (1955), 347-359; and the articles by I. Sevčenko and D. Geanakoplos in the same issue of the same journal.

10. N. K. Gudzy, *History of Early Russian Literature*, trans. Susan

198 ROBERT LEE WOLFF

Wilbur Jones (New York: The Macmillan Company, 1949), pp. 258-259.

11. A. Popov, *Istoriko-Literaturnyi Obzor Drevne-Russkykh Polemicheskikh Sochinenii protiv Latinyan* (Moscow, 1875), pp. 394-395; this book is inaccessible to me, and I cite from the review by A. Pavlov, *Otchet o Devyatnadtsatom Prisuzhdenii Nagrad Grafa Uvarova* (St. Petersburg, 1878), pp. 293-294.

12. P. Pierling, *La Russie et le Saint-Siège* (Paris, 1896), I, p. 171.

13. The three passages are confronted by Schaeder, *op. cit.*, p. 51, who quotes all three in the original. Strémooukhoff (*loc. cit.*, p. 86, n. 13) challenges this interpretation (but unconvincingly to me and to Toumanoff, *loc. cit., p.* 437, n. 67).

14. Malinin, *op. cit.*, pp. 62 ff. of texts at the end; commentary in Schaeder, p. 55, and Strémooukhoff, pp. 98-99.

15. Gudzy, *op. cit.*, pp. 261 ff.

16. See the splendid recent book by F. Dvornik, *The Idea of Apostolicity in Byzantium and the Legend of the Apostle Andrew* (Cambridge, Mass.: Harvard University Press, 1958), on the legend in general; on its origins in Russia, see A. Pogodin, "Povest o khozhdenii Apostola Andreya v Rusi," *Byzantino-slavica* 7 (1937-1938), 128-148.

17. I have not seen *Pamyatniki Diplomaticheskikh Snoshenii Drevni Rossii s Derzhavami Inostrannymi*, of which Part I is "Snoshenii Knyazei Ioanna Vasilievicha i Vasilya Ioannovicha s Imperatorimi Germanskimi, 1488-1517" (St. Petersburg, 1851), so I cite this passage from F. Adelung, *Kritischliterarische Ubersicht der Reisenden in Russland* (St. Petersburg-Leipzig, 1846), I, p. 153.

18. Sigismund, Baron Herberstein, Neyperg, and Guettenhaag, *Rerum Moscovitarum Commentarii* (Basel, 1551), p. 17. He goes on to speculate as to whether the physical mass of the Russian nation required tyranny, or whether tyranny had rendered them hulking and cruel: "Incertum est an tanta immanitas gentis tyrannum principem exigat; an tyrannide principis gens ipsa tam immanis tamque dura crudelisque reddatur" (p. 18).

19. The Patriarch of Constantinople, in *Sobranie Gossudarstvennykh Gramot i Dogovorov* II (Moscow, 1819), p. 97, col. 2. The most recent discussion of Nikon and the *Epanagoge* is in Medlin, *op. cit.* The text of Peter's "Reglament" is in *Polnoe Sobranie Zakonov Rossiiskoi Imperii*, I, 6 (St. Petersburg, 1830), no. 3718, p. 314; see also V. M. Gribovskii, *Pamyatniki Russkago Zakonodatel'stva XVIII Stoletiya* (St. Petersburg, 1907), pp. 176 ff.

20. *The Letters of the Tsaritsa to the Tsar* 1914-1916 (London: Duckworth & Co., 1923), pp. 145, 150, 156-157, 168, 455.

12. The Myth of Nazism

HENRY HATFIELD

I. THE HISTORICAL BACKGROUND

SINCE SO MANY myths were involved in what finally resulted in
the ideology of National Socialism, perhaps the reader may feel
that the word "myth" should appear in the plural in the title of
this essay. Yet, as I hope to show, the various elements which
contributed to the Nazi Weltanschauung were finally fused into
a fairly consistent "philosophy"; and it has seemed convenient to
treat the various motifs, beliefs, archetypes, etc., as the components or themes of one vast, hideously effective myth. I can
hardly deal here with two almost unanswerable questions: were
the Nazi leaders sincere in upholding some or all of their out-
rageous doctrines? More important: did these dogmas actually
determine events, or were they a mere ideological façade? Even
if they were only that, it would remain a matter of some importance to discover why one façade was chosen rather than another,
and why it impressed so many people, not all of them Germans,
by any means. Furthermore, the Nazi leaders varied greatly in
temperament: Hitler was an entirely different type from Goering;
the visionary Rosenberg had little in common, psychologically,
with that extraordinarily efficient hangman, Himmler. As I shall
argue below, quite possibly the notions of the hero stabbed in the
back and the *Götterdämmerung* meant as much to Hitler, subjectively at least, as the financial support of the Ruhr barons or
the intrigues of certain East Prussian landowners. Probably the

latter were decisive in bringing him to power; quite possibly the former—the psychological or mythic factor—ensured not only his defeat but the almost total destruction of Germany.

This "historical survey" is necessarily rapid, and in parts no doubt sketchy.* Though I am familiar with much that has been written about National Socialism[1]† by writers ranging from Konrad Heiden and Aurel Kolnai to Peter Viereck, F. L. Schuman, and Alan Bullock, it has seemed best to rely mainly on primary material. Of necessity, many figures, some of them of great importance, have been discussed briefly or not at all.[2] Fundamentally, I am in agreement with Viereck and Fritz Stern[3] that Nazism derived less from the authentic German tradition than from cranks, dilettantes, and "armed Bohemians,"—basically from men second-rate at best. While one cannot absolutely separate Wagner the great musician from Wagner the paranoiac who wrote *Jewishness in Music* (1850) and seemed to take sado-masochistic pleasure in contemplating and representing the annihilation of the world, it is the latter Wagner who will figure as one of the two or three arch-villains of this essay. Of course there are dangerous elements in Luther's thought, as in Herder's and still more in Fichte's. Someone even found seeds of Nazism in Friedrich Schlegel, of all people. Generally, however, an idea like Herder's concept of the *Volk*, for example, was exaggerated and indeed perverted by the time it trickled down to the level of Nazism. Furthermore, most of the leading Nazis did not read the

* I have not attempted to give the full story or to document all my assertions. Some of my ideas are frankly speculative. To give a reasonably thorough account would require yet another long book on Nazism.

† The most important literary treatment of the theme is that symbolic account of the rise and fall of Nazism, Mann's *Doctor Faustus*. Inevitably, Mann's view of Germany and German culture, while in a sense profoundly true, is one-sided. It was natural that Mann excluded the most civilized of the great Austrians—Mozart, Haydn, Hofmannsthal. Beyond that, German culture in *Doctor Faustus* has lost all real contact with figures like Lessing, Goethe, Kant, Bach, and Beethoven. When the great themes and the great figures are mentioned, they are either parodied or rejected. Today we may feel that this view is too black, but only a very foolish person could have stated categorically, in 1947, that Mann's pessimism was fundamentally mistaken.

classic German books during their formative years, if they read them at all. (The highly educated Goebbels, who took his doctorate at Heidelberg[!], was a striking exception.) In the index to *Mein Kampf,* Nietzsche is not mentioned, nor are Luther, Herder, or Fichte. Like many of his henchmen, Hitler drank from such impure fountains as the prose works of Wagner, the writings of H. S. Chamberlain and Dietrich Eckart,* and the example of Viennese anti-Semites like Karl Lueger and perhaps G. A. J. Lanz von Liebenfels.[4] Not all of the "intellectual" forerunners of Nazism, it will be observed, were Germans. Chamberlain, the renegade Briton and pluperfect Wagnerite, is probably the most morally despicable of the whole unsavory crew. He was less dangerous than Wagner because he lacked the genius of the "old magician" of Bayreuth: he could not use the seductions of music to endow his myth with an emotional charge. Thus it is possible, though by no means certain, that Mann was wrong in sensing in Nazism the logical, indeed the inevitable, end result of German history and culture. And even in *Doctor Faustus* we are left with a "hope beyond hopelessness, the transcendence of despair, not its betrayal."[5]

Much has been written about Luther's relation to Nazism. While there were certainly crude, authoritarian, and even "daemonic" elements in his nature, only one serious charge can be established, I believe, about his political impact on the German tradition.† He took too simplistically the Biblical injunction to "render unto Caesar the things that are Caesar's." His Erastianism —the dogma that the church must give in to the secular authorities in *every* secular matter—had disastrous consequences. It is at least one of the major sources of that "non-political" attitude which we find in Goethe, the mature Schiller, Schopenhauer, and

---

* An obscure dramatist who was a convinced Nazi.

† Similarly, his equally exaggerated emphasis on the commandment "Honor thy father and thy mother . . ." very probably did much to make the German family an authoritarian one. Beyond inducing sinister psychological effects in the individual, this may well have inclined Lutheran Germans to accept political authoritarianism; but I am not qualified to deal with this complex cluster of problems.

many others. Eventually the "non-political man"* comes to feel
that, since he considers himself intelligent and decent, politics
must be left to those who are not. Traces of this attitude persist
today, especially in German academic circles.

To leap into the eighteenth century: the impact of Herder on
German (and Slavic) nationalism has been an ironic one indeed.
Probably the most important of the German "pre-Romantics,"
Herder was indeed sympathetic with the aspirations of each
ethnic group to form its own nation and its own culture. Undoubtedly he idealized the Middle Ages and the *Volk* as well as
the folk song. Yet at the same time he was basically a man of the
Enlightenment, committed to the freedom of the individual. He
was also a sincere if non-dogmatic Christian—someone well
called him "an inspired Unitarian"—who loathed war and the
authoritarian state. As a man who criticized Frederick II of
Prussia repeatedly, his contribution to the rise of Hitlerism was
obviously involuntary. By the cruel dialectic of history, however,
his works did foster, indirectly, the rise of fiercely nationalistic
states. If the Slavs and Hungarians of the former Austro-
Hungarian Empire, for example, find their present status rather
less agreeable than their lot before 1918, they have Herder as well
as the equally well-meaning Woodrow Wilson to thank, to say
nothing of the fatal mistakes of the Austrian ruling class† and
the excessively radical nationalism of some of their own leaders.
Herder's error seems the more forgivable; unlike Wilson, he had
not had the chance to observe what nationalism had become by
1918.

Despite widely held beliefs to the contrary, the earlier German
Romanticists were by no means reactionary or anti-intellectual in
their speculations about political matters. Thus, while Novalis'

* Thomas Mann's *Reflections of a Non-Political Man* (1918) is an extreme statement of this attitude. This book, because of which Mann was
unfairly attacked during the Second World War, served a cathartic function; within a few years he had become one of the most "political" of the
important writers of his time.

† The basic responsibility, of course, lay within the faults of the Hapsburg
system itself.

Christendom or Europe (1799) glorifies the Middle Ages and has harsh things to say about "book learning" and even the invention of printing, this rather naïve tract is, in intention at least, forward-looking; Novalis manages to find dialectical reasons for defending the French Revolution. Most of the other members of the "first" Romantic group, indeed, were non-political with a vengeance. Only with the Heidelberg school-men like Arnim, Brentano, and Görres—does German Romanticism become reactionary, chauvinistic, and indeed pre-Nazi. The historical reasons are obvious: from the triumph of the French revolutionary forces at Valmy in 1792 to the final defeat of Napoleon at Waterloo, Austria and the various German states lived in perpetual fear of French aggression. When Napoleon crushed the "invincible" Prussian army at Jena, in 1806, many German intellectuals became quite suddenly interested in politics; patriotism was the order of the day.

Actually, one can make a rather strong case that the French invaders did more good than harm to their German neighbors: they liquidated numerous petty principalities, introduced the *Code Napoléon,* emancipated the Jews, and gave the *coup de grâce* to the long moribund Holy Roman Empire. (In fact, one of the great architects of modern German unity—and militarism—was Napoleon I; later, Napoleon III was to add his own involuntary contribution.) One can hardly expect men whose country is being overrun, however, to view such matters with dispassionate objectivity; still less, that they miraculously attain, by anticipation, the historical perspective of a later age.

For various reasons, Goethe remained calm. On the younger writers and philosophers, the effect of political events, especially of the humiliation of Prussia, was electric. Josef Görres changed from an extreme left-wing sympathizer with the Revolution to an equally extreme reactionary.* The myth of a medieval Germany, inhabited by a musical, virtuous, contented, and poetic if illiterate *Volk,* acquired real political mana. Arnim contrasted this ro-

---

* The parallel to certain American ex-Communists seems unavoidable.

mantic-conservative vision to a France damned to materialistic decay because, among other reasons, her peasants had forgotten their old songs.[6] Burkean conservatism became the vogue. Kleist appealed to a whole series of myths: the old Empire, the ideal of Prussian military virtue, the "heroic" figure of Arminius luring Augustus' legions to their doom in the Teutoburg forest. A few years after he had planned, in one of his frequent bouts of psychosis, to join Napoleon's invasion of England, Kleist seriously considered assassinating the Corsican and employed propaganda devices as radical as any devised by the Nazis; he even recommended the manufacture of atrocity stories and the murder of prisoners of war. The notion of northern superiority, an outgrowth of the mid-eighteenth-century "Nordic renaissance,"* also took on increased importance; Siegfried made his fateful entrance into nineteenth-century literature.

In the German states the dominant mood was one of romantic enthusiasm for national unity and in some cases a considerable degree of political liberalism. In conservative Austria, as one would expect, the appeal was a different one; restoration not freedom was the great goal. Those two most unmilitary characters, the brothers Schlegel, became psychological warriors for the Hapsburg cause, working with Gentz[7] and Metternich. The Austrian aim included not merely the defeat of Napoleon but the overthrow of all the achievements of the French Revolution. But the clock could not be turned back that far.

Broadly speaking, the German Romanticists display two related tendencies of much interest: the almost Faustian search for the original, the "Ur"; and the habit of thinking mythically, rather than in more or less precise, logical terms. In the search for origins, the Grimm brothers, Friedrich Schlegel, Görres, and Fichte are dominant figures. This enterprise combined a great deal of patient, scholarly work—one thinks of the fabulous industry of the Grimms—with reckless speculation, some of it

---

* Ironically, the main instigator of this movement, which was to lead to the highly dangerous cult of "the blond and the blue-eyed," was a French-speaking Swiss, Paul-Henri Mallet (1730-1807).

highly chauvinistic. The Romantic scholar searched for the *"Ur"* myth, folk tale, language, and nation. Even the Grimms, conscientious scholars though they were, were often moved by a prejudice in favor of all things Germanic.* The philosopher Fichte, like Görres a lapsed liberal, proclaimed that the Germans were the *Urvolk*, and German the *"Ur"* language.[8]

Less easy to pin down is the cult of "mythic" thinking for its own sake, as it were. The search for symbols, which were then interpreted with wild abandon, is a case in point. One thinks of the mythological interpretations invented by Schelling and Creuzer. (Goethe loathed this sort of thing and satirized it in the second part of *Faust*.)† Bachofen with his interest in mother-cults is a later heir of this mythologizing. And F. Schlegel opposed the Dionysiac to the Apollonian long before Nietzsche was born.

One can speak here of anti-intellectualism and *Irrationalismus* in the worst sense. The ruinous German tendency to think that what is "deep" cannot be clear, and *vice versa*, became fully apparent. In Hamann's writings as in some of Herder's, it had existed long before, but now it was a really widespread intellectual disease. One of its more unpleasant results was the decline of the quality of German prose. To compare the style of Winckelmann or Lessing with that of Hegel or Schelling is a painful but enlightening exercise.**

The role played by that belated Romantic, Friedrich Nietzsche, is most difficult to describe. He was one of the most self-contradictory of writers, and one can support almost any interpretation of his thought with quotations from his works. Certain of his concepts—the superman, the blond beast, the will to power, the glorification of war, the distinction between "master" and "herd"

* Germanistic studies, which did not become a recognized discipline until the Romantic period, have been influenced by this bias ever since; fortunately, many scholars have resisted it.

† When he wanted to, Goethe could always beat the Romantics at their own game; see the "mythic" thinking in *Faust*.

** There are great exceptions, like Heine and Schopenhauer, but these are few indeed.

morality—do seem to anticipate National Socialism; but one must
beware of taking too literally a writer who spoke in metaphors
and had "a touch of the poet." (Mann finally came to view
Nietzsche as primarily an aesthete, after having regarded him for
years, by an ingenious though tortured interpretation, as a Christian *malgré lui*, who died a vicarious death, "crucified on the
cross of thought.")* The "gentle" Nietzscheans, to use Crane
Brinton's phrase, emphasize rather his idea of the "good European," his opposition to Bismarck, Wagner, and anti-Semitism,
and his highly sophisticated psychology. It may well be that
Nietzsche's "Dionysian" affirmation of life, breaking sharply with
the cult of death fostered by Novalis, Schopenhauer, and Wagner,
is his greatest contribution. Yet when he states that "life" cannot
be judged by any other value, he opens the door to complete
relativism, and in fact to utter ruthlessness.

It is typical that such perceptive critics as Brinton and Walter
Kaufmann arrive at radically different conclusions. The only hope
of a valid reading lies in a careful chronological and topical approach, which attempts to regard each of his works in its proper
context and to give due weight to historical and pathological
factors. While the view that Nietzsche's works may be divided
into three parts is out of fashion, one can nevertheless distinguish
between the young author of *The Birth of Tragedy*, still much
under the spell of Schopenhauer and Wagner; the skeptical, rationalistic aphorist who wrote books like *Human, All Too Human;*
and the megalomaniac author of *Ecce Homo* and *The Will to
Power*. On one point Nietzsche appears reasonably consistent:
the rejection of Christian ethics in favor of a hard, aristocratic,
"Greek" morality. To judge by the texts, the late, half-mad
Nietzsche meant rather literally his praise of brutality, war, and
a sort of Prussian-socialist state. Especially as "edited" by his
highly unreliable sister and interpreted by that intelligent but
notorious Nazi Alfred Bäumler, Nietzsche's late work is a heady
and poisonous brew. It is not surprising that he appealed to

* Contrast "Nietzsche's Philosophy in the Light of Contemporary Events"
(1947) to the "Speech in Nietzsche's Honor" (1924).

Mussolini, Goebbels, and the more sophisticated propagandists of the SS. His impact on later writers, political and literary, was enormous, but almost everyone has his own image of the Nietzschean ideal. If he has been misinterpreted, the blame rests primarily on his own ambivalences, secondarily on the activities of Elisabeth Förster-Nietzsche, the wife of a notorious anti-Semite, who distorted his texts to make them conform the better to her own chauvinistic views. In any case, few German intellectuals, from Rilke and George to Spengler and Jünger, escaped his influence.

Count Gobineau (1816-1882) exerted a great influence on pre-Nazi and Nazi racist theories. His four-volume *Essai sur l'inegalité des races humaines* (1853-55) flattered the Germans by its stress on the alleged superiority of the Germanic and/or Aryan peoples; it appealed to Nietzsche, Wagner, and Chamberlain. He distinguished sharply between primitive Semites and the later, "degenerate" Jews of the modern world, and made a cult of "pure" blood. While he distrusted Bismarck's empire and Wagner's ideas,[9] his impact on German thought was not diminished by such mental reservations. Doubtless it was all the greater because he was a Frenchman, an aristocrat, and a creative writer of some standing, not merely another German crank. Duly grateful for this praise from an "enemy," Gobineau's translator Ludwig Schemann founded a "Gobineau Union" to propagate the racist faith.

Paul de Lagarde[10] (1827-1891) was a formidable scholar, particularly in the field of Semitics, a human being of considerable force, and—a pronounced anti-Semite as well as the declared enemy of all liberalism. "Liberalism," described by him as a deadening, leveling, egalitarian movement, he denounced in a famous essay as "the gray international." In fact, he tended to call anything he disliked—even the Prussian school system—"liberal," but he usually reserved the term for persons who had no feeling for the continuity of history, for national tradition, and the ideal of *Gemeinschaft*. Politically he was a belated romantic reactionary, looking back like Arnim and others to a medieval Empire which was really Holy though in no sense Roman. Projecting this idea into the future, he conceived the notion of a vastly expanded "Germania," ruled by a God-inspired Kaiser.* This wish-dream, along with the more practical proposals of the economist Friedrich List, was one of the main sources of the movement to establish a Middle Europe, of course under German domination. This ideal of *Mitteleuropa* was popularized by Friedrich Naumann and others, particularly during the First World War; Hitler, Rosenberg, and Himmler labored, in their own fashion, to realize it during the Second.

Lagarde was too much of an individualist, and in some ways too much of a Christian, to be ranked among the direct ancestors of Nazism. He was closer to Carlyle than to Wagner or Chamberlain. Like so many other disappointed Gentiles, he made a scapegoat of the Jews, but his anti-Semitism was not based on the notion of "blood." He once wrote a testimonial on behalf of certain Hungarian rabbis accused of ritual murder.[11] While his works were taken very seriously during the Thirties,[12] he might well himself have ended his days in a concentration camp had he been alive during the Nazi era. Such was actually the fate of not a few romantic conservatives and other nationalists† who strayed too far from the party line.

Julius Langbehn, who owed a great deal to Lagarde's political tracts, stressed the theme of individualism more insistently than the older writer had done. The superior minority was to rule; only thus could rebirth be achieved. Quite consistently, he was a hero-worshipper who owed something to Carlyle. As the title of his widely read *Rembrandt as Educator* (1890) indicates, it was the "northern" hero whom he held up as a model for his

* "Germania" was to be an aristocratic agrarian state which yet preserved a maximum of freedom for its inhabitants, and so strong that it need be no longer bullied by Russia and France! (*Deutsche Schriften:* Göttingen, 1892, p. 246.) This passage was written in 1878, at which time the Germany of Bismarck and Moltke was hardly defenseless. Lagarde's "persecution complex" is typical of the attitude of many German nationalists.

† Thus the conservative novelist Ernst Wiechert was sent to a concentration camp by Dr. Goebbels. Wiechert's account of this experience in *Der Totenwald* (1946) is probably his best book.

countrymen; he was very much the Anglophile. Like Nietzsche and Lagarde, he inveighed against specialization and sterile knowledge. He resembled them also in warning against "vulgar" anti-Semitism; but his linking of the Jews, professors, and the older generation[13] ominously anticipates the dogmas of the *Hitlerjugend.* Usually, Langbehn is not offensively fanatical, but when he exclaims: "Die Jugend gegen die Juden!"[14*] his alliteration has a strikingly demagogic ring.

Whatever the impact of figures like Langbehn and Lagarde may have been, it was presumably minor compared to that of Wagner. There are at least three reasons that the influence of the composer was so great: the intrinsic appeal of the Germanic legends he used; his musical genius; and his skill in gathering a clique—one can almost call it an organization—of patrons, ideological allies, and disciples around him. Not many composers have had private periodicals at their disposal; Wagner had the *Bayreuther Blätter,* in its way a distinguished journal. He had also a real gift for finding men of means, talent, or prestige to assist him. One thinks of Hans von Bülow, of the "mad king of Bavaria" Ludwig II, and of poor Herr Wesendonck, who played a generous King Mark to Wagner's Tristan. Among his allies and apostles, Gobineau and H. S. Chamberlain stand out, but there were numerous others. Not the least influential were the two prominent bluestockings of the movement: Cosima Liszt von Bülow Wagner and Elisabeth Förster-Nietzsche. The latter received official recognition from the Third Reich when she was already an overage Valkyrie. From Hitler's point of view, she had richly deserved her honors.

Like many other half-educated persons, Wagner had a predilection for sweeping assertions which sound "deep." Such men as he tend toward mythic thinking in the worst sense; the conscious mind is insufficiently trained to put up the proper amount of rational resistance to wild assertions and fancies. (Many of the Nazi ideologues, including Hitler himself and the lunatic fringe of various "irrational" groups, particularly among the Munich

* "Youth against the Jews!"

Bohemians and certain Expressionist cliques, and the wilder practitioners of depth analysis, to say nothing of nudists, vegetarians, and worshippers of Wotan, are cases in point.) Thus we find Wagner praising Gobineau for finding "the blood in the veins of contemporary mankind incurably spoiled"[15]—though this did not prevent the composer from proclaiming, in other moods, his hope of regeneration. Like Schopenhauer, he believed that animals were holy—more holy than human beings, one gathers. (Surely Nietzsche was right in finding the Christianity of *Parsifal* spurious.) The virulence of Wagner's anti-Semitism is frightening. Towards the end of *Jewishness in Music* he speculates on the possibility of "casting out by force the decomposing alien element,"[16] but adds with apparent regret that he does not know whether forces exist to perform this task. Rather grudgingly, he concedes in the next sentence that the assimilation of the Jews may be possible, but the intention of the whole passage is such that one must agree with the epigram that Wagner "forged the uncreated conscience of the Third Reich."[17]

It was doubtless the *Ring* which most affected that conscience. Whether we interpret it in Schopenhauer's terms or agree with Shaw that it reflects the decay of capitalism, we sense that here a dark, treacherous, violent world is moving toward its doom. However exaggerated Paul Henry Lang's wartime essay may be, he is right in stating that "the sun of Homer does not shine"[18] upon these gods, heroes, and dwarfs.

In fairness, it must at once be stated that the world of *Die Meistersinger* is far saner and brighter. Yet a generation which had experienced war, defeat, and social ruin could hardly find the solid Nuremberg burghers particularly relevant. The young, largely nourished on romantic notions and militaristic propaganda, naturally found the sturdy figure of Hans Sachs or even the glamorous Walther von Stolzing less charismatic than the heroic Siegfried, vulnerable only to treachery. As Elmer Davis once suggested, the implausible notion that Germany had been defeated in the First World War by a "stab in the back" must have drawn much of its credibility from the story of the betrayal of Siegfried. The birth of Nazism from the spirit of Bayreuth!

Clearly, it was no accident that Hitler was fascinated by Wagner. (The beliefs and attitudes of H. S. Chamberlain, Wagner's son-in-law and to some extent his intellectual heir, formed an added link.) I would seriously propose that certain of Hitler's gross blunders can best be explained in terms of the myth of the *Ring*. Why did he fail to seal off the Mediterranean by sending his troops through Spain; or to conclude a separate peace with Stalin, for example? Quite possibly because, on one level of his psyche, he believed that heroes must eventually end in a *Götterdämmerung*. There was to be sure the countervailing myth of Frederick II of Prussia, victorious in the Seven Years War against an overwhelmingly powerful coalition. But to the hyperromantic mind, total defeat is nobler than partial victory. One is driven to believe in the operation of a will to self-destruction, a "death-wish."

Of H. S. Chamberlain, much less need be said. His main work, *The Foundations of the Nineteenth Century* (1899), is on the whole less extreme and far better informed than Wagner's essays. Yet it fosters the attitudes typical of the pre-Nazi (and Nazi) tradition: preoccupation with race and with the national hero. His anti-Semitism is less virulent than Wagner's, but by linking "Jewish intellectualism" with Marxism, he was to provide Nazi propaganda with one of its most telling slogans. In celebrating the glories of the Germanic peoples, he went even farther than Gobineau. *Ex septentrione lux!*

There would be little point in analyzing separately the dogmas of minor predecessors of Nazism like A. Moeller van den Bruck and Hans Grimm, or in recounting the contents of works like Rosenberg's *The Myth of the Twentieth Century* or Goebbels' curious novel *Michael*. Two figures, however, demand separate if brief treatment: Oswald Spengler[19] and Stefan George. Neither was a Nazi; George indeed went into voluntary exile in 1933. Yet each contributed, more or less indirectly, to the triumph of Hitlerism.

In Spengler's *Decline of the West* (1918), as in his lesser works, there prevails a harsh insistence on the central importance of power, especially of military power. His rather crude historical determinism seemed to make superfluous all moral judgments on political matters. Similarly, his denigration of cultural creativity, as opposed to "practical" achievement, encouraged the attitude that the erstwhile "land of poets and thinkers" should concentrate its energies on building factories—and armies. Yet his somewhat brutal concept of "Prussian socialism" seems to be directed more at the aristocrats than the masses, at the future officer rather than the potential storm trooper.

Most of George's involuntary contribution to Hitlerism can more conveniently be discussed below. Two paradoxes, however, demand attention. It seems strange that a believer in the "leadership-principle," in a tough ethic inherited from Nietzsche, in the unique mission of the Germans to unite Greek and Nordic elements in an anti-Christian synthesis, should reject Nazism completely. It is also curious that the "George Circle" should influence a man like Goebbels, and yet include among its younger members some of the most dedicated figures of the German resistance. The answers to both are closely interrelated. Whether George was primarily the aesthete or the aristocrat, he was deeply averse to mass movements and "vulgarity" of any sort; National Socialism was too brutal and in a sense too democratic for his taste. (It is also probable that his highly autocratic nature made it impossible for him to accept a leader who was not the product of his own group.) While a few Nazis, like Goebbels, admired his Nietzschean stance, and possibly his poetry as such, they were, at the most, borrowers of certain of his attitudes. Having sworn fealty to another leader, they were never Georgeaner in the full sense.

Finally, one may well ask what elements in Hitler's personality and circumstances led him first to accept and then to embody the myth in its most extreme form. The answer lies primarily, I think, in the fact that he was an "outsider," in several senses. Though intuitive and in some ways highly intelligent, his mind had never been trained to discriminate between ideas. An autodidact, he was attracted by sweeping and cloudy abstractions. Both socially and nationally, he felt himself déclassé. He was one of those German-Austrians who bitterly resented the fact that he did not live in a purely German state. (It is significant that several of the leading Nazis were born outside the *Reich;* they tended to become more German than the Germans.) Hitler was thus psychologically predisposed to look down on the "inferior" races of Austria-Hungary, and was particularly vulnerable to Viennese anti-Semitism of the early 1900's. Finally, the German defeat in a war for which he had fought, apparently very bravely, as a volunteer, shook him profoundly. Unable to accept this reverse as an authentic fact, socially and sexually insecure, he threw himself into a fanatic effort to redress the situation. Any propaganda, any method was justified in his mind. Undoubtedly, he rationally accepted certain of the mythic dogmas and was indifferent to others. Given the set of his mind around 1919, however, the question of his sincerity has little objective importance.

II. THE COMPONENTS OF THE MYTH

Hitler took very seriously the racist beliefs of the "tradition," particularly its anti-Semitism. Quite probably he would have won the war by abandoning, or even modifying, his anti-Jewish policies. After all, some of Germany's best physicists were Jews;* and the loyalty of many Jews to the *Reich,* even after 1933, was heartbreaking, if at times irritating to non-Germans. In Paris, the refugees were known to some as "les *bei-uns,*" because of their habit of remarking that "with us in Germany" or even, in one authentic case, "with us in Dachau" things were managed more intelligently. It is bitterly ironic to consider that some of them might have made good Nazis had Hitler been less consistently the fanatic.† Nazi racism may be regarded as an involuntary parody of a certain type of fanatical Judaism. And, if one adds to the arrogance of so many Germans after the victories of

---

* The race to build the first atom bomb could hardly have been won by the United States without the help of refugees from central Europe.

† Goering, always more interested in *Realpolitik* than in ideology, protected a handful of Jews whose talents he thought particularly useful. One of them was a noted general of the German Air Force.

1870 a literal belief in being in every sense the chosen people, the result, in Gentile or Jew, is formidable.

The hysterical character of much Nazi and pre-Nazi anti-Semitism is revealing, going far beyond dislike, social snobbery, or religious bias. Possibly this paranoia was based not only on the fear of superior Jewish intelligence but on the belief that the Jews, with their allegedly superior sexual powers, would "defile" Gentile women. Such fears are not exclusively German; Lillian Smith attributes the fierce hatred felt towards the Negroes by many Southerners to a similar obsession.[20]

Clearly the obverse of anti-Semitism is the cult of the Germanic, especially the Nordic "race." This ranges from Thomas Mann's harmless weakness for the "blond and blue-eyed" to the wildest theories of Hitler and Rosenberg and the attempts of the SS to produce the maximum number of "Aryan" children, "natural" or even legitimate. Nietzsche's image of the blond beast was taken very literally, George established a link between Apollo and Baldur, and of course Siegfried was a blond. Racist theorists often ranked the Scandinavians and the English above the "Alpine" South-German types. Vienna, the most cosmopolitan and civilized of German-speaking cities, was anathema to Hitler.

The cult of the soil was allied to that of blood. The glorification of the peasant grew out of the rather harmless—and mainly very dull—vogue of regional literature. Ultimately it may be traced back at least as far as those two very dissimilar Swiss writers, Rousseau and Albrecht von Haller.

The nation-state, in true romantic fashion, was considered to be a living organism. Democracy was of course rejected; as Nietzsche had demanded, the elite should rule. In theory the *état machine* was almost equally abhorrent. In practice it flourished, just as it did, even more paradoxically, in Communist Russia. Partly the cult of the "organic" folk was based on an authentic desire for solidarity and for the end of the bitter class conflict of the last years of the Weimar Republic. The once well-publicized "anticapitalist yearnings" of many Germans represented in many cases a sincere conviction that a socialist state was desirable and indeed necessary. On this conviction Goebbels and other "left" Nazis, like Gottfried Feder, the author of the "Party Program," played skillfully. The genuinely socialist leaders of the party were intimidated by the "blood purge" of June, 1934. Many were killed, some fled, many retired into obscurity. From that time on, the SA, which formed the popular militia of the party, had very little real power.

Another source exploited by the Nazis was the "experience of the front" shared by millions of veterans of the First World War. The evil memories of those days were increasingly suppressed, first by the individual ego, then by political censorship. Many of the veterans of the first conflict were indeed rather admirable people. One recalls Mann's tribute in *The Magic Mountain* to the dedicated young officer Joachim Ziemssen: "the best of all of us." A respected friend told me in 1933 that the best, as well as the worst, of his university students were Nazis. But the "best" were either disillusioned or, more frequently, corrupted. The effect of the systematic, sentimental glorification of war was bound to be disastrous.

In appropriating the symbol of the "third kingdom,"[21] the Nazis degraded one of the most fascinating concepts of European thought. The idea that there is a third, still higher achievement open to man than any he has yet achieved, goes back to the Church Fathers, but it is primarily associated with the name of Abbot Joachim a Fiore (died c. 1201). Lessing's *The Education of Mankind* envisions a third (Spinozistic) religion, superior to Judaism and Christianity. In this final stage, man will do good for its own sake, with no thought of rewards or punishments. In Goethe, as later in Ibsen's *Emperor and Galilean* (1873) and in other writers, the concept denotes the attainment, or at least the attempt, of a reconciliation of Christian and Pagan values. The Nazis first narrowed the reference to German history: the Third Reich was to be the successor of the Holy Roman Empire and of Bismarck's creation. Then they proceeded to make the term roughly synonymous with Hell, in most of the non-fascist world.

Another aspect of the concept of the military-socialist state was the fundamentally Nietzschean notion that both workers and soldiers should outrank the bourgeoisie. Ernst Jünger, with his belief in the hardening and somehow ennobling effect of the "storm of steel" on the survivors of modern war, was the most effective spokesman for this particular form of militaristic propaganda.[22]

Such ideas of the state obviously imply a powerful ruler or "leader." The all-out Nazis endowed the *Führer* with the god-like qualities of omnipotence, omniscience, and infallibility. Nietzsche's superman and George's Maximin are obvious proto-types. (George declared that the youthful and mediocre poet Maximilian Kronberger, with whom he had been in love, was literally a God. In part George's motives may have been tactical, but that way madness lay.) A possibly more important source of the German weakness for "leaders" lies in the tradition, ex-tending back to the eighteenth century, of ascribing more or less divine attributes to cultural as well as political heroes. To name but a few: Klopstock, Goethe, Wagner, George, Klages, and Freud* were all the objects of intense reverence to many of their followers; the Nazis popularized the series Frederick "the Great," Bismarck, Hindenburg, Hitler—thus cleverly exploiting the Prus-sian myth for their own purposes. (In Wagnerian terms, Hinden-burg played the role of an aging Wotan to Hitler's Siegfried.)†
The United States has not been immune to the same tendency: in the religious field, we have had Fathers Coughlin and Divine in recent years; in the political, Generals MacArthur and Eisen-hower, not to mention Franklin Roosevelt.

Linked to government by dictator is an extreme "medievalism" which frankly upholds terror, blind faith, and absolute authori-

* It may well be significant that the idea of making the psychoanalyst an all-powerful "father-image" was conceived in a German-speaking country. In a successful Freudian analysis, the father-image maintains its potency only for a limited period. How fortunate that Freud was a Viennese rather than a "Prussian"!

† He was of course no blond hero, but the myth is no respecter of common sense.

tarianism. As a safety valve for the relief of the otherwise enslaved individual, the Nazis frankly encouraged sexual promiscuity.

During Hitler's years of power, the sense of national superiority was deliberately fostered, in part to offset that haunting sense of inferiority which goes back at least to the days of the Thirty Years War. To cite a rather amusing example: Goethe's Wilhelm Meister is sincerely flattered when he is taken for an Englishman! A special complex exists vis-à-vis the French: even the enlightened Lessing was not free of strong cultural resentment. There is of course some historical justification for this unhappy tradition: the German policies of Louis XIV, the two Napoleons, and Clemenceau are not completely above reproach. When Hitler made a leitmotif, in his early speeches, of the exclamation: "German people, you are *not* inferior!" his demagoguery was shrewd indeed. The self-pity expressed in the title of Hans Grimm's widely read novel *People Without Space* (1927) comes to mind. Presumably the propaganda for *Mitteleuropa*, Greater Germany, and colonies, served as a psychological compensation.

The countervailing belief in superior German efficiency, energy,* and military prowess is obviously intimately related to the sense of being late-comers and outsiders. As recent events have shown, this national pride is all too well founded, though it often degenerates into blind arrogance.

As the myth of Nazism gained increasing acceptance, Burckhardt's prophecy that "dreadful simplifiers" would take over the world became more relevant. "Intellectual" was a nasty word to Nazi ears. One thinks furthermore of the rejection of all "psychology"—especially of psycho-analysis—as nineteenth-century softness, of modern art and humanistic culture generally, and of humanitarianism. Here the Prussian cult of hardness made itself felt. Far more sinister than the student duels was the highly

---

* There is much justification for stressing the "Germanness" of Faust. Goethe's version held up eternally restless dynamism as an ideal. See also Spengler's "Faustian man."

successful "education for barbarism," practiced especially by the SS in its *Ordensburgen*. In the case of the assassination of Rathenau and of the later "Potempa murders," the most naked political terror was openly defended. While many Germans did not know, until 1945, the *details* of what went on in the concentration camps, almost everyone, at least in my experience, knew enough to be very much afraid of spending any time there. Watching parades of perfectly trained SS elite troops, one often recalled Goethe's description of the Duke of Alba's troops: "machines with a devil inside."

Finally, Nazism marked a climax of the revolt against Christianity which has been such an important part of German (and European) intellectual life since the mid-eighteenth century. This is a complicated affair, and some of its aspects are hardly relevant to this essay.* "Nordic" neo-paganism, leading from relatively innocuous beginnings through Wagner to Rosenberg, is obviously an important factor. It ended in the most unrestrained endorsement of hardness, brutality, and the extermination of other races. Perhaps most significant of all is the fact that anti-Semitism leads logically to the rejection of all Judaeo-Christian values. To paraphrase one of Lichtenberg's aphorisms: all of us Christians, after all, are only a sect of Jews.

* At least two other movements entered into the German (and European) revolt against Christianity: the Enlightenment, with its attempt to displace faith by reason; and the aesthetic neo-Paganism of Winckelmann and his intellectual heirs, which appealed to Greek rather than Christian norms.

REFERENCES

1. Some of the more interesting books on the subject are Bentley, Eric Russell, *A Century of Hero-Worship* (Boston, 1957); Bullock, Alan, *Hitler* (London, [1952]); Butler, Rohan, *The Roots of National Socialism, 1783-1933* (London, 1941); Heiden, Konrad, *A History of National Socialism* (New York, 1935) and *Hitler; a Biography* (London, 1936); Klemperer, K. W. v., *Germany's New Conservatism* (Princeton, 1957); Kolnai, Aurel, *The War against the West* (London, 1938); Neumann, Franz, *Behemoth* (Toronto, New York, and London, 1944); Petersen, Julius, *Die Sehnsucht nach dem dritten Reich in deutscher Sage und Dichtung* (Stuttgart, 1934); Rauschning, Hermann, *The Conservative Revolution* (New York, 1941), *Gespräche mit Hitler* (New York, [1940]), and *The Revolution of Nihilism* (New York, [1939]); Santayana, George, *Egotism in German Philosophy* (New York, 1916); Schuman, F. L., *The Nazi Dictatorship* (New York, 1935); Stern, Fritz R., "Cultural Despair and the Politics of Discontent: a Study in the Rise of the 'Germanic' Ideology" (diss. Columbia, 1953); and Viereck, Peter, *Metapolitics* (New York, 1941).

2. A long list of figures, some of them highly important in the pre-history of Nazism, and in themselves, has been dealt with briefly if at all. These include, in rough chronological order: F. K. von Moser, Justus Möser, Adam Müller, Arndt, Körner, and other heroes of the "Wars of Liberation," Hegel, Bachofen, Carlyle, Adolf Stoecker, Treitschke, Eugen Dühring, Georges Sorel, d'Annunzio and other pre-Fascist and Fascist "thinkers," Klages, Ernst Bertram and several other members of the "George Circle." Nor have I dealt with nationalistic tendencies among the German Naturalists at the end of the nineteenth century, or among the liberals and even the Social Democrats. "Sunt certe denique fines."

3. An excellent dissertation; should be published.

4. See Wilfried Daim, *Der Mann, der Hitler die Ideen gab* (Munich, 1958), a fascinating if one-sided book. Lanz was only one of many who "gave Hitler his ideas." I am indebted to Walter Grossmann and Reginald Phelps for this reference.

5. (New York: Alfred A. Knopf, 1948), p. 491.

6. In the preface to that famous collection of folk songs, *Des Knaben Wunderhorn*.

7. See Gottfried Mann's excellent though highly conservative book: *Secretary to Europe* (New Haven and London, 1946).
8. In his *Addresses to the German Nation* (1807-08).
9. See Oscar Levy, Introduction to Gobineau's *The Renaissance* (New York, 1913), pp. xxx f., xli.
10. The authoritative life of Lagarde was written by the same Schemann who translated Gobineau. Schemann, who was also close to Wagner and Chamberlain, played an important if relatively obscure role in the pre-Nazi intellectual underground. For a more negative evaluation, see H. Hatfield, "The Political Ideas of Paul de Lagarde," M.A. thesis, Columbia University, 1938.
11. See Lagarde, *Mittheilungen* (Göttingen, 1884-91), II, 323.
12. See especially Fritz Hippler, *Staat und Gesellschaft bei Mill, Marx, Lagarde* (Berlin, 1934) where Lagarde emerges as easily the first among the three theorists.
13. *Rembrandt als Erzieher* (Leipzig, 1890), pp. 350 f.
14. *Ibid.*, p. 351.
15. *Gesammelte Schriften* (Leipzig, 1898), X, 34.
16. *Das Judenthum in der Musik* (Leipzig, 1869), p. 57.
17. Harry Levin, *James Joyce* (Norfolk, Conn., 1941), p. 211.
18. "Background Music for *Mein Kampf*," SRL (Jan. 20, 1945), pp. 5-9.
19. See H. Stuart Hughes, *Oswald Spengler* (New York, 1952).
20. See *Killers of the Dream* (New York: Norton, 1949).
21. On this theme see especially J. Petersen's brochure (cited in note 1).
22. See Eugen Schmahl, *Der Aufstieg der nationalen Idee* (Stuttgart, 1933), pp. 142-44.

13. The World Impact of the West: The Mystique and the Sense of Participation in History

JOHN T. MARCUS

EVERY CULTURE has its values which direct the activities of its members and provide the community with a sense of purpose. In modern times, the impact of Western values upon other societies has been one of the dominant themes of the movement of history. It is the nature of this effect in the contexts of India and China which we shall presently consider.

I. THE MYSTIQUE AND THE WESTERN WORLD-SENSE

In Western civilization, the world-sense has generally been based on the consciousness of history. Thus Christianity has involved, since St. Augustine, the convictions of an historical destiny moving towards Judgment.[1] In this concept, Providence is immanent in history, and history is given meaning through God's Will.[2] Alternative formulations of Western ideals have generally shared the messianic sense of the Christian faith they were seeking to re-interpret or replace. Significantly, such ideals as the perfectibility of man through good-will or reason, the progress of humanity towards universal democracy, the manifest destiny of the nation or "race," or the vision of a Socialist society all have held in common the sense of time moving towards an historical goal. In short, the Western *Weltanschauung* has been characteristically both "historical" and "messianic."[3]

Such a perspective assumes the inter-penetration of history with an ultimate ideal vision, much as Bergson conceived of the inter-penetration of successive instants in the unbroken continuum of time. The messianic outlook therefore rests upon the belief in some historical myth-ideal. In other words, this form of historical consciousness is actually permeated, whether crudely or with infinite subtlety, by a myth-sense. But myth is a reality in its own right, a psychic reality as Carl Jung states, no less "real" than physical reality.[4] What characterizes the historical myth is not that it is necessarily false but that its "truth" cannot be established from historical evidence. As Cassirer writes: "The problem is not the material content of mythology but the intensity with which it is experienced, with which it is *believed*—as only something endowed with objective reality can be believed."[5]

This myth-sense is not only an historical reality, it is also an historical force. Georges Sorel in his reaction against the materialist emphasis of the orthodox Marxist school proclaimed historical myths to be the critical moral and psychological determinants of history as it moves towards a syndical-socialist goal. His historical sense was fired by "the respect for that fundamental mystery [of history] which only a superficial science presumes to ignore."[6] And Sorel's one-time friend, Charles Péguy, found in the mystique of the Revolution the true historical embodiment of a messianic Christian-socialist ideal. We have thus come to what we may call the "mystique-sense": the identification of an historical ideal with an historical event and, conversely, the transmutation of an historical event into an historical ideal.

A vivid illustration of the mystique can be found in the outlook of the Communist regarding the events that began in Petrograd in October, 1917. These events have become the myth of revolutionary tradition while his Marxist faith has been incarnated in the historical process by the October Revolution. It is this consciousness of History—the conviction that the ideal is not only immanent in history but has actually been materialized, at least in part, in particular myth-events[7]—that constitutes the essence of the mystique. At the same time, the mystique postulates a messianic "meaning" in history which the myth-event symbolizes. The myth-event is the "break-through" in society of the inherent values to which history itself is believed committed. The storming of the Bastille, for example, has played this dual role in the revolutionary mystique in France. As the characteristic of the mystique-sense, the ideal acquires "presence" in the historical process, and that process is endowed with a universal purpose.[8] One may conclude that a mystique is the result of the transformation of an event, specifically defined in time and place, into a transcendental value.[9]

The mystique-consciousness has certain consequences which have had a major effect on the Western world-sense. Thus in our society, it is the mystique which has performed the functions of giving the individual the sense of a meaningful relationship to his world, as well as a place and a role in the scheme of things. It has related him to his historical environment and to the continuous process of historical change. It has also provided him with a framework of values which integrates the apparently fortuitous incidents of history and the actions of individuals into the transcendental goal. For the group, the mystique has performed the task of providing the essential cohesive force in the community. This it has done by creating a sense of unity in purpose and of continuity in time.[10] At most, it has generated a common ideal and the vision of a shared goal; at least, it has furnished an essential substructure of historical assumptions about the nature of the world without which purposeful action in our society would become virtually impossible.[11]

It appears that a central function of the mystique has been to hold together and give coherence to the seemingly unrelated, meaningless or even contradictory manifestations of history. Thus with the denial of all historical universals which the pragmatist draws from the contradictions of specific evidence, the role of historical accident and discontinuities that the empiricist tends to stress, or the skepticism of the historical relativist: these

remain in the mystique nothing more than the transitory manifestations of incidentals that have no bearing on the universal,
immanent "truth" in history.[12] The mystique even bridges conflicting ideological positions in its basic psychology. For example,
the typical liberal of the mid-19th century was a staunch
individualist, fearing above all else the despotism of the state.
In mid-20th century, the liberal has been primarily conscious
of the group and of the responsibility of the community for social
welfare. Yet they both have shared a fundamental *Weltanschauung*, the ethos of the liberal mystique, namely the expectation of universal Progress.

From these considerations, it appears that the mystique has
provided the changing framework of values in Western society
and has acted as a primary ideological determinant of European
history. Even the significant material forces have acted in part
through the mystiques they generated. That is why the passing
of one mystique in our history has always been accompanied by
the birth of another[13]—or by chaos. As an illustration of the
latter, it is the disillusionment with history, and particularly with
the mystique of progress, which largely accounts for the crisis
of values of the 20th century. It may be concluded that the
mystique has provided the *élan vital* of Western history.

The force of the mystique has resided in the fact that it gives
history coherence.[14] In turn, this coherence implies that the
mystique offers a rationale of history and an over-all explanation
of change and stability in society. Generally, the explanation has
taken the form of a dialectic of opposites. The poles of such a
dualism may be reason and the irrational, dominant race and
inferior beings, the goodness of men or nature and original sin,
or exploiting class and wage-slave; this is important to the life
of the society, but it is only incidental to the basic mystique-
psychology of the *Weltanschauung*. What is significant here is
not the dualism itself; indeed, such a bi-polar vision is found in
numerous civilizations. What matters, rather, is the concept of
an inevitable historical movement leading through ever-changing
antitheses to a teleological goal. Hegel but stated explicitly a

perspective long ingrained in various strands of the Western tradition. It is the mystique-view of the immanence of the ideal in history and of the transcendental "meaning" of particular myth-events that is the cause of the teleological outlook. In fact, the primary significance of the mystique-sense is precisely this: that it is the source and vehicle of the messianic consciousness of history crucial to Western civilization.

II. THE WESTERN WORLD-SENSE AND
THE MYSTIQUE OF MOVEMENT AND ORDER

In Western history, there have appeared countless mystiques, many of them "private" or shared only by small "inner groups," and others characteristic of the culture as a whole, yet each causing and reflecting in part the ever-changing climate of opinion and the ideological determinants of history. At the same time, the mystique has been seen to provide also that continuity in time which has produced the Western sense of a meaning in history and of the messianic historical limit. It is the particular property of mystiques that they furnish in the West both the essence of distinctiveness in the identity-sense of individuals, and the conviction of historical unity and coherence. Indeed, the mystique acts simultaneously as the vehicle of individuality —the personal contribution to historical purpose—and as the coordinating force in society. In its role of furnishing an identity-sense, the mystique has assumed various forms of ethnocentrism peculiar to the historical perspective of the West, among which one may cite primarily the modern mystiques of national and racial identity.[15]

The two basic functions of distinguishing and integrating the Self in history are mutually in a permanent state of tension. This tension is one of the primary forces behind the "activism" characteristic of Western society, behind the sense of a direct personal involvement in the course of events. Parenthetically, this tension also lies at the heart of the contemporary dilemma to which existentialist philosophers, and theologians like Niebuhr,

Tillich and Bultmann, have sought a meaningful resolution.[16] In the mystique, however, the two basic functions are joined: if history as a whole has a "real" value, then conscious action by the particular in history can acquire "real" significance and can provide a "real" identity. Thus the two functions are merged in the mystique by virtue of the fact it combines within itself and transfigures both the differentiated particulars of the historical process and the ultimate one-ness of the trans-historical goal.

It appears that the mystique acts simultaneously as a crucial source of the "tension" of history and as a primary source of the psychological "release" of the individual. Consequently, the historical fulfillment of a mystique deprives the society both of what Toynbee identifies as the internal challenge, and of the release previously found by the individual in his "self-reference" to a transcending ideology. In mid-19th-century Italy, for example, the ideal of unification, partially expressed in Mazzinian romanticism, acted as a dominant mystique for politically conscious elements. The achievement of unification during the sixties "completed" the mystique and thereby destroyed it, or made it historically irrelevant. The consequence of this destruction was a crisis of values and the collapse of the ideological scaffolding of the political order. In the ensuing politico-ethical degeneration, the "new" Fascism, with its pseudo-historical aping of ancient Rome, was subsequently to proclaim itself as the saving force of "moral" integration for the nation and was to provide the individual with what Durkheim called "solidarity." Thus it fulfilled once more two of the central roles of the mystique.[17]

In its functions of giving relevance to the particular and of providing a sense of individuality, the mystique emphasizes the individual Self as the creative agent of historical destiny. Thus in the realm of the mystique, the Hero reigns. Prophet, martyr, charismatic leader of Incarnate Deity, one of these stands at the heart of every mystique.[18] National-Socialism, for instance, is inconceivable without Hitler, or Fascism without Mussolini. Yet more revealing than either of these two examples, the development of Socialism has shown that, as a mystique-force, it cannot be divorced from the role of Marx, or some of his messianic precursors such as Blanqui or Proudhon. It is, indeed, striking that even a doctrine like Marxism, which proclaims itself the science of an inevitable course of history, blind to the idiosyncrasies of individual personalities,[19] has nonetheless been obliged in its mystique-form to develop what has been called "the cult of personality."[20] Even French Socialists, who perhaps have gone further than most groups in striving to maintain a rationalist framework, built much of their program on a quasi-religious exegesis of Marx's messianic doctrines and upon the prophetic stature of Jaurès' mission.

Around the Hero there develops an elite of disciples.[21] They are marked by the consciousness of a "calling" and that personal identification of the prophet-type with the mystique-ideal. It is usually they who give the mystique its initial form. As long as the mystique survives, it must replenish constantly the inner circle of the elite. A central function of the elite is to develop and preserve, in ever-changing form, a particular rationale of history. This role is of crucial significance to the operation of the mystique; it causes the ideological responses to the specific issues that characterized the period of the original Hero to be perpetuated in the mystique long after the conditions out of which these responses grew have disappeared. Thus the mystique tends to "freeze" society in one or another particular dialectical conflict; it is inclined to act as a conservative force, not in the sense that it resists change in society but rather in the sense that it resists change within its own structure and rationale of history. This static quality has been fully evident in the mystiques of revolution which reject with particular violence heterodox interpretations of their mystique-ideal.[22] Hence while the mystique, like every element in history, is always undergoing change,[23] it does so reluctantly and often with violent convulsions.

Yet if the mystique is on the one hand a factor preserving the status quo—not necessarily the social equilibrium, but the psychological climate—it is on the other a primary force of historical movement. Certain mystiques act primarily as preservers of stability, others as promoters of change. The interplay between these general types has been decisive to the course of Western civilization and to that "tension" of history which has appeared as one of the central elements of the mystique-function. Indeed, in a civilization which has long regarded the course of events through the mystique-perspective of a dialectical dualism, the conflict between Movement and Stability has been a great and ever-recurrent *leitmotiv* of society. Consequently whether the ethos of a mystique falls primarily into the one or the other category is crucial to the nature of its specific action upon history.[24] The answer clearly depends upon the historical context, or upon the specific coordinates of time and place, in which the mystique appears. In fact, the categories of Conservation and Movement are not sharply defined, and virtually every mystique contains significant elements of both. The meaningful question then becomes: what specific aspects of a cultural "total" does a particular mystique seek to change, and what aspects is it directed to preserve? In the context of a given historical situation, what effect does this mystique exercise upon the central issue of its day?—that is the determinant point. But even the dominant tendency of a mystique seldom is crystallized or permanently fixed. Has the mystique of nationalism, for example, been primarily an expression of Movement or a manifestation of Conservatism? In Jacobin France, and in the France of Gambetta, it was obviously an instrument and an ideology of revolutionary change; in the France of the Dreyfus Case, of Drumont, Barrès and Maurras, it was strikingly the expression of preservation of a previous socio-political status quo.[25] In short, the attributes of Movement and Order can have only a relative historical meaning, referring to a particular social structure and specific cultural context.

Nevertheless, a mystique such as Liberalism has been seen to provide, within changing socio-economic patterns, a transcending sense of continuity that bridges the conflicting liberal beliefs of the 19th and 20th centuries. How can two such apparently contradictory characteristics of the mystique be reconciled? The

answer is that the essence of the mystique lies not in its content
—nationalism, or the liberal concepts of civil liberties and political rights—but in its perspective of the historical process. In
the psychology of conservatism the essential elements of the
mystique-ideal have already been incarnated and partially realized in history. In the psychology of movement, the essential
elements are seen as imperfectly incarnate and largely unrealized
in the historical reality. Thus the former tends to preserve a
psychological status quo, or equilibrium point of values; the
latter tends to change it. The Conservative mystique seeks to
"etherealize" into a transcending, permanent ideal the essential
historical qualities of its time; the mystique of Movement seeks
to "materialize" in the historical process a pattern of values that
it regards as still immanent rather than permanently manifest in
the actual events. It is these converse processes in the basic
Weltanschauung of the mystique that distinguish the inherent
attributes of Movement and Order. The basic perspective, in
turn, provides the unifying power of the mystique over the
changing historical content of particular and transitory socio-
political tenets. And it is by embodying these respective perspectives of Movement and of Stability that mystiques have acted
in Western civilization as a fundamental instrument of the tension
and the changes of history.

The ethos of the mystique was found to lie in its messianic
conception of history. Even mystiques of Stability reveal this
feature. In fact, it is the presence of this characteristic which
constitutes the conservative mystique-sense and distinguishes it
from mere conservatism. It has been noted that only as long as
a mystique is not "completed" and thus does not become wholly
past-directed can it continue to exist. In Burke, for example, one
finds the conviction that history has a meaning and a messianic
purpose, and that it is, indeed, the agent of Divine Will. Here
one finds also a view of the immanence of Providence in history
itself and the implicit sense of an eschatological goal. And finally
one can find, built on the moral and historical foundations of the
past, Burke's expectation of inevitable socio-cultural change.[26]

Other great heroes of conservative mystiques reveal the same sense of immanent purpose in history, of Providence or of historical meaning, and of a teleology which looks to the future. Bossuet, the Catholic conservative, shares with Condorcet, the rationalist liberal, and Comte, the Positivist "radical," the vision of a universal history moving to a definite climax.[27] Such is also the vision that characterized Bismarck's concept of his role in Germany and in Europe.[28] Churchill and de Gaulle, each in his own way, express still more decisively the combination of ideological conservatism and an eschatological "expectation" of history. Thus even the Conservative mystique, which holds that the "meaning" of history has been partly materialized, is intrinsically, if unconsciously, future-oriented because it is implicitly messianic.

III. THE MYSTIQUE-SENSE AND
THE NON-WESTERN WORLD

We have seen that the mystique acts as a motivating force for the individual, an integrating frame of values for the group, and an ideological determinant of history. We have noted, further, that the central attribute of the mystique is the conviction that history has a meaning and a direction predetermined by its teleological goal. And finally, we have observed that this eschatological perspective is embodied in the essence of the mystique: the transubstantiation of the ideal vision into the historical process, and the metamorphosis of the historical event into an ideological value.

From this, it is apparent that the mystique can be present only in a society that is conscious of the historical process. In other words, the mystique demands as pre-requisites an awareness of the significance of the particular historical instance and an assumption of the transcendent meaning of history itself.

It has been observed by philosophers and historians that a consciousness of history and a sense of meaning in history have been the particular attributes of Western civilization.[29] It is this society which developed an outlook merging the vision of the ideal with the evolution in time of an historical reality.[30] In most other societies, the sense of time and of the past evolved largely in the form of cyclical patterns, the principle of which was emulative repetition rather than linear evolution.[31] In China, for example, a strongly developed sense of the past involved primarily a chronicler's interest in particular changes within a frame of values presumed to be static and a moralist's concern with the threatened degeneration of the idealized ethical standards of a previous Golden Age.[32] Here "history" meant less inevitable change than emulation of the harmony of nature; its purpose was the attempt to preserve a permanent equilibrium point.[33]

This Confucian *Weltanschauung* may seem to be the epitome of the mystique of stability. In fact, it is not. Indeed, it largely lacks the sense of evolution—the cumulation of previous change within time—and that conviction of an ultimate meaning in history necessary to the mystique-sense. The Sinic world-view is largely devoid of the concept of a convergence of the ideal with the actual process of historical change, or of a teleogical goal and messianic function.[34] It stands in striking contrast to the mystique of order as we noted it in the particular historical consciousness of Burke, Bismark, Churchill, de Gaulle and other great conservatives in the Western tradition. In Confucian China, future generations of sons were important because they would serve the past by honoring their ancestors; in Burke's view, the cumulative experience of the past had purpose because it would serve by guiding the inevitable changes of the future.[35]

In the actual annals of China, to be sure, repeated violent changes in the "Mandate of Heaven" characterized a record of events scarcely less cataclysmic than that of Europe. Furthermore, modern scholarship is revising the old view of a Chinese culture almost static over a millennium of history. But the framework of these changes was generally believed to be, in the classical values of the mandarinate, the immutable Order of Nature and the unchanging pattern of ideal social relations. Such was the essence of the Sinic outlook.[36] The consequence was that a *Weltanschauung* based on a yearning for the preservation of the static equilibrium was alien to that sense of historical movement which characterizes the messianic essence of Western mystiques.

Against the tradition of Indian civilization, the emphasis on particular phenomena and on the distinctness of unique events and personalities in the Western consciousness of history appears still further removed from the classical way of experiencing life.[37] Here the very nature of historical consciousness has been rejected in the common assumption of fundamentally cyclical, or pulsating, rhythms of universal change,[38] themselves illusory, which leave no room for a linear and messianic view of historical evolution.[39] Consequently the mystique, consisting of that historical perspective, could not exist in a society that did not conceive of a directioned historical line. One may conclude that within the scope of the major contemporary cultures of Eurasia, the mystique has been the specific attribute of Western civilization which developed a conception of change based on historical time. Only in such a society could the mystique integrate the ideal, partly embodied in the events of the past, with a future-oriented perspective of change and the assumption of an historical destiny.

It is self-evident that one of the great movements in the history of civilizations has been the impact of the West during the 19th and 20th centuries upon the non-Western world.[40] Accompanying the effects of the technology and the new socio-economic determinants of the West's industrial system have been ideologies born in Europe such as nationalism, individualism, and socialism.[41] And accompanying these, in turn, have been the historical mystiques—specifically the mystiques of Movement—in which they are contained: faith in potential control over a utopian, material environment, the expectation of progress, and the sense of a messianic historical purpose leading to an ideologically inspired activism.

The consequence has been the virtually world-wide penetration, especially among the elites of non-Western civilizations, of the psychology of the Western "mystique-sense." This is perhaps the most significant aspect of the European impact upon other cultures. The primary manifestation of such a psychology has been the attitude that history has an implicit or revealed "meaning" and the expectation that the eschatology of this Ideal—whether Judgment or secular Utopia—is actually immanent in the historical process.[42]

To conclude, a critical element in the partial Westernization of the world has been the imposition of a linear time-perspective and an historical consciousness through the newly-acquired mystique-sense manifested in the idea of Progress that the West exported. This has reflected itself in the subtle but revolutionary change from a cyclical to a linear, or future-oriented, outlook. Thus one finds developing in many of the former colonial areas of Asia and Africa the attitude that the present is not a recurrence or re-evocation of the past, but rather that there exists an irreversible purposeful orientation of the past into the present and of the present into the future.

The importance of this new attitude towards history in the mystique-psychology of change now penetrating the non-Western world is seen in the creation of certain critical mystique-born values that have traditionally characterized the Western *Weltanschauung*. Among these one may note particularly: 1) the sense of activism, that is to say conscious participation in the evolution of history; 2) the conviction that individual action can affect the direction of historical movement; 3) the sense that the respective contributions to history give moral purpose to the life of the individual and to the existence of the group; and 4) the equating of the supra-historical Ideal with the limit of the actual historical process.

Such are the attitudes that typify the ideal of Sun Yat-sen's republic, Gandhi's campaign for Indian independence, Nehru's activism for a national democracy and Nasser's pan-Arab messianism. It is noteworthy that all of these names and movements have been enlisted into historical myth-situations; the Hero's life is seen in the context of an historical mission, the history of his movement and times as an exemplification of progress and fulfillment. Indeed, in each of these otherwise disparate instances, the heterogeneous composite of autonomous and Western-imported values, significantly different from the previous outlook, has come about through the creation of a mystique-sense. Thus the messianic *Weltanschauung* contained in the mystique-psychology of Western civilization constitutes the most profound legacy of historical consciousness and of the sense of historical destiny to non-Western civilizations. And this legacy is embodied in the nature of the mystique itself: that transcendental "etherealization" of historical events and "materialization" of the ideal which produces a vision of the eschatological convergence of ideal Being and historical Becoming.

REFERENCES

1. Mircea Eliade, *The Myth of the Eternal Return,* trans. by Willard R. Trask (New York: Pantheon Books, 1954). Ernst Cassirer, *The Philosophy of Symbolic Forms,* 3 vols., trans. by Ralph Manheim (New Haven: Yale University Press, 1953-1957), II, 120-22.

2. Denis de Rougemont, *Man's Western Quest: The Principles of Civilization,* trans. by Montgomery Belgion (New York: Harper & Brothers, 1957), pp. 88-91, 93-96. D. de Rougemont, "Le sens de nos vies, ou l'Europe," *Quaderni Aci* (Turin), VIII (1952), pp. 46-47.

3. Reinhold Niebuhr, *Faith and History: A Comparison of Christian and Modern Views of History* (New York: Charles Scribner's Sons, 1949), pp. 139-70.

4. Carl Jung, *Modern Man in Search of a Soul,* trans. by Cary F. Baynes (New York: Harcourt-Brace, 1933), pp. 186-87.

5. E. Cassirer, *The Philosophy of Symbolic Forms,* II, 5.

6. Georges Sorel, *Les illusions du progrès* (Paris: M. Rivière, 1908), p. 2.

7. Max Radin, "Tradition," *The Encyclopedia of the Social Sciences* (1942 ed.), IV, 64.

8. John T. Marcus, "The Mystique in History," *The Centennial Review of Arts and Science* (East Lansing, Mich.) IV (Spring, 1960), pp. 267-79.

9. For a contemporary Protestant comment, see Paul Tillich, *The Interpretation of History,* trans. by N. A. Rasetzki and Elsa Talmey (New York: Charles Scribner's Sons, 1936), pp. 274-75. See also R. Niebuhr, *Faith and History,* pp. 139-70.

10. Pitirim A. Sorokin, *Social and Cultural Dynamics,* 4 vols. (New York: American Book Co., 1937-1941), I, 19-21, 25; IV, 587-602 ff. P. A. Sorokin, *Society, Culture and Personality: Their Structure and Dynamics* (New York: Harper & Brothers, 1947), pp. 360-62, 555-62. Harold D. Lasswell and Abraham Kaplan, *Power and Society: A Framework for Political Inquiry* (New Haven: Yale University Press, 1950), p. 119. E. Cassirer, *The Philosophy of Symbolic Forms,* I, 285.

11. Carl Becker, *Everyman His Own Historian* (New York: F. S. Crofts, 1935), pp. 235-36. R. M. MacIver, *The Web of Government* (New York: The Macmillan Company, 1947), pp. 4-5.

12. Karl R. Popper, *The Poverty of Historicism* (London: Routledge & Kegan Paul, 1957), pp. 159-61.

13. Francis Delaisi, *Political Myths and Economic Realities* (London: N. Douglas, 1925), p. 64.

14. Max Weber, *Ancient Judaism*, trans. and ed. by Hans H. Gerth and Don Martindale (Glencoe, Ill.: The Free Press, 1952), pp. 326-27, 329, 361-62, 375-76, 397-98. P. A. Sorokin, *Social and Cultural Dynamics*, I, 29, 32-33 ff., 39-40 ff.; IV, 11-40 ff., 60-62. P. A. Sorokin, *Society, Culture and Personality*, pp. 147-51.

15. E. Cassirer, *The Myth of the State* (New Haven: Yale University Press, 1946), chs. XVI-XVIII, esp. pp. 277-87 ff., 297-98. Harold D. Lasswell, "World Politics and Personal Insecurity," pp. 29-51 in H. D. Lasswell, Charles Edward Merriam and T. V. Smith, *A Study of Power* (Glencoe, Ill.: The Free Press, 1950). Hans Kohn, *The Idea of Nationalism: A Study of Its Origins and Background* (New York: The Macmillan Co., 1944), pp. 3-7, 10-13, 16-17, 18-19, 21-24. Especially interesting in this regard are the contemporary studies of the psychological and sociological aspects of nationalism. See for example Louis L. Snyder, *The Meaning of Nationalism* (New Brunswick, N. J.: Rutgers University Press, 1954), esp. Ch. IV; and particularly Florjan Znaniecki, *Modern Nationalities: A Sociological Study* (Urbana, Ill.: University of Illinois Press, 1952). See also L. L. Snyder, *Race: A History of Modern Ethnic Theories* (New York: Longmans, Green, 1939).

16. Rudolf Bultmann, *Essays, Theological and Philosophical* (New York: The Macmillan Co., 1955), pp. 14-16, 18-20, 103-6, 117-18. R. Bultmann, "New Testament and Mythology," in Hans Werner Bartsch, ed., *Kerygma and Myth: A Theological Debate*, trans. by Reginald H. Fuller (London: S.P.C.K., 1953).

17. For an indication, sympathetic to the "new" mystique of Fascism, of this point, see Michael Oakeshott, *The Social and Political Doctrines of Contemporary Europe* (Cambridge, Engl.: The University Press, 1939), pp. 164-68, 169-75 ff., 177-78. See also René Albrecht-Carrié, *Italy from Napoleon to Mussolini* (New York: Columbia University Press, 1950), pp. 43-44, 46-47, 53-61, 64-65, 75-76, 81-87, 95, 120-21, 123-24, 127, 129-31. This point is not intended to minimize the economic, social and political factors which most historians of Italy, including Albrecht-Carrié, emphasize.

18. See Talcott Parsons' discussion of "charisma": M. Weber, *The Theory of Social and Economic Organization*, trans. and ed. by A. M. Henderson and Talcott Parsons (Glencoe, Ill.: The Free Press, 1947), pp. 64-66, and Weber's own discussion, *ibid.*, pp.

358-62; and M. Weber, *The Religion of China: Confucianism and Taoism,* trans. and ed. by H. H. Gerth (Glencoe, Ill.: The Free Press, 1952), esp. pp. 226 ff. See also F. Znaniecki, *Modern Nationalities,* pp. 83-86.

19. Karl Kautsky, *Die Materialistische Geschichtsauffassung,* 2 vols. (Berlin: J. H. W. Dietz nachf., 1927), II, 703; also cited in Sidney Hook, *Towards the Understanding of Karl Marx: A Revolutionary Interpretation* (New York: John Day, 1933), pp. 164-72. Georgii V. Plekhanov, *The Role of the Individual in History* (London: Lawrence and Wishart, 1950), pp. 38-49, 55-62.

20. T. V. Smith, "Power and Conscience; Beyond Conscience," pp. 292-94 ff., 328-30, in H. D. Lasswell *et al., A Study of Power.*

21. Arnold J. Toynbee, *A Study of History,* 10 vols. (London: Oxford University Press, 1934-1954), III, 117-377. M. Weber, *The Theory of Social and Economic Organization,* pp. 367-70. M. Weber, *The Religion of China,* pp. 129-64. P. A. Sorokin, *Social and Cultural Dynamics,* III, 140-49.

22. C. E. Merriam, *The Role of Politics in Social Change* (New York: New York University Press, 1936), p. 89. See also S. Hook, *Towards the Understanding of Karl Marx,* Part I.

23. R. M. MacIver, *The Web of Government,* p. 6.

24. For a more detailed historical investigation of this point, see J. T. Marcus, "The Mystique: Movement and Order," *The American Journal of Economics and Sociology* (New York), XIX (April, 1960), 231-39.

25. René Rémond, *La droite en France de 1815 à nos jours: Continuité et diversité d'une tradition politique* (Paris: Aubier, 1954), pp. 150-68, 169-73 ff., esp. 150-52. Carlton J. H. Hayes, *The Historical Evolution of Modern Nationalism* (New York: R. R. Smith, 1931), *passim.* C. J. H. Hayes, *France: A Nation of Patriots* (New York: Columbia University Press, 1930), pp. 10-14, 22-23. H. Kohn, *The Idea of Nationalism,* pp. 205-6, 218-19 ff., 237-52, 259. H. Kohn, *Revolutions and Dictatorships; Essays in Contemporary History* (Cambridge, Mass.: Harvard University Press, 1939), pp. 72-80.

26. Edmund Burke, "Reflections on the Revolution in France," in *Burke, Select Works,* 3 vols., ed. by E. J. Payne (Oxford: Clarendon Press, 1888-1892), II, 101-2, 107-9; III, 114-16 ff., 291-93. See especially Alfred Cobban, *Edmund Burke and the Revolt Against the Eighteenth Century: A Study of the Political and Social Thinking of Burke, Wordsworth, Coleridge and*

Southey (London: Allen & Unwin, 1929), pp. 42-43, 80-84, and esp. 92-94. Charles Parkin, *The Moral Basis of Burke's Political Thought: An Essay* (Cambridge, Engl.: The University Press, 1956), Chs. VI and VII, esp. pp. 130, 138. The same point is developed in the enthusiastically partisan analysis of Burkean conservatism by Peter J. Stanlis, *Edmund Burke and the Natural Law* (Ann Arbor, Mich.: University of Michigan Press, 1958), pp. 57-58, 74, 83-84, 109-110 ff., 166-67, 173-74, 176-94, 200-4, 205-8, 219-30, 239-40, 247. See also E. Burke, *Burke's Politics: Selected Writings and Speeches of Edmund Burke on Reform, Revolution and War*, ed. by Ross J. S. Hoffman and Paul Levack (New York: Alfred Knopf, 1949), pp. XIII, XIV-XVII.

27. Jacques Bénigne Bossuet, *Discours sur l'histoire universelle* (Tours: Cattier, 1875), Part III, Ch. VII, esp. pp. 450-51. Marquis de Condorcet, *Esquisse d'un tableau historique des progrès de l'esprit humain: Nouvelle édition suivis de fragments de la quatrième époque, et d'un fragment sur l'Atlantide* (Paris: Bibliothèque Choisie, 1829 [2nd edit.]), throughout, but esp. pp. 7-8 ff., 18-19, 247-99.

28. Alan J. P. Taylor, *Bismarck, The Man and the Statesman* (New Yord: Alfred Knopf, 1955), pp. 13, 21-22, 122, 151, and esp. 265.

29. Albert Béguin, "La révolte de l'Asie et la conscience européenne," *Esprit* (Paris), XXIII (1955), 1803, 1804 ff., 1812, 1818-19.

30. Oswald Spengler, *The Decline of the West*, 2 vols., authorized translation by Charles F. Atkinson (New York: Alfred Knopf, 1926-1928), I, 131-36; II, 26-31, 291-94.

31. M. Eliade, *The Myth of the Eternal Return*, Ch. II.

32. Charles S. Gardner, *Chinese Traditional Historiography* (Cambridge, Mass.: Harvard University Press, 1938), pp. 7, 13-14, 71-72, 76, 77-78.

33. Derk Bodde, "Dominant Ideas," in Harley F. McNair, ed., *China* (Berkeley, Cal.: University of California Press, 1946), pp. 20-21 ff.

34. A. Cobban, *Edmund Burke and the Revolt Against the Eighteenth Century*, pp. 90-91 ff. E. Burke, *Burke's Politics*, pp. XXVI-XXVII.

35. J. T. Marcus, "Time and the Sense of History; West and East," to be published in *Comparative Studies in Society and History* (The Hague, Netherlands), III (January, 1961), No. 2.

36. M. Weber, *The Religion of China*, Parts II and III.

37. F. S. C. Northrop, *The Meeting of East and West: An Inquiry Concerning World Understanding* (New York: Macmillan, 1946),

pp. 366-70 ff., 391-401 ff. René Guénon, *Man and His Becoming According to the Vedanta,* trans. by Clark Whitby (London: Rider & Co., 1928), pp. 34-35.

38. Heinrich Zimmer, *Myths and Symbols in Indian Art and Civilization,* ed. by Joseph Campbell (New York: Pantheon Books, 1946), p. 17. Sir Charles Eliot, *Hinduism and Buddhism: An Historical Sketch,* 3 vols. (London: E. Arnold, 1921), I, 334-36.

39. H. Zimmer, *Philosophies of India,* ed. by Joseph Campbell (New York: Pantheon Books, 1951), pp. 224n-25n, 226-28, 275-76, 348, and esp. 450.

40. For an Asian view of a relationship usually considered in the perspective of the West, see K. M. Panikkar, *Asia and Western Dominance: A Survey of the Vasco da Gama Epoch of Asian History, 1498-1945* (London: Allen & Unwin, 1953).

41. E. R. Hughes, *The Invasion of China by the Western World* (London: A. & C. Black, 1937). See also John Stewart Burgess, "Cultural Change in China," *Sociology and Social Research* (Los Angeles, Cal.), IV (1931), 373-78.

42. P. Tillich, *The Interpretation of History,* pp. 272, 282-84.

14. A Modern Mythmaker*

PHILIP RIEFF

WITH *Psychoanalysis and the Unconscious* and again with *Fantasia of the Unconscious,* Lawrence made his main efforts to explain the doctrine otherwise expressed in his art. As doctrinal counterpoints, these books together take on the importance, if not the excellence, of his art.

When first given in 1921, Lawrence's doctrinal explanations were laughed away by the reviewers, without exception; what scant notice *Psychoanalysis and the Unconscious* received was good humored, treating it as a bizarre and often incomprehensible new testament in the religion of Sex, ardent to supersede the then not very old testament of psychoanalysis. In the first few pages it does appear that Freud is cast down quickly to the role of Judas, fingering the gentle Jesus of an Unconscious for the police forces of civilization, leaving Lawrence alone in his true discipleship. The attack on Freud, however, is incidental to the presentation of his own doctrine. After Lawrence discovered how completely his presentation had been misunderstood, he immediately tried again—belligerently, even somewhat peevishly. "I stick to the solar plexis," he announces, thus challenging the "dear reader" of the second volume with the fact that his message is the same as in the first. Only the "few" will understand, he proclaims, in an unhappy effort to appeal to the snobbishness of his readers. Apparently very few even pretended to understand, despite the fact that this was their second chance, coming only a year after the first.

* What follows is the first draft of a chapter from a book, tentatively titled *Advocates and Analysts of the Unconscious: Studies in the Religious Problem of Our Time,* on which I have embarked.

Fantasia is a restatement and elaboration of his doctrine of the Unconscious as it was stated in *Psychoanalysis;* it had an equally bad press. To the evident pleasure of his meaner critics, Lawrence the artist had strayed too far from his art and thus exposed the incompetence of the prophet who urged the artist on. Those few critical friends Lawrence had at the time kindly ignored both books, preferring to avoid the embarrassment of defending the artist against his urges toward prophecy. The embarrassment lingers; friendly readers generally assume still that the artist in Lawrence can be distinguished from the prophet, that his fiction can be properly enjoyed without the pathos of learning from it those lessons that Lawrence considered were uniquely true to life.

The critical enemies of Lawrence were never thus confused. T. S. Eliot and Wyndham Lewis, to name only two, attacked the lyric fiction of Lawrence precisely because of the moral polemic embodied in it. In *After Strange Gods,* and in a number of articles, Eliot shows toward Lawrence all the cold intellectual fury of an inquisitor close on the hunt for a major heretic and yet never quite able to trap him. Even Eliot's customary ecclesiastic coolness as a critic fails him whenever he approaches Lawrence. For his genius in explaining himself imaginatively in prose fiction, poetry and essays, the reputation of D. H. Lawrence has been plastered with some very ugly labels: essentially a bad writer, Eliot announced, and moreover, also sexually morbid, a snob, boor, uneducated, wrongheaded—finally, worst of all, rather unintelligent. The name-calling in which Lewis indulged shows that writer in more than customary bad temper. Lawrence is said to purvey "Freudian hot-sex-stuff," to write a prose that is little more than an "eloquent wallowing mass of mother-love and self-idolatry," to support the cults of "homo" and "child," to be a consummate "nigger-lover"; for relish, Lewis adds the judgment that "Mr. Lawrence is, in full hysterical flower, perhaps our most accomplished English communist."[1] No other writer in the twentieth century, except Freud, has been subjected to so much abuse from so many otherwise intelligent people.

* Surely Lewis, whose talent was mainly for invective, is one of the most over-rated figures in the world of modern art and literature.

That these two men of genius have been treated with such excited stupidity marks that protective value which Bagehot notes as the essential cultural function of stupidity. Because each, in his own way, had gotten down to fundamentals, each stood accused of being at once irrelevantly eccentric and directly dangerous to the generality. To the literary and scientific guardian classes of mediocrity in our culture, genius is always a thing of the past; it may be discovered in books, but not in the flesh. Freud resented the separation from society that his genius caused him. Lawrence sought, as well as suffered, his messianic alienation. "Entire separation, that is what must happen to one: not even the nominal shelter left, not even the mere fact of inclusion in the host. One must be entirely cast forth." This alienation he advises his friend Bertrand Russell to seek, if Russell hoped to become something more than an academic philosopher. Lawrence's withdrawal represents the religious seriousness with which he took himself. His "utter hatred of the whole establishment—the whole constitution of England" was not merely a consequence of his bitter personal and social experience first as a lower class man and then as a misunderstood writer. Rather, Lawrence's isolation was also self-imposed. As an isolate, desperately seeking community, he self-consciously transformed himself into a representative man of our culture. Underneath the dead levels of the conformity which he saw decades before the knowledge became popular, Lawrence detected in himself the panic of isolation that grips modern man.

Rationalists, whether, like Eliot, defenders of the inherited churchly civilization of authority, or, like Lewis, defenders of less aged institutional varieties of Reason, were bound to oppose Lawrence's doctrine and therefore criticize with open malice his art. In turn, Lawrence opposed with something less than detachment the doctrine of a rationalist such as Freud. In these two books, the confrontation between Freud and Lawrence recapitulates the historic controversy that divides western culture still; what is man and what ought to be the character of his existence. Lawrence is the most profound spokesman in our century for the irrationalist minority position, defended heretofore by religious mystics living on the emotional and intellectual boundaries of a church civilization. On the other hand, Freud bequeathed to the rationalist majority position that analytic subtlety in which it has been wanting for more than a century.

For these hundred years, there had been sporadic attempts to encompass within rational science the irrational, from which the specifically religious emotion grows. Quite apart from the anti-scientific line followed by Nietzsche and Schopenhauer in philosophy and by Hamann in theology, the psychologist Carl Gustav Carus pioneered in this scientific effort, which was originally French. Prosper Enfantin made the most strenuous efforts among the French scientists of moral life, aiming specially to incorporate the rational and irrational into a scientific movement that would also be religious in character. In England, a book titled *Mental Physiology*,[2] written by William Carpenter, made the original English approach to the Unconscious. The capstone of this approach to the irrational from the scientific side was Freud's. The approach was not continuous; the various figures are not directly related but independent sports of the rationalist era. Freud does not spring from them, although he plainly had read Carus and others had been less directly known. He simply superseded them.

From the other side, the approach to the Unconscious was in advocacy of it. As an advocate, Lawrence derives from the powerful tradition of religious mysticism, both Christian and non-Christian. Despite the frequent violence of his literary voice, there is an interior tranquility in Lawrence's prose, a confident walking in the darkness of understanding that will seem odd only to those who have no familiarity with the imagery of mysticism. Mystics have never been afraid of the dark, as rationalists always are. Nor have they avoided the use of sexual imagery. On the contrary, even in the Christian tradition, sexual imagery was freely used to symbolize the relation between the inner man and his God. Mysticism bred acceptance of what the more ascetic rationalist tradition called the "animal" in man, and mystics of all schools often decry the isolate and manipulative view of life bred by intellectualizing about it. The continuity of all creation is a fundamental apprehension of Mysticism, and to that apprehension Lawrence held throughout his life and work. From this continuity mankind has fallen through its own fatal assignment of omnipotence to thought, Lawrence believed. Against all abstractions Lawrence inveighs as a sin against life.

The two books are rather unevenly divided between analyses of the effects of over-rationalizing our lives and the advocacy of the religious mood, which is specifically irrational and erotic. Freud is the object of the Laurentian polemic precisely because he was the genius who took the longest step toward rationalizing even our erotic lives. Lawrence's analytic powers were limited by the passion of his advocacy; Freud remained always supremely analytical because he advocated nothing. His analysis of the erotic life is no more an advocacy than an attack. For this reason, as Lawrence says early in *Psychoanalysis and the Unconscious,* Freud can never "get down to the rock on which he must build his church."

The psychoanalytic movement cannot develop a cultic, passional character. Being analytical, the movement can never become communal. This is, at once, its limit and salvation. It must remain, even at best, something less than a movement, which, upon maturing, can express itself in fledging social and political communities. The personal problems which psychoanalysis confronts are also communal, but, according to Freud, these problems can only be settled personally.

Because, to Freud no less than to Lawrence, a rational religion is a contradiction in terms, the psychoanalytic movement has no religious potential. It is this potential for which Lawrence pleads, once he leaves the polemic against Freud behind and takes up his own position. No one before Freud had made so precisely for "the origins"; for this stroke of genius Lawrence does not grudge his admiration for Freud. But Freud had plunged alone and farthest into the religious depths for a purpose that seems sacrilege to Lawrence: in order to tap these depths with more powerfully rational controls, distributed, like oil derricks, along the self-conscious surfaces of life. It is the rationalist ambition to strengthen the machinery of control that Lawrence opposes. His attack on Freud, in the opening pages of *Psychoanalysis and the Unconscious*, really assaults the latest Jewish law-giver, now wearing the smock of the scientist, but all the more dangerously compelling than his predecessors because he has forgotten the prayerful attitude that man ought to have towards himself; instead, Freud went most profoundly to the issue of whether man still needs such an attitude, even towards himself. Lawrence, on the other hand, suggests the prayerful attitude, without anyone to whom to pray. In those halcyon days, before the full impact of 1914 had registered on the genius of the twenties, it appeared (as it had to advanced minds since the enlightenment) that religion could be divorced from theology. Lawrence went further. There are long paragraphs, especially in the *Fantasia*, in which he suggests what became, from the twenties to nowadays, the personal position of advanced sensibility: feeling divorced from responsibility. Thus, in two books that were written soon after the war that shattered once and for all the Christian moral frame of western culture, Lawrence gave the lead that is still followed by our unchurched religious virtuosi and by our anti-social men of feeling. It sits strangely to read Lawrence's moral indignation against Freud.

"First and foremost," writes Lawrence, "the issue is a moral issue. It is not a matter here of reform, new moral values. It is the life and death of all morality." Freud knew what he had to do, even if his followers did not. Knowing or unknowingly, "psychoanalysis is out, under a therapeutic disguise, to do away entirely with the moral faculty in man." Thus strangely did our foremost novelist, censored for his literary immoralities, defend the "old religious faculty," which is the source of our moral emotions, against a psychologist as widely censored for the immorality of his therapeutic interpretations of that same religious faculty at the end of its strength. Here, if anywhere, it would appear, is a perfect case of the pot calling the kettle black. But Lawrence knew what he was about, as surely as did Freud. The "moral faculty" that Lawrence sets out to defend is, for him as for Freud, dependent on the religious one beneath—specifically irrational, an activity of the Unconscious. "We are in for a debacle," Lawrence announces. It is an announcement in which Freud could believe, given the clinical evidence he had collected from private sources and noticed as well all around him in public relations. The "old world" of Reason was indeed "yielding under us," its thin dried crust of morality cracking up above. But it was this debacle that Freud strove to help our civilization avoid, by shoring up Reason against further perverse outbreaks of the religious Unconscious.

Coming to the Unconscious armed with his rationalist suspicions of it, Freud found there none of the "wonder of wonders" for which, Lawrence believed, men always wait. Rather when Freud came back from his journey he brought with him, Lawrence writes, "sweet heaven, what merchandise! What dreams, dear heart! What was there in the cave? Alas, that we ever looked! Nothing but a huge slimy serpent of sex, and heaps of excrement, and a myriad repulsive little horrors spawned between sex and excrement. Is it true?"

Lawrence offers, repetitively, his "No" for an answer. Of course, these "gagged, bound, maniacal repressions, sexual complexes, faecal inhibitions, dream monsters" that "ate our souls and caused our helpless neuroses" were there. But we have planted them there. Psychoanalytic rationalism found what it was trained to suspect in the religious recesses of which it is afraid. To achieve knowledge of this "true unconscious," science would have to abandon its "intellectualist position" and embrace the "old religious faculty," becoming thereby not less scientific but at last "complete in knowledge." Here is the ancient self-confidence of the mystic, revived. Knowledge, in the mystical sense, is primarily self-knowledge.

But rationalism had learned this intimate fact about the nature of knowing a century before Lawrence accused it of ignorance. In the nineteenth century, rationalism lost its arrogance precisely by making dignified sense of the apparent insanities that eighteenth-century rationalism had smugly exposed as the folly characteristic of even the highest religious belief. The Resurrection, for example, was no longer dismissed simply as a deliberate fraud. Such an early rationalist story (which Lawrence reversed in his own about *The Man Who Died*) as the one about Christ recovering from a coma, after which he could not convince his disciples that he was still a natural man, did not survive later rationalist sophistication. The transition from the rationalism of a Voltaire or a Gibbon to that of a Strauss or a Renan conforms to a transition from a special hostility toward Christian religion to a general sympathy toward the need for mythic explanations felt by a mankind not yet educated in Reason. Lawrence's sympathy for the religious need is not really different; his departure from the rationalist tradition lies in a reversal in the direction of his suspicion; perhaps his suspicion of any universal claims for Reason, in contrast to the suspicions of eighteenth-century rationalism against the universal claims of Religion, marks the difference between the hope of that century and the experience of our own.

That Lawrence took no specific religious statement seriously, except as symbolic, brings him uncomfortably close to his opponent, Freud, who also took no religious statement seriously—except as symptom. The difference between symbol and symptom is only that between advocacy and analysis. In Lawrence, the compassionate nineteenth-century science of religion was transformed into the characteristic religious poetry of the twentieth. Our poetry, with its inclinations to evoke creedal worlds without end, is a lyrical kind of rationalism (or "Idealism," as Lawrence prefers to call it), beginning with an intellectual decision to tap the resonances of belief and working from these sounds further and further from the discordant secular music of modern life. At least those rationalists who return, with Freud, to a therapeutic examination of the religions which held their fathers, grant that every article of faith—every myth, every projection—yields an important kind of self-knowledge, upon which their own kind depends, as theory depends on the criticism of data. Without an

intimate touch of the irrational, science grows ever colder and
more remote, more in control of life than useful for controlling it.
As rationalists obsessed with examining the ejects of dying and
corrupt religiosities, too weak for life and yet too strong for death,
the Freuds of our world were really engaged in just that research
into their own unconscious from which the secular paradigm of
religious self-knowledge derives. The psychological man of our
time struggles to make his deeper and more subjective processes
clearer as neuroses, rather than, as formerly his ancestors did, as
gods. Lawrence admits that such objectifications must differ from
time to time. He has no more faith in the Christian God who died
finally in 1914 than in any of the far longer dead Aztec ones he
tried to revive, experimentally in the fiction of *The Plumed
Serpent*. Gods have lives that are historically limited. What Lawrence really dislikes are the religious procedures of our time: he
could not rightly claim that we have no god terms. Our Holy
Ghost, as he knew, is in the machine, where it took refuge when
its home in the soul was condemned as too ancient and rundown
by modern housing ordinances.

The way the Ghost got in the machine is remarkably similar to
the way that God got into heaven. Whatever the differences are
between the mythic and the scientific, they are not so great as
Lawrence believed. Freud was aware how little the differences
mattered, and that his own science in the end comes down to
myth. Two myths may oppose each other, one claiming to be more
scientific, but the scientific myth arises no less from within the
Unconscious than does the unscientific one. Reality principle not-
withstanding, the *esse* of the external world remained its *percepi*.
The rationalist tradition experienced a chastened culmination in
Freud. His is very opposite from the crude rationalism of the
eighteenth century which rejected all psychic products as somehow fraudulent. Understanding his patient's perceptual and social
world as expressions of the percipient's intelligence and emotion,
Freud really erases the gap between therapeutic rationalism and
self-assertive romanticism. This subtle reconciliation Lawrence
did not understand. The implied condescension in Lawrence's

criticism of Freud's "idealism" exhibits Lawrence's impatience as a critic. A patient approach to Freud would indicate with what genius he conducted rationalism to its self-transformatic reconciliation with romanticism. Lawrence suffers from the fundamentalism of his faith in the irrational; so strict in his advocacy that he fails to appreciate the final sinuous turn that Freud gave rationalism.

On the other hand, with their ignorant irreligions, the fundamentalists of rationalism are still with us; they are frequently to be met among the most highly trained and emancipated people, who, in their yet unspoiled bigotry, fail to realize that everything great and good springs, as Lawrence believed, from man's inner life and not from changes in social and scientific arrangements. This faith in the externals of life has had the effect, despite its coating with the religion of humanity, which Lawrence despised as a rank sentimentalism no less profoundly than Freud, of making man think less than highly of himself. Such pride of place was not missing in the religious epochs of our emotional history. But now that pride has been completely abandoned. Compare Lawrence's daring to place the self not only at the center of the universe but imagining it literally as the hot creative stuff from which even the remotest cold stars derive, with his friend Russell's characterization of man as a passing and miserable accident in an indifferent creative universe. On the contrary, Lawrence proclaims, "it is the [life of the] universe which has resulted from the death of individuals." In its anthropomorphism, this mythic effort is breath-taking in its challenge to the scientific downgrading of man. The myths here presented, as the doctrinal intuitions animating his art, are sometimes carried along by a high good humor; but even when he is frolicsome Lawrence never loses his essential lyric seriousness of purpose.

In the fundaments of social theory, Lawrence stands alone with Freud, although he himself remained unaware of this agreement. As a literary man, Lawrence cannot be expected to contribute anything more fundamental than intuitive agreement to that complete and inspiriting reversal of the trend of scientific social theory with which Freud has upset the rationalist temper of our century; but such agreement is remarkable enough for its very rarity. Consider the theory that has dominated our sense of the relation between man and society since the second quarter of the nineteenth century. For figures in the rationalist tradition as far apart as the conservative Auguste Comte and the radical Karl Marx, the self is society individualized. The object of scientific devotion, which infuriated Lawrence to the opposite advocacy and drove Freud to the opposite analysis, is the individualized social self. Freud's historic revision against the entire rationalist doctrine, as it expresses itself still in all the social sciences, is his analysis of the socialized individual self, in all the painful vicissitudes of that socialization. It is precisely against this rationalist ideology, or "mental consciousness" or "social consciousness," as Lawrence variously calls it—that he argues throughout the chapters that follow. How sad that Lawrence did not understand Freud. But genius has a way of not recognizing the character of that genius closest to its own; carried away by the rhetoric of his alienated situation in the twenties, Lawrence marked Freud down as the leader of the enemy rationalist camp. Aiming as he did to liberate the religious impulse in his dogmatically rationalist readers, Lawrence failed to understand how undogmatic was his chosen rationalist opponent. Deliberately taunting his readers with examples of their own rigid dichotomizing of the categories of life, Lawrence commits what should be to him the sin of dichotomizing; Freud is put too strictly in the rationalist camp.

In advocating the irrational during a time he considered fatally rationalist, perhaps Lawrence carried his artist's sense of alienation from his culture too far. For thus he expressed his uncertainty about the quality and worth of his own participation in the unconscious. Like Whitman,* in whom he was greatly interested, Lawrence was not a primitive expressionist of the Unconscious but a painfully self-conscious protagonist of what Hegel first called "mansoul." It is questionable, I think, whether any great

---

* The sentences that follow reflect the profit of a fortunate chance conversation with Henry Nash Smith.

modern artist can escape the double burden of having to relate himself analytically as well as expressively to his culture, no matter how profoundly he himself may manage to remain on intimate terms with it, as a participant observer of its unconscious life. The modern artist cannot belong where there are no communities in which membership can be taken for granted. With his sense of blood ties, Shakespeare participated in the unconscious life of his time perhaps more profoundly than any other man who has ever expressed himself in writing. But in that first Elizabethan age, just before rationalism moralized as "freedom" and "individuality" the alienation of man from God, the self or community, such direct and publicly cognizable transformations as Shakespeare's of the irrational into art were still possible. Lawrence had to be stimulated to his polemical rather than participant observations by reading Frazer's *Golden Bough* and *Totemism and Exogamy*. Shakespeare needed no armchair anthropologist to recall the sacred heart of genuinely popular culture. The signs of its life were then still all about him. Lawrence had no such luck; the organic community of extended families had been superseded by societies of mutual manipulation. The family had lost both economic function and emotional authority; the role of the mother had been grotesquely distorted into dominance, and the father's degraded to that of permanent *other*. Only in private erotic relations, thought Lawrence, was it still possible to achieve the silent capacity for "passional communion" once natural in families. Nothing has changed since Lawrence's time, but only become more so.

Yet, with his imagery of blood, sun and earth Lawrence came closer than any other modern artist to a sense of what the simplicity of passion might have been. "Blood" is perhaps the most common metaphor for passion in our literary language. The rhetoric of Shakespeare runs with consciousness of blood. Having to be didactic, Lawrence writes awkwardly of "blood consciousness." But the time needed a teacher desperately, as he knew. Lawrence is the lesser artist because of his pedagogic inclinations. But his blood metaphors remain traditional, expressing for him, as for Shakespeare and others between, the possibility of leading the impassioned life. There is nothing sinister in Lawrence's use of the ancient blood metaphors. Pathetically, he raised them from long disuse to compete against the contemporary machine-metaphors of human passion, which, according to Lawrence, had corrupted passion itself. What is sinister, as symptom, is our revulsion against blood metaphors when not kept under glass, as approved museum pieces.* Such metaphors have been dismissed as dirty or reactionary—even fascist. Thus manipulative self-consciousness—to use Laurentian terms for alienation —has progressed to that stage of moral sickness which Freud confronts. For this progress of the disease, Lawrence blames the rationalized machine civilization into which he was born. But alienation, as he elsewhere sensed, was characteristic of the human condition long before the rationalizing of life by technological science.

Alienation is originally neither a Marxist nor a psychiatric tool of understanding the human condition, but theological and specially Christian. In the act of knowledge, of being rather than merely continuing to be, the old Adam disobeyed God and thereby became estranged from the divine in himself. That inner part of life thus became unknown to him, repressed by man's new commitment to the outer part. In the original version of the doctrine of alienation, man can cure himself only by accepting God's forgiveness, through Christ, and thus, in imitation of the divine mood, love not only his neighbors but also himself. When Catholic institutional theology of the Middle Ages had thoroughly rationalized human misery, and made reconciliation a routine, the early Luther recalled western man to the necessity of leading an inner life; the doctrine of justification by faith alone derives from Luther's rejection of Catholic rationalist theology, and from his sensitivity to the overwhelming need of man to love himself for his own sake, as God had loved him.

---

* The pleasure of Shakespeare has been destroyed for generations of schoolboy readers, who have encountered him thus with the blood let out, under the sterile guardianship of old maid teachers.

When Luther saw what violence his liberation of the religious faculty had let loose, he hedged in remorse against the consequences of his own position. The later Luther became far more the institutional Catholic than the revolutionary Protestant. In his polemical enthusiasm for the same liberation, and without that experience of organizational responsibility which is thrust like an object lesson upon every revolutionary, Lawrence rejects all hedgings. Welcoming as he did the imminent end of a culture created out of divine ordering words (*Logos*), he is not appalled by the "scream of violence," which to him expresses not death but the birth in "pain and splendor," of true individuality.

The freedom for which Lawrence argues especially in the later parts of *Fantasia* is not the civil freedom sought by political philosophers; rather Lawrence returns to the more traditional, religious conception of freedom as a condition of the inner life. Truly to Lawrence man is everywhere born free and not all the cleverness of constitutional checks and balances, or more equitable distributions of property, can protect this original uncorrupted state of mind. The "bread question," as Lawrence mocks our politics, is not the essential one. In his advocacy of the Unconscious—the essential unique nature of every "individual creature" which appears in "defiance of all scientific law, in defiance even of reason"—Lawrence renders a modern version of the religious sense of freedom. In its intuitions of what freedom really is, "religion was right and science is wrong." According to this "fearfully religious" man, as Lawrence once described himself, the human is captive not of regimes but of his own lust for reasoning. Finally, to Lawrence, freedom in our time consists in the liberation of the inner man from his own "idealism."

The Laurentian politics resembles in remarkable ways that of Prosper Enfantin and other Saint-Simonians about whom Lawrence apparently knew nothing whatever. In a letter of 26 July, 1915, to Russell, he writes out his sketch of a new hierarchal organic society that would permit communal passion. This society would culminate, as for Enfantin, in "one real head, as every organic thing must—no foolish republics with foolish presidents, but an elected King, something like Julius Caesar. And as the men elect and govern the industrial side of life, so the women must elect and govern the domestic side. And there must be a rising rank of women governors, as of men, culminating in a woman Dictator, of equal authority with the supreme Man." Of this hierarchy, Lawrence, again like Enfantin,* at times imagined himself the head. Lawrence thus fits into that underground tradition of speculation about the religious rehabilitation of modern society which informed significant political as well as literary movements in nineteenth-century Europe. Note that a woman governor of the "inner half of life" really gives women the main say: over the private life. There is a tremendous envy of women in Lawrence—an envy which psychoanalysis has explained superbly in case histories of religiously burdened man.[3]

In the course of his correspondence with Russell, Lawrence declared himself unequivocally on the relation between religion and society. "There is no living society possible but one which is held together by a great religious idea." Rid as Lawrence thought he was of all Christian metaphysics, he argued gratuitously with the embarrassed intellectual Russell for just the "opposite principle to Christianity: self-fulfillment and social destruction, instead of self-love and self-sacrifice." That opposite Laurentian principle would, for the sake of immediacy in the expression of the intimate self, admit the scream of violence, as natural to man as the arched and stiffened back of a baby having a temper tantrum and of animals showing their teeth. Our culture had enforced the pretense that every show of teeth is a smile, that love is benevolent in character. To teach us differently, there was a period in Lawrence's life when he felt messianic enough to hope for an assembly of men and women who would form the "nucleus of a new belief," launching a "new center of attack" far removed from politics. In this respect, Lawrence shows himself as the most genuine of modern heresiarchs, chief and father, although only long after his death, over all the little heresiarchs—father-killers,

---

* Who actually put his fancy into experimental, institutional practice.

ambivalent mother-lovers, culture-breakers, beat generators—who swarm along the literary horizon. In his criticism of the tyrannous publicity of modern life he is truly the revolutionary of the private life.

Perhaps Lawrence would have been a less happy auditor of the scream of violence, which he could not himself learn to utter, had he lived a little longer. He missed the noises from Nuremburg; he could not hear the screams in the neighborhood from which Freud was extricated, despite his reluctance to leave for Lawrence's still idealist England. Rationalist distrust of the irrational finds good cause in the bloody history of mankind. Lawrence read more than enough history to know better.

Yet, as it has turned out, no age has been more horrific than this age of science. The Unconscious has revenged itself for the repressions it has suffered at the hands of rationalist science. Repressed as theology, the Unconscious has manifested itself in all sorts of perverse religions, as we saw in Germany, the great center of rationalism in the nineteenth century. We have paid dearly for the victory of rationalism—a victory that Freud, in his wisdom, wished to meliorate if only for the sake of preserving the weak hold over life that secular, uncommitted Reason had achieved in the course of fairly recent maneuvering. With his tremendous intuitions into a historical development of which he had little grasp in any precise or scholarly way, Lawrence knew that reason defends mainly against impulse, and against what he considered the legitimate and undeniable power of love. An argument, as he rightly sensed, is rationalist, or "ideal," when it is pressed against the possibility of some religious affirmation of our lives.

Where not only was his own English human community rationalized, but all communities alike are now well along in the same process of rationalization, it is futile, if not dangerous, for Lawrence to insist as he did that men ought not to arbitrate their passions primarily through their analytic intelligences. Analysis can judge not only passion but also itself; as the common judge of both, it can be superior to passion without killing it, as the

Romantics feared. On the other hand, passion is the common divider of men—in particular when it becomes attached to the world of ideas. A fresh wave of religiosity, in the form of an indifference to public ideas while teasing out the *pneuma* of intimate relations, will not of itself bring either social peace or at last crown the power of love. To thus save mankind from remaining fixated upon its ideological follies demands an intellectual grasp of the issue no less profound than the experience of the power of love that Lawrence communicates in his art. Merging again the intellectual and the experiential, theory with therapy, Freud's appears to me a far more realistic genius than Lawrence's. By contrast, in its deliberate avoidance of a restraining intellectualism, Lawrence's erotic doctrine permits violences of expression in which anger and hatred represent thereby ultimately more powerfully encouraged motives than that of love. Nothing is less loving than the still Laurentian message of the beat generation writers.

His message may be futile, as it can be dangerous; nevertheless the prophet in Lawrence deserves the widest possible reading. This is, after all, the most talented believer in the irrational yet born of the wedlock of power with profit that is rationalist culture in contemporary Europe and America. This culture has survived mainly by taking up religious rejections into itself. The Protestant Reformation revitalized it; after suffering the spurious revolutions of Socialism (Lawrence knew them to be spurious before they occurred, and Freud, unlike some of his followers, was never taken in by them), it is time again for the thoughtful of the culture to realize that genuine revolutions are basically religious in character. In our time, again, not science but religion carries the power of criticism as well as love. Being religious, the Laurentian criticism at least goes to fundamentals, however little it may appear to explain them usefully. It is inevitable that the Laurentian criticisms, enseamed as they are in a network of affirmative myths, should be disputed; but they cannot be, except at our peril, entirely rejected, let alone ignored.

For Lawrence, the religious problem is identical with the

moral and the aesthetic. In these two books he strives to preserve on the religious and moral level what elsewhere he protects on the aesthetic level: that aura of divinity around the person which Christianity has left behind. Lawrence follows the ancient theologically-rooted distinction between person and personality; the latter, in its usage by the scientific and liberal of our culture, is in process of destroying the former, by pulling it to pieces and showing it to be composed of nothing except social parts. The person has been diagnosed as a kind of intersection of environments and influences. Everything, in fact, is thought to exist in the modern individual except his own "pristine consciousness," his hidden self, soul. Lawrence dares to propose a fresh franchise for the incommunicable, inalienable soul—in which, incidentally, our traditional culture once could see its most beautiful self-image. What a mixture of traditional and revolutionary motifs Lawrence has composed for a doctrine.

The "old religious faculty" of which Lawrence writes in advocacy, and in defense against science, is specifically the irrational power of love. With such praise, the pallid reasonable religions favored by the educated classes for two centuries are implicitly criticized. Our ethical religions were originally developed in direct conflict with a religiosity that Lawrence raised up from a grave long shared with mysticism, the religions of primitive peoples, the ancient Egyptians and scattered heretics in Christian culture. Thus, if as I believe, these two books argue for a revival of religiosity, they for the same reason argue against any revival of a church-centered civilization. Lawrence was not a religious intellectual in the sense we can apply the term to Eliot. But it is not unknown for the profoundly religious intellectual to oppose churchliness, as, for example, Kierkegaard opposed the Christendom of his time.

It is the religiosity of living, in conjugal love and with the natural event of children, of which Lawrence seeks to remind us. Evidently the one institution left behind by Christianity which, in Lawrence's mind, still lives is the family. That institution is also the crux of the Freudian analysis. Love, in the family way:

this is the main problem to which both Lawrence and Freud, despite their differing approaches, address themselves.

If his religion is not ethical, and neither is it theological, then in what sense can we rightly speak of the religious dimension in Lawrence's work? By advocating the "old religious faculty," Lawrence had in mind the freer expression of man's basically erotic character. But in doing so, Lawrence locates the religious capacity in man at that level of life which is, say, for Kierkegaard, only the first stage on the way to a genuinely religious attitude: the aesthetic.

The stage of his religious development being aesthetic, Lawrence considers the divine as essentially erotic in character; it is a position advanced at least since the time of Plato. But Lawrence is a very modern advocate of eros, and therefore very direct: the divine is realized characteristically in the sexual relation between a man and one woman—and then, in pathos, only fleetingly. Being far better educated than many of his detractors, Lawrence is also aware of alternative conceptions of the Divine, both pagan and Christian variants. But he seriously experimented with imaginative reconstructions of a culture dominated neither by *Agape* nor by *Reason*—the Christian sense of love and the Greco-Christian-scientific *logos*—but by eros. Deliberately, *The Plumed Serpent* is a novel of pagan religiosity, centering on the possibility of converting a western woman to a primitive Indian cult. In his imaginative rehabilitation of Aztec ritual, Lawrence rightly understands their sun-dancing as an imitation—or a dramatic representation—in assistance of the divine's procedure with the human. The lady, Kate, is very advanced; she knows all about socialism and is quite beyond religion in its western institutional appearance. But she accepts her religious duty when it is presented to her sexually, and enters the social enjoyment of marriage to the high priest of the cult. Thus, she chooses to participate directly in a passional community instead of merely observing it, as her European upbringing inclines her to do. An embarrassment even to defenders of Lawrence, *The Plumed Serpent* runs together just those motifs—the sexual, instinctual unconscious and the religious—which in European culture have been strenuously kept apart. On the whole, the European compartmentalization of the sexual and religious motifs has been successful, but perhaps at great cost not merely to the sexual but also to the religious quality of western culture.

The Christian possibility had ceased entirely in 1914, Lawrence felt. His great story, *The Man Who Died*, written a decade afterward in contemplation of the definite historic ending of the Christian passion, has a therapeutic intention. It portrays Jesus himself admitting the error of becoming a Christ. Upon his resurrection, Jesus vaguely understands that he cannot return to his former public role. He rediscovers his amatory humanity— the true divine in him—in a directly sexual way, taught that much by a blond votary of the Isis cult. Thus is Christ resurrected as Jesus. As a man, he has recovered his divinity. Lost before in an ideologically encouraged confusion about his mission, Jesus now has no mission; he has achieved, in his encounter with an oriental erotic religion, his own innocence of consciousness. Jewish passion for carrying a public message has entirely evaporated. He understands now that he has misled his poor followers by searching for God the Father in the wrong way. Salvation lies only in the intimate, private life.

In *The Man Who Died*, Lawrence is at once the most religious and most revolutionary writer in modern English literature. In *Psychoanalysis*, and at greater length in *Fantasia*, he tried to explain what his revolutionary religiosity amounted to. In sum: he declares his trust in the irrational, in precisely that human energy which this civilization most distrusts. Moreover, he declares for an innocence of mind that will permit western man to relocate himself again in connection with the rest of natural life. His passion is for the private message, often esoterically given. But the message is absolutely clear in his own intimate correspondence with men he considers candidates for his revolutionary moral instruction on how to save themselves, and thus possibly the world. "For heaven's sake," he writes, in all seriousness, to the supremely intellectual Bertrand Russell, "don't think . . . be a baby, and not a savant any more. Don't *do* anything any more—but for heaven's sake begin to *be*—start at the very beginning and be a perfect baby: in the name of courage."

The rhetoric of "child consciousness," which runs through *Fantasia* and *Psychoanalysis*, will puzzle only if not put in the context of Lawrence's pre-Freudian view of the innocence of the child. Not that Lawrence believed that the child was innocent of sexuality. Rather, precisely this sexuality is the permitting condition of the innocence of childhood. For in its unconsidered sexual drives—to and from objects—a child cannot abide in any fixed ideals. From this Lawrence makes it follow that little children can, if understood, lead men toward the good life. Taking thought is not, to Lawrence, a virtue. The very nature of goodness, of the relation of goodness to truth, is that men stop taking so much thought of themselves. Of the cardinal virtues, Lawrence would preserve only two, it appears: fortitude and justice. Restraint and prudence do not seem to him conducive to the good life, as they were considered by Christian moralists—and by Freud. More important, theorizing about life conspires with vice to render all virtues ambiguous. Lawrence prefers the purity of ignorance to the impurities of our civilizing educations. Such faith in the natural man has not appeared so importantly in literature since the early Rousseau.

Because Freud trusted civilization, however burdensome, more than the natural man, it is understandable that Lawrence should oppose so vehemently the Freudian doctrine. Freud too intended to help mankind break away from its habitual fixation upon ideals; but from long clinical experience he knew better than to present the child as a counter-ideal. There is nothing in the man, except his intelligence, that is not already in the child. In order to overcome the child in himself, while not denying it, a man can only resort to his added quality: intellect. No two doctrines could be more opposed in this respect about how to treat in maturity the quality of childhood than the Laurentian and the Freudian.

Lawrence never really knew children. He saw them without the aid of either clinical or parental intimacy. Otherwise, he would have noticed their tremendous craving for order. However changeable, under manipulation by more adult minds, the passions of a child are so dogged that they remain powerful in adult memory—or so painful, in frustration, that they have to be repressed. The passions of childhood far outlast their objects and at times therefore develop the quality of an obsession. Badly informed as Lawrence is about children, he could with confidence, and for his own didactic purposes, commend to adults the spontaneous and arbitrary purposiveness of the childlike in man.

From his idealization of the passions as he supposed they are—fresh in childhood—Lawrence derived, in part, his two main criteria for the living of life: first, the capacity to unite with another in the alternately straining and easing relation of love; second, the special masculine need for a "passionate purpose" in life, beyond meeting the erotic demands in a relation with one woman. The second purpose is in tension, as Freud thought too, with the first. For both Lawrence and Freud, women distract men from the missions in the world upon which they must embark. The feminine is the specifically anti-cultural force. Given his ambivalent attitude toward high culture, Lawrence's peculiar envy of the feminine, and his awe of it, becomes more understandable. But his manliness constantly serves as a critical balance of his envy of the feminine, permitting him to reject it. Alone, or in a company of like-minded men, the husband must set out from his home to make something new and better in the world. If they are to be effective, passionate purposes must be steady; and if they are steady, then they develop inevitably into "fixed ideals." Yet just this steadiness of purpose, Lawrence considers, needs breaking. This second and higher satisfaction of the religious need in the working half of mankind, through passionate purpose, dissolves under analysis into mere passion for purpose. A nostalgia—passion once removed from purpose—informs Lawrence's private life. Many of the projections of himself in the male protagonists of his novels, as well as in the exhortatory poetry, reflect his own sterile passion for purpose. Like those for whom faith means mainly a continuing capacity to believe in the possibility of finding themselves, not in finding something beyond themselves, Lawrence's personal religion is all going to church and never getting there. The first criterion, which can be satisfied only in the erotic life, seems more strongly argued. In one respect, this strength compensates for the weakness of his second argument: toward the investment of passion in purpose.

Ultimately, Lawrence believed, each self in its distinctiveness has one purpose only: to come into the "fullness of its being." From this fulfillment any fixed direction can only distract. To recognize "the fact of otherness," to accept the good life as an erotic crucible that can, for sacred moments, fuse together self and other—these alone can proximate fulfillment. Thus to take for granted both the distancies and proximities of love completes in maturity the innocent eroticism of childhood.

In such fulfillments, Freud, with his modern genius for suspicion, no longer believed. He begins really where Lawrence, for lack of sufficient analytic patience, leaves off—at the compatibility of love and hatred in the family relation, at the mystery of the ambivalent relation that unites man and woman, and from which they patch their domestic arrangements. It is not at all clear that even the higher animals are not self-divided into both subject and object, burdened with the rudiments of double consciousness. Lawrence's piety toward the possibility of living in continuity with the universe, which he elaborates in his discussion of the alienation from true selfhood that loads the latter half of *Fantasia*, specifies his religious hope for a condition of innocence, a return to that naïvete which can persist beyond the oceanic feelings of identity known at times to mystics and perhaps (Lawrence thought) to life in the womb. The Laurentian God represents precisely what Freud called an "oceanic feeling."[4] In fact, elsewhere Lawrence explicitly invokes the "Oceanic God."[5] Nowhere if not in man, does the Oceanic God represent that state of feeling in the residual psychological womb which cossets early infancy. Then the human ordinarily experiences unqualified and unreflective love, in particular from the mother (or, at least, from the pre-Freudian mother). For this unmanipulative state of consciousness Lawrence makes his plea elaborately in *Fantasia*, having considered that he had failed to put across the same point to the readers of *Psychoanalysis*. Such a state was better known to ages before the emancipation of women—an advance in society which, like the political enfranchisement of the masses, Lawrence bitterly regretted for the corruptions of innocence it had imposed on its beneficiaries. Limited by their sexuality, both women and the masses have only been made unhappy by the political responsibilities conferred upon them. The biological warmth that kept families together was more and more missing from modern democratic culture. The family, more than most institutions, was atomized by the new free individual in search of as many of his selves as he could find. To Lawrence, not the freedom of self-searching but only a biologically warm family could preserve "the human being all his life fresh and alive, a true individual." Compared to this individual consciousness of continuity with all other selves, our polite social consciousness created individuals in relations of manipulative tension with one another. The modern tolerant, atomized family represented to Lawrence our lowest point of alienation from other selves and not our harmony with them. The alternative to the family naturally hot for each other is the cool democratic family which we now, characteristically, have: one educated in the liberal art of togetherness, well-tempered love, mutual consideration and the modern option of treating first marriages as trial runs—a sort of growing-up period for grownups, with children as evidence of the inconvenient nature of the experiment.

To save themselves from false otherness, in which an immoral intellectualism miseducates them, individuals are urged to follow their own particular "Holy Ghost." In burnishing this pale mirror of the Christian self-image, Lawrence shows something more than literary artifice. As a post-Christian, he was profoundly troubled by the problem of how men in this time shall find their own God.[6] Now, patently, there is no Savior. As the novels expressing his own fantasies of leadership indicate, the best answer to our religious need would be for the Oceanic God to send a fresh Savior. Lawrence fascinated himself with the possibility of bringing religiosity back into politics; the theme is adumbrated in *The Plumed Serpent, Aaron's Rod* and *Kangaroo*. But, except in his literary fantasies, no erotic leader appeared. He gave up on politics, and on the possibility of a rehabilitation of the soul through the agency of one fatherly man. The search for God would have to be conducted inwardly, through each man coming to terms with the incommunicable love that is his own soul.

Lawrence's sense of the incredible divinity in loving appears anything but Christian. Pagan fertility meant more to him than Christian charity. Yet in his deliberate revolt against it, the Christian inheritance dominates Lawrence. This dominance is expressed not least in his fiction by the pathetic groping for charity between his violent lovers. The more violent is their erotic feeling, the more they grope after charity. There are passages enough in Lawrence's writing where he thunders no less loudly against the contemporary confusion of "mental lust" with fleshly love than to satisfy the strictest old Christian postmaster.

The desire Lawrence built into the uncomplicated having of an *other* is the more pathetic for his irresistible intuitions of the impossibility of such satisfactions. Desires that bring genuine union also bring marriage. Sexual union puts the partners in a family way. Love, when complete, complicates life further; for it involves a group that grows along the line drawn by the original love relation. The final question which tests erotic behavior is whether one can become a good parent. Bad lovers make bad parents. Especially in *Fantasia*, Lawrence concentrates on the consequences of the original love relation for those loved. Without that sense of otherness which balances the capacity for warmth between lovers, they, as parents, kill their children with domineering kindness; on the other hand, alienated from each other, they may use their children as substitute lovers, as Lawrence knew mothers often do.* It is not the child but the parent

---

* Or, as an alternative, the alienation of the parents may be expressed in the "freedom" permitted their children. Lawrence noted the decline of immediacy not only in love but in authority. Instead of direct relations of authority, the family is run by oblique manipulations of guilt feelings, which train the child to congenital dishonesty in later life as well as often to wearing confusions of sex role.

(and, in particular, the modern mother) who invents the incest problem. Only near the end of these volumes will the attack on Freud's idea of the incest taboo, with which Lawrence begins, turn clear and more plausible. The reader will have to be patient with Lawrence, who was never a systematic writer but something better—a seer. As a concept, the incest taboo like other Freudian hypotheses, represents projections as science of the false standards governing erotic relations in the family. Thus the incest taboo articulates the training in possessive love with which modern mothers, no longer libidinally related to their husbands, manage to keep their sons even after they become mothers-in-law. The sons, when they marry, remain bound to the one true love they have known, as infants. Freud merely "idealized" this failure of parental willingness to recognize the child too as an inviolate other, and thus thought the incest taboo into universal existence. The experience of anthropologists and psychologists with pre-modern and un-Christian cultures no more confirms the Laurentian criticism of Freud than it conclusively confirms the Freudian concept. But the weight of evidence inclines to the side of Freud. The ubiquity of the incest taboo, in cultures without our peculiar mother fixations, indicates that the Freudian concept is no mere public projection as science of some occasionally exaggerated notion of the intimacy appropriate between the generations.

Nevertheless, Lawrence's practical advice on the conduct of family life seems to me healthy; it is also sad, for in the personal life of this deliberately prophetic figure the love relation with his wife, Frieda, was childless. As a prophet, Lawrence drove himself, as much as he was driven, in search of the exemplary life. His rejection of England just equals his acceptance of himself. Yet, in his own private relations, he failed of completion in what was to him a most fundamental way. Not that, viewed from the perspective of prophecy, the personal life of D. H. Lawrence was a failure. Rather, because of his ambition to be an exemplar, his life, more than most, shows up its patches of familiar compromise. He was a second husband. His wife had already had her two children by a man whom she no longer loved—if ever she did.

This preacher of family as well as conjugal passion never experienced, in his own childhood, that which he advocated. His own family example could only have taught him what it is he had to criticize, not, except by abstract negation, what to praise. Moreover, while preaching sheer physical exuberance, Lawrence was a sick shell of a man. The gospel of health was carried in a thin hollow vessel. If ever strength of will and intelligence triumphed over weakness of body, this triumph belongs to Lawrence, panegyrist of the body.

Further against his own stated doctrine, Lawrence could not avoid transforming the love relation between man and woman into a religious one. It helps, in reading Lawrence on love, to remember that in his inherited religious sense the object of love is by the nature of the case incapable of being possessed; the worshipper has no means of completely satisfying his desire. For Freud, incompleteness is in the nature of satisfaction; for Lawrence, incompleteness derives from the object of satisfaction. Lawrence divinizes the sense of otherness. Men and women must naturally want to possess each other completely, just as they must also want to be free of each other. They are unable to accomplish either side of the duality of life to their satisfaction. Through his sense of the other, remote and yet tense with erotic capacity, Lawrence portrays people as most exquisite isolates—finally even from themselves: the self, being the God in every man, cannot be fully entered into. Between the moments of advance and withdrawal, there is the painful middle distance upon which the manner of western civilization depends. Notice the suffering of husband and wife in the story, "New Eve and Old Adam," another of the many Lawrence stories translating the Christian search for God into a secular search for the *other*. In this story, wife accuses husband of withdrawing into himself at the same time that she has succeeded in disengaging herself from him and becomes "in the deepest sense . . . free of him" so that "above, in the open, she [could] live." Such an isolate life of freedom must, Lawrence feels, corrupt the very individuality of the soul, whose nature it is to seek another. The corruption of freedom is nothing like the innocence of one "private, sacred heart" seeking the beating rhythm of another. Expect more than a complementarity of separate life rhythms and every marriage must seem a "comparative failure"—as the "Old Adam" concludes about his own. Once accept the "real separation of souls" and marriage becomes all it can be. Eros must be cherished, tenderly pursued, loved for the exercise that it gives in the chase and prized in the moments of capture. Lawrence believed in the ultimacy of means and in the illusoriness of ends. His moral doctrine is of the most modern sort: neither an ethics of responsibility nor an ethics of conscience, but an ethics of action. Figures as far apart as Sorel and Dewey would have understood perfectly this aspect of the Laurentian gospel.

In the act of love is, for Lawrence, perfect action; in it we become free of both conscience and responsibility. We merely *are;* we cease to care, consider, reflect. This ecstatic doctrine of erotic action is in no way original to Lawrence. He could have read it in Nietzsche's *Birth of Tragedy,* for which he developed a youthful enthusiasm. For brief moments, wrote Nietzsche, we become "Primordial Being itself, and feel its indomitable desire for being, and joy in existence. The struggle, the pain, the destruction of phenomena appear to us something necessary . . . considering the fertility of the universal will." Generation is holy. Passion is holy. Screams of violence are more full of life than the hushed tones of tolerance. Only the isolate quieters of life, in the name of thought and care, offend Lawrence. "Blood consciousness" is nothing new in the English literary tradition; Shakespeare had it, as I have said. And, of course, it is a staple of European, and especially, German *lebensphilosophie.* What is new in Lawrence is his hymn-singing attitude toward the physicality of life. Lawrence's piety for the body is not vulgar; it is merely gratuitous. The world affirms itself. No religion of affirmation is needed; rather, a vital religion of denial remains ever necessary. I do not suggest by "denial" a religion that withdraws man further from life but an attitude that permits the human, tempted as he is to constant affirmations, to criticize them all freely from the treacherous middle of life. Nevertheless, Lawrence's hymns of affirmation are understandable, particularly in their insistence on the sexual. All such affirmations are not, as for the Greeks, an expression of aesthetic sensibility. Rather, in modern culture, the emphasis on the sexual, the obsession with the private parts of life, are an implicit criticism of the ugly and deforming thing that our sociability has become.

Lawrence's erotic fiction has the function of critical myth. Narrow subscribers to the rationalist tradition therefore find him a morally subversive writer, for they are inevitably advocates of living on the surface of consciousness, as far away from the religious unconscious as they can get. Lawrence's entire psychology is based upon his critical religious sensibility. Ultimately, his psychology and religion merge. The "pure Unconscious" contrasts sharply to the impure Unconscious, defined by its repressed contents, that Freud proposes. In its purity, the Unconscious is identical with (in Lawrence's further explanatory phrase) the "pristine consciousness," which in turn describes the state of "innocence" which man must seek. Here, in the ultimate term "innocence," the psychological and religious terms in Lawrence's vocabulary become one.

As critical myth, it is the purpose of Lawrence's fiction to permit an experience of the divine to be encountered anew. Outside art, the numinous experience is not ordinarily available to modern men of culture. In this sense, all great art is therapeutic. Myth, and an art which expresses the mythic, permits a second level of experience; this time indirectly, the experience of the divine comes to the reader through the imagination of the writer, and is endowed with the form of his own life and special concerns. For this reason the interest in the personal history of the writer is inextricable from an interest in his fiction; the two dimensions live and die together.

The Freudian therapeutic process parodies the mythic. As a second experience, it is intended to reduce rather than renew the meaning of the first. Lawrence, too, is therapeutic, but with the intention of renewal rather than reduction. Art, as therapy, takes on a certain theurgic quality, exactly the reverse of therapy scientifically intended. Thus, in his theurgic capacity as an artist, Lawrence could write that "a book is a holy thing, and must be made so again." For this reason only, Lawrence's life is part of his art, for it went obviously into the making of his books. Correspondingly, his art reveals the pathos of his life, for the two are as far apart as an interpretation can be from that which is interpreted.

Fiction has taken over the teaching functions of myth in modern culture; that describes its importance. Lawrence's fiction reproduces the activity of myth in many places throughout the works discussed here. In fact, *Fantasia* opens with a critical little "just-so" story about the creation of our world as the opposite of the beautiful world that once was. Where seas are, there was land; what knowledge was, now is "ritual, gesture, and myth-story." The entire Laurentian art has the prophetic intention of recalling us to this "half-forgotten" knowledge, buried as emotion in the unconscious.

Lawrence would not have approved the odor of sanctity that now surrounds art work. Yet that odor is as inevitable as the odor of churches. The cultured of this era strive to relate themselves to art as a way of recapturing the experience of the divine in which otherwise they no longer believe and cannot feel participant in, even indirectly. Through the mediation of a writer, painter, composer, movie director, the work of art is experienced as a thing in itself, bracketed and raised above the ordinary workaday world, yet related to that world as revelation is related to that which is revealed—superior and saving. The work of art becomes that *wholly other*, present and yet inviolate, through which the cultivated may escape, for the time of the relation, their self-isolation. Thus, for significant numbers of people in contemporary culture, the aesthetic relation takes on religious import. To some it may become even more important than directly human contacts, as somehow superior to such contacts because of the relative frequency with which passional communions occur in confronting the surrogates of life in art. There is certainly a parallel between the neurotic and the artistic process: surrogates in each case may become more satisfying than the real thing.

That such passion may actually be reserved for relating to works of art is even more likely to occur among its producers than among its consumers. A painter may now consider it more important to paint a fine picture than to raise a fine family. With his sense of "vocation," the artist himself becomes the exemplary individualist, justified in his self-isolation, by a culture aware of the decline of vocations into jobs. But even an art that preaches life, as Lawrence's did, may perversely sacrifice life to art. For when art becomes invested with religious meaning, it may become the vehicle of nothing other than its own continuance. In art, the producer of it may secure for himself the communion missing from his lived life. Although a mere consumer undergoes a milder therapy through his relation to the finished work of art, the cult of the art object in modern society, quite apart from its dynamics of prestige, illustrates just that vicariousness of the erotic which Lawrence opposed.

The scientifically inclined in our culture may suffer an even more corrupting vicariousness: in the deliberate withdrawal of the scientist from his object, and his pretense of non-involvement with it. Such pretenses of neutrality ease the mind of the scientist in his characteristic relation to an object in nature—which is more sadistic than participative. No alienation of the knower from that which he knows is more systematically encouraged than that of the scientist, engaged as he is mainly in coaxing out the transformative use value of the object under study.

Lawrence, for his own part, detested the scientist precisely for his transformative function. Nor did he value the role of the artist as myth-mediator much more highly. Yet, despite his pro-grammatic statements urging everyone to his own numinous experience of continuity with the *other*, Lawrence has become a major myth-mediator in our time. The continuing excitement about his work and life measures the emotional investment this culture has made in the invisible church of literary men.

Coming our from behind the fictional arts to speak directly for himself in these polemics, Lawrence argues vigorously for each man steering toward his own sort of collision with the power of emotions; this Lawrence considers the very core of religious experience—an experience of self. It is this ruthless driving inward, toward the hidden self, rather than outward, toward society, that characterizes at once the motif of Lawrence's fiction and the motif of Freud's psychotherapy. Both, in very different ways and for opposing purposes, encourage as well as express the dominant inward movement of our time.

With all the heated polemic, Lawrence did not exaggerate the difference between his own and the psychoanalytic encounter with instinct. In the therapeutic situation, psychological man apparently achieves a variety of that encounter of conflict in wills that the religious man must always have experienced. But the Freudian contact with the Unconscious is in effect a homeopathy of religious experience, an effort to eliminate it by paralleling and subjecting it to the closest intellectual scrutiny and review at decisive stages of its development. As an experience of self-encounter, the therapy is bracketed and controlled; in the transference, the sources of erotic feeling are made transparent. Held up to the intellectual light, every motive, including the intellectual one, is seen through and thus put in question. To Lawrence, such approaches intellectualize the genuinely erotic out of life, thus destroying the possibility of achieving innocence. So, in fact, Freud intended. Lawrence is right to pose his own religiosity against Freud's scientific approach to the Unconscious. In the psychoanalytic situation, Freud guides a therapeutic collision between Reason and that force which religious men have long recognized and agreed to call divine: force in its definitively irrational form, love.

During the shaping period of western culture, it was in the Christian way that the encounter with love was critically represented. Augustine's *Confessions* explain the encounter as it occurred in one man; but they explain, at the same time, how the Christian myth did for so long stabilize the encounter, not as art, but as theology. Truly the greatest expressant of the religious experience as it was felt in the Christian era, Augustine fully recognized the erotic drive, which comes upward from below

into every aspect of ordinary life at the superficies of consciousness. In the Christian myth of encounter, as exemplified in the
personal experience of Augustine, the violence of erotic feeling
is pierced by the counter-eroticism of God, which descends from
above to below and assumes the aspect of authority, through
the "Word" or "Reason" or "Logos" incarnate in one man. Just
this rationalizing element in the Christian erotic myth Lawrence
rejected. The Logos, the commanding order of the universe, was
for him neither the first word nor the last. Love cannot be identified with reason; this is precisely the "mental consciousness"
which Christianity criticizes in the myth of the fall of man from
innocence to knowledge. The new Eve of Science, linked ances-
trally with rationalist theology, continues to recapitulate the
myth of the first fall in such efforts as Freud's to link erotic
experience with a technique of knowing.

In the writing of Lawrence, love is made both to permit and
to heal the separation between subject and object which he
considers the original sin of "mental consciousness" through
which all men daily recapitulate the first fall, led on to more
and more self-destructive knowledge by science. When, through
erotic experience, we repair the damage done by abstract
thought, we are in fact loving the divine substance in things.
Lawrence's mystical intuitions are, as I have said, post-Christian.
In the Christian myth, loving oneself derives from experiencing
the fact that one is loved by God. But, in the Laurentian version,
God having died, nothing remains except self-love. Coming thus
at the very end of the personalistic tradition—as one finds it
variously expressed in the Song of Solomon, in Augustine, in
the doctrine of Luther—Lawrence deliberately played on the
Christian mythology. He is caught in his time, a Trinitarian who
understood that the first two Persons had gone the way of all
myth figures and that only the third, the Holy Ghost, had some
chance of survival.

Lawrence's harping on the Holy Ghost is no cheaply-bought
reasonance of the religious motif essential to the doctrine informing his art. After all, trinitarian Christianity is responsible for
our present inclination to attribute an aura of divinity to the

person as such—an inclination which derives from the original attribution of personality to God. The Hebrew God was a distinct person: in the Christian myth, that person became more complicated, in order to express a growing awareness of the complexity of love, which could no longer be understood merely under the rubric of Law. Thus, in Augustine, the three persons of the Trinity—Father, Son and Holy Ghost—become analogous to the three parts of love. The Father is the original Him who loves; the Son originally Him who is loved, as God-man, and therefore (as Jung rightly says) an archetype of the Self; finally, the Holy Ghost is the power of love in that Self. In another place, Augustine analogizes the Trinity to memory, intelligence and will. All that remains alive in this myth is the third person, will, upon which is founded both the Freudian science and the Laurentian art. Freed from theological encumbrance, will—the third person, Holy Ghost, power of love—survives as the object of Freud's analysis and Lawrence's advocacy. But as Freud knew and Lawrence did not, behind the Holy Ghost is the figure of the Mother, the original third person of the Trinity, now returning to psychological power. In the age-old struggle between Father and Son, Lawrence, through his art, enacted the role of the rebel son and sided with the figure of the Mother, as Christianity did in its struggle against the patriarchal faith that is Israel. Having abandoned that patriarchal faith, yet feeling the gravity of his loss, Freud became a conservative of culture in the name of science rather than faith, reconciling father and son at the expense of the mother. On the other hand, like every true revolutionary, Lawrence, in his avowed anti-Christianity, himself expresses a powerful unconscious motif in the very tradition against which he reacted. In Lawrence's art, as in the Christian unconscious, the Holy Ghost is specifically the sexual agency, which traces back, as Ernest Jones brilliantly said, to the "fantastic 'woman with the penis,' the primal Mother."[*] It is to this primal Mother that both of Lawrence's books on the Unconscious are

[*] Yet the Holy Ghost is male, a change of sex which psychoanalysis has explained as at once an accommodation to the Hebraic maleness of the Christian god-term and a symbolic resolution of the Oedipus complex.

really devoted. And by reason of this devotion, Lawrence is called sex-mad by those who unconsciously worship gods rather than goddesses. Yet Lawrence is himself not an unqualified worshipper of the mother-goddess, in her disguise as the Holy Ghost, which Freud insisted on further depersonalizing as Libido. There is an ambivalence in Lawrence's art that almost shatters it, for although Lawrence is self-converted to the underlying feminism of the tradition of the Holy Ghost he is nevertheless unwilling to accept the homosexual consequences of that conversion when it occurs outside the Christian symbolic frame. In his ambivalent advocacy of the returning feminine, Lawrence found in Freud an ideal enemy: for, far from advocating the sexual anti-culture for which Lawrence stands, Freud set out to devise explicitly masculine (read "rational") means for its control.

Freud possessed a coherent and conservative imagination, the one conservative genius of modern culture, defending only what can possibly be defended. Lawrence's was an incoherent and revolutionary imagination—incoherent because revolutionary. In our own immediate time, the incoherence of the revolutionary imagination, as we find it exhibited in art and poetry, is a consequence of the decline of the necessary and permitting condition out of which revolutionary imaginations can develop: the vitality of tradition. The continuity between tradition and revolution having been shattered, the revolutionary imagination has been distorted. Because we really have no churches, we can have no reformations.

What ties the Lawrence of this volume close to an ancient reforming tradition is his belief that the decisive function in man is will, desire—not intellect. Here, in his polemic against Freud, Lawrence reproduces the great struggle in Western culture between voluntarism and intellectualism. Lawrence, the voluntarist, trusts will; Freud, the intellectualist, trusts reason. To Lawrence, therefore, Freud is the great enemy spokesman, engaged to the analysis but not the advocacy of the Unconscious.

REFERENCES

1. Wyndham Lewis, *Paleface* (London, 1929).
2. William B. Carpenter, *Principles of Mental Physiology*, 4th ed. (London, 1876). See, in particular, Part II, pp. 515-543, Chap. XIII, "Of Unconscious Cerebration"; see also his discussion of the "myth-making tendency in dreams," p. 584, *et seq.*
3. See Freud's analysis, in the form of a case history, of Judge Schreber's *Memoirs*, in "Psychoanalytic Notes on an Autobiographical Account of a Case of Paranoia," in the Standard Edition of the Complete *Works* (London, 1958), Vol. XII, pp. 12-82.
4. See Sigmund Freud, *Civilization and Its Discontents* (London, 1939), pp. 7-9.
5. See *Phoenix, The Posthumorous Papers* (New York, 1936), pp. 720-23, *et passim*, in which Lawrence states explicitly through the course of his essay, "The Proper Study," that the proper study of man can only be conducted through a study of man's search for God.
6. Cf. *Phoenix, op. cit.*, p. 727: "How Shall Man *find* God? That's the real problem."
7. See "A Psychoanalytic Study of the Holy Ghost," in Ernest Jones's *Essays in Applied Psychoanalysis* (London: 1923), pp. 415-430.

15. *Myth and Identity*

JEROME S. BRUNER

WE KNOW NOW a new origin of the faint hissing of the sea in the conch shell held to the ear. It is in part the tremor and throb of the hand, resonating in the shell's chambers. Yet, inescapably, it is the distant sea. For Yeats, it would have been a reaffirmation of his proper query:

> O body swayed to music, O brightening glance,
> How can we know the dancer from the dance?

And so with myth. It is at once an external reality and the resonance of the internal vicissitudes of man. Richard Chase's somewhat cumbersome definition will at least get us on our way: "Myth is an esthetic device for bringing the imaginary but powerful world of preternatural forces into a manageable collaboration with the objective [i.e., experienced] facts of life in such a way as to excite a sense of reality amenable to both the unconscious passions and the conscious mind."

That myth has such a function—to effect some manner of harmony between the literalities of experience and the night impulses of life—few would deny any longer. Yet I would urge that we not be too easily tempted into thinking that there is an oppositional contrast between *logos* and *mythos,* the grammar of experience and the grammar of myth. For each complements the other, and it is in the light of this complementarity that I wish to examine the relation of myth and personality.

Consider the myth first as a projection, to use the conventional psychoanalytic term. I would prefer the term "externalization," for I do not refer solely to the tendency to project outward simulacra only of those impulses that we cannot accept in ourselves. We might begin, rather, with the human preference to cope with events that are outside rather than those that are inside. Freud long ago remarked on this preference, noting that in so far as we were able to do so, we converted inner stimuli into seemingly outer events as if better to protect ourselves. So it is in the dream, where impulse is transduced into image and symbol, where an internal plight is converted into a story plot. So, too, even in rather simple forms of motor learning, where, after mastery, a pattern of muscular movements is rendered into a visualized image of a path of movement. And when we are painting a picture or writing a poem or constructing a scientific theory, there comes a moment when "it," the product we are producing, takes over and develops an autonomy of its own, an external existence. It is now the theory that requires the revision, not the theorist, the picture that needs this line here, and not the painter's whim.

What is the significance of this externalizing tendency? It is twofold, I would urge. It provides, in the first instance, a basis for communion between men. What is "out there" can be named and shared in a manner beyond the sharing of subjectivity. By the subjectifying of our worlds through externalization, we are able, paradoxically enough, to share communally in the nature of internal experience. By externalizing cause and effect, for example, we may construct a common matrix of determinism. Fate, the full of the moon, the aether—these and not our unique fears are what join us in common reaction. But perhaps more important still, externalization makes possible the containment of terror and impulse by the decorum of art and symbolism. Given man's search for art forms, it must surely be no accident that there is no art of internal feeling or impulse. We seem unable to impose what Freud once called the artifice of formal beauty upon our internal sensations or even upon our stream

of seemingly uncontrolled fantasy. It is in the act of fashioning
an external product out of our internal impulses that the work
of art begins. There is no art of kinesthesis, and for all Huxley's
fantasies, there will not be an art of the "feelies." Sharing, then,
and the containment of impulse in beauty—these are the possibilities offered by externalization.

Let me illustrate my point by reference to Homer, particularly
to the madness of Ajax in the *Iliad*. Recall the occasion of the
death of Achilles and the determination of Thetis that the bravest
man before Ilium shall have her slain son's arms. Agamemnon
must make the fateful decision, and it is Odysseus and not Ajax
who receives the gift of Hephæstus-forged armor. Ajax is lashed
by human anger and a craving for vengeance in a proportion to
match his heroic capacities. But before these impulses can be
expressed, there is an intervention by Athene: Ajax is struck mad
and slaughters the captive Trojan livestock, cursing Agamemnon,
Odysseus, and Menelaus the while, in a manner that would be
described today as a massive displacement of aggression. It is
Athene, then, who saves Ajax from a more direct expression of
his fury and saves the Greeks from a slaughter of their leaders.
Again the ingenious and rational intervention of the gods, a
formal working out of internal plight in a tightly woven and
dramatic plot. It is much as Professor Dodds has suggested in
examining the containment of irrationality in Greek myth. The
clouding and bewildering of judgment that is *ate*, or the seemingly unnatural access of courage that is *menos*—both of these
sources of potential disruption of natural order are attributed to
an external agency, to a supernatural intervention, whether of
the gods or of the Erinyes.

I suggest that in general the inward monition, or the sudden unaccountable feeling of power, or the sudden unaccountable loss of
judgment, is the germ out of which the divine machinery developed.
One result of transposing the event from the interior to the external
world is that the vagueness is eliminated: the indeterminate daemon
has to be made concrete as some particular personal god.[1]

These were the gods that the Greeks shared, by virtue of whom a sense of causation became communal, through the nurturing of whom an art form emerged. The alternative, as Philip Rahv comments in discussing the governess in *The Turn of the Screw* and the chief protagonist in *The Beast in the Jungle*, is to give up one's allotment of experience. If one cannot externalize the daemon where it can be enmeshed in the texture of aesthetic experience, then the last resort is to freeze and block: the over-repression and denial treated so perceptively by Freud in *The Problem of Anxiety*.

What is the art form of the myth? Principally it is drama, yet for all its concern with preternatural forces and characters, it is realistic drama that in the phrase of Wellek and Warren tells of "origins and destinies." As they put it, it comprises "the explanations a society offers its young of why the world is and why we do as we do, its pedagogic images of the nature and destiny of man."[2] Ernst Cassirer senses a proper antinomy when he notes that the myth somehow emphasizes the physiognomic character of experience while at the same time it has the property of compelling belief. Its power is that it lives on the feather line between fantasy and reality. It must be neither too good nor too bad to be true, nor must it be too true. And if it is the case that art as a mode of knowing has precisely the function of connecting through metaphor what before had no apparent kinship, then in the present case the art form of the myth connects the daemonic world of impulse with the world of reason by a verisimilitude that conforms to each.

But there is a paradox. For on the one side we speak of myth as an externalization, on the other we speak of it as a pedogogical image. This is surely a strange source of instruction! But it is precisely here that the dramatic form of the myth becomes significant, precisely here where Gilbert Murray was so perceptive of the genius of Homer and of the Greeks: "This power of entering vividly into the feelings of both parties in a conflict is . . . the characteristic gift."[3]

Let me revert for a moment to a consideration of the human

personality, to the nature of the vicissitudes that are externalized in myth. It is no longer novel to speak of personality as a cast of characters, although in the last decades we have oversimplified the drama they enact in the summary image of Freud's morality play of the ego, superego, and id. In his telling essay on "The Poet and the Daydream," Freud recognizes the potential complexity of the internal cast when he speaks of the art of the playwright as one of decomposing this cast into the dramatis personae of the staged drama. It is far from clear why our discordant impulses are bound and structured in a set of identities —why one pattern of impulse is the self-pitying little man in us, another the nurturing protector, another the voice of moral indignation. Surely it is something more than the sum of identifications we have undertaken in the course of achieving balances between love and independence, coming to terms with those who have touched our lives. Here myth becomes the tutor, the shaper of identities; it is here that personality imitates myth in as deep a sense as myth is an externalization of the vicissitudes of personality.

Joseph Campbell, in his *The Hero with a Thousand Faces*, writes:[4]

In his life-form the individual is necessarily only a fraction and distortion of the total image of man. He is limited either as male or as female; at any given period of his life he is again limited as child, youth, mature adult, or ancient; furthermore, in his life role he is necessarily specialized as craftsman, tradesman, servant, or thief, priest, leader, wife, nun, or harlot; he cannot be all. Hence the totality—the fullness of man—is not in the separate member, but in the body of the society as a whole; the individual can be only an organ.

But if no man is all, there is at least in what Campbell calls the "mythologically instructed community" a corpus of images and identities and models that provides the pattern to which growth may aspire—a range of metaphoric identities. We are accustomed to speaking of myth in this programmatic sense in reference to history, as when Sorel invokes the general strike of all workers as a dynamizing image, or when Christians speak of the Second Coming for which men must prepare themselves. In the same sense one may speak of the corpus of myth as providing a set of possible programmatic identities for the individual personality. It would perhaps be more appropriate to say that the mythologically instructed community provides its members with a library of scripts upon which the individual may judge the internal drama of his multiple identities. For myth, as I shall now try to illustrate, serves not only as a pattern to which one aspires, but also as a criterion for the self-critic.

Let me use as an example the myths that embody and personify man's capacity for happiness. They are not infinite in variety, but varied enough. An early version is the Greek conception of the Five Ages of Man, the first of which is the happy Age of Gold. In Robert Graves's transliteration:[5] "These men were the so-called golden race, subjects of Cronus, who lived without cares or labor, eating only acorns, wild fruit, and honey that dripped from the trees . . . never growing old, dancing, and laughing much; death to them was no more terrible than sleep. They are all gone now, but their spirits survive as happy genii." This is the myth of happiness as innocence, and in the Christian tradition we know it as Man before the Fall. Innocence ends either by a successful attempt to steal the knowledge of God or by aspiring to the cognitive power of the gods, *hubris*. And with the end of innocence, there is an end to happiness. Knowledge is equated with temptation to evil. The issue appears to revolve around the acquisition and uses of knowledge.

Let me oversimplify in the interest of brevity and say that from these early myths there emerge two types of mythic plot: the plot of innocence and the plot of cleverness—the former being a kind of Arcadian ideal, requiring the eschewal of complexity and awareness, the latter requiring the cultivation of competence almost to the point of guile. The happy childhood, the good man as the child of God, the simple plowman, the Rousseauian ideal of natural nobility—these are the creatures of the plot of innocence. At the other extreme there are Penelope, the suitors, and Odysseus. In Gilbert Murray's words:[6]

Penelope—she has just learned on good evidence that Odysseus is alive and will return immediately—suddenly determines that she cannot put off the suitors any longer, but brings down her husband's bow, and says she will forthwith marry the man who can shoot through twelve axeheads with it! Odysseus hears her and is pleased! May it not be that in the original story there was a reason for Penelope to bring the bow, and for Odysseus to be pleased? It was a plot. He [Odysseus] meant Eurycleia [the old maidservant] to recognize him [by his scar], to send the maids away, and break the news to Penelope. Then husband and wife together arranged the trial of the bow.

Again and again in the Greek myths there are cleverness, competence and artifice—Herakles, Achilles, Odysseus, Perseus— wherever you may look. It is the happy triumph of clever competence with a supernatural assist. And yet there is also the ideal of the Age of Innocence. So too in the later Christian tradition and in our own times. The manner in which superior knowledge shows itself changes: the ideal of the crafty warrior, the wise man, the interpreter of the word of God, the Renaissance omnicompetent, the wily merchant, the financial wizard, the political genius. If it is true that in some way each is suspect, it is also true that each is idealized in his own way. Each is presented as satisfied. New versions arise to reflect the ritual and practice of each era—the modifications of the happiness of innocence and the satisfaction of competence.

I would like to submit that the manner in which man has striven for competence and longed for innocence has reflected the controlling myths of the community. The medieval scholar, the Florentine prince, the guild craftsman alike, as well as the withdrawn monastic of Thomas à Kempis and the mendicant of St. Francis—all of these are deeply involved with the myths of innocence and competence, and are formed by them. Indeed, the uncertainty in resolving the dichotomy of reason and revelation as ways to a knowledge of God reflects the duality of the myth of happiness and salvation. It is not simply society that patterns itself on the idealizing myths, but unconsciously it is the individual man as well who is able to structure his internal clamor of identities in terms of prevailing myth. Life then produces myth and finally imitates it.

In our own time, in the American culture, there is a deep problem generated by the confusion that has befallen the myth of the happy man. It reflects itself in the American personality. There still lingers the innocent Christian conception that happiness is the natural state of man—or at least of the child and of man as innocent—and that it is something that we have done or failed to do as individuals that creates a rather Protestantized and private unhappiness. The impact of Freud has begun to destroy this myth, to replace it. Our popular films may now, with artistry, depict the child as murderer. A generation of playwrights have destroyed the remnant of Horatio Alger, replacing it with the image of Arthur Miller's salesman dying by entropy, an object of compassion. We are no longer, in Professor Campbell's words, "a mythologically instructed community." And so one finds a new generation struggling to find or to create a satisfactory and challenging mythic image as aspiration.

Two such images seem to be emerging in the new generation. One is the myth of the "hipsters" and the "squares." The other is the myth of creative wholeness. The first is the myth of the wandering hero as uncommitted, as capable of the hour's subjectivity—its "kicks"—sharing in a new inwardness. It is the theme of reduction to the essentially personal, the hero capable of filtering out the clamors of an outside world, an almost masturbatory ideal. Eugene Burdick in a recent issue of *The Reporter* (3 April 1958) gives the following account of a conversation in a San Francisco café between two practitioners of the cult of the Beat Generation:

"Man, I remember something when I was little, a boy," somebody named Lee says. He is hunched forward, his elbows on the table, a tumbler of wine between his hands. "About a dog. Little miserable dog of mine."

"Yeah, man, go on," Mike says, his eyes lighting up.

"I get up real early to do my paper route. Los Angeles *Examiner*," Lee says. "Streets always empty, just a few milk trucks and bakery trucks and other kids like me. My dog goes along, see? Every day he trots along with me. Little mongrel dog."

"Yeah, yeah, go on, man," Mike says, impatient for the story, sure that it has meaning.

"There we are in all those big empty streets. Just me and the dog. Sun coming up, papers falling on the porches, me dreaming and walking and the dog trotting," Lee says. "Then far away, about as big as a black mosquito, I see this hopped-up Model A. Wonderful pipes on it, blatting so sweet I could hear them for six blocks. I stand there on the curb, listening to that sweet sound and watching that car come weaving down that empty street. And the dog stands in the gutter, watching too. That Model A gets bigger and I can see the chrome pipes on the side, the twin Strombergs sucking air, just eating up the asphalt."

He pauses and Mike leans forward and says urgently, "Now, man, come on, go. I wanna hear this."

"This Model A is a roadster and there is a Mexican driving and his girl with him," Lee says slowly, stalking the climax. "It weaves across the street, and me and the dog stare at it. And it comes for us in a big slow curve and hit that dog. His back broke in mid-air and he was dead when he hit the street again. Like a big man cracking a seed in his teeth . . . same sound, I mean. And the girl stares back at me and laughs. And I laugh. You see why, man?"

The two of them sit quietly, looking down at the wine and listening to the jazz. Mike glances once at Lee and then back at his glass. He has learned something secret and private about Lee, and that is good enough. After a while they sit back, smiling, and listen to the jazz.

It is not easy to create a myth and to emulate it at the same time. James Dean and Kerouac, Kingsley Amis and John Osborne, the Teddy Boys and the hipsters: they do not make a mythological community. They represent mythmaking in process as surely as Hemingway's characters did in their time, Scott Fitzgerald's in theirs. What is ultimately clear is that even the attempted myth must be a model for imitating, a programmatic drama to be tried on for fit. One sees the identities of a group of young men being "packaged" in terms of the unbaked myth. It is a mold, a prescription of characters, a plot. Whether the myth will be viable, whether it will fit the internal plight, we do not know. There are temporary myths too. There was a myth of the supernatural birth of a dead woman's son, a myth Boas found in 1888 and again in 1900. By 1931 there was no trace of it.

What of the renewal of the myth of the full, creative man? It is even more inchoate than the first, yet perhaps more important. It is, for example, the young middle-aged executive sent back to the university by the company for a year, wanting humanities and not sales engineering; it is this man telling you that he would rather take life classes Saturday morning at the Museum School than be president of the company; it is the adjectival extravaganza of the word "creative," as in creative advertising, creative engineering, creative writing. It is as if, given the demise of the myths of creation and their replacement by a scientific cosmogony that for all its formal beauty lacks metaphoric force, the theme of creating becomes internalized, creating anguish rather than, as in the externalized myths, providing a basis for psychic relief and sharing. Yet, this self-contained image of creativity becomes, I think, the basis for a myth of happiness. But perhaps between the death of one myth and the birth of its replacement there must be a reinternalization, even to the point of a *culte de moi*. That we cannot yet know. All that is certain is that we live in a period of mythic confusion that may provide the occasion for a new growth of myth, myth more suitable for our times.

Indeed, one may ask whether the rise of the novel as an art form, and particularly the subjectification of the novel since the middle of the nineteenth century, whether these do not symbolize the voyage into the interior that comes with the failure of prevailing myths to provide external models toward which one may aspire. For when the prevailing myths fail to fit the varieties of man's plight, frustration expresses itself first in mythoclasm and then in the lonely search for internal identity. The novels of Conrad, of Hardy, of Gide, of Camus—paradoxically enough, they provide man with guides for the internal search. One of Graham Greene's most tormented books, an autobiographical fragment on an African voyage, is entitled *Journey Without Maps*. Perhaps the modern novel, in contrast to the myth, is the response to the internal anguish that can find no external constraint in the form of myth, a form of internal map. But this is a matter requiring a closer scrutiny than we can give it here. Suffice it to say that the alternative to externalization in myth appears to be the internalization of the personal novel, the first a communal effort, the second the lone search for identity.

Let me conclude by reiterating the general line of my thesis. It is simple enough. The first premise is that the externalization of inner impulse in the form of myth provides the basis for a sharing of inner experience and makes possible the work of art that has as its objective to contain and cleanse the terror from impulse. The myth as a work of art has as its principal form the shape of drama. So too the human personality: its patternings of impulse express themselves as identities in an internal drama. The myths that are the treasure of an instructed community provide the models and the programs in terms of which the growth of the internal cast of identities is molded and enspirited. And finally, when the myths no longer fit the internal plights of those who require them, the transition to newly created myths may take the form of a chaotic voyage into the interior, the certitudes of externalization replaced by the anguish of the internal voyage.

REFERENCES

1. E. R. Dodds, *The Greeks and the Irrational* (Boston: The Beacon Press, 1957), pp. 14-15.
2. René Wellek and Austin Warren, *Theory of Literature* (New York: Harcourt, Brace & Co., 1942), p. 180.
3. Gilbert Murray, *The Literature of Ancient Greece* (Chicago: University of Chicago Press, Phoenix edition, 1957), p. 43.
4. Joseph Campbell, *The Hero with a Thousand Faces* (New York: Meridian Books, Inc., 1956), pp. 382-383.
5. Reprinted from *The Greek Myths,* by Robert Graves. Published by Penguin Books Inc., 3300 Clipper Mill Road, Baltimore 11, Maryland.
6. Murray, *op. cit.*, pp. 39-40.

16. Myth and Mass Media

MARSHALL McLUHAN

WHEN AN ATTEMPT is made to bring the relatively articulated concept of "myth" into the area of "media"—a concept to which surprisingly little attention has been given in the past—it is necessary to reconsider both "myth" and "media" in order to get at relevant data. For example, English is itself a mass medium, as is any language employed by any society. But the general use of the phrase "mass media" would seem to record an unfavorable valuation of new media, especially since the advent of the telegraph, the telephone, moving pictures, radio, and television. These media have had the same kind of drastic effect on language and culture that print had in Europe in the sixteenth century, or that it is now having in other parts of the world.

It might even be well to avoid so highly charged a phrase as "mass media" until a little more thought can be given to the problem. Languages as human artifacts, collective products of human skill and need, can easily be regarded as "mass media," but many find it difficult to consider the newer media deriving from these languages as new "languages." Writing, in its several modes, can be regarded technologically as the development of new languages. For to translate the audible into the visible by phonetic means is to institute a dynamic process that reshapes every aspect of thought, language, and society. To record the extended operation of such a process in a Gorgon or Cadmus myth is to reduce a complex historical affair to an inclusive time-less image. Can we, perhaps, say that in the case of a single word, myth is present as a single snapshot of a complex process, and that in the case of a narrative myth with its peripety, a complex process is recorded in a single inclusive image? The multilayered montage or "transparency," with its abridgement of logical relationships, is as familiar in the cave painting as in cubism.

Oral cultures are simultaneous in their modes of awareness. Today we come to the oral condition again via the electronic media, which abridge space and time and single-plane relationships, returning us to the confrontation of multiple relationships at the same moment.

If a language contrived and used by many people is a mass medium, any one of our new media is in a sense a new language, a new codification of experience collectively achieved by new work habits and inclusive collective awareness. But when such a new codification has reached the technological stage of communicability and repeatability, has it not, like a spoken tongue, also become a macromyth? How much compression of the elements of a process must occur before one can say that they are certainly in mythic form? Are we inclined to insist that myth be a reduction of collective experience to a visual and classifiable form?

Languages old and new, as macromyths, have that relation to words and word-making that characterizes the fullest scope of myth. The collective skills and experience that constitute both spoken languages and such new languages as movies or radio can also be considered with preliterate myths as static models of the universe. But do they not tend, like languages in general, to be dynamic models of the universe in action? As such, languages old and new would seem to be for participation rather than for contemplation or for reference and classification.

Another way of getting at this aspect of languages as macromyths is to say that the medium is the message. Only incidentally, as it were, is such a medium a specialized means of signifying or of reference. And in the long run, for such media or macromyths as the phonetic alphabet, printing, photography, the movie, the telegraph, the telephone, radio, and television, the social action of these forms is also, in the fullest sense, their message or meaning. A language is, on the one hand, little affected by the use individuals make of it; but, on the other hand, it almost entirely patterns the character of what is thought, felt, or said by those using it. And it can be utterly changed by the intrusion of another language, as speech was changed by writing, and radio by television.

Is, then, what concerns us as "myth" today a photograph or "still" shot of a macromyth in action? As a word uttered is an auditory arrest of mental motion, and the phonetic translation of that sound into visual equivalence is a frozen image of the same, is not myth a means of static abstraction from live process? A kind of mythmaking process is often associated with Hollywood and with Madison Avenue advertising agencies. So far as advertisements are concerned, they do, in intention at least, strive to comprise in a single image the total social action or process that is imagined as desirable. That is, an advertisement tries both to inform us about, and also to produce in us by anticipation, all the stages of a metamorphosis, private and social. So that whereas a myth might appear as the record of such extended metamorphosis, an advertisement proceeds by anticipation of change, simultaneously anticipating causes with effects and effects with causes. In myth this fusion and telescoping of phases of process becomes a kind of explanation or mode of intelligibility.

What are the myths by which men have recorded the action of new media on their lives? Is there significance in the fact that the Oedipus myth has so far not been found among the preliterate? Is the action of literacy in the shaping of individualism and nationalism also severe on kinship structures? Is the Gorgon myth an account of the effects of literacy in arresting the modes of knowledge? Certainly the Cadmus myth about letters as the dragon's teeth that sprang up armed men is an image of the dynamics of literacy in creating empires. H. A. Innis in his *Empire and Communications* has given us a full exegesis of the

Cadmus myth. But the Gorgon myth is in much greater need of exegesis, since it concerns the role of media in learning and knowing. Today, when by means of a computer it is easy to translate a mere blueprint of an unbuilt plane into a wind-tunnel test flight, we find it natural to take all flat data into the domain of depth interpretation. Electronic culture accepts the simultaneous as a reconquest of auditory space. Since the ear picks up sound from all directions at once, thus creating a spherical field of experience, it is natural that electronically moved information should also assume this spherelike pattern. Since the telegraph, then, the forms of Western culture have been strongly shaped by the spherelike pattern that belongs to a field of awareness in which all the elements are practically simultaneous.

It is this instantaneous character of the information field today, inseparable from electronic media, that confers the formal auditory character on the new culture. That is to say, for example, that the newspaper page, since the introduction of the telegraph, has had a formally auditory character and only incidentally a lineal, literary form. Each item makes its own world, unrelated to any other item save by date line. And the assembly of items constitutes a kind of global image in which there is much overlay and montage but little pictorial space or perspective. For electronically moved information, in being simultaneous, assumes the total-field pattern, as in auditory space. And preliterate societies likewise live largely in the auditory or simultaneous mode with an inclusiveness of awareness that increasingly characterizes our electronic age. The traumatic shock of moving from the segmental, lineal space of literacy into the auditory, unified field of electronic information is quite unlike the reverse process. But today, while we are resuming so many of the preliterate modes of awareness, we can at the same time watch many preliterate cultures beginning their tour through the cultural phases of literacy.

The phonetic alphabet, which permits the translation of the audible into the visible, does so by suppression of meaning in the sounds of the letters. This very abstract technology has made

possible a continuous one-way conquest of cultures by the
Western world that is far from finished. But it would seem that
with the commercial use of the telegraph during more than a
century we have become accessible to Eastern art and technology
as well as to preliterate and auditory cultures in general. At
least, let us be prepared to consider carefully the formally auditory character in the telegraph and in subsequent electronic
forms of codifying information. For the formal causes inherent
in such media operate on the matter of our senses. The effect of
media, like their "message," is really in their form and not in
their content. And their formal effect is always subliminal so far
as our ideas and concepts are concerned.

It is easy to trace some of the effects of phonetic writing since
they are coextensive with the most familiar features of the
Western world.

The phonetically written word, itself an abstract image of a
spoken word, permits the prolonged analysis of process but does
not greatly encourage the application of knowledge to action
beyond the verbal sphere. It is not strange, therefore, that the
ancient world should have considered applied knowledge under
the mode of rhetoric. For writing made it possible to card-
catalogue all the individual postures of mind called the "figures"
of rhetoric. And these became available to all students as direct
means of control over other minds. The oligarthic reign of these
figures was swiftly liquidated by printing, a technique that
shifted attention from the audience to the mental state of the
individual reader.

Writing has given the means of segmenting many phases of
knowing and doing. Applied knowledge by the lineal segmenta-
tion of outward motion comes with print, which is itself the first
mechanization of an ancient handicraft. And whereas writing had
fostered the classification of the arts and sciences in depth, print
gave access to the arts and sciences at high speed and on one
plane at a time. While manuscript culture required gloss and
commentary to extract the various levels of meaning it held for
the awareness, because of the very slow reading necessary, print

is itself commentary or explanation. The form of print is single-leveled. And the print-reader is greatly disposed to feel that he is sharing the movements of another mind. Print drove people like Montaigne to explore the medium as a new art form providing an elaborate means of self-investigation in the act of learning as well as self-portraiture and self-expression.

By contrast, today we live in a postliterate and electronic world, in which we seek images of collective postures of mind, even when studying the individual. In some respects, myth was the means of access to such collective postures in the past. But our new technology gives us many new means of access to group-dynamic patterns. Behind us are five centuries during which we have had unexampled access to aspects of private consciousness by means of the printed page. But now anthropology and archæology give us equal ease of access to group postures and patterns of many cultures, including our own.

Electronic tape permits access to the structure and group dynamics of entire languages. My suggestion that we might regard languages on one hand as mass media and on the other hand as macromyths seems obvious to the point of triteness to the structural linguists to whom I have mentioned these approaches. But it may be useful to point to some of the many nonverbal postures, both individual and public, that accompany changes in the media. That is to say, a new form is usually a cluster of items. For example, in the very first decades of printing at the end of the fifteenth century, people became vividly aware of the camera obscura. The relation of this interest to the new printing process was not noted at the time. Yet printing is itself just such a camera obscura, yielding a private vision of the movements of others. While sitting in the dark, one has in the camera obscura a cinematic presentation of the outside world. And in reading print, the reader acts as a kind of projector of the still shots or printed words, which he can read fast enough to have the feeling of re-creating the movements of another mind. Manuscripts could not be read at a speed sufficient to create the sense of a mind actively engaged in learning and in self-expression. But here, centuries before the movie, is the ultimate magic and myth of the movie in the camera obscura. Perhaps as the camera obscura was the first, the movie is the last phase of print technology.

The movie, which has so little in common with television, may be the last image of the Gutenberg era before it fuses via the telegraph, the telephone, radio, and television, and fades into the new world of auditory space. And as the habits of reading print create intense forms of individualism and nationalism, do not our instantaneous electronic media return us to group dynamics, both in theory and in practice? Is not this shift in media the key to our natural concern with the concept and relevance of myth today?

Printing evoked both individualism and nationalism in the sixteenth century, just as it will do again in India, Africa, China, and Russia. For it demands habits of solitary initiative and attention to exactly repeatable commodities, which are the habits inseparable from industry, and enterprise, production and marketing. Where production precedes literacy, there is no uniform market and no price structure. Industrial production without well-established markets and literacy makes "communism" necessary. Such is the state of our own ignorance of our media that we are surprised to find that radio has very different effects in an oral society than it had in our highly literate culture. In the same way the "nationalism" of an oral world is structured quite differently from the nationalism of a newly literate society. It would appear that to see one's mother tongue dignified with the precise technology of print releases a new vision of unity and power, which remains a subliminal devisive force in the West even today. Unawareness of the effects of our media these past two thousand years and more would seem to be itself an effect of literacy that James Joyce designated as "ab-ced" or absent-mindedness.

The sentiment of spatial and territorial nationalism that accompanies literacy is also reinforced by the printing press, which provides not only the sentiment but also the centralized bureaucratic instruments of uniform control over wide territories.

Perhaps we tend to define myth in too literary a way, as something that can be verbalized, narrated, and written down. If we can regard all media as myths and as the prolific source of many subordinate myths, why cannot we spot the mythic aspect of the current hulahoop activity? Here is a myth we are living. Many people have puzzled over the fact that children refuse to roll these hoops on roads or walks. A mere thirty years ago a hoop was for rolling. Today children reject the lineal use of the hoop in an external space. They use it in a nuclear mode as a means of generating their own space. Here, then, is a live model or drama of the mythic power of the new media to alter sensibility. For this change in child behavior has nothing to do with ideas or programs.

Such a changed attitude to spatial form and presence is as definitive as the change from the photographic to the television image. In his *Prints and Visual Communication* (London: Routledge and Kegan Paul, 1953), William M. Ivins explains how the long process of capturing the external world in the "network of rationality," by the engraver's line and by ever more subtle syntax, finally reached conclusion in the photograph. The photograph is a total statement of the external object without syntax. This kind of peripety will strike the student of media as characteristic of all media development. But in television the striking fact is that the image is defined by light *through,* not by light *on.* It is this fact that separates television from photography and movie, relating it profoundly to stained glass. The spatial sense generated by television experience is utterly unlike that of the movie. And, of course, the difference has nothing to do with the "content" or the programming. Here, as ever, the medium itself is the ultimate message. The child gets such messages, when they are new, much sooner than the adult. For the adult instinctively retards awareness that will disturb a cherished order of perception or of past experience; the child would seem to have no such stake in the past, at least when he is facing new experience.

It is my point that new spatial orientation such as occurs in the format of the press after the advent of the telegraph, the swift disappearance of perspective, is also discernible in the new landscapes of Rimbaud in poetry and Cézanne in painting. And in our time Rouault anticipated the mode of the television image by decades. His use of stained glass as a means of defining the image is what I have in mind.

The mythmaking power of a medium that is itself a myth form appears now in the postliterate age as the rejection of the consumer in favor of the producer. The movie now can be seen as the peak of the consumer-oriented society, being in its form the natural means both of providing and of glorifying consumer goods and attitudes. But in the arts of the past century the swing has been away from packaging for the consumer to providing do-it-yourself kits. The spectator or reader must now be cocreator. Our educational establishment naturally lags behind the popular media in this radical change. The young, when exposed to the television image, receive at once a total orientation in spatial matters that makes the lineality of the printed word a remote and alien language. Reading for them will have to be taught as if it were heraldry or some quaint codification of reality. The assumptions about reading and writing that accompanied the monarchy of print and the related rise of industrial forms are no longer valid for, or acceptable to, those being re-formed in their sensibilities in the electronic age. To ask whether this is a good or a bad thing is to express the bias of efficient causality, which is naturally that of the man of the printed word. But it is also a futile gesture of inadequacy to the real situation. The values of the Gutenberg era cannot be salvaged by those who are as unaware of how they came into existence as they are of why they are now in the process of liquidation.

Philosophic agreement is not necessary among those who are agreed that the insistent operation of media-forms on human sensibility and awareness is an observable, intelligible, and controllable situation. Today, when ordinary consciousness is exposed to the patternmaking of several media at once, we are becoming more attentive to the unique properties of each of the media. We can see both that media are mythic "images" and that they have the power of imposing subliminally, as it were, their own assumptions. They can be viewed at the same time as intelligible explanations of great tracts of time and of the experience of many processes, and they can be used as a means of perpetuating such bias and preference as they codify in their structure.

It is not strange that we should long have been obsessed with the literary and "content" aspect of myth and media. The "form" and "content" dichotomy is as native to the abstract, written, and printed forms of codification as is the "producer" and "consumer" dichotomy.

Unfortunately for the direction and control of education, such a literary bias is quite unable to cope with the new "images" of the postliterate age. As a result of our using literary lenses, the relevant new data have escaped our scrutiny. My book, *The Mechanical Bride: Folklore of Industrial Man,* is a case in point. Turning literary guns on the new iconology of the Madison Avenue world is easy. It is easy to reveal mechanism in a postmechanical era. But I failed at that time to see that we had already passed out of the mechanistic age into the electronic, and that it was this fact that made mechanism both obtrusive and repugnant.

One of the great novelties effected by printing was the creation of a new sense of inner and outer space. We refer to it as the discovery of perspective and the rise of representation in the arts. The space of "perspective" conditioned by an artificially fixed stance for the viewer leads to the enclosing of objects in a pictorial space. Yet so revolutionary and abstract was this new space that poets avoided it in their language for two centuries after painters had accepted it. It is a kind of space very uncongenial to the media of speech and of words. One can gain some idea of the psychic pressures exerted by print in the work of William Blake, who sought new strategies of culture to reintegrate the segmented and fractured human spirit. In fact, the explicit mythmaking of Blake is the greatest monument and antidote to the mythic pressures of the printing press, to "single vision and Newton's sleep." For the matrix of movable type contains the totality of industrialism as well as the means of global conquest, which, by peripety, brought the preliterate world once more into the heart of the industrial metropolis.

The prevalent concept that the mass media exert a baneful influence on the human spirit has strange roots. As Marjorie Nicolson has shown in *Newton Demands the Muse,* it was Newton's *Opticks* that taught poets the correspondence between the inner and outer worlds, between the structure of seeing and the structure of the scene. This notion planted in poets the ambition to gain control over the inner life by a calculus of landscape composition. The idea of verbally constituted landscape, as a lever upon the psychic eye of man, was a dichotomy quite congenial to the culture of the printed word. And whereas external landscape has been abandoned for inner landscape since Rimbaud, Madison Avenue clings to the earlier Romantic concept of consumer control by means of externally arranged scenes. The recent flutter about "subliminal" advertising indicates the delayed shift of attention from outer to inner landscape that occurred in many of the arts in the later nineteenth century. And it is this same shift that today focuses attention on myth in all its modes. For myth is always a montage or transparency comprising several external spaces and times in a single image or situation. Such compression or multilayering is an inescapable mode of the electronic and simultaneous movement of information, whether in popular media or esoteric speculation. It is, therefore, an everyday occurrence for academic entertainment to stress "content," while displaying complete illiteracy with regard to media old and new. For we have now to possess many cultural languages for even the most ordinary daily purposes.

The newspaper will serve as an example of the Babel of myths or languages. When information from every quarter arrived at the same time, the paper became a daily snapshot of the globe, and "perspective" in news became meaningless. Editorials could still try to tie some items together into a chain or sequence with a special point of view or vanishing point. But such views were really capsules for passive readers, while, paradoxically, the unprocessed, uninterpreted, raw news offered far more challenge to the reader to find his own meanings. Today it is easy to see how Edgar Allen Poe, both in his symbolist poems and in his detective stories, had anticipated this new mythic dimension of producer orientation by taking the audience into the creative process itself. Likewise, it is easy to see how the spot news of the telegraph press really acts like the yes-no, black-white dots of the wire-photo in creating an inclusive world image. Yet even now the sponsors of pre-electronic media continue to overlay the new myth by injections of earlier myth, creating hybrids of the "horseless carriage" variety in the interests of superior culture.

The same type of confusion exists in education in the concept of "audio-visual aids." It would seem that we must do in education what the poets, painters, and composers have done, namely, to purge our media and test and define their unique powers before attempting Wagnerian concerts. The Gutenberg myth was not a means of modifying the Cadmus myth, any more than the Henry Ford myth modified the horse and buggy. Obliteration occurred, as it will with the movie under the impact of television, unless we choose to restrain the operation of form on form by due study and strategy. We now stand at that point with regard to all myth and media. We can, perhaps we *must*, become the masters of cultural and historical alchemy. And to this end, we can, I suggest, find means in the study of media as languages and languages as myths. For our experience with the grammar and syntax of languages can be made available for the direction and control of media old and new.

17. The Possible Nature of a "Mythology" to Come

HENRY A. MURRAY

A. AIM

THE TITLE of this paper may be taken as evidence of a prejudice in favor of expanding the meaning of the term "mythology" so as to include products of modern imaginations provided these are comparable, in certain essential respects, to mythologies of ancient origin. The title also suggests anticipation of periodic generations and integrations in the future of a multiplicity of variant myths, rather than of the advent of any single myth. But the quotation marks around Mythology are meant to indicate uncertainty as to whether this is the term which will be ultimately preferred and hence the absence of any compulsion to push or pull you to this usage.

Briefly stated, what I have in mind are first, the images (imagined scenes or objects) and *imagents* (imagined actions or events) underlying, sustaining, and activating some conceptually represented, developmental philosophy of life, or ideology, individual and social, and second, more particularly, a large assemblage of narratives in prose or poetry, each illustrative of a better or worse course of action, a better or worse state of being, or a better or worse mode of becoming, for an individual, for a society, or for the world at large. Some of the imagery, or imaginative symbolism, of these parables would come from the "depths" of human nature and appeal to the "depths," so that the whole Self, heart and mind in unison, would be awakened and drawn to this or that represented way of functioning. Of course, allegories of this potency cannot be manufactured; they must come, if they ever do come, out of a procession of passionately lived lives. All of this, as I envisage it, roughly corresponds to Schorer's definition of myth (given in the Appendix) combined with some of the views of myth set forth by Campbell in his memorable book, *The Hero with a Thousand Faces;*[1] and this correspondence is all the terminological justification I require for the present.

I would be ready to agree with Schorer's 1946 opinion that the definition of myth "must be both broad and loose," had not the broadness and the looseness of recent usage—particularly since 1946 in literary circles—gone so far as to deprive the term of cognitive utility. It seems to have lost connection with its inherited domain and come to mean almost any product of the imagination and hence nothing distinguishable from other things, since the imagination, as we now realize, is involved in all but the simplest sensations. The question is whether this most notorious semantic hobo of our time can ever be persuaded to stick to a few habitats, each of them susceptible of definition in a way that will diminish, if not abolish, the confusion that currently exists in many circles as to the conceptual places in which it is, or should be, its privilege and duty to abide.

A comprehensive definition of myth should certainly include the various accredited meanings of the word since its introduction by the Greeks—as presented to us, for example, in Levin's admirable chapter—as well as the more recent and exact meanings proposed by anthropologists. In fact, it may be held that some already published definitions come close enough to meeting these requirements. But, to my knowledge, no definitions of primitive and classic myths make room for any kinds of novel emanations from contemporary minds. And so, since it has not been unanimously decided that a "modern myth" is a contradiction in terms, I am strongly disposed to take account of those eminent literary critics and serious creative writers, such as Lawrence and Yeats, who have seized on "myth" as a word they cannot do without, as well as of the often expressed current "need for myths" and hence for mythmakers. With these wants in mind, then, I shall in due course endeavor to construct a set of definitions starting with "tales about the gods," which will be as useful and inviting to authors of today and of tomorrow as I can make them: not so loose as to refer to almost anything—any little image, idea, or attitude—not so rigid as to impale or suffocate imaginations. It is no easy task and, as things now stand, perhaps only an imprudent amateur would refuse to be checked by inner qualms and by outer auguries of futility such as those which are implied by "The Modern Myth of the Modern Myth," title of Stauffer's gently squelching essay of 1947.[2]

There is a sign ahead of me which reads: "Beware of booby traps, pitfalls, bogs, quicksand, canebrakes, and the Slough of Despond. Enter at your own risk." But this warning did not stop Chase[3] and other valiant ones who have recently struggled for a language that would order the existing chaos. Although each of these came out with admirable illuminations of certain issues, it seems that there is still something to be done, since their several concluding definitions are neither obviously equivalent nor obviously complementary, and many literary men are implicitly resistant or explicitly opposed to them: preferring to cleave to their own diction, or, like Rahv, for example, antipathetic to the whole idea of our "returning" to myth or "modernizing" myth.

Rahv's thesis, forcefully set forth in "The Myth and the Powerhouse,"[4] is briefly this: first, that today's mythomaniacs have failed to distinguish three radically different entities—myth, metaphysics, and poetry—and second, that the amorphous composite that has come from melting these together has engendered a spurious religiosity, and third, that the present craze for myth is merely the recurrence of a known form of romantic primitivism, motivated by a yearning to escape from the "powerhouse" of history and to experience the static complacence of passivity in circular mythic time. Since it is not possible to summarize with justice this smashing polemic by one of the most articulate and informed antagonists of modern mythophiles, I can do no better than suggest that you read it at your leisure. Personally I agree with many of Rahv's judgments relative to the existing situation —the meretricious scent of sanctity, for example, that adheres to the word "myth" in certain circles—, but, by my measures, some of his views are as mistaken as those which he denounces.

With this prospect, this jungle of contradictions ahead of me, what basis do I have for hope? Nothing but the thought that the explanation of the present multiplicity of dissonant definitions, especially in the humanities, is not far to seek: their authors have had different classes of myths in mind (fallacy of limited class focus), or have had different aspects of a myth in mind (fallacy of limited aspect focus), or have described these classes or aspects in non-referential language (fallacy of misplaced emotive diction). Schorer's excellent definition, for example, does not embrace primitive (daemonic) myths, whereas the definition adopted by Rahv is only applicable to these (fallacy of limited class focus). In Rahv's case the assumption seems to be that the very earliest form in which a named entity (e.g. myth) appears is its "true" form and therefore only when found in this first form can the entity be legitimately designated by the given name (fallacy of phylogenetic primacy). Also, in claiming that myths are never concerned with history and progress, Rahv is excluding numberless future-oriented myths (e.g. myth of the Promised Land, Persian, Judaic, and Christian apocalyptic myths, myth of the Second Coming, etc.). In short, many of the current definitions are adequate so far as they go, as supplements or complements to each other. They are contradictory only when they are implicitly or explicitly proposed as general definitions. Perhaps Campbell is or will be an exception to everything I have just said, since he, in one vast, masterful, metaphorical embrace, surrounds every definition. My work, then, may prove to be no more than the pedestrian endeavor of a professional psychologist to reduce Campbell's poetry to prose.

Anyhow, armed with nothing but the few elementary principles I have named plus one other idea reserved for later mention, I am proposing to proceed at a slow pace, scarcely mindful of the probability of my boring the majority of readers and of the penalty I incur in doing so—risking all this in the hope of arriving at a little clarity, order, dignity, and vision. But first let us look quickly down the centuries—with the help of Chase[3] and others—in order to be reminded of the different views of myths, especially of primitive myths, that have successively prevailed.

B. HISTORICAL SURVEY OF SOME PERTINENT VIEWS OF MYTH

Through twenty-five centuries of Western history the myths of Greece have magnetized the minds of men. Originally received as indubitable revelations of divine powers determining the course of natural events, they have been successively regarded as supreme models of heroism and virtue for youth to emulate, setting limits to the intemperance of mortal pride; as pithy and enchanting stories for the nourishment of the imagination; as childish fables unworthy of serious attention; as enigmas whose genesis required explanation by detached, speculating theorists, such as Thales and Pythagoras in the sixth century B. C., Zeno in the fifth, Euhemerus in the third, and Cicero in the first; as abominable Pagan superstitions to be refuted and denounced in the name of Christianity; and then again as stories to be enjoyed and interpreted in ancient ways—as entrancing fictitious narratives of the interplay of personified cosmic forces (Thales), or as providers of knowledge, however hyperbolic and distorted, of great pre-historic personages (Euhemerus), or as edifying moral allegories and parables (Zeno). In later eras myths were seized as opportunities for grandiose delusions on the part of kings and princes and as sources of inspiration for the compositions of architects, painters, sculptors, poets, and scholars, not only during and after the Renaissance, but, as Seznec[5] has made so visually apparent to us, throughout the Middle Ages.

In the seventeenth and eighteenth centuries—after scores of travelers and missionaries had returned to Europe laden with fabulous myths and folk-tales from remote peoples—these bizarre stories, together with the ancient myths of Greece, Rome, and the Near East—including some equally-incredible, slyly-mentioned, sacred tales of Christianity—became objects of keen analysis and veiled derision by such anti-clerical rationalists as Fontanelle and Bayle. In due course, however, this trend of denigration and disdain was partly offset by advocates of other views, starting with Vico's insights and culminating in Herder's celebration of myth as the central, creative, culture-shaping product of every distinctive collectivity, or *Urvolk*, the formative agent of its unique character. In the nineteenth century, subsequent to these reducing and elevating waves of judgment—most recently and fully set forth for us by Manuel[6]—, myths became one of the strategic problems to be solved by methodical investigators working in the name and mode of some neutral, scientific discipline—one or another branch of anthropology, in the broadest sense.

From the researches and inductions of anthropologists—including archaeologists, folklorists, and historians of religion—we have learnt: a) that almost every primitive society composed and conserved for ages, through oral transmission and artistic representation, multifarious mythic stories, the more or less coherent sum of which may be said to have constituted their mythology—this being an undifferentiated compound, as we analyze it now, first and foremost of primitive religion and secondly of primitive law and morality, primitive art and drama, and primitive science and techniques of a magical nature; and b) that primitive peoples continued to value their major myths, believed in some of them as sacred truths, were moved and edified by them, emulated and enacted them in religious rituals and ceremonies, defended them, fought and died for them, implanted them in the minds of conquered peoples, and were convinced that unfaithfulness in these regards would be severely punished. It may be said, in other words, that myths are simple or compound narrative units, many of which, carried in the mind, have had extraordinary permanence and potency, inasmuch as generations of people have been disposed to live—feel, think, and act—to a considerable extent in these terms, and hence that knowledge of the myths of any given society should enable us—has enabled anthropologists—to explain many of the otherwise unintelligible conceptions, emotional reactions, and modes of behavior of its members. In short, as Malinowski[7] and other field workers have made plain to us, a live or *vital* mythology, composed of graphic and dramatic stories about gods and heroes, has all the principal properties—the socially formative, unifying, solidifying, and sustaining functional capacities—of an effective social philosophy or religion. This might stand as one possible *functional* definition of an operative *collective* mythology. An *inert* mythology, on the other hand —like a forsaken ideology or theology—is one that has lost its efficacy, lost the power to invoke belief, kindle the heart, and orient endeavors.

At first the attention of anthropologists was directed less constantly to the various effects of myths—primitive myths being incredible to them—than it was to their referents and attributes, particularly to their countless incongruities with the perceptible phenomena of nature as well as with modern scientific explanations of these phenomena. Competent interrogation of members of primitive societies led to the unequivocal conclusion that one large class of myths, *etiological* myths, consists of firmly and sincerely held beliefs as to the origins of things (e.g. creation of the world or of human beings), that another class, *unique natural event* myths, consists of supposedly true descriptions of some momentous occurrence experienced in man's past (e.g. story of deluge), and that a third class, *interpretive* myths, represents beliefs as to the superhuman agents responsible for recurrent natural events (e.g. movements of celestial bodies, procession of the seasons). Myths of these classes have been termed *nature* myths.

To scientists of the West, trained in the rituals of precise perception, these sorts of stories were amazing and baffling in so far as the amount of sheer imagination exceeded that of objective observation. All of them told of *preternatural* events: actors with preternatural *anatomies,* in preternatural *places* and *situations,* manifesting preternatural *capacities,* resulting in preternatural *effects.* They abounded in portrayals of miracles of strength, agility, and speed, of winged flights, conquests of gravity, and of descents into regions below ground, miracles of invisibility and of invulnerability, of penetration through solid barriers, of incarnations, transfigurations, and metamorphoses, miracles of mere thought, of conception, creation, and destruction, of death and resurrection. This might stand as a possible *formal* descriptive definition of a *primitive* myth.

Next it became apparent that non-literate peoples—strangers to Greek thought, say to the analytic and synthetic, evolutionary speculations of Democritus and Epicurus—had no conception of variously combined atomic constituents of matter and no conception of purely physical forces operating imperceptibly through space or on a minute scale within natural objects. Instead of the difficult concept of invisible physical energy, in one or another form, determining all changes in the universe, pre-scientific peoples had inserted what was closest to their own immediate experience, namely felt *psychic energy*—that is, something comparable to the human will magnified to the required degree of intensity and provided with the required variety of powers. It was Fontanelle, I believe, who first suggested the idea—so lucidly illustrated and elaborated in Topitsch's chapter—that the mind is most naturally disposed to conceive of what is remote, strange, or difficult to explain in terms of what is near, familiar, or self-evident, namely (in this case) subjective experiences of feeling, deciding, moving in space, and manipulating objects as well as of empathically perspecting similar activities in others. Thus "savages" so-called—not to speak of many of their more civilized descendants if they had any—lived in a world that was populated by numerous imperceptible but often imagined psychic beings, however named—spirits, souls, ghosts, devils, angels, demi-gods, supreme deities—some of whom were immanent in nature, usually inhabiting a particular region or body, such as the earth, sea, sky, mountain, or sun, and some of whom were more mobile—floating or moving freely in the ether—and capable of appearing almost anywhere, or of influencing, simultaneously and from a distance, events at many separate spots. The fluid, intraceptive, primordial state of mind conducive to this mode of apprehension constitutes a general *structural psychic determinant* of mythic compositions of this class, especially when combined with continuous, direct exposure to the wild vicissitudes of nature in its most maleficent and gracious aspects (general *positional situational* determinant).

So far as I know, it was Max Muller—whose farfetched, linguistic theory of the genesis of myth may be set aside—, it was Max Muller who first suggested the notion of "the fundamental metaphor," outcome of the process of projection, to account for the attribution of human passions and actions to cosmic bodies. Or the credit should go to Tylor, who proposed the more comprehensive concept of *animism*—animation of the inanimate —, which includes many, but by no means all, of the products of *projection* as now defined. No doubt Muller was projecting to a considerable degree himself when he conceived of primitive Aryans as poets indulging in the delights of metaphorical expression, and, in their use of it, one gathers, as self-conscious as William Blake when he made his famous avowal that it was not the sun he saw rising above the horizon but "an Innumerable company of the Heavenly host crying 'Holy, Holy, Holy is the Lord God Almighty'."

But for all his errors—as judged by today's experts—Muller did not assume that etiological and interpretive myths were resultants of serious and deliberate efforts of the mind to understand natural phenomena dissociated from emotion. He left this intellectualist theory for adoption, to a varying extent, by a number of his contemporaries and successors, who, being reared in the tradition of science, were naturally inclined to project into primitive minds a large measure of their own differentiated and disciplined form of curiosity. With this exclusive assumption, it was scarcely possible to regard myths as anything but prime samples of man's innate propensity for madness—for absurdity, delusion, folly, ferocity, and self-torture. Thus the marriage of myth and falsehood, cemented by the Church Fathers, was certified once more with the now-more-respected stamp of science, most definitely and authoritatively by the great autocrat of mythology, Frazer himself: "By myths I understand mistaken explanations of phenomena, whether of human life or of external nature. Such explanations originate in that instinctive curiosity concerning the causes of things which at a more advanced stage of knowledge seeks satisfaction in philosophy and science, but being founded on ignorance and misapprehension they are always false, for were they true, they would cease to be myths."[3] According to this *evaluative* definition, myth is a false explanation (theory) "concerning the causes of things," the product of an ignorant and misguided attempt to arrive at a valid explanation. The acceptance of this view might almost lead to the conclusion that Frazer's explanation of myth is itself a myth (false theory), since it is clearly "founded on ignorance and misapprehension" as to other than cognitive psychic determinants of mythic compositions. Why, we may ask, should the most gifted stylist of his profession—who often sacrificed accuracy for vividness and force —exclude, *among other things,* the demands of emotional (empathic and dramatic) needs which even for post-Newtonians have been better satisfied by the graphic diction of poetic myth than by the cold, insensible abstractions of the sciences?

Besides etiological and interpretive myths, chief topic of the above discussion, there is a multiplicity of primitive myths or legends of other types, a sizable proportion of which are primarily concerned with the life and exploits of a man-god or culture-hero, the charismatic possessor of preternatural energy, or "mana," as well as of certain special preternatural abilities— a compound of dispositions and powers which once upon a time enabled him to contribute in some remarkable way to the foundation, survival, or development of his society. One may reasonably suppose that out of admiration, wonder, awe, and gratitude for his signal benefactions, and out of compassion and sorrow at his death, the image of the king or hero was raised from the cortical tomb where memories decompose and perish, and with the aid of crystallizing and magnifying imaginations was made the radiant center of an orally transmitted and elaborated mythic narrative, and sometimes of a mythic cult and rite. Myths that are primarily of this class may be called *heroical historical* myths, and in so far as they are offered to later generations as models for emulation, *exemplar*, or *eductional*, myths. It is easy to understand—even in an age when it is more fashionable to reduce than to elevate the characters and talents of our benefactors—how an amazing and compelling innovator (e.g. the discoverer of fire, agriculture, or music) could in this way be transformed into a man with superhuman powers, and then into a god-man or man-god, and perhaps finally into a deity of the highest order.

If this is correct, it seems that a god can be created either by projecting a psyche, or personality, into an object or process that is already endowed with everlasting superhuman powers (e.g. earth, sun, volcano, lightning), or by raising for all time the extraordinary awesome powers of some departed mortal to a superhuman level. The two processes could combine to produce myths of divine beings (or of souls) who have descended from sky to earth and/or ascended from earth to sky. Thus, both the theory attributed to Thales—myths are stories about the interaction of personified natural forces—and the theory attributed to Euhemerus—myths are stories about greatly idealized historic characters—conform, in the main, to the accredited facts and theories of contemporary anthropological science. It should be added that a myth may be both heroical and interpretive or heroical and etiological; for instance, when a narrative attributes the founding of a society (etiological historical myth) to the brave and sagacious acts of a particular ruler—father of his country—including in the account a number of impressive biographical items (heroical historical myth).

From the researches of anthropologists (in the broadest sense) we have also learnt that a number of myths—constituents of the mythologies of different societies—have had, from a very ancient origin, a temporal span (duration down the ages) and a spatial scope (distribution over the globe) of such great extent that they may be regarded as virtually universal, or "archetypal." The universality of certain mythic themes is the topic of Kluckhohn's substantial contribution to this volume.

Finally, to end this preliminary abstract of relevant anthropological findings and hypotheses, I should mention the famous theory—first proposed by Robertson Smith and subsequently espoused by a host of other scholars—to the effect that every myth—or every major myth—in its original crude form was associated with the performance of a religious ritual. According to this view, the composition and performance of the ritual—whose purpose, let us say for short, was to encourage and support certain beneficent divine powers in their timely efforts to produce some urgently needed state of nature and society (e.g. return of lost vitality, fertility, re-invigoration of the pharaoh)—the ritual came first in point of time, the myth later, its role being to describe in words and thereby to assist the enactions of the performers of the rite. Since here the theorist is pointing to the conditions (place, time, occasion, speaker) under which the recital of a myth occurs, we might call this a *conditional* definition of myth.

From psychoanalysts—Freud, Rank, Jung, and many others—we have learnt that numerous themes commonly represented nowadays in the dreams, fantasies, story compositions, play enactions, and art forms of children are essentially similar to the themes of widely known primitive myths. A modern child may dream or daydream of being the offspring of a parent far superior to his own, of a miraculous conception and miraculous birth, of an idyllic environment, of imminent annihilation by monster, flood, or fire, of preternatural exploits and experiences—subterranean locomotions, metamorphoses, rising and floating in the air, being invisible and invulnerable—of spectacular achievements and piteous defeats, of incest and murder, crime and punishment, death and resurrection. From numerous correspondences of this sort we may provisionally assume that dispositions to imagine events conforming to these thematic patterns (mythmaking tendencies) are basic, genetically transmitted *potentialities* of the human mind, shared by all children from prehistoric times. In modern children these recurrent patterns of imagination are understandable as products of wishes or dreads linked with one or more needful and emotional dispositions (*dynamic psychic* determinants), such as hunger, sex, love, curiosity, admiration, ambition, anxiety, or hate. In many cases these needs and emotions are clearly related to one or another evident *instigational* determinant—some type of bodily experience or of treatment by mother, father, or sibling, or some type of disturbing family event, enigma, accident incurred, or striking natural phenomenon, many of which are virtually universal (e.g. birth, oral gratification and privation, walking and falling, transgressions and punishments, advent of younger sibling, loss of monopoly of mother's love, enigma of birth, thunder and lightning, successes and failures of multifarious endeavors, and so forth). Such instigating experiences and such potentially reactive dispositions, common to all children past and present, would partially account for the great spatial scope and temporal span of certain patterns of dramatic thought.

The imaginations of children are marked not only by the prevalence of these common thematic trends but also by distinctive formal attributes. Characteristically, they consist of *autonomous* (involuntary, not consciously directed), *disjunctive* (incoherent, uncoordinated) processions of extravagant and *incongruous* (preternatural, unrealistic) *images* (instead of words) which approach perceptions in their *vividness* and therefore are experienced as momentarily *credible representations* of the environment (as in a dream). The incongruity of these representations of the external world may be explained partly by reference to the greater impressiveness and appeal of *autistic* (self-centered), wish-engendered, and hence distorted or magnified, imaginations (*dynamic psychic* determinant) relative to the appeal of selfless, detached perceptions, and partly by reference to a primordial, fluid, "unstructured" state of mind typical of the earlier prerational stages of mental development in all children, a psychic state which is conducive to empathic participations with natural objects and events, coupled with animistic projections of all sorts (general *structural psychic* determinant).

But the supposed similarity in these respects of modern and pre-historic children is not enough to explain the noted similarities between the fragmentary and transitory fantasies of modern children and the more integrated and enduring myths of pre-historic adults. An additional assumption is required, namely, that in ancient times the development of the minds of youth was not marked (as it is with us today) by a radical change of cognitive standards and dispositions combined with changes of the mental entities in terms of which natural (physical, physico-chemical, physiological, pathological) phenomena were originally interpreted. Without doubt pre-historic children, not unlike the Geneva boys and girls studied by Piaget, explained the movements of inanimate bodies—that were not only "remote, unknown, or difficult to understand," but also experienced *later* in their lives—by reference to the emotions and intentions of animate beings (themselves and parents), that were not only "near, well known, and self-evident," but also experienced *earlier* in their lives. In ancient times, according to this view, such projections of known psychical events into unknown physical events—especially common, say, among children who are least shielded from and hence most affected by the vicissitudes of nature (general *positional situational* determinant)—were not side-tracked or abandoned in later years of life, but propagated as initially received in one or another reconstructed or elaborated guise.

The Uranus and Gaea myth of creation, for example, could easily have had its genesis in the mind of a child who, after witnessing sexual intercourse between his parents, imagined that god-and-human life began once upon a time as the consequence of a comparable conjugation between the male sky and the underlying female earth. Likewise, the Babylonian Biblical myth of creation—still accepted in certain quarters as literal truth—might have originated in the imagination of a child who had once been particularly impressed by the way his venerated, bearded grandfather, monarch of his clan, fashioned a life-like idol out of mud.

The here-relevant differences between Westernized adults of today and adults of the pre-historic past can be partly attributed to the more complete submersion, or dislodgment from consciousness, in the West of the child's mode of experiencing the environment (Schachtel⁹), and its replacement during the course of education by other modes of perception and mentation, derived in part from Greek philosophy and from modern science. To highlight four phylogenetic and ontogenetic mental transformations that are pertinent to the present issue—all of them clear consequences of the advance of the physical sciences—I might speak of a) emotional identifications with nature and projections into space displaced in due course by a stage of cognitive detachment permitting dissections of the environment into concepts of material particles and energy; b) a progression from feelings and images without words to words which evoke images and feelings (emotive diction), then to concepts which become increasingly abstract (theoretical diction), and ultimately to symbols dissociated from images and feelings; c) an initial cognitive state of trustful receptivity to visions, sensory impressions, and authoritative statements changing with cultural evolution and with age toward a state of constant distrust, with suspension of judgment, in the absence of indubitable proof; d) an ever-higher standard as to what constitutes sufficient basis or evidence for a statement.

Let this rough, brief sketch of historic mental trends—marked by rhythms of progression and regression—suffice as indicator of one psychological determinant of the excommunication of the psyche and its feelings from air, water, fire, earth and other forms of matter, and hence the banishment of mythic (animistic) diction from the domain of the physical sciences. Long in disrepute is the mental state of that early chemist who described the result of triturating mercuric chloride with mercury in these words: "The fierce serpent is tamed and the dragon so reduced to subjection as to oblige him to devour his own tail."¹⁰ Somewhat comparable is the partial expulsion from humanistic philosophy and from the various social sciences of the graphic diction and magnifying projections of mythology. In these domains, instead of vivid and dramatic stories (emotionally logical at best) about the extraordinary doings of extraordinary beings, we find cool, imageless conceptual statements (intellectually logical at best) about the ordinary doings of an abstract "average man," of the majority of men, of a class or of a group of men. Since here the objects of primary concern are personalities in societies, it is still considered proper to attribute to them psychic states and processes. Only in the extreme case of Watsonian Behaviorism do we come upon a concerted effort to chase the psyche out of man.

Obviously, I am not talking, at this point, about the arts, however much they too have been affected by the above-enumerated trends. I am talking about the referential (fact-pointing) ideas of social science and about the referential ideas plus the orientational (preferred goal-pointing) ideas of social and political ideologies. Although in both cases we are confronted by general concepts, most of these require criterial or operational definitions, that is, definitions in terms of images of visible and audible persons, actions, qualities, and outcomes, as well as of inferred mental states and forces. By way of definition of an abstract symbolic model, we are given a story in concrete, sensible language of an "ideal" event (in these respects similar to a myth). In short, if one purposes to arrive at a usable meaning of any sociological or psychological theory it is necessary to compose *imaginal* representations of events which illustrate the given theory. Likewise— particularly when it comes to a goal-oriented social philosophy, such as Marxism—, if one wants to discover some of the chief psychic determinants and potencies of a sequence of ideas, one must try to identify, if possible, the underlying imagery, because, as Schorer has reminded us, imagery is "neither the negation nor the contrary of ideas, but their basis and their structure, the element by which they are activated."

Since some of the identifiable imagery supportive of great ideas and ideologies obviously conforms to well-known mythic patterns, the trend of this discussion has brought us round again to psychoanalytic theory, specifically, in this case, to Freud's conceptualization of the gradual repression, or elimination from consciousness and the "ego" system, of those primitive psychic states and processes which generate mythic imaginations, coupled with his theory of their continued, unconscious operation in the "id" system, and, under certain conditions, of their penetration of the hypothetical boundary between the "ego" and the "id" and their invasion of the stream of thought. Numerous adult dreams marked by spectacular, preternatural, archaic imagery, numerous adult visions of a similar nature produced in certain extraordinary states of mind, as well as multifarious, insane hallucinations and delusions add up to a considerable body of evidence in favor of Freud's revolutionary proposition. According to this formulation, then, the condition of mind conducive to primitive, autonomous, disjunctive, feelingful modes of thought and to the production of primitive images and themes exists, for all of us, in that hypothetical "region" or excluded sub-system of the mind known as the "id." Of this mental condition we are generally not aware except while experiencing dreams or trances of a certain kind— especially those which are engendered during periods of excessive strain, anxiety, resentment, or despair, or in a season of love, adoration, or intense creative productivity. In saying that a myth is a "collective dream"—a reconstructed, composite dream of many members of a society—emphasis is laid on the state of mind out of which myths are born (general *structural psychic* determinant) and—since dreams, according to Freud, are expressions of wishes—on the motivating force which directs the flow of imagery (*dynamic psychic* determinant). Such determinants might constitute a part of a *causal* definition of myth.

A boy's unconscious or half-conscious wish to possess his mother sexually and the wish to eliminate his interfering father (basis of the Oedipus myth) are the prime motivating forces of the "id" in psychoanalytic theory. Less emphasized and sometimes overlooked are a) hatred and the wish to kill, directed against a rejecting, "devouring," or "sinful" mother or against some non-paternal alter (psychic source of the matricidal Orestes myth, and the fratricidal Cain and Abel myth, and many others); b) erotic love and the wish for union directed toward the self or toward some non-maternal alter (psychic source of a variety of myths, phallic, orgiastic, conjugal—e.g. Narcissus, Krishna, Tristan and Isolde myths); c) state of need and helplessness in a perilous, unnourishing, or hostile environment and the wish for an omnipotent, omniscient, and benevolent protector, provider, and director (psychic source of various theistic myths); d) narcism and the wish to be omnipotent and superior to others (psychic source of countless self-glorification and heroical myths); e) curiosity and the wish to obtain an appealing *graphic* explanation of how babies are created (first of a series of etiological myths); f) dread of temptation and punishment (psychic source of numerous images of demonic (satanic) tempters, threatening indignant deities, and myths of crime and punishment—e.g. Sodom, Gomorrah, and the Deluge); not to speak of such basic, *collective* motivations as g) fear of starvation and a consequent decline of social and regal vigor in a barren, dry environment leading to ardent wishes for the revival of fertility and of vigor (psychic source of the important death and resurrection myth).

These interior determinants of mythic imaginations may also be determinants of overt behavior, and most of the actions I have mentioned—patricide, murder of tyrants, matricide, fratricide, incest, revengeful punishments, heroic combats, cultural innovations, and so forth—must have occurred in this and that society at least as frequently as they occur with us. Indeed, a single sensational incident (*instigational* determinant) might be quite enough to start a host of magnifying flights of imagery, resulting eventually in several recurrent versions of essentially the same tale. Certain catastrophe (*unique natural event*) myths (e.g. myth of a great flood) probably have their source—as indicated by archaelogical findings—in some destructive natural event suffered in the past, although to account for the wide propagation of the story it may be necessary to include a supplementary somatic determinant. One more word before leaving this wish-fulfillment and dread-eventuation theory of dreams and myths: many myths, such as those enacted in Greek drama, are stories of severely punished wishes, the recital of which was, to some extent, intended as a lesson (e.g. Zeno's parable theory) in support of the accepted moral order. Narratives of this class may be called *deterrent* myths.

Up to this point it has been tacitly assumed or explicitly stated that myths refer to occurrences in the external world (etiological or interpretive nature myths) or to overt interactions between persons or societies and their environment (heroical, historical, educational, or deterrent myths). But Jung, among psychoanalysts, as well as numerous Oriental scholars, such as Coomaraswarmy, Zimmer, and Campbell, have shown us that many of the referents of Indian myths are endopsychic states, dispositions, and dispositional relationships, and, when this is the case, the whole question of the external incongruity (lack of correspondence with natural events) of mythic imagery is eliminated. These symbolic *intrapsychic* myths portray conditions, conflicts, and victories within the soul of man.

C. A SET OF DEFINITIONS

In the preceding section I did not aim to map the vast territory of mythology, or to distinguish myth from saga, legend, and fairy tale, or to enumerate all of the major conceptions and interpretations of myths that have been offered by learned scientists and scholars. I included only what was relevant to my present purpose: the discrimination of different *aspects* and of different *kinds* of myths and the framing of a set of suitable definitions with an eye to the possibility of mythic compositions in the future.

Before proceeding I should say—in order to forestall misunderstanding—that most mythic narratives consist of fusions (*complex* myths) or of sequences (*serial* myths), or of both fusions and sequences of *simple* (component) myths. Each of these simple myths can stand alone and constitute a separate tale, or be incorporated as a part in an otherwise non-mythic narrative. The myth of miraculous birth, for instance, is a component of various heroical, *serial* myths, but it is nonetheless often recited and celebrated by itself in its own right, as it is with us on Christmas day. Anyhow, from now on I shall generally be using —for brevity's sake—the singular form, "myth," "story," or "event," rather than repeating in each instance, "myth or compound of myths," "story or series of stories," "event or chain of events."

The following definitions are arranged according to aspects, under each of which one or more kinds, or classes, of myths may be distinguished.

1. *Formal, descriptive definition. A myth manifestly consists of the essential features of an important, more or less natural/ preternatural situation or event (that has a basic thema) in which at least one extraordinary, more or less natural/preternatural psychic entity is involved—all this as sensibly represented in one channel or another.* Let us consider this definition part by part.

1.1. *an event (series of actions or interactions) sensibly represented in one channel or another,* that is, a myth is *not* an actual occurrence, but an occurrence (more or less actual/imaginary) represented in sensory terms, *not* in conceptual, theoretical terms. To the early Greeks *mythos* meant "the thing spoken" or uttered by the mouth (Spence,[11] including "the thing spoken during a religious ceremony." Since these were magical words identical with their meanings, one could say that *mythos* referred to *both* the actual *words* which represented the preternatural (imagined) event enacted by the mute performers of the rite, *and* the preternatural (imagined) *event* represented by the words. The preternatural event consisted chiefly of the imagined actions of one or more gods, the audible imitation (description) of which by means of words and the visible imitation (enaction) of which by means of muscles was felt to be unquestionably efficacious. From these sacred tales and rituals, in imitation of the imagined actions of *superhuman* beings, evolved the written and then audibly spoken and visibly enacted secular tragedies of the Greek theater in imitation of the imagined actions of unusual *human* beings. The term that Aristotle gave to the events or series of actions represented by the masked actors of the drama was *mythos* (translated "plot").

Research indicates that many of the stories incorporated in the works of Homer and Hesiod were descended from ritual narratives. Though greatly altered in the course of transmission, these were still called "myths" and, in subsequent centuries, characters and episodes from these mythic tales were depicted time and time again in vase-paintings and in sculpture. Thus, it is not contrary to Greek usage to say that a myth may be not only a story, or event represented in words, but also an event enacted in a ritual or drama, and that a part-myth may be one or more climactic moments of an event depicted in some durable medium. Besides these, there is another channel of representation which is central to them all, namely the imagination. This is so because an event must be covertly visualized (recollected, dreamt, or consciously fabricated in the mind) before (or during) its theatrical enaction, its narration, or its depiction in a bas-relief or drawing. Furthermore, an overtly represented event must be registered in the mind by its receptors (spectators, auditors, readers); and, then, if it is to endure in a state of readiness for numerous subsequent transmissions, it must be recurrently reproduced in the stream of consciousness. In short, to account for the creation and propagation of myths in variant versions, there must be composers, transmitters, receptors, conservers, and re-composers of mythic patterns. I am proposing, then, that we distinguish the following channels of representation:

(i) an imagined (visualized) representation of a mythic event: a *mythic imagent* (imagined event). This approaches the definition of myth as a "large controlling image." (Schorer)

(ii) a verbal (visualizable) representation of a mythic event in speech or writing: a *mythic narrative.*

(iii) a quasi-actional (visible and audible) representation of a mythic event: an *enacted myth, a mythic drama or rite.*

(iv) a material (visible) representation of a mythic situation or of one or more mythic characters or moments of a mythic event: a *depicted myth* or *mythic icon.*

Here my first purpose is to substitute "event sensibly represented" for "story," because the latter, though usually more convenient, is ambiguous: it points (too exclusively) to spoken or written language as well as to the actions described by the language. My second purpose is to introduce *imagent* (an imagined—dreamt, fantasied, recollected, predicted, or fabricated—event), in preference to "image"—which points to a single, more or less stationary entity or configuration, a still-shot of a moment in the sequence of events—as a suitable word to designate the covert unit central to all mythic transactions. A book of mythic stories on a shelf in the library is inoperative—a mere residue of past imaginations—so long as it is never read, never generates influential imagents in other minds. "Imagent" is also consonant with the psychoanalytical conception of myth as a collective dream or fantasy.

What is common to all the above-listed channels of representation (some of which are nowadays commonly combined—in cinema, TV, comics, etc.) is their appeal to the emotions through the senses, chiefly through internal or external vision, but also through the ear, and even through the nostrils (e.g. incense in a religious ceremony). For this, "sensible" (sensuous) seems to be a suitable term, indicating that myth belongs in the domain of art in the broadest sense, that is, belongs with what is art to children, to primitives, to the multitude, to professional critics, or to the artist, whether or not it serves the aims of religion, morals, politics, or commerce. Its concrete, "sensible" (graphic, figurative, visualizable) representations distinguish it from the general, conceptually-abstract, imageless, and emotionally-uninvolving diction of science and philosophy, as well as of much ordinary thought and speech. The utility of the word "sensible" is that it is not (like "artistic" or "aesthetic") restricted to the sense-qualities enjoyed and valued by gifted and experienced appreciators, the sense-qualities say, of acknowledged works of art, of impressive religious ceremonies or monuments, of eloquent political rhetoric, and so forth. "Sensible" is equally applicable to tawdry, unartistic, visual representations (e.g. a cheap "chromo" of the Crucifixion), to low-grade, commercial art, such as advertising (cf. *The Mechanical Bride*, McLuhan[12]), and indeed, to all grades of graphic portrayals, from the lowest to the highest, encountered, for example, in today's mass media. Thus, according to this view, every myth is an event sensibly represented; but only a relatively few, sensible representations can be properly called "myths," and of these some are cherished as great art (e.g. certain poetical passages in *Isaiah*), whereas others lack aesthetic properties. Whether or not a mythic narrative or mythic icon (e.g. cave-painting, picture of Madonna and Child) is *valued* as a work of art, depends, in each case, on the genius of the composer.

1.2. *a represented event in which at least one extraordinary psychic entity is involved*, that is, *every* actor in a mythic event is *not* an average, all-too-human mortal. Among the early Greeks "myth" came to mean a story "about the gods," that is, about supposedly supernatural, immortal beings. But not exclusively, because in a large number of their mythic stories the immortal gods, either by conjugating among themselves or by conjugating with mortal beings, begot human sons and daughters with whom they were thenceforth almost necessarily involved. Furthermore, these immortals of the Hellenic imagination, being often more quarrelsome than peaceful and very interested in mankind, were constantly meddling and taking sides in the disturbed affairs on earth—giving victory to some favored hero, impeding the endeavors of a person who angered them, rewarding the virtuous, humbling the vain, or elevating some abused heroine or hero to the high bowl of heaven to survive there in the form of an immortal constellation. Hence, a "story about the gods" was a story which had one or more genuine gods or goddesses in its cast, and *also*, in most cases, other less exalted characters, say, a demi-god or demi-goddess, a mortal hero or heroine, a prophetess, an old crone, a nondescript hermit, a few animals, or a monster of one fabulous variety or another. Later there were so-called "myths" in which the veritable gods were not at all involved (e.g. Narcissus, Daedalus, Icarus, and so forth) or no more than the God of Christianity would be involved in a modern story about the general of an army who devoutly prayed for victory. In due course, as mentioned earlier, *mythos* was applied by Aristotle to dramas about men and women of superior estate (e.g. Agamemnon and Clytemnestra), who were believed to be actual, historical persons. They became purely fictional to later "more sophisticated" generations; but now once again, since the excavations of Schliemann and his successors, they have been restored in many minds to the status of authentic human beings. Anyhow, do we not find inseparable gradations between venerated human beings (culture heroes, founders of religions, kings, emperors) and unmistakable gods? Alexander the Great was a god at the oasis of Ammon, Captain Cook a god in the Hawaiian Islands.

Although these considerations make it impossible to assert that all or most myths, in the Greek sense, are stories about the gods, it can be said that the vast majority of them are about one or more very *extraordinary* psychic entities. By "psychic (anthropopsychic rather than anthropomorphic) entity" I mean an animate creature or even an inanimate object that is described as perceiving, feeling, thinking, or intending as a human person does. This or some equivalent expression is required in order to embrace all the principal participants in primitive myths. An anthropopsychic entity may have a natural anatomy (animal or human), a preternatural anatomy (gigantic, weird, some combination of animal and human features), or no designated anatomy at all (a bodiless psyche, Holy Ghost, God). But whatever his or her embodiment or lack of embodiment, at least one psychic creature (hero or heroine) in a mythic story has cynosural, charismatic potency, that is, attracts and binds attention, interest, wonder, awe, dread. This attractive force is generated by the recognition that the being is in some or most respects *extraordinary*: omnipotent, omniscient, or uncommonly beautiful, powerful, brave, reckless, wise, virtuous, or evil—a creator, progenitor, provider, seductress, leader of a great migration, founder of a society, law-giver, ruler, warrior, implacable enemy, priest-king, prophet, seer, magician, healer, savior, killer of killers, technical inventor or benefactor, victor in a decisive contest. Often the decisive factor is the degree to which receptors become identified with the hero of the story. It seems that myth-makers have since time immemorial been almost exclusively interested in natural or preternatural superior beings, say in the aspirations of a king or of an elite group. In some myths a highly valued sect or a whole collectivity is "hero."

1.3. *the essential features of an important event that has a basic thema*, that is, a represented *mythic event* is distinguished from all other events (represented in dreams, fantasies, folktales, novels, dramas, ceremonies, pictures, and carvings) by its great "importance" to human beings, its relevance to their origin, survival, development, happiness, or glory. Furthermore, although the representation of a mythic event may contain any number of non-essential features, it must include its "essential features," that is, it must set forth concrete, sensible exemplifications of its complete *thema* (thematic pattern).

Later on I shall bring up the problem of *partial* representations of a complete event and representations of an *incomplete* event. A single mythic image in the mind, in a poem, or depicted in a painting (e.g. Axis Mundi, Tree of Knowledge, Angel, Virgin Mary) is, in my terminology, a *part* of a myth (*mythic object, mythic character, mythic symbol*, or *moment* of a myth), a part which is very commonly sufficient to bring the complete mythic event to the consciousness of those who are familiar with it. In other cases, we may be dealing with a myth in process of formation and hence with the imagination of an as-yet-incomplete event.

For lack of suitable English words pertaining to processes in time (in contrast to material configurations in space) "event" is commonly used to designate a single process completed in a fraction of a second (micro event) as well as to designate a manifold of proceedings with a far greater temporal span (macro event, e.g. the Thirty Years War). For present purposes, how-ever, an event may be defined as an arbitrarily selected *chrono-logical series of interdependent activities* (succession of inter-acting endeavors) which has a *unitary character*, marked by a definable beginning, middle, and ending, the nature of which (beginning, middle, and ending) differentiates this temporal unit (time segment) from preceding and succeeding happenings, and in terms of which (beginning, middle, and ending) this unit may be sufficiently formulated. According to this view, an event may be of any *span* (duration) and of any spatial *scope* (size and distance of the terrains of action), and of any social *compass* (number of characters involved), provided it can be suitably designated by a single formula (*thema*), simple or complex. For example, the simple formula, oProhibition→sTransgression→oPunishment, might abstract the essential features of a myth with a span of a few minutes, or one, such as the famous Garden of Eden interaction, in which the passage of time between the beginning and the middle or between the middle and the ending terms was apparently much longer.

Since a *simple* thema is apt to be a very general statement, not sufficiently specific and distinctive for most purposes, one usually requires a more or less *complex* thema. For instance, the above-given formula for the Garden of Eden story might be supplemented with terms indicating that the prohibitor was God, that the prohibition was not to eat of the fruit of the Tree of Knowledge, that a tempter (serpent) was involved, that there were two transgressors, male and female (both "extraordinary" in being the first human creatures on this earth and progenitors of our species), that the transgression was prompted by curiosity, and finally that the form of punishment was expulsion from an idyllic environment, with no promised possibility of forgiveness and re-admission. So much for a single temporal unit and its simple or complex formulation.

Most mythic narratives and dramas, however, are composed of two or more *different* temporal units, and hence cannot be epitomized by a single formula, simple or complex. These may be called *serial* myths, consisting, as they do, of a progression of causally related single myths, a progression which can be formulated only by a chain of simple or complex themas. The myth of the hero is a typical *serial* myth. Eventually we may have to go further, and distinguish myths which have a single, superordinate (overall, major) thema and a number of minor, component themas, sub-themas, and sub-sub-themas, some of which may be irrelevant to the major thema. More of this later.

This usage of "myth" and "thema" seems to conform to Aristotle's "myth" and "plot-structure," because for him "myth" was synonymous with "plot" and "plot" meant the sequence of concrete dramatic transactions, or, in other words, "the chain of incidents which are gradually unfolded in the story of a play" (Webster). A "plot" in this sense could be set forth by giving a reasonably full account of the enacted events, divorced from other aspects of the drama, such as the spectacle, diction, thought, and so forth. But "plot," for some critics, means "the plan or scheme of a literary creation" (O.E.D.), not the theatrical execution of the plan. In this sense, "plot" corresponds to Aristotle's "structure of the plot," an abstract, let us say, of the essential components of the enacted course of events, with special emphasis perhaps on the climactic enaction. Thus my *serial thema* (series of thematic patterns) is equivalent to Aristotle's "structure of a plot," or "structure of a myth," except that "thema" (a somewhat-more-technical word) is presented in terms which are usually more abstract than Aristotle's and always more abstract than the conventional "synopsis" of a dramatic story. This distinction between a) "plot" as the chain of events visibly and audibly enacted and b) "plot" as an abstract model of this chain is considered crucial, because the former is something "given" in the drama, something about which almost all receptors can agree, whereas the latter is the "construct" of a formulating critic; and, as Weisinger in his chapter illustrates with such lucidity, differences between constructs of this nature may be fundamental enough to generate protracted arguments among scholars. A myth, then, is an imagined event characterized by a certain thema (the best statement of which may be a matter of debate), but *not* the thema *per se;* because a thema is a *brief, conceptual* (imageless and undramatic) formula, which by itself lacks the myth's power to evoke emotions.

A *mythic event* is "important" partly because it involves an extraordinary, interest-binding psychic entity (e.g. Whale), but mostly because it is or has been *critical* and *consequential* to the welfare of a society as a whole or of most of the individual members of a special cult or great religion. Because the presence or absence of this characteristic is usually obvious to a reader of a written myth, it is included in this *formal*, descriptive definition; but the acid test is whether the represented event was or is felt to be important by its composers, receptors, conservers, and transmitters (part of a *functional* definition).

Generally speaking, a represented situation and endeavor is felt to be important if there is much at stake: if it is a question of non-existence (nothingness) or existence (creation), chaos or order, extinction or survival, being killed or killing, decay or renewal, death or resurrection; a question of gaining, preserving, or losing some highly valued region, position, thing, person, or internal state of grace; a question of glory or humiliation, of the right to supreme authority, of ruling or being ruled, submission or defiance, being accepted or rejected; a question of prolonged captivity, liberation or escape; a question of moral good or evil, of transgression, punishment or pardon, of forgiveness or revenge, salvation or damnation; or a question of stagnation, death-in-life, or evolution, of challenge, catastrophe or creative coping.

A *mythic event*, as indicated earlier, is distinguished from all other, variously represented (non-mythic) events by the fact that it exemplifies a *basic* thema, clearly and dramatically, the themas involved in other classes of events being not only less fundamental or universal (basic), but less striking (harder to apperceive), because the engaged dispositions of the actors are mixed and weaker, adulterated by irrelevant elements, shaped by a particular culture in time, tempered by civilized restraints, and hence less primitive and deeply moving. Some day there may be some agreement as to the most acceptable criteria of "basic"; but in the meantime I shall define a "basic" thema as one which involves to a marked degree and in a dramatic form, emotions, wants, and actions, which are present as potential tendencies in virtually all men and women of all societies and times, a pattern of conflicting endeavors emanating from dispositions such as these: the craving for peace, security, serenity, or ecstasy; the force of lust, love, jealousy, or hate, of rage or fear, of hunger or avarice, suspicion or curiosity, of worldly ambition or lofty aspiration, envy, vanity, or pride, of exultation or creative zest, of loyalty, adoration, or compassion, grief or joy. Some of such strongly expressed dispositions will be embodied in the hero and some in other participants in the procession of events.

Before proceeding to other definitions of myth it might be clarifying to describe a little more explicitly than I have so far one possible way—a somewhat more detailed version of Aristotle's way—of analyzing a myth (plot, event) and formulating its thema (structure of plot). A reasonably complete statement of a thema should include:

(i) *Beginning*: *an abstract statement of the initial situation.* This might involve the specification of such variables as the state of the physical, social, cultural environment (e.g. the scene is laid in Hell, or the country is in a state of war, or a bitter religious controversy is in progress), or of such variables as the sex, age, relationships, position, traits, capacities, recent actions and present emotional state of each of the major characters (e.g. the life of a male child is threatened by a ruler who fears that the boy will eventually supersede him; or an intellectual recluse, satiated and enervated by years of orthodox scholarship, invokes the Devil; or a young prince is both outraged and depressed by the confirmed surmise that the new husband of his recently widowed mother is none other than his father's murderer).

(ii) *Middle*: *the thema proper*: *an abstract of the body of the represented event.* This consists of a brief specification of the major aim and endeavor of the hero, or, in more detail, if necessary, his successive proactions and reactions in relation to the environment, particularly in relation to one or more specific interacting entities, or characters (e.g. the vengeful hero searches for his injurer (a malevolent whale), encounters and attacks him; or the hero leads his people out of captivity and searches for land on which to settle).

(iii) *Ending: an abstract of the outcome, the terminal situation.* This defines the effects and consequences, or fate, of the hero's actions, the final state of affairs (e.g. the hero triumphs and marries the king's daughter; or the hero, overcome by guilt, puts out his own eyes; or the hero dies and is transported to heaven).

This is no more than a sketch of one among many modes of thematic analysis. Since, so far as I know, there is no widely preferred mode, decisions are bound to be largely arbitrary, a matter of taste or aim.

Although my own preferred method is to classify myths, whenever possible, in terms of the *thema proper* (middle term), most mythologists use a variety of methods, naming myths according to their most striking feature, at one or another level of abstraction (generality-specificity): initial mythic situation (e.g. idyllic environment, Eden), mythic hero or protagonist (e.g. androgynous deity, Herakles), mythic antagonist (e.g. were-wolf, Satan), relationship of mythic characters (e.g. brothers, Cain and Abel), mythic *press,* or environmental force (e.g. flood, prohibition), mythic interaction (e.g. encounter with monster), terminal mythic situation (e.g. creation of the world, resurrection, paradise regained) and so forth. In Eliade's illuminating chapter one perceives the advantages, if not the necessity, of classifying at least some myths according to a certain kind of environmental situation or enjoyed inner state (e.g. Paradise), since this has been, on the one hand, a retrospected, preternatural *initial* situation from which humans were long ago expelled, and, on the other hand, a prospected preternatural *terminal* situation toward which their hopes have stretched: this progress into the future being equivalent to a regress into the past aiming at the ultimate restoration of the once-experienced, lost beatitude.

1.4. *a more or less natural/preternatural situation, event, or psychic entity involved,* that is, myths vary all the way from narratives almost all parts of which are preternatural (never been perceived, experienced, or known to occur—fantastic places, anatomies, capacities, and effects), such as the story of the creation of the world by a lizard, to narratives which are entirely natural (possible though not necessarily probable) except, say, for the intervention of a single preternatural being (god). And here the question is whether or not it is advisable to extend the traditional definition of a myth to include imaginations of important events with basic themas which are represented naturally, say, a realistic portrayal of the failure of a reckless astronaut to reach the moon—the myth of Icarus in modern dress. My proposal would be to call this a story with a *mythic thema* which was not mythically represented. In this connection we might note that a kind of achievement (e.g. flight) that would be preternatural (miraculous, impossible) in all preceding eras may suddenly become natural and commonplace.

The forces that are responsible for the course of mythic events are always psychic forces (agents, actors), never physical or chemical forces, and the representation is always concrete and sensible (not conceptual). The thema that a myth exemplifies, however, is abstract (a virtual universal), in the sense that it is a composite or generalization of countless human experiences or imaginations, divorced of all particulars.

2. *Referential definition.*

2.1. *Phenomenal reference. The manifest components of a myth—the represented situations, events, and actors—may mean what they literally appear to mean or may stand for anything else that is conceivable by man.* It is here that we run into the wars of the schools—many besides those mentioned by Dorson and Ackerman—in regard to the relative validity or significance of one or another mode of interpretation.

When we dream, everything we envisage is literally given, the real thing; but as soon as we awake, it becomes either meaningless, trivial, or symbolic of something else, and the nature of this "something else" depends on our choice of analyst. To the one who experiences it, a vision or hallucination may come as an animate actuality, the very presence, say, of the creator and director of the universe; but to a psychiatrist it may be nothing but an obvious wish fulfillment, the projection of a bad conscience, or a powerful archetype heralding an inflated psychic state. Who decides? There have been times when a man's life might hang on whether he took a sacred image or object literally or symbolically (e.g. the forced confession of Berengarius that "the bread is not merely a sacrament but the true body of Christ that is chewed with the teeth"). A little later the orthodox way of taking it might be the exact opposite. Evidently, what is literal truth to one person, or to a person in a primitive state of mind, or to members of a particular cult, may be one or another variety of symbolic truth to others, or sheer nonsense. To its composer, a mythic composition may be consciously symbolic of one or more things and unconsciously symbolic of several others, none of which might correspond to the interpretations of its receptors. Think of the many proposed meanings of the White Whale. To Starbuck Moby-Dick was "natural," because the traumatic mutilation of Captain Ahab's leg was merely the involuntary reaction of a dumb brute. But to Ahab the Whale was preternatural, the superhuman embodiment of a human psyche, or god, who acted deliberately out of malice.

A mythic narrative, then, is usually susceptible of several interpretations, some on different levels, each of which is likely to contribute to our understanding of the full significance of the story. Of the major varieties of referents, it seems that the largest consists of descriptions of the imagined psychic causes of natural phenomena (although Freudian psychoanalysts do not seem to believe that the imagination, even of primitive peoples, is responsive to perils, harms, or benefits coming from the physical or biological environment). Leaving aside the question of which entities or kinds of entities were more influential in the composition of myths—the weather, sun, moon, Sirius, Orion, Milky Way, earth, mountain, volcano, sea, river, rain, fire, and so forth—*nature* myths can surely be distinguished as one great class, with *meteorological, astronomical, terrestrial, chemical,* and *biological* (totem, monster) myths as sub-classes. All of these involve patent psychic projections (charming "pathetic fallacies") and hence nowadays can be entertained only on an emotional, poetical "as if" basis. They may contribute to our "feeling" for nature, but they add nothing to our understanding, and diminish, if anything, the effectiveness of our dealings with phenomena of these varieties. Perspectives of a psyche in the earth have been replaced by knowledge of soil chemistry.

Besides animistic *nature* myths, there are those which refer to the states, actions, aspirations, and fortunes of a particular cult or whole society (*collective* myths); those which refer more particularly to the birth, experiences, endeavors, death, and after-death of an extraordinary human being or demi-god—hero, king, savior (*individual* myths); those myths, social or individual, in which the prime actor is a transcendental preternatural being without embodiment in nature (*theistic* myths), and, finally, those which are chiefly concerned with internal, or endopsychic, occurrences or states (*intrapsychic individual* myths). Of course, these types are not mutually exclusive: a single, compound serial myth might include exemplifications of each variety. In fact, in primitive psyches, internal and external states are apt to change concurrently: the vigor of the earth, the vigor of the king, the vigor of the whole society decline together, the god of the past year, the old sun, is obviously dying; and when the young new god arrives, or the old one is rejuvenated, vigor and fertility are restored on all levels.

Analogous, in certain respects, to the visible cyclic transformations of the flora and fauna of the earth, of human bodies and of social groups, are the invisible but intimately experienced transformations of the psyche, self, or personality. It is to these that *intrapsychic* myths refer by means of imagery derived primarily from greatly modified percepts of external objects and events, much of which imagery had been projected into the environment. Thus myths of this sort involve a partial or complete withdrawal of projections, the projections of an earlier age, and a concentration on interior, intrapersonal developments: consequential subjective experiences, states of being or becoming, mutations of emotion and evaluation, interior conflicts and their resolutions. Poetic, mythic diction is not only the most natural and satisfying mode of expressing, representing and recording experiences of this sort, it is the only verbal means—particularly with the aid of ritual—of educing comparable emphatic experiences in other suitably receptive persons. Each mythic thema of this class is an abstract of countless personal experiences, set forth in concrete figurative language, all of which experiences, though necessarily both private and unique, are similar in certain significant respects, and thus common to a large number of self-conscious persons, generation after generation. In the last analysis, myths of this sort may be said to tend toward emotional and evaluational unanimity, toward shared subjective states and shared subjective knowledge through internal transformations. In contrast, science might be said to tend toward perceptual and conceptual unanimity, toward shared impartiality and shared objective knowledge through experimental manipulations of the environment. Mythic stories and symbols that depict the "night journey" of the intraverted soul, the encounter with the monster in every person's "depths," liberation from imprisoning modes of feeling and of thought, reconciliation, spiritual rebirth, the beatific state of grace and redemption—experiences of this nature—are expressed in language that must be taken figuratively, symbolically, and imaginatively. Though the imagery is necessarily derived from the external world, the reference is internal. In no other way, as Plato insisted, can certain profound truths be genuinely conveyed to others.

This is a class of myths that were first generated and elaborated with the greatest subtlety in India. There, it seems, the solitary ascetic was inevitably more engaged in heroic encounters with his instincts—grown monstrous through perpetual frustration—than he was in dealing with the monsters of whatever environment he had deserted. This seclusive, inward, concentrated, private, and spiritual Hindu orientation may be seen as the direct antithesis of the gregarious, outward, expansive, public, and material orientation of contemporary Soviet Russians as well as of Westerners generally, especially North Americans. It is Jung more than anyone perhaps who has worked with distinct success toward a synthesis of these opposites by applying Indian mythic images, modes of thought, and wisdom in modified forms to the dilemmas of Western man. One of his present theses, for example, is that our real enemies are within us—a horde of frantically ambitious, vainglorious, and destructive dispositions—and our prime obligation is to cope with them at their source rather than to project them into our ideological opponents. Here intrapersonal (intranational) and interpersonal (international) conflicts are mutually dependent, as they are generally. But instead of holding that the international conflict must be settled before intrapersonal and intranational serenity and good-will are possible, the order is reversed.

2.2. *Temporal reference. Myths are the essential features of imagined situations or events a) that occurred once upon a time in the past, b) that are destined to occur in the future, or c) that are now recurring, or have recurred and will continue to recur at regular intervals or in chronological order.* All etiological myths (e.g. creation), unique environment or event myths (e.g. paradise, catastrophe), social historical myths (e.g. migration), and individual historical myths (e.g. life of a savior) belong to the first type (*retrospective* myths). Interpretive myths descriptive of the forces responsible for recurrent seasonal changes (e.g. movements of celestial bodies, fertility) or for a recurrent, chronological series of social or personality changes (e.g. transformations of the self) belong to the third type (*perennial* myths). Terminal, prophetic, promissory, and apocalyptic myths (social or individual), descriptive of a unique mission, great encounter, and ultimate better world (e.g. utopia, kingdom of heaven, world socialism, salvation, immortality, nirvana) belong to the second type (*prospective* myths). All three types may be combined in a complete metahistory of a society or metabiography of an individual.

3. *Functional definition. A myth is an influential representation whose powers may be estimated in terms of the social scope, the*

temporal span, and the average intensity of its effects, these effects being of five classes: *a*) *cynosural-emotional-memorable-inspirational*, *b*) *convictional*, *c*) *evaluational*, *d*) *conational*, and *e*) *integrational*. Let us examine this definition part by part.

3.1. *cynosural, emotional, memorable, inspirational effects:* a mythic representation is peculiarly and mysteriously attractive to the senses and imagination (vivid, impressive, enchanting, spectacular, dramatic, marvelous). It becomes the focus of rapt attention, excitement, wonder, thought, and talk (cynosure), and leaves a durable and recurrent imprint in the minds of its receptors (memorable). Its power in these respects is often difficult to explain. Besides wonder, one or more other emotions are generally involved: an affect corresponding to that of the hero or heroine of the drama (empathic identification) or an affect, reciprocal or complementary, to that of some represented entity (e.g. awe, fear, guilt in the presence of an indignant deity). The representation may console, encourage, relieve anxiety, increase self-respect, or engender hope, and, in addition, evoke and bind positive affection (fellow-feeling, love, gratitude, compassion, admiration, adoration) for a major character in the story (e.g. Osiris, Astarte, Adonis, Buddha, Job, Christ, Tristan, St. Joan, Don Quixote, Hamlet, etc.).

Futhermore a myth inspires receptors with artistic gifts to reproduce it in its original form or in variant forms and thus, through chains of transmission, to propagate it down the generations. One measure of the value of a myth, then, is the quality of the imaginative symbolism and of the works of art which it inspires.

3.2. *convictional effects:* a mythic representation has a cognitive property, or function, in so far as it elicits belief or faith in its essential validity or authenticity. Contrary to the tenet of several of the foremost mythologists of the past century, this is not the primary function of most myths (it may be the primary function of etiological myths); but it is a necessary secondary or subsidiary function. A representation of an event in which nobody has ever believed, literally or symbolically, and/or in which nobody believes today, is not a myth. Although it is generally agreed that a myth is a story which "purports to be true," most people are quick to add that a myth is, in fact, false, however true it may once have seemed or may now seem to its adherents. For those who say this, the stories or visions of the future in which they themselves believe and take to heart are not myths; only the stories or visions cherished by those with whom they disagree are myths. This major source of confusion and dissension calls for a concerted effort to arrive at some acceptable solution.

First, let us note that the O.E.D.'s definition of "myth" as a "wholly fictitious story" has no basis in antiquity, the term having been initially employed to denote the exact opposite: a sacred story, or an *hierophany*, as Eliade has called it—an impressive, compelling manifestation of a spiritual force, an epiphany of the superhuman psychic determinant of a critical event. The fact that animistic nature myths and primitive myths generally have been invalidated by science is not sufficient reason for asserting that *all* myths are false, by definition. Countless scientific theories have been similarly invalidated, but this does not lead us to assert that *all* theories are false. We say that theories are the best things science has invented, even though the latest and best of these best things are not considered to be wholly and precisely true.

It has already been pointed out that the linkage of "myth" (the sacred truth of pagans) with "falsehood," as well as the linkage of "gospel" with "truth," was hammered in by generations of Christian writers for reasons that are quite obvious. But now that it is generally acknowledged that Christianity itself has its ineradicable roots in myth, it is no longer the religionists, but those whose conception of truth is restricted to perceptible, objective facts who are most inclined to tie myth and falsehood in one package. This is to be expected, since myth is a product of imperceptible (but no less real and true) psychic states and dispositions and, in many of its best forms, has reference to these; and, furthermore, a large class of myths (*prospective* myths) refer to possibilities in the as-yet imperceptible future.

According to the definition here submitted, then, a live or *vital* myth is a representation of a state, situation, or event (past, current, or future) which, at its lowest, is accepted by its carriers as sufficiently valid (credible, satisfying), or, at its highest, is embraced as "the nearest approach to absolute truth that can be stated" (Coomaraswamy). Like a theory, however, a myth may not be credible to others, and it may cease to be credible, literally or symbolically, to those who formerly adhered to it; in which cases we might speak of an abandoned or *inert* myth. But it should be stressed that the convictional function of a myth is, in most cases, subsidiary to its conational function: it may be most effective when it provides no more than what is necessary in the way of an historical and contemporary perspective—say, a description of relevant antecedent events, of the current crisis, and of the desired outcome—to give meaning, significance, and urgency to some individual or social endeavor.

3.3. *evaluational effects:* one function of a myth is to propagate and periodically revive and re-establish veneration for the entities and processes it represents. Also, the myth itself, being highly valued, will ordinarily attain a superordinate, "sacred" position in the conscience of its carriers.

3.4. *conational effects:* these are of two kinds; the first is to excite and orient certain valued actional dispositions, guide conduct, and sustain effort (*eductional* myth); the second is to do the opposite: to weaken or suppress certain disvalued actional dispositions (*deterrent* myth). By illustrating a basic aimful need, its actuation, and its outcome, undesirable or desirable, a myth presents a model, as does a parable, of what should be done if possible or of what should not be done under the given circumstances. It provides, one might say, a graphic exemplification of a precept, or even an operational definition of a possible scientific proposition: if in a *situation* of class 13, a man attempts an action of class 27, the *outcome* will be one of class 9. If the aim or action of an otherwise admirable hero is extravagant, vainglorious, shameful, or immoral and its outcome tragic, the story should produce, in susceptible receptors, an empathic discharge and a subsequent reduction (weakening or suppression) of comparable, latent dispositions (*cathartic and deterrent* function). But if the aim and action of the hero or heroic group is admirable and the outcome happy (or even tragic), a potent myth will serve to encourage or sometimes imperatively impose comparable behavior. This I am calling the *eductional* (drawing forth) function of a myth. We have such words as "imitation," "emulation," "actional identification" to describe what a witness of a conspicuous act may do; but, so far as I know, there is no common word— no word as suitable as "educe" ("eduction," "eductive")—to describe what the conspicuous actor (exemplar, eductor) is doing, intentionally or unintentionally. Eductional myths may be individual or collective.

Collective eductional myths of an especially potent species describe the alignment of forces already engaged or soon to become engaged in a crucial and decisive conflict, perennial or final. The forces which are in line with the group's welfare, with its hopes for the future, being beneficent in direction, are exalted as the good powers. The opposing and hence maleficent forces are portrayed as evil. It is a struggle-to-the-finish, then, between the forces of good and evil in one or another guise—light and darkness, renewal and decay, evolution and stagnation, unity and disunity, conservation and destruction, life and death—forces which have been commonly embodied in two opposing supernatural beings (e.g. God and Satan, Christ and anti-Christ, God and Allah), and more recently in two opposing -isms (e.g. Communism and Capitalism). According to this myth the triumph of the good force is inevitable, provided all become empathically identified with its objective and by certain prescribed co-actions assist in its achievement. Here the convictional function of the myth gives place to its conational function. The myth is conationally successful if it sets forth the confronting situation in such a way as to evoke social participation in acts which ultimately accomplish something.

3.5. *integrational effects:* a potent myth has the property of engendering unanimous passionate participation of all functions of the personality (*individual* myth), or of all members of a society (*collective* myth), and thereby of unifying and strengthening the person or the group. According to this criterion of the potency of a collective mythic ideology, the truth or falsehood of its representation of the group's present situation and future destiny, or the merit of the goal of the endeavor (as judged by posterity), or even the external effectiveness or ineffectiveness of the prescribed actions (ritual or actual) are of secondary importance: what counts is the achievement and maintenance of social solidarity (Durkheim). A myth is valuable if it prevents disintegration, decadence, or civil war.

4. *Conditional definition. A ritual myth is an imagined event represented in words spoken by an appointed agent (e.g. shaman, priest, medicine man) during the event's ceremonial enaction at a prescribed place and time. Not all veritable myths are of this type.* Those who assert that "myth" means primitive *ritual* myth and nothing else are arbitrarily limiting the term to what is assumed to be the first public occasion and first purpose of a recited myth—say, to cooperate with the performers of a religious rite (enactors of the myth) in their efforts to imitate, assist, and influence a beneficent god or spirit in bringing about a desired state of society and of nature. I have called this type of semantic restriction the fallacy of phylogenetic primacy, because if we confine the referent of a word (e.g. myth) to the first *known* appearance of a certain entity, this referent must be abandoned (e.g. ritual myths can no longer be called myths) if an earlier appearance of the entity is subsequently discovered. Furthermore, if we do this, every later appearance of the entity (e.g. the same sacred story recited under other conditions or with different aims, or various successive modifications of the story) must be designated by another name. My procedure has been to use adjectives to distinguish different kinds of myth.

I can see no good reason for excluding from the category "myth" all stories, no matter how primitive or sacred, whose association with a rite is neither traceable nor probable (e.g. numerous myths collected by anthropologists); exclude all stories which, during their descent from primitive, sacred (and maybe ritual) narratives, lost much of their primitiveness and compelling sacredness as a result of the refinements and elaborations of story-tellers, poets, and dramatists—stories which were still about the gods (sacred in this sense) but which were no longer evocative of belief and veneration (not sacred in this sense)—e.g. the classical myths of Greece and Rome); exclude all less primitive stories about a person, such as Buddha, or the Virgin Mary, who made no claims to supernatural parentage and powers (not sacred in this sense), and yet is worshipped by millions as a supreme being (sacred in this sense); exclude all sublimated and symbolically re-interpreted descendants of early myths, which, though still held sacred and, in some cases, associated with a religious ceremony, have been purged of much of their original primitiveness (e.g. myths of Christianity, the Eucharist); and also exclude all cherished and widespread secular stories with mythic roots and characteristics that were composed within the last two thousand years in response to some state of affairs which, in certain respects, was unexampled in primitive societies (e.g. Faust myth in relation to Christianity, the Communist "apocalyptic" myth, Nazi myths).

As to the question of the priority of ritual and the invariable linkage of myth and ritual, it appears that those who cleave to this view are basing their judgments on documents drawn almost exclusively from the Near East (especially those descriptive of the death and rebirth rite); and though the theory is supported by many of the findings of recent, world-wide surveys, the amount of disconfirming data is at present so substantial that the rite-myth hypothesis can no longer be accepted as applicable around the globe. In the most comprehensive examination and judicious weighing of the evidence from primitive cultures that I have read, Kluckhohn[13] cites several instances of the composition of myths antecedent to the inauguration of a correlative ceremony, and of myths that are not associated and apparently have never been associated with ritual performances.

"To a considerable extent," Kluckhohn concludes, "the whole

question of the primacy of ceremonial or mythology is as meaningless as all questions of 'the hen or the egg' form." A statement with which I heartily concur, because, as I see it, a mythic imagent (imaginal event: dream, fantasy, vision, trance, apperception, recollection), mythic narrative (event described in words), and mythic rite (event enacted physically), are interdependent, and all three related in some way to a given environmental situation or event. A mythic imagent—being either an imaginative apperception (interpretation) of an environmental situation or event, or this *plus* a vision of modifying the event in progress, of coping with the situation, improving or transforming it, or of escaping to a better situation—a mythic imagent constitutes the central variable in all transactions of this class, the patterned process intermediate between the environment and any overt endeavor to respond to it effectively. Undisputed is the insight—generative of the profound rite-myth theory—that an act (say an instinctive act—analogous to a ritual—which is empathic with a movement in nature) precedes, in the chronology of a child's development, any—analogous to a recited myth —verbal description of the act. But here we are discussing elaborate *collective* rituals performed by adults, which evolved, we may suppose, from the simple to the complex down the generations; and it seems hardly possible that throughout this long history of ritualistic enactions, there were no dreams, fantasies, or visions (mythic imagents) about the gods to whom these ceremonies were addressed and no exchanges of these visions (mythic narratives) among those who were periodically participating in the elaboration of the rites. These considerations lead to a theory of interdependence, with any temporal order of the three overt channels of representation—narration, enaction, and depiction (e.g. cave paintings, figurines of Earth Goddess)—being possible, though not equally probable, and with the covert channel of representation—imagination—being almost inevitably prior to the other three.

5. *Causal definition. A myth is a product of imaginations oriented and sustained by one or more basic needs and feelings*

(*dynamic psychic determinants*) *in response to a critical situation* (*instigational determinant*) *which is experienced, consciously or unconsciously, by the society as a whole, by members of a certain class, or by numerous individuals as persons.* I have already given illustrations of these and other classes of determinants, and a brief summary should be sufficient at this point.

The sense of empathic (mystical) participations with surrounding nature, projections of psychic beings, states and processes into environmental phenomena (e.g. Jehovah's voice in the hurricane), and the incongruous, preternatural figures and effects— exhibited in primitive myths, in the fantasies of children, the dreams of adults, the visions of highly creative people (e.g. Blake, Melville, Nietzsche), and the hallucinations of psychotics —may be partly attributed to the nature of the mental processes —the autonomous, disjunctive, undirected and uncorrected sequences of imagents—that occur in primitive, fluid, intraceptive, dream-like states of mind (general *structural psychic determinant*). In other words, the psyche of a myth-maker, ancient or modern, must be open *at times* to influxions from the "depths" of the "unconscious" ("id" system). By primitives, such influxions were taken literally (as in a dream), but by modern poets they are eagerly received and judged as possible symbolic or metaphorical expressions.

To explain primitive man's awe of nature—fear of the dark, biting animals, hurricanes, floods, and so forth—as well as his daylight feelings of participation and reciprocation, another factor should be added, namely, direct, unsheltered exposure to the caprices of environmental forces (general *positional, situational determinant*). But I have already said a good deal—too much perhaps—about nature myths, and since man has now gained considerable knowledge and control of physical and chemical forces, and succeeded in constructing artificial environments in which to live, nature has become less intimate and less threatening to the majority of people and only in our more poetic moods is it endowed with psychic attributes. Henceforth, then, I shall confine myself to myths whose referents are societies, special groups, two persons, a single person, or components of a person.

I have already presented examples of critical situations (*instigational determinants*) as well as of the fundamental needs and emotions (*dynamic psychic determinants*) which down the centuries have recurrently been involved in human responses to these situations. The simplest formula is Freud's (expanded to some extent): distressful stimulation leading to a dream or fantasy of an object or person (e.g. breast, mother, father, god, savior), of an external situation (e.g. idyllic environment, better world), of an external event (e.g. death of enemy or rival), or of an act (e.g. murder, copulation, glorious achievement) that will reduce the distressful stimulation (e.g. appease the aroused need). If the imagined, wish-fulfilling act is consciously or unconsciously felt to be sinful or criminal (e.g. parricide, incest), provoking to others or extremely dangerous (e.g. flight), the dream is likely to include the dreaded resultant of the act—retaliation, punishment, fall—and thus serve as a deterrent. But now the person (dreamer) will be involved in another type of stressful state, namely, that of internal conflict between a strong primitive drive and an inhibiting fear of the consequences of its actuation. The kind of response that is now called for is one which will resolve the painful conflict, abolish anxiety, and restore the harmony of the personality as well as the harmony of whatever interpersonal relationships were involved.

Religions, myths, philosophies, and systems of psychotherapy have been largely or partly devoted to the achievement of unifying resolutions of this type and of more complicated types, in the society as a whole and/or in its individual members; and to the degree that any one of these systems succeeds in doing this—in preventing or relieving intolerable conflicts, curing "sick souls"—people will trust it, cling to it, believe in it, and conform to its prescriptions. Furthermore, to the extent that such high evaluations are shared by the population at large, the system will serve as a cohesive force. Thus, the relief of suffering, the gratification of the wish for spiritual unity and health, might well be added to the above-given *functional* definition of a myth. Here we happen to be viewing this achievement as one of the determinants of the myth's power to generate conviction and orient behavior. But clearly the two factors are mutually dependent: if a person is cured of an ailment he is more likely to be convinced of the truth of the correlative myth, and if he believes the myth he is more likely to be cured. As Julius Caesar is supposed to have said, "Most people believe what they want to believe."

What can be said about the origination or genesis of a myth? We are apt to talk—thinking of archetypes and the perennial philosophy—as if universal myths had been residing in man's mind since time immemorial. A better conception would be that of *mythic genes*—elements of mythic compositions—as very stable, potential image-tendencies, and yet perpetually engaged from generation to generation in a procession of compositions, decompositions, and novel re-compositions, so that it would be virtually impossible to point to a single mind as the place in space-time where a new, unexampled combination of mythic genes occurred for the first time.

A somewhat comparable difficulty is encountered in tracing the genealogy and allocating the credit for a new scientific proposition, such as the theory of evolution. But still we do point, with justice, to particular individuals as the ones who presided, each in his own way, over a revolutionary synthesis of ideas that occurred, unconsciously and consciously, in his head. Locating the origin of new mythic compositions is another matter: impossible in the case of prehistoric myths and not easy when it comes to modern myths. Myths are more likely to be formed unconsciously by slow degrees in many contemporary minds and must wait for their acceptance and propagation until the psyches of others are prepared for their reception. Also, recent myths are harder to identify: they are either veiled by the conceptual, discursive language of social ideology and social science (e.g. Marxism, Freudianism), or they are fragmentary, being still in process of cultural evolution.

In summary it may be said that the creative imaginations

which participate in the formation of a *vital* myth must be those of people—often alienated and withdrawn people—who have *experienced,* in their "depths" and on their own pulses, one or more of the unsolved critical situations with which humanity at large or members of their own society are confronted. In other words, suffering in "representative men" may be one of the necessary determinants of an adequate response to challenge.

6. *Summary of definitions.* Disregarding nature myths (whose referents, in today's scientific terms, are physical, chemical, biological, and physiological entities and events), the following slight reconstruction of what has been said in this section may prove useful:

6.1 *mythic representation:* a sensible (sensuous, graphic), symbolic representation of an imagined situation or series of events, especially, today, a story or drama in poetic prose—not an abstract, conceptual (scientific) model of a certain class of events, nor an accurate, factual report of a specific event.

6.2 *mythic content:* a story which is manifestly about one or more extraordinary persons or preternatural psychic beings (e.g. god, whale, Frankenstein) or about a group or society as a unit, earnestly and wholly engaged in a series of important, critical endeavors (matters of physical, social, or spiritual vitality or death)—not about trivial people involved in inconsequential interactions.

6.3. *mythic thema:* a story which clearly, dramatically, and memorably exemplifies a basic or crucial (archetypal, virtually universal, or emergent and creative) plot structure—not a confused medley of several artificial, minor plots.

6.4. *mythic referent:* a story whose symbolism refers to intrapersonal, interpersonal, intrasocial, intersocial, or human-environmental states, forces, establishments, and interactions (conflicts), or to supernatural beings (e.g. extra-natural deities).

6.5. *mythic function*

6.51 *evaluational and conational function:* a) *eductional function:* a story which offers better values to its receptors, and—by presenting an example of a better type of action in a given type of situation, or of the solution of a distressful conflict, or of a better way of life or better target of endeavor—educes emulative efforts and thereby changes personalities and/or their modes of living. This is the chief criterion of a *vital* myth as contrasted with an *inert* myth. b) *deterrent function:* a story which produces a catharsis and subsequent inhibition of an actional disposition.

6.52 *convictional function:* a story which is literally or symbolically credible to its receptors, congruent with reality, a story which portrays a form of interaction or a state of being which is realizable or conceivable, an outcome that is not impossible. Like a fable, it may be "a lie which tells the truth," or, like a parable, it may convey a particle of the wisdom of the ages or new wisdom.

6.53 *cynosural, emotional, or memorable function:* a story or drama in poetry or prose which "rejoices the aesthetic imagination" and leaves an indelible and recurrent impression.

6.54 *integrational function:* a large collection of sensible representations of events (mythology) which serves to unify a whole society.

Many modern works of literature satisfy a number of these criteria: 6.1, *mythic (symbolic) representation;* 6.4, *mythic referent;* 6.53, *mythic cynosural and emotive function;* and even 6.52, *mythic convictional function*—astonishing "the intellect with a new aspect of the truth." Of these, some are veritable exemplifications of 6.3, *a mythic thema* in modern dress. As for 6.2, *mythic content,* it seems that most artists and writers of our time are consciously oriented in the opposite direction, intent on describing trivial, impotent, neurotic, decerebrate, or hollow non-heroes, engaged in an essentially inconsequential sequence of events, who go out "not with a bang but a whimper." It is true that many highly intelligent young men—"Beats" in the broadest sense—have been empathically drawn in this general direction, but not with much zest and hope; and it would be hard to name a modern work which genuinely fulfills 6.51, *mythic evaluational and conational function* (either eductional or deterrent). Of course we are a long way from 6.54, *mythic integrational function* (either individual or social).

This brings me to a question which, for certain obscure reasons, was postponed until this point: How shall we classify the numberless stories which exhibit some characteristics of a myth, however defined, as well as some characteristics of a non-myth? Is there the slightest possibility of agreeing on a rule which will tell us what proportion of what characteristics (say, of the above-listed criteria) must be identified for a story to be called a myth rather than a non-myth? Would it not be better, at least in debatable instances, to discriminate the mythic and the non-mythic parts or aspects of a story, instead of trying to decide into which of the two categories the whole medley should be forced? Personally, I would say "yes for the time being," and, instead of "myth," speak of "mythic contents," or "mythic thema," or "mythic function," and so forth.

Quite different from composing myths in mythic diction for mythic functions is the craftsman's use of one or more inert myths of antiquity as scaffolding for image sequences, or in order to supply the learned with opportunities to identify recondite allusions, or to imbue his work with some flavor of profundity—to do this, tongue in cheek, without conviction or commitment.

No plenitude of mythic images, references, symbols, names, or parallels can constitute a living myth, and, if used in this sense, however sanctimoniously, "myth" will deteriorate into a five-cent term and a counterfeit at that.

7. *Covert myths.* Very likely I have given the impression that I am looking forward to the time when poets and artists will collaborate in creating a saving mythology for mankind. This is partly true, since out of admiration—and ignorance no doubt— I am bent to the belief that the world cannot be changed in a desirable direction and remain changed for successive generations without the free and spontaneous collaboration of every form of art. Witness Christian art. But I surmise—anyhow for our time—that creative ideas and creative lives will more generally precede it, though not by a long span. What will inevitably come

first are *covert* myths—mythic imagents (visions)—which may be translated into theoretical language (the dominant diction of our time) and simultaneously or somewhat later into action, after which the arts will come, and make the heretofore covert myths visible to all.

Pertinent at this point is Whitehead's famous comment that Christianity "has always been a religion seeking a metaphysic, in contrast to Buddhism which is a metaphysic generating a religion."[14] If we substitute "mythology" for "religion," and "metapsychology" or "metasociology" for "metaphysic," a discernible, ongoing cultural trend can be formulated in this way: (i) a developmental metapsychology, (ii) partly corresponding patterns of child-rearing, self-development, and interpersonal relations, and (iii) partly corresponding mythic themes represented in poetry, prose, and works of art. In other words, these trends indicate an almost synchronous and interdependent middle course between Buddhism and Christianity, closer to the former than the latter sequence. An obvious example is psychoanalysis with its novel, theoretical reconstruction of the Hebraic-Christian mythology (e.g. the inherited trace of the original sin of parracide from the prehistoric past, the imaginal recurrence in each child of the Oedipus drama, the upper superego in place of Heaven and Jehovah, the lower id in place of Hell and Satan, etc.). Also to be noted is the mutual influence of psychoanalysis and literature, and of psychoanalysis and personalities in process, the former shaped by observations of the latter and the latter shaped by the theories and practices of the former.

On the societal level we can observe in Marxism comparable, interdependent evolutions in the three spheres of activity: (i) an historical metasociology, (ii) corresponding patterns of social action, and (iii) a partly corresponding literature, all initiated and sustained by a secular form of the apocalyptic myth.

Communism, a mystique which tends toward war, tries to make the healthy into more effective social agents; and hence will have no truck with Freudianism, which is primarily concerned with the experiences of individual children, and with the disturbances of childhood as determinants of mental illness in adults as individuals. In process, possibly, is a mythology for peace and concord on the societal level, and, on the personal level, a mythology for successive stages of optimal development from adolescence to old age, as indicated by Erikson[15] for example.

8. *Part-myths.* Whoever is interested in modern myths will necessarily be alert to myths in the making, and hence to mythic fragments—covert images veiled by theoretical statements, symbols, metaphorical expressions, new enthusiasms, trends of thematic content in mass media, "explosions" of new slang, and so forth. The task is to extract mythic images and imagents from a large number of heterogeneous partial exemplifications and, if possible, to make a coherent whole of them.

D. SUMMARY OF ENDEAVOR

The definitions and formulations I have given are by no means complete or comprehensive; but I trust they are sufficient to the aims that I have had in mind, namely:

(i) To distinguish various aspects of a myth (formal, functional, etc.) and various kinds of myths (etiological, eductional, etc.), and thereby to make places for many dissimilar current definitions, which, when placed where they belong, will be seen to be complementary or supplementary rather than mutually contradictory. The largest variety of definitions culled from various literatures are those which are expressed in emotive metaphors, each of which conveys in unique diction a subjective *experience* of a myth. Some of these statements are choice and valuable in their own right and could have served as illustrations of the emotional or convictional effects of myths on a number of sensitive receptors; but since they were not strictly germane to my more pedestrian objective, these were not incorporated. I myself have tried to inhibit rhetoric whenever possible, convinced that in this endeavor cognitive clarity, however flat, was the one desideratum.

(ii) To furnish adequate reasons for rejecting three arbitrary tenets; namely, that the meaning of the term "myth" should be limited a) to stories composed by prehistoric man, and/or b) to stories recited in conjunction with a sacred ritual, and/or c) to false beliefs (graphically represented) which purport to be true. It has seemed best to differentiate each of these fundamental classes with an appropriate adjective, and thereby to free "myth" for further usages, such as European witchcraft myths, the Tristan and Isolde myth, the metaphysical myths of India, and modern myths in process of creation. A myth never reproduces the perception of a specific, overt (historical) event, and hence it is never true or false in these terms. Its function is to evoke a total empathic experience of the essential features of a series of prototypical events, often accompanied by the belief that conduct should be guided (activated or inhibited) by this vicarious experience. Here "truth" may mean, "essentially and importantly true to life," or "true value," "true path," or "true goal."

(iii) To show in what respects a possible modern myth might resemble a primitive myth—first and foremost in its functional properties—, and, in so doing, provide links between what people do not hesitate and what they do hesitate to call a myth.

E. CHALLENGE

Among the interrelated instigating situations which distress the world today, more particularly the Western world and Western individuals as persons, the following are perceived by many people: a) the probability of the mutual extermination of the technologically more advanced nations of the two Northern Hemispheres; b) the aggressive, world-ambitious mystique (apocalyptic ideology) of Communism in the East and the absence of any comparably dynamic, world-unifying vision in the West; c) the hypertrophy of greed for material possessions and comforts, and for individual and national power and prestige based on such possessions, constituting, on the one hand, the principal, irresistible forces productive of fierce, global competitions for markets and resources, and eventually of a genocidal war; and on the other hand, within each nation, resulting in a gigantic, heart-breaking disproportion of matter, mechanisms, and shallow, regulated social contacts *over* spirit, depth of thought and feeling, joyous spontaneities, and quality of interpersonal relations; d) the senescence of the traditional religions and their present incapacity in the face of the world's strait to bring forth a new vision of a better world, to generate widespread passionate belief in their own doctrines, or, in all sincerity, to guide individual self-development and conduct in the light of an acceptable ideal, and *partly* because of the unfilled vacuum left by the decay of these religions, the spread of existential anxiety, affectlessness, meaninglessness, spiritual loneliness, hollowness, alienation, and regressive emotional drift (the "Beat" phenomenon).

Instigations of these vast dimensions are too appalling to be held steadily in mind by more than a few people. The majority, made anxious by such prospects, repress them and go about their own affairs. But this being one of the most momentous instances in human history of Challenge, as Toynbee would say, there must be some potential, creative Response latent in the unconscious depths of a good many Western people. I have already discussed several channels of response—covert mythic visions, theoretical and ideological constructions, experimental actions and directions of individual development, and, in conjunction with these, mythic works of art. But, so far as I can see, there are no known mythic patterns which are appropriate to the magnitude and exigency of the confronting situation. To succeed, I would surmise, they will have to be as radical and revolutionary as the antibiological Sermon on the Mount.

Would it be less revolutionary or more revolutionary, from the point of view of our innate store of self-serving, egocentric instincts, to suggest that the mystique of the hero, savior, charismatic leader, or great man—Christ or Caesar—and the mystique of the elect minority with a mission, of inflated nationalism, or the great nation are all obsolete? If so, what would our instincts say to a procession of myths in which there were never less than two chief characters—two leaders meeting amicably at the summit, two nations settling their disputes, rituals cementing international reciprocities and concord; and, on the personal level also, never less than two chief characters, man and woman, in a creative, mutually self-developing relationship?

REFERENCES

1. Joseph Campbell, *The Hero with a Thousand Faces,* Bollingen Series XVII (New York: Pantheon Books, 1949).
2. Donald A. Stauffer, "The Modern Myth of the Modern Myth," *English Institute Essays,* 1947 (New York: Columbia University Press, 1948).
3. Richard Chase, *Quest for Myth* (Baton Rouge: Louisiana State University Press, 1949).
4. Philip Rahv, "The Myth and the Powerhouse," *Partisan Review,* November-December, 1953.
5. Jean Seznec, *The Survival of the Pagan Gods,* Bollingen Series XXVIII (New York: Pantheon Books, 1953).
6. Frank E. Manuel, *The Eighteenth Century Confronts the Gods* (Boston: Harvard University Press, 1959).
7. B. Malinowski, *Myth in Primitive Psychology,* Psyche Miniatures, General Series No. 6 (London: Kegan Paul, Trench, Trubner & Co., 1926).
8. Frazer, quoted in Herbert Weisinger, "Some Meanings of Myth," *Comparative Literature, Proceedings of the ICLA Congress in Chapel Hill, N. C.* (Chapel Hill: University of North Carolina Press, 1959), p. 6.
9. Ernest G. Schachtel, *Metamorphosis* (New York: Basic Books, Inc., 1959).
10. J. W. Mellor, *A Comprehensive Treatise on Inorganic and Theoretical Chemistry* (London: Longmans, Green & Co., 1922), p. 3.
11. Lewis Spence, *The Outlines of Mythology* (London: Watts & Co., 1944), p. 1.
12. Herbert M. McLuhan, *The Mechanical Bride* (New York: Vanguard Press, Inc., 1951).
13. Clyde Kluckhohn, "Myths and Rituals: a General Theory," *The Harvard Theological Review,* Vol. XXXV, No. 1, January, 1942.
14. Alfred North Whitehead, *Religion in the Making* (New York: Macmillan Co., 1926), p. 50.
15. Erik H. Erikson, *Childhood and Society* (New York: W. W. Norton & Co., 1950).

Appendix

I

THE WORD "MYTH" is subject to many variant and often opposing definitions, in particular as it is applied to the products of modern man's imagination. It has seemed fitting, therefore, to recall a memorable passage from Mark Schorer's *William Blake*. It provides, so far as we know, as complete and concise a view of current usage of the term as recent literature affords.

The Necessity of Myth

MARK SCHORER

THE DEFINITION of mysticism, to be useful at all, must be stringent, for mysticism is in itself a highly specialized experience. But the definition of myth, if the term is to be used in the discussion of modern poets, particularly of William Blake, must be both broad and loose, for myth operates universally and diversely. The term must include such varying manifestations as the sharply formed figures of classic fable and the malformations of delusion and neurosis. Even a loose definition does not include, however, the current journalistic sense of falsehood, nor does it imply anti-intellectualism or any other such pejorative. The term denotes, in fact, neither the negation nor the contrary of ideas, but their basis and their structure, the element by which they are activated. "The doctrines which men ostensibly hold," wrote Leslie Stephen, "do not become operative upon their conduct until they have generated an imaginative symbolism."

Myths are the instruments by which we continually struggle to make our experience intelligible to ourselves. A myth is a large, controlling image that gives philosophical meaning to the facts of ordinary life; that is, which has organizing value for experience. A mythology is a more or less articulated body of such images, a pantheon. Without such images, experience is chaotic, fragmentary and merely phenomenal. It is the chaos of experience that creates them, and they are intended to rectify it. All real convictions involve a mythology, either in its usual, broad sense or in a private sense. In the first case it is embodied in literature or in ritual or in both, in which it has application to the whole of a society and tends to be religious. In the second, it remains in the realm of fantasy, in which it tends to be obsessive and fanatical. This is not to say that sound myths of general application necessarily support religions; rather that they perform the historical functions of religion—they unify experience in a way that is satisfactory to the whole culture and to the whole personality. Philip Wheelwright, from the point of view of an uncommon philosophical theism, argues understandably that "the very essence of myth" is "that haunting awareness of transcendental forces peering through the cracks of the visible universe." Durkheim pointed out that myth suggests the sacred rather than the profane; that is, the enormous area of experience into which technology cannot usefully enter rather than the relatively small area into which it does. Yet this does not make religious experience proper more than a portion of the larger area. That myth cannot be so limited is made clear by our own civilization, which seems to be struggling toward a myth that will be explicitly ethical, even political. Today, Thomas Mann has said, "the question of the human conscience . . . is presented to us essentially in its political form; perhaps more than in any other epoch of history, it wears a political face." Wars may be described as the clash of mythologies; and a basically disorganized society such as ours is the result of a number of antithetical and competing mythologies that fail to adjust themselves.

Rational belief is secondary. We habitually tend to overlook the fact that as human beings we are rational creatures not first of all but last of all, and that civilization emerged only yesterday from a primitive past that is at least relatively timeless. Belief organizes experience not because it is rational but because all belief depends on a controlling imagery, and rational belief is the intellectual formalization of that imagery. . . . As a basic set of images, Christianity has commanded the unanimous faith of millions; as a system of belief capable of a wide variety of dogmas, it has commanded the intellectual assent of hostile sectarian groups. Such a more recent mythology as socialism, which as a faith presents an international hope for the full development of democratic man, is rent by schisms as dogma.

All those systems of abstractions which we call ideologies activate our behavior, when they do, only because they are themselves activated by images, however submerged. An abstraction is a generalization, and the essential antecedents of generalizations are *things*. Jung, writing of language, has made the useful observation that "Speech is a storehouse of images founded in experience, and therefore concepts which are too abstract do not easily take root in it, or quickly die out again for lack of contact with reality." Are not ideas, like language itself, supported by the "submerged metaphor"? In this sense, myth is indispensable to any form of belief. And in this sense, one may even concur with Hume's offensive remark that "there is no such passion in human minds, as the love of mankind, merely as such"; for this passion, like all others, must have an image, real or ideal, as its correlative. Myth is fundamental, the dramatic representation of our deepest instinctual life, of a primary awareness of man in the universe, capable of many configurations, upon which all particular opinions and attitudes depend. Wallace Stevens writes: ". . . we live in an intricacy of new and local mythologies, political, economic, poetic, which are asserted with an ever-enlarging incoherence." Even when, as in modern civilization, myths multiply and separate and tend to become abstract so that the images themselves recede and fade, even then they are still the essential substructure of all human activity.

Most profoundly they apply in literature. Great literature is impossible without a previous imaginative consent to a ruling mythology that makes intelligible and unitive the whole of that experience from which particular fables spring and from which they, in turn, take their meaning. Literature ceases to be perceptual and tends to degenerate into mere description without adequate myth; for, to cite Malinowski, myth, continually modified and renewed by the modifications of history, is in some form an "indispensable ingredient of all culture." Thus, for example, the prevailing and tiresome realism of modern fiction. When we feel that we are no longer in a position to say what life means, we must content ourselves with telling how it looks. Those of our novelists who have transcended realism have done so by a bootstrap miracle, by supplying the myth themselves. Mann has made a possibly artificial use of literary myth. Joyce attempted to distil their mythical essences from specifically modern developments such as psychology. Kafka disturbingly dramatized neurosis. In a disintegrating society such as this, before it can proceed with other business, literature must become the explicit agent of coherence. In the realm of the imagination serious artists must be like Hart Crane's tramps in their cross-country freight cars: "They know a body under the wide rain." All readers are aware that the chief energies of modern poets have been expended not simply in writing poetry but in employing poetry to discover its indispensable substructure. They have been compelled to build a usable mythology, one that will account for and organize our competing and fragmentary myths. T. S. Eliot is the most familiar example; here excursions into anthropology and Orientalism preceded and enriched the final embrace of Christian orthodoxy. The example of Yeats is no less spectacular and is even more systematic: Years devoted to the exploration of magic and spiritualism and all the disreputable purlieus of mysticism were combined with the results of a late interest in politics, and the curious mixture seems to have served its purpose. Americans generally have found the material for their myths nearer at hand than have modern Europeans. Hart Crane ingeniously but unsuccessfully utilized a combination of American legend and modern American industrialism in the construction of his single sustained work. Older poets and poets less given to self-questioning, like Robert Frost, were apparently quite comfortable in employing the available myth of the independent American democrat for which younger men no longer find historical sanction. Among younger men, the quest is apparent in such diverse examples as W. H. Auden, Delmore Schwartz, and Karl Shapiro, and one could multiply the instances. The hunt for the essential image goes on everywhere today—but the problem is hardly new.

II

GEORGES SOREL noted that those who are actively committed to the promotion of a great revolutionary movement invariably envisage a critical conflict in which their cause will triumph. This product of the apocalyptic imagination—this "myth," in Sorel's language—is of all factors the most potent in converting people and motivating them to action, despite the rational analyses and invalidations of intellectuals.

We are reprinting here a few passages from Sorel's most influential book *Réflexions sur la violence* (published in 1908), a work to which both Fascists and Communists have acknowledged their indebtedness. We do this partly because it is possibly the first sophisticated and explicit statement—pessimistic, Sorel would say, yet confident and impassioned—in favor of the deliberate use of such a myth in bringing about a radical transformation of society; and partly as a reminder of the spirit of importunate and ruthless mythic fervor. Sorel describes the myth of "the general strike" as endowed with the character of *infinity*, "because it puts on one side all discussion of definite reforms and confronts men with a catastrophe" that signifies "absolute revolution."

Reflections on Violence
GEORGES SOREL

AND YET without leaving the present, without reasoning about this future, which seems for ever condemned to escape our reason, we should be unable to act at all. Experience shows that the *framing of a future, in some indeterminate time,* may, when it is done in a certain way, be very effective, and have very few inconveniences; this happens when the anticipations of the future take the form of those myths, which enclose with them all the strongest inclinations of a people, of a party or of a class, inclinations which recur to the mind with the insistence of instincts in all the circumstances of life; and which give an aspect of complete reality to the hopes of immediate action by which, more easily than by any other method, men can reform their desires, passions, and mental activity. We know, moreover, that these social myths in no way prevent a man profiting by the observations which he makes in the course of his life, and form no obstacle to the pursuit of his normal occupations.

The truth of this may be shown by numerous examples.

The first Christians expected the return of Christ and the total ruin of the pagan world, with the inauguration of the kingdom of the saints, at the end of the first generation. The catastrophe did not come to pass, but Christian thought profited so greatly from the apocalyptic myth that certain contemporary scholars maintain that the whole preaching of Christ referred solely to this one point. The hopes which Luther and Calvin had formed of the religious exaltation of Europe were by no means realised; these fathers of the Reformation very soon seemed men of a past era; for present-day Protestants they belong rather to the Middle Ages than to modern times, and the problems which troubled them most occupy very little place in contemporary Protestantism. Must we for that reason deny the immense result which came from their dreams of Christian renovation? It must be admitted that the real developments of the Revolution did not in any way resemble the enchanting pictures which created the enthusiasm of its first adepts; but without those pictures would the Revolution have been victorious? Many Utopias were mixed up with the Revolutionary myth, because it had been formed by a society passionately fond of imaginative literature, full of con-

Reprinted by permission from Georges Sorel, *Reflections on Violence.* Translated by T. E. Hulme and J. Roth, with an introduction by Edward A. Shils. Copyright, 1950, The Free Press of Glencoe, Illinois.

fidence in the "science" and very little acquainted with the economic history of the past. These Utopias came to nothing; but it may be asked whether the Revolution was not a much more profound transformation than those dreamed of by the people who in the eighteenth century had invented social Utopias. In our own times Mazzini pursued what the wiseacres of his time called a mad chimera; but it can no longer be denied that, without Mazzini, Italy would never have become a great power, and that he did more for Italian unity than Cavour and all the politicians of his school.

A knowledge of what the myths contain in the way of details which will actually form part of the history of the future is then of small importance; they are not astrological almanacs; it is even possible that nothing which they contain will ever come to pass— as was the case with the catastrophe expected by the first Christians. In our own daily life, are we not familiar with the fact that what actually happens is very different from our preconceived notion of it? And that does not prevent us from continuing to make resolutions. Psychologists say that there is heterogeneity between the ends in view and the ends actually realised: the slightest experience of life reveals this law to us, which Spencer transferred into nature, to extract therefrom his theory of the multiplication of effects.

The myth must be judged as a means of acting on the present; any attempt to discuss how far it can be taken literally as future history is devoid of sense. *It is the myth in its entirety which is alone important:* its parts are only of interest in so far as they bring out the main idea. No useful purpose is served, therefore, in arguing about the incidents which may occur in the course of a social war, and about the decisive conflicts which may give victory to the proletariat; even supposing the revolutionaries to have been wholly and entirely deluded in setting up this imaginary picture of the general strike, this picture may yet have been, in the course of the preparation for the Revolution, a great element of strength, if it has embraced all the aspirations of Socialism, and if it has given to the whole body of Revolutionary thought a precision and a rigidity which no other method of thought could have given.

To estimate, then, the significance of the idea of the general strike, all the methods of discussion which are current among politicians, sociologists, or people with pretensions to political science, must be abandoned. Everything which its opponents endeavour to establish may be conceded to them, without reducing in any way the value of the theory which they think they have refuted. The question whether the general strike is a partial reality, or only a product of popular imagination, is of little importance. All that it is necessary to know is, whether the general strike contains everything that the Socialist doctrine expects of the revolutionary proletariat.

To solve this question we are no longer compelled to argue learnedly about the future; we are not obliged to indulge in lofty reflections about philosophy, history, or economics; we are not on the plane of theories, and we can remain on the level of observable facts. We have to question men who take a very active part in the real revolutionary movement amidst the proletariat, men who do not aspire to climb into the middle class and whose mind is not dominated by corporative prejudices. These men may be deceived about an infinite number of political, economical, or moral questions; but their testimony is decisive, sovereign, and irrefutable when it is a question of knowing what are the ideas which most powerfully move them and their comrades, which most appeal to them as being identical with their socialistic conceptions, and thanks to which their reason, their hopes, and their way of looking at particular facts seem to make but one indivisible unity.

Thanks to these men, we know that the general strike is indeed what I have said: the *myth* in which Socialism is wholly comprised, *i. e.* a body of images capable of evoking instinctively all the sentiments which correspond to the different manifestations of the war undertaken by Socialism against modern society. Strikes have engendered in the proletariat the noblest, deepest, and most moving sentiments that they possess; the general strike groups them all in a co-ordinated picture, and, by bringing them together, gives to each one of them its maximum of intensity; appealing to their painful memories of particular conflicts, it colours with an intense life all the details of the composition presented to consciousness. We thus obtain that intuition of Socialism which language cannot give us with perfect clearness —and we obtain it as a whole, perceived instantaneously. . . .

The professors of the *little science* are really difficult to satisfy. They assert very loudly that they will only admit into thought abstractions analogous to those used in the deductive sciences: as a matter of fact, this is a rule which is insufficient for purposes of action, for we do nothing great without the help of warmly-coloured and clearly-defined images, which absorb the whole of our attention; now, is it possible to find anything more satisfying from their point of view than the general strike? But, reply the professors, we ought to rely only on those realities which are given by experience: is, then, the picture of the general strike made up of tendencies which were not obtained directly from observation of the revolutionary movement? Is it a work of pure reason, manufactured by indoor scientists attempting to solve the social problem according to the rules of logic? Is it something arbitrary? Is it not, on the contrary, a spontaneous product analogous to those others which students of history come across in periods of action? They insist, and say that man ought not to let himself be carried away by his impulses without submitting them to the control of his intelligence, whose rights are unchallenged; nobody dreams of disputing them; of course, this picture of the general strike must be tested, and that is what I have tried to do above; but the critical spirit does not consist in replacing *historical data* by the *charlatanism of a sham science*. . . .

We are perfectly well aware that the historians of the future are bound to discover that we laboured under many illusions, because they will see behind them a finished world. We, on the other hand, must act, and nobody can tell us to-day what these historians will know; nobody can furnish us with the means of modifying our motor images in such a way as to avoid their criticisms.

Our situation resembles somewhat that of the physicists who work at huge calculations based on theories which are not destined to endure for ever. We have nowadays abandoned all hope of discovering a complete science of nature; the spectacle of modern scientific revolutions is not encouraging for scientists, and has no doubt led many people, naturally enough, to proclaim the bankruptcy of science, and yet we should be mad if we handed the management of industry over to sorcerers, mediums, and wonder-workers. The philosopher who *does not seek to make a practical application of his theories* may take up the point of view of the future historian of science, and then dispute the absolute character of present-day scientific theses; but he is as ignorant as the present-day physicist when he is asked how to correct the explanations given by the latter; must he therefore take refuge in scepticism?

Nowadays no philosophers worthy of consideration accept the sceptical position; their great aim, on the contrary, is to prove the legitimacy of a science which, however, makes no claim to know the real nature of things, and which confines itself to discovering relations which can be utilised for practical ends. It is because sociology is in the hands of people who are incapable of any philosophic reasoning that it is possible for us to be attacked (in the name of the *little science*) for being content with methods founded on the laws that a really thorough psychological analysis reveals as fundamental in the genesis of action, and which are revealed to us in all great historical movements.

To proceed scientifically means, first of all, to know what forces exist in the world and then to take measures whereby we may utilise them, by reasoning from experience. That is why I say that, by accepting the idea of the general strike, although we know that it is a myth, we are proceeding exactly as a modern physicist does who has complete confidence in his science, although he knows that the future will look upon it as antiquated. It is we who really possess the scientific spirit, while our critics have lost touch both with modern science and modern philosophy; and having proved this, we are quite easy in our minds. . . .

Morality is not doomed to perish because the motive forces behind it will change; it is not destined to become a mere collection of precepts as long as it can still vivify itself by an alliance with an enthusiasm capable of conquering all the obstacles, prejudices, and the need of immediate enjoyment, which oppose its progress. But it is certain that this sovereign force will not be found along the paths which contemporary philosophers, the experts of social science, and the inventors of *far-reaching reforms* would make us go. There is only one force which can produce to-day that enthusiasm without whose co-operation no morality is possible, and that is the force resulting from the propaganda in favour of a general strike. The preceding explanations have shown that the idea of the general strike (constantly rejuvenated by the feelings roused by proletarian violence) produces an entirely epic state of mind, and at the same time bends all the energies of the mind to that condition necessary to the realisation of a workshop carried on by free men, eagerly seeking the betterment of the industry; we have thus recognised that there are great resemblances between the sentiments aroused by the idea of the general strike and those which are necessary to bring about a continued progress in methods of production. We have then the right to maintain that the modern world possesses that prime mover which is necessary to the creation of the ethics of the producers.

I stop here, because it seems to me that I have accomplished the task which I imposed upon myself; I have, in fact, established that proletarian violence has an entirely different significance from that attributed to it by superficial scholars and by politicians. In the total ruin of institutions and of morals there remains something which is powerful, new, and intact, and it is that which constitutes, properly speaking, the soul of the revolutionary proletariat. Nor will this be swept away in the general decadence of moral values, if the workers have enough energy to bar the road to the middle-class corrupters, answering their advances with the plainest brutality.

I believe that I have brought an important contribution to discussions on socialism; these discussions must henceforth deal exclusively with the conditions which allow the development of specifically proletarian forces, that is to say, *with violence enlightened by the idea of the general strike.* All the old abstract dissertations on the Socialist *régime* of the future become useless; we pass to the domain of real history, to the interpretation of facts—to the ethical evaluations of the revolutionary movement.

The bond which I pointed out in the beginning of this inquiry between Socialism and proletarian violence appears to us now in all its strength. It is to violence that Socialism owes those high ethical values by means of which it brings *salvation* to the modern world.

III

THOMAS MANN was among the foremost advocates of the "necessity for myth" to modern man. Nevertheless, he did not hold that all myths were valid and beneficent. The following excerpt from *Doctor Faustus* illustrates their contrary aspect. Here we have a gripping portrayal of a group of representative German rationalists in the years immediately following World War I, and of how they became debauched by the myth of Might, merciless and unrestrained.

Doctor Faustus
THOMAS MANN

I HAVE called attention above, quite apart from these evenings, to the disturbance and destruction of apparently fixed values of life brought about by the war, especially in the conquered countries, which were thus in a psychological sense further on than the others. Very strongly felt and objectively confirmed was the enormous loss of value which the individual had sustained, the ruthlessness which made life today stride away over the single person and precipitate itself as a general indifference to the sufferings and destruction of human beings. This carelessness, this indifference to the individual fate, might appear to be the result of the four years' carnival of blood just behind us; but appearances were deceptive. As in many another respect here too the war only completed, defined, and drastically put in practice a process that had been on the way long before and had made itself the basis of a new feeling about life. This was not a matter for praise or blame, rather of objective perception and statement. However, the least passionate recognition of the actual, just out of sheer pleasure in recognition, always contains some shade of approbation; so why should one not accompany such objective perceptions of the time with a many-sided, yes, all-embracing critique of the bourgeois tradition? By the bourgeois tradition I mean the values of culture, enlightenment, humanity, in short of such dreams as the uplifting of the people through scientific civilization. They who practised this critique were men of education, culture, science. They did it, indeed, smiling; with a blitheness and intellectual complacency which lent the thing a special pungent, disquieting, or even slightly perverse charm. It is probably superfluous to state that not for a moment did they recognize the form of government which we got as a result of defeat, the freedom that fell in our laps, in a word, the democratic republic, as anything to be taken seriously as the legitimized frame of the new situation. With one accord they treated it as ephemeral, as meaningless from the start, yes, as a bad joke to be dismissed with a shrug.

They cited de Tocqueville, who had said that out of revolution as out of a common source two streams issued, the one leading men to free arrangements, the other to absolute power. In the free arrangements none of the gentlemen conversationalists at Kridwiss' any longer believed, since the very concept was self-contradictory: freedom by the act of assertion being driven to limit the freedom of its antagonist and thus to stultify itself and its own principles. Such was in fact its ultimate fate, though oftener the prepossession about "human rights" was thrown overboard at the start. And this was far more likely than that we would let ourselves in today for the dialectic process which turned freedom into the dictatorship of its party. In the end it all came down to dictatorship, to force, for with the demolition of the traditional national and social forms through the French Revolution an epoch had dawned which, consciously or not, confessedly or not, steered its course toward despotic tyranny over the masses; and they, reduced to one uniform level, atomized, out of touch, were as powerless as the single individual.

"Quite right, quite right. Oh indeed yes, one may say so!" zur Höhe assured us, and pounded with his feet. Of course one may say so; only one might, for my taste, dealing with this description of a mounting barbarism, have said so with rather more fear and trembling and rather less blithe satisfaction. One was left with the hope that the complacency of these gentlemen had to do with their recognition of the state of things and not with the state of things in itself. Let me set down as clearly as I can a picture of this distressing good humour of theirs. No one will be surprised that, in the conversations of this avant-garde of culture and critique, a book which had appeared seven years before the war, *"Réflexions sur la violence"* by Sorel, played an important part. The author's relentless prognostication of war and anarchy, his characterization of Europe as the war-breeding soil, his theory that the peoples of our continent can unite only in the one idea, that of making war—all justified its public in calling it the book of the day. But even more trenchant and telling was its perception and statement of the fact that in this age of the masses parliamentary discussion must prove entirely inadequate for the shaping of political decisions; that in its stead the masses would have in the future to be provided with mythical fictions, devised like primitive battle cries, to release and activate political energies. This was in fact the crass and inflaming prophecy of the book: that popular myths or rather those proper for the masses would become the vehicle of political action; fables, insane visions, chimaeras, which needed to have nothing to do with truth or reason or science in order to be creative, to determine the course of life and history, and thus to prove themselves dynamic realities. Not for nothing, of course, did the book bear its alarming title; for it dealt with violence as the triumphant antithesis of truth. It made plain that the fate of truth was bound up with the fate of the individual, yes, identical with it: being for both truth and the individual a cheapening, a devaluation. It opened a mocking abyss between truth and power, truth and life, truth and the community. It showed by implication that precedence belonged far more to the community; that truth had the community as its goal, and that whoever would share in the community must be prepared to scrap considerable elements of truth and science and line up for the *sacrificium intellectus*.

And now imagine (here is the "clear picture" I promised to give) how these gentlemen, scientists themselves, scholars and teachers—Vogler, Unruhe, Holzschuher, Institoris, and Breisacher as well—revelled in a situation which for me had about it so much that was terrifying, and which they regarded as either already in full swing or inevitably on the way. They amused themselves by imagining a legal process in which one of these mass myths was up for discussion in the service of the political drive for the undermining of the bourgeois social order. Its protagonists had to defend themselves against the charge of lying and falsification; but plaintiff and defendant did not so much attack each other as in the most laughable way miss each other's points. The fantastic thing was the mighty apparatus of scientific witness which was invoked—quite futilely—to prove that humbug was humbug and a scandalous affront to truth. For the dynamic, historically creative fiction, the so-called lie and falsification in other words, the community-forming belief, was simply inaccessible to this line of attack. Science strove, on the plane of decent, objective truth, to confute the dynamic lie; but arguments on that plane could only seem irrelevant to the champions of the dynamic, who merely smiled a superior smile. Science, truth—good God! The dramatic expositions of the group were possessed by the spirit and the accent of that ejaculation. They could scarcely contain their mirth at the desperate campaign waged by reason and criticism against wholly untouchable, wholly invulnerable belief. And with their united powers they knew how to set science in a light of such comic impotence that even the "beautiful princes," in their childlike way, were brilliantly entertained. The happy board did not hesitate to prescribe to justice, which had to say the last word and pronounce the judgment, the same self-abnegation which they themselves practised. A jurisprudence that wished to rest on the popular feeling and not to isolate itself from the community could not venture to espouse the point of view of theoretic, anti-communal, so-called truth; it had to prove itself modern as well as patriotic, patriotic in the most modern sense, by respecting the fruitful *falsum*, acquitting its apostles, and dismissing science with a flea in its ear.

"Oh yes, yes, certainly, one may say so"—thump, thump.

Although I felt sick at my stomach, I would not play the spoilsport; I showed no repugnance, but rather joined as well as I could in the general mirth; particularly since this did not necessarily mean agreement but only, at least provisionally, a smiling, gratified intellectual recognition of what was or was to be. I did once suggest that "if we wanted to be serious for a moment," we might consider whether a thinking man, to whom the extremity of our situation lay very much at heart, would not perhaps do better to make truth and not the community his goal, since the latter would indirectly and in the long run be better served by truth, even the bitter truth, than by a train of thought which proposed to serve it at the expense of truth, but actually, by such denial, destroyed from within in the most unnatural way the basis of genuine community. Never in my life have I made a remark that fell more utterly and completely flat than this one. I admit that it was a tactless remark, unsuited to the prevailing intellectual climate, and permeated with an idealism of course well known, only too well known, well known to the point of bad taste, and merely embarrassing to the new ideas. Much better was it for me to chime in with the others; to look at the new, to explore it, and instead of offering it futile and certainly boring opposition, to adapt my conceptions to the course of the discussion and in the frame of them to make myself a picture of the future and of a world even now, if unawares, in the throes of birth—and this no matter how I might be feeling in the pit of my stomach.

It was an old-new world of revolutionary reaction, in which the values bound up with the idea of the individual—shall we say truth, freedom, law, reason?—were entirely rejected and shorn of power, or else had taken on a meaning quite different from that given them for centuries. Wrenched away from the washed-out theoretic, based on the relative and pumped full of fresh blood, they were referred to the far higher court of violence, authority, the dictatorship of belief—not, let me say, in a reactionary, anachronistic way as of yesterday or the day before, but so that it was like the most novel setting back of humanity into mediaevally theocratic conditions and situations. That was as little reactionary as though one were to describe as regression the track around a sphere, which of course leads back to where it started. There it was: progress and reaction, the old and the new, the past and the future became one; the political Right more and more coincided with the Left. That thought was free, that research worked without assumptions: these were conceptions which, far from representing progress, belonged to a superseded and uninteresting world. Freedom was given to thought that it might justify force; just as seven hundred years ago reason had been free to discuss faith and demonstrate dogma; for that she was there, and for that today thinking was there, or would be there tomorrow. Research *certainly* had assumptions—of course it had! They were force, the authority of the community; and indeed they were so taken for granted as such that science never came upon the thought that perhaps it was not free. Subjectively, indeed, it was free, entirely so, within an objective restraint so native and incorporate that it was in no way felt as a fetter. To make oneself clear as to what was coming and to get rid of the silly fear of it one need only remind oneself that the absoluteness of definite premises and sacrosanct conditions had never been a hindrance to fancy and individual boldness of thought. On the contrary: precisely because from the very first mediaeval man had received a closed intellectual frame from the Church as something absolute and taken for granted, he had been far more imaginative than the burgher of the individualist age; he had been able to surrender himself far more freely and surefootedly to his personal fantasy.

IV

IN THE FOLLOWING excerpts from a speech delivered in Vienna, 9 May 1936, in celebration of Freud's eightieth birthday, Thomas Mann comes forth with eloquence as advocate of the "lived" myth. Here it is not the collective, or social, myth, with which he was concerned in the above-quoted passage from *Doctor Faustus*, but the individual exemplar myth in the light of which a "depth" biographer or creative writer may choose to view and represent his hero's personality and role and the vicissitudes of his career. Finally, he speaks of the possibility of a fresh incarnation of a mythic character consciously accepted as a way of life.

Freud and the Future
THOMAS MANN

FOR THE MYTH is the foundation of life; it is the timeless schema, the pious formula into which life flows when it reproduces its traits out of the unconscious. Certainly when a writer has acquired the habit of regarding life as mythical and typical there comes a curious heightening of his artist temper, a new refreshment to his perceiving and shaping powers, which otherwise occurs much later in life; for while in the life of the human race the mythical is an early and primitive stage, in the life of the individual it is a late and mature one. What is gained is an insight into the higher truth depicted in the actual; a smiling knowledge of the eternal, the ever-being and authentic; a knowledge of the schema in which and according to which the supposed individual lives, unaware, in his naïve belief in himself as unique in space and time, of the extent to which his life is but formula and repetition and his path marked out for him by those who trod it before him. His character is a mythical role which the actor just emerged from the depths to the light plays in the illusion that it is his own and unique, that he, as it were, has invented it all himself, with a dignity and security of which his supposed unique individuality in time and space is not the source, but rather which he creates out of his deeper consciousness in order that something which was once founded and legitimized shall again be represented and once more for good or ill, whether nobly or basely, in any case after its own kind conduct itself according to pattern. Actually, if his existence consisted merely in the unique and the present, he would not know how to conduct himself at all; he would be confused, helpless, unstable in his own self-regard, would not know which foot to put foremost or what sort of face to put on. His dignity and security lie all unconsciously in the fact that with him something timeless has once more emerged into the light and become present; it is a character; it is native worth, because its origin lies in the unconscious.

Such is the gaze which the mythically oriented artist bends upon the phenomena about him—an ironic and superior gaze, as you can see, for the mythical knowledge resides in the gazer and not in that at which he gazes. But let us suppose that the mythical point of view could become subjective; that it could pass over into the active ego and become conscious there, proudly and darkly yet joyously of its recurrence and its typicality, could celebrate it role and realize its own value exclusively in the knowledge that it was a fresh incarnation of the traditional upon earth. One might say that such a phenomenon alone could be the "lived myth"; nor should we think that it is anything novel or unknown. The life in the myth, life as a sacred repetition, is a historical form of life, for the man of ancient times lived thus. . . .

The Spanish scholar Ortega y Gasset puts it that the man of antiquity, before he did anything, took a step backwards, like the bull-fighter who leaps back to deliver the mortal thrust. He searched the past for a pattern into which he might slip as into a diving-bell, and being thus at once disguised and protected might rush upon his present problem. Thus his life was in a sense a reanimation, an archaizing attitude. But it is just this life as reanimation that is the life as myth. Alexander walked in the footsteps of Militiades; the ancient biographers of Caesar were convinced, rightly or wrongly, that he took Alexander as his prototype. But such "imitation" meant far more than we mean by the word today. It was a mythical identification, peculiarly familiar to antiquity; but it is operative far into modern times, and at all times is psychically possible. How often have we not been told that the figure of Napoleon was cast in the antique mold! He regretted that the mentality of the time forbade him to give himself out for the son of Jupiter Ammon, in imitation of Alexander. But we need not doubt that—at least at the period of his Eastern exploits—he mythically confounded himself with Alexander; while after he turned his face westwards he is said to have declared: "I am Charlemagne." Note that: not "I am like Charlemagne" or "My situation is like Charlemagne's," but quite simply: "I am he." That is the formulation of the myth. Life, then—at any rate—significant life—was in ancient times the reconstitution of the myth in flesh and blood; it referred to and appealed to the myth; only through it, through reference to the past, could it approve itself as genuine and significant. The myth is the legitimization of life; only through and in it does life find self-awareness, sanction, consecration. Cleopatra fulfilled her Aphrodite character even unto death—and can one live and die more significantly or worthily than in the celebration of the myth? We have only to think of Jesus and His life, which was lived in order that that which was written might be fulfilled. It is not easy to distinguish between His own consciousness and the conventionalizations of the Evangelists. But his word on the Cross, about the ninth hour, that *"Eli, Eli, lama sabachthani?"*

was evidently not in the least an outburst of despair and disillusionment; but on the contrary a lofty messianic sense of self.
For the phrase is not original, not a spontaneous outcry. It stands
at the beginning of the Twenty-second Psalm, which from one
end to the other is an announcement of the Messiah. Jesus was
quoting, and the quotation meant: "Yes, it is I!" Precisely thus
did Cleopatra quote when she took the asp to her breast to die;
and again the quotation meant: "Yes, it is I!"

Let us consider for a moment the word "celebration" which I
used in this connection. It is pardonable, even a proper usage.
For life in the myth, life, so to speak, in quotation, is a kind of
celebration, in that it is a making present of the past, it becomes
a religious act, the performance by a celebrant of a prescribed
procedure; it becomes a feast. For a feast is an anniversary, a
renewal of the past in the present. Every Christmas the world-
saving Babe is born again on earth, to suffer, to die, and to arise.
The feast is the abrogation of time, an event, a solemn narrative
being played out conformably to an immemorial pattern; the
events in it take place not for the first time, but ceremonially
according to the prototype. It achieves presentness as feasts do,
recurring in time with their phases and hours following on each
other in time as they did in the original occurrence. In antiquity
each feast was essentially a dramatic performance, a mask; it
was the scenic reproduction, with priests as actors, of stories
about the gods—as for instance the life and sufferings of
Osiris. . . .

Infantilism—in other words, regression to childhood—what a
role this genuinely psychoanalytic element plays in all our lives!
What a large share it has in shaping the life of a human being;
operating, indeed, in just the way I have described: as mythical
identification, as survival, as a treading in footprints already
made! The bond with the father, the imitation of the father, the
game of being the father, and the transference to father-
substitute pictures of a higher and more developed type—how
these infantile traits work upon the life of the individual to mark

and shape it! I use the word "shape," for to me in all seriousness the happiest, most pleasurable element of what we call education (*Bildung*), the shaping of the human being, is just this powerful influence of admiration and love, this childish identification with a father-image elected out of profound affinity. The artist in particular, a passionately childlike and play-possessed being, can tell us of the mysterious yet after all obvious effect of such infantile imitation upon his own life, his productive conduct of a career which after all is often nothing but a reanimation of the hero under very different temporal and personal conditions and with very different, shall we say childish means. . . .

And no less firmly do I hold that we shall one day recognize in Freud's life-work the cornerstone for the building of a new anthropology and therewith of a new structure, to which many stones are being brought up today, which shall be the future dwelling of a wiser and freer humanity. This physicianly psychologist will, I make no doubt at all, be honoured as the pathfinder towards a humanism of the future, which we dimly divine and which will have experienced much that the earlier humanism knew not of. It will be a humanism standing in a different relation to the powers of the lower world, the unconscious, the id: a relation bolder, freer, blither, productive of a riper art than any possible in our neurotic, fear-ridden, hate-ridden world. Freud is of the opinion that the significance of psychoanalysis as a science of the unconscious will in the future far outrank its value as a therapeutic method. But even as a science of the unconscious it is a therapeutic method, in the grand style, a method overarching the individual case. Call this, if you choose, a poet's utopia; but the thought is after all not unthinkable that the resolution of our great fear and our great hate, their conversion into a different relation to the unconscious which shall be more the artist's, more ironic and yet not necessarily irreverent, may one day be due to the healing effect of this very science.